THE AVIATION FACTFILE
CONCEPT AIRCRAFT

THE AVIATION FACTFILE

CONCEPT AIRCRAFT
Prototypes, X-Planes, and Experimental Aircraft

GENERAL EDITOR: JIM WINCHESTER

THUNDER BAY
P·R·E·S·S

San Diego, California

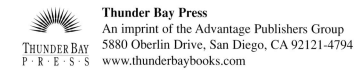

Thunder Bay Press
An imprint of the Advantage Publishers Group
5880 Oberlin Drive, San Diego, CA 92121-4794
www.thunderbaybooks.com

All notations of errors or omissions should be addressed to Thunder Bay Press, Editorial Department, at the above address. All other correspondence (author inquiries, permissions) concerning the content of this book should be addressed to Amber Books Ltd., Bradley's Close, 74–77 White Lion Street, London N1 9PF, England, www.amberbooks.co.uk.

ISBN-13: 978-1-59223-480-6
ISBN-10: 1-59223-480-1

Library of Congress Cataloging-in-Publication Data available upon request.

Printed in Singapore

1 2 3 4 5 09 08 07 06 05

Contents

INTRODUCTION

Left: In the early 1950s, Britain's Royal Aircraft Establishment investigated controlled vertical jet flight with this remarkable and dangerous machine, the Thrust Measuring Rig, known commonly as the 'Flying Bedstead'.

Right: Burt Rutan designed the Voyager to fly non-stop around the world without refuelling, a feat achieved in December 1986.

Below: The vectored-thrust Hawker P.1127 Kestrel, the forerunner of the Harrier.

Below right: Bell's X-15 was the first truly successful tilt-rotor – an aircraft that takes off vertically like a helicopter but flies horizontally like a fixed-wing machine. It was the ancestor of today's V-22 Osprey.

In mathematics and physics 'X' stands for the unknown. In aeronautics an 'X-plane' is an experimental or research aircraft, designed to explore the unknown boundaries of aerodynamics, powerplant technologies or materials science. 'X' was first used in the USA in the mid-1930s as a prefix to aircraft designations, meaning 'prototype', such as the XB-15 bomber. After the war, a series of purely experimental aircraft was begun in the US,

initially by the United States Army Air Forces (later USAF) in cooperation with the civil agency NACA, the National Advisory Committee on Aeronautics. The first of these was the Bell XS-1 ('S' standing for 'Sonic'), usually known as the X-1. Nearly 50 craft in this series have followed, with the best known probably being the X-1 series, the hypersonic X-15 and the X-29 with its distinctive forward-swept-wing. Half of the US X-series

aircraft have been unmanned rockets, aerodynamic shapes or Unmanned Air Vehicles (UAVs), but those piloted aircraft intended for high-speed and high altitude flight have inspired legends, and created heroes of the pilots who risked – and sometimes lost – their lives while 'pushing the outside of the envelope' as Tom Wolfe put it in *The Right Stuff.*

The US Air Force Flight Test Center's motto is 'Toward the Unknown' and the

golden age of rocket aircraft at Edwards Air Force Base from the 1940s to the 1970s was an exciting era that captured the public's imagination, and was celebrated in fiction, film, comics, and in the model kits of the day.

NACA became NASA (the National Air and Space Administration) when the 'space race' proper took off in the late 1950s. Their involvement ensured that civil as well as military aviation benefited from

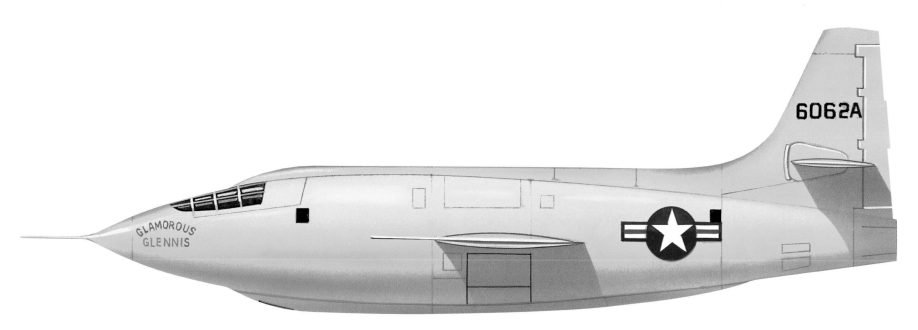

6062A

GLAMOROUS
GLENNIS

Top: Probably the most famous X-plane of all, the Bell X-1 took Chuck Yeager to Mach 1 at 12,800 m (42,000 ft.) on the morning of October 14, 1947.

Right: De Havilland designed the DH.108 Swallow to break the sound barrier, but both prototypes were destroyed in fatal high-speed crashes, putting an end to the programme.

Far right: The SR.A/1 was a radical design for a jet-powered flying boat fighter. Designed by Saunders-Roe, the first aircraft flew in 1947, too late for World War II.

the work of these and other experimental craft, although military concepts took precedence in the X-series proper. The spin-offs for commercial flight were mainly in the realm of material science and aircraft systems. Other NASA sponsored programmes explored quiet and short take-off engine technologies, slew wings, 'morphing' wings, and solar-powered and man-powered flight, among other groundbreaking concepts.

X-Planes Around the World

The United Kingdom led the world in jet engine development for many years, and supplied most other countries (including the USSR) with engines and licences to build them. A number of aircraft were modified as engine testbeds but relatively few pure research aircraft were built after the loss of the De Havilland DH.108s in 1946 and 1950. The Miles M.52 would probably have been the first Mach 1 aircraft

if it had not been cancelled before completion, ostensibly because of the perceived risk to its pilot. British post-war research efforts were mainly in support of particular programmes, such as the V-bombers (Vulcan, Victor and Valiant) and Concorde. Realising that slow flight can be as dangerous as that at supersonic speeds, the UK built several testbeds to explore the low-speed handing of new configurations as well as high-speed research aircraft.

In 1945 the French aircraft industry barely existed, although some design work had gone on in secret under Nazi occupation.

The industry was rebuilt from scratch, using German jet engines to begin with, then British engines, and finally French engines. France built so many varied and short-lived experimental aircraft up to the late 1950s that it was dismissed of being 'an industry of prototypes' by outside observers. In the end the best designs won

Top: Based on the captured Messerschmitt P.1101 prototype, the Bell X-5 was the first aircraft able to vary its wing sweep in flight.

Left: A giant white elephant, the Saunders-Roe Princess was a ten-engined flying boat designed for transatlantic luxury. The development of the faster and cheaper Boeing 707 condemned it to the breaker's yard.

Far left: Combining the capabilities of a helicopter with the performance of a jet fighter, the Ryan XV-5A Vertifan showed enormous potential.

out and the industry rationalised itself from a plethora of regionally based concerns into one major aircraft manufacturer and participation in or leadership of various European joint ventures.

Having built some remarkable aircraft in the war years, the German aircraft industry took longer to get back on its feet after 1945. After the war, Germany relied mainly on the United States for its military aircraft and devoted little effort to experimentation,

but in one field it did take a lead – jet vertical take-off and landing (VTOL) aircraft. Ultimately, despite their merits, the three German VTOL designs (the VJ-101C fighter, VAK-191 attack aircraft and Do 31 transport) which reached the test-flight stage did not enter production or operational service.

The Soviet Union explored many of the same concepts as Western designers, including rocket and mixed-powerplant

interceptors, delta wings, forward-swept wings, swing wings and VTOL fighters. Unlike the US, the USSR seems to have not bothered too much with VTOL transports or observation aircraft, relying on large numbers of helicopters of all sizes for its huge army.

Return of the Flying Boat
The jet age saw a revival (of sorts) of the flying-boat. New turboprop and turbojet

engines seemed to offer higher performance for fighters (SR.A/1 and Sea Dart), bombers (Seamaster), patrol aircraft ('Mallow') and transports (Tradewind). For military applications, these promised to overcome some of the limitations of contemporary aircraft carriers, allowing navies to compete for the strategic role which historically would have fallen to air forces. Only the Russians persisted with the jet amphibian, with a brief sojourn into an

Left: This Swiss-registered VariEze is an example of one of Burt Rutan's remarkable designs for the civil aviation market.

Right: Reclusive millionaire Howard Hughes almost died when the XF-11 reconnaissance prototype he was piloting crashed into a house on its maiden flight in 1946.

Below: The French-designed Hermes spaceplane concept, designed to be launched into low earth orbit by an Ariane rocket. Intended to support the International Space Station, the project was cancelled in 1993.

entirely new type of vehicle: the wing-in-ground-effect 'Ekranoplan', a series of machines that remained unknown in the West until the 1990s.

VTOL

The quest for vertical flight has lead to more 'solutions' than just about any other type of aeronautical problem. Rotorcraft development began during World War I with unmanned prototypes for observation platforms, but did not reach true practicality until the 1940s, with a few helicopters seeing service with the US and German armies. Almost as soon as conventional rotorcraft appeared, their limitations of speed and range became apparent. The mechanical complexity of rotor and transmission systems also encouraged aircraft makers to seek simpler solutions, most of which (such as tip jets and rigid rotors) proved more complicated or expensive than conventional rotors.

Combining vertical lift with wing-borne cruise flight proved the great challenge of the 1950s and '60s. One approach was 'tail-sitters' like the Pogo and the Salmon, although the difficulties of landing them ruled out their operational use. The many combinations of propellers and wings included tilt-wings, tilt-rotors, tilt-fans and tilt-engines, embodied in a range of experimental craft, many of them sponsored by the US Army, which wanted its own 'organic' battlefield transports, scout aircraft and attack platforms. The US Air Force saw this as encroaching on their turf and the Army satisfied itself with conventional helicopters.

Jet-lift VTOL (Vertical Take-Off and Landing) experiments produced almost as many configurations as did propeller-driven lift systems. Almost all were

Left: One of the strangest aircraft ever to fly, the Convair XF2Y Sea Dart was a Mach 1 fighter able to take off and land on water.

Right: An artist's impression of the Junkers Ju 322 Mammut (Mammoth), a vast glider tested by Germany during World War II.

Below: The ungainly looking Bell X-22A proved the potential of the VTOL concept in the 1960s.

inefficient flying machines because they used multiple (up to eight) small lift engines in addition to propulsive engines. These took up space and weight that could have been better used for fuel and weapons. The answer proved to lie in vectoring the thrust of the main engine so it could be used for both lift and thrust, as introduced on the Hawker P.1127, predecessor of the Harrier. A variation of this theme, using the main engine to drive a lift fan, will power the version of the F-35 Joint Strike Fighter due to enter service with the US Marines and the Royal Air Force and Royal Navy.

Despite all this effort, and the construction and testing of over 40 different experimental aircraft types since the war, the number of non-helicopter VTOL aircraft to reach operational service can be counted on the fingers of one hand – namely the Harrier, the Yak-36M and the V-22 Osprey.

Make-do and Mend

Experimental aircraft programmes often have to make do with limited budgets and are frequently constructed using off-the-shelf (sometimes off-the-scrapyard) components. Landing gears, ejection seats, canopies, instruments and flight control systems, even large structural sections, are 'borrowed' from other aircraft. The Grumman X-29 has the nose and cockpit of a Northrop F-5A, The British Aerospace EAP used the fin, engines and other parts from the Panavia Tornado. The Rockwell XFV-12 seemed to have largely built from spare parts (but never actually flew). Several British experimental aircraft were derived from or rebuilt from examples of the Sea Hawk and Attacker naval fighters.

Civil X-Planes

Compared to aircraft built for military research programmes, fewer research

Above: The VFW-Fokker VAK 191B was an advanced German VTOL fighter concept with three engines, abandoned on grounds of cost.

Right: Convair's NB-36H was built to test the technology behind nuclear-powered aircraft, and required tons of lead shielding for the crew.

Left: At a time when most aircraft were biplanes, Deperdussin's sleek monoplane racers were a remarkable sight.

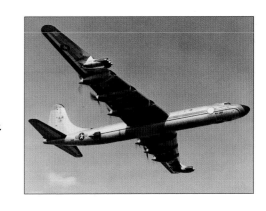

aircraft have been built for purely civil purposes. Generally speaking, governments do not build airliners, the private sector does (the exception being in communist countries, but few civil 'X-planes' have appeared there either). The Avro Canada Jetliner remained a one-off, largely because the factory space was needed for building fighters. Even while the Jetliner, based on the design of the piston-engined Tudor, was still flying, the parent company in the

UK was building Ashton jet testbeds, also based on the Tudor. These performed useful test work, but did not lead to any production aircraft either.

One civilian designer has made a remarkable contribution to civil aviation, particularly in the use of composite materials. Burt Rutan's extraordinary designs, built for various customers, have ranged from kits for the homebuilder to the only aircraft to fly non-stop unrefuelled

around the world, to the first private-venture spacecraft. His designs are instantly recognisable and his influence on other makers immeasurable.

Conventional naturally stable aerodynamic forms had just about reached their limits by the 1970s when computerised fly-by-wire control systems allowed new configurations to be built that could never be flown by an unaided human pilot. This meant that some earlier

layouts, such as the XB-35 and YB-49 flying wings of the 1940s, could be revived, leading to the B-2 Spirit, the most sophisticated (and expensive) warplane ever built. Despite wind tunnel testing and computer aided design and modelling, unexpected glitches can still crop up after an aircraft enters service. Real world experimentation and flying testbeds (and the brave men and women who fly them) will always be needed.

AIRSHIP INDUSTRIES

SKYSHIP

● Non-rigid airship ● Camera platform ● Advertising

Developed from the Skyship 600, the Sentinel 5000, known to the Navy as the YEZ-2A, is the last word in affordable airborne early warning platforms for the Fleet. With this non-rigid airship, technology has gone full circle, providing a vehicle that can hover over the valuable assets providing an eye-in-the-sky to spot low-observable, sea-skimming cruise missiles. It is a relatively cheap solution to a potentially expensive problem in lives and equipment. Developed by Airship Industries using a hangar in England that once housed the once-famous airships R100 and R101, the now U.S.-built Sentinel looks set to make its mark around the world.

▲ *The Skyship 500 was marketed around the world. This example is seen on its maiden flight over Toronto airport in Canada. North America has been one of the prime markets for Airship Industries.*

AIRSHIP INDUSTRIES SKYSHIP

Coming to rest ▶
Manoeuvring such a large craft close to the ground can prove difficult. Once in position it is secured to a mooring mast.

▼ Working down-under
The first production Skyship 500 shows its advertising potential. It resulted in sales of two Series 600s to Australia.

▲ Modern gondola
The gondola is a one-piece molding of Kevlar reinforced plastics. The Series 500 has accommodation for two pilots with five standard seats and a three-person bench seat at the rear.

Cardington base ▶
The production facility at Cardington has a long association with airship production. The huge hangars were built in the 1920s for the early hydrogen airships.

▲ Military market
The Skyship was also targeted at the military market. This series 600 was demonstrated to the French navy for maritime patrol.

◀ Skyship family
Both the Skyship 500 and 600 were demonstrated at trade shows such as Farnborough and Paris. Spectators were impressed by their serene displays.

FACTS AND FIGURES

➤ Proposed military uses have included airborne early warning, mine countermeasures and maritime patrol.

➤ The first production Skyship 500 took to the air in September 1981.

➤ This type made the first scheduled passenger airship service in 49 years.

➤ Following the collapse of Airship Industries, the company was acquired by Westinghouse Electric Corporation.

➤ Westinghouse has based their Sentinel 5000 for the Navy on the Skyship 600.

➤ Skyships are still regularly seen over big cities advertising different products.

PROFILE

Billboards in the sky

Interest in airships, which peaked during the first 30 years of this century, never died out altogether despite their apparent obsolescence. Of the most recent developers of the idea, Airship Industries of England, has been at the forefront of the lighter-than-air craft business since the early 1980s with the Skyship 500 and

600. These two models carved a small niche as camera ships, where their stability is appreciated for sports events and as airborne advertising billboards. Overseas sales were made in Australia, South Korea and Japan.

In a joint venture with the U.S. firm Westinghouse, the Sentinel 5000 was then developed for the U.S. Navy for

airborne early warning (AEW), over-the-horizon targeting and drug surveillance. This will be the largest non-rigid airship ever built. Sadly, the British firm failed in 1990. Westinghouse acquired the company's 50 percent stake in the programme, but more than a decade later, the Sentinel 5000 has not yet flown.

Left: In 1986, Skyship inaugurated the first scheduled airship passenger service in 49 years flying sightseeing trips.
Below: The larger Skyship 600 can carry up to 13 passengers and is the basis for the Navy's Sentinel project.

Skyship 600

Type: Non-rigid helium-filled airship.

Powerplant: Two 190 kW (255-hp.) turbocharged Porsche 930/10 air-cooled piston engines.

Maximum speed: 107 km/h (66 m.p.h.)

Still air range: 1017 km (632 mi.) without auxiliary tanks.

Pressure ceiling: 3050 m (10,000 ft.)

Endurance: Over 13 hr.

Weight: Gross disposable load 2343 kg (5,155 lb.)

Dimensions:

Max diameter	15,20 m	(48 ft. 10 in.)
Length	59 m	(193 ft. 6 in.)
Height	20,30 m	(66 ft. 7 in.)
Volume	6666 m³	(235,410 cu. ft.)

SKYSHIP 600

G-SKSC was the Skyship 600 prototype and made its first flight at Cardington in March 1984. It was subsequently used as a company demonstrator.

The envelope of the Skyship series is manufactured by Aerazur in France, from a strong single-ply polyester fabric and is coated with a titanium dioxide loaded polyurethane to reduce ultraviolet degradation.

Curtains fitted to the roof of the envelope on the inside carry 14 main cables of Kevlar within the envelope for the suspension of the gondola.

The tail unit is of conventional cruciform layout, each surface being attached to the envelope at its root and braced by four wires on each side. All four surfaces are constructed from interlocking ribs and spars. The control surfaces are cable operated, and each has a spring tab.

Two ballonets, which together comprise 26 percent of the envelope volume, are installed fore and aft. Differential inflation of these ballonets allows the pilot to trim the airship to gain the correct attitude in flight.

The gondola is constructed of Kevlar in a one-piece mold. It has dual controls for the pilot and accommodation for 13 passengers. On the ground, the airship rests on a single wheel mounted beneath the rear of the gondola.

The two Porsche 930/10 engines are turbocharged to provide extra power. Each drives a ducted fan with a Hoffman five-blade propeller. The fans can be rotated through an arc of 210 degrees.

Skyship's rotating propulsor

1 FORWARD FLIGHT: With the fan in the horizontal position, the airship is driven forward up to a maximum speed of 107 km/h (66 m.p.h.).

2 CLIMBING AND HOVERING: The fan can be rotated 120 degrees downward, allowing the airship to hover or climb in conjunction with the elevators.

3 DESCENDING: Rotating the fan downward allows the Skyship to descend. This vectoring of the fan gives the airship a V/STOL capability.

ACTION DATA

LENGTH

The massive Hindenburg of the 1930s was typical of the golden era of airships. It was envisaged that hundreds of these massive craft would make luxury trips across the Atlantic. Unfortunately after a series of disasters these hydrogen-filled monsters were consigned to history. The modern-day Skyship is filled with helium for safety and is approximately one-quarter of the size.

HINDENBURG 245 m (803 ft. 7 in.)

SKYSHIP 600 59 m (193 ft. 6 in.)

ANTONOV

AN-70

● Commercial transport ● Propfan engines ● Composite structure

Filling a Russian air force requirement for a transport to replace the venerable An-12, the An-70 is the world's first aircraft powered entirely by propfans. Development began in 1975. The new design followed the configuration of the An-12, but incorporated new technologies into the much larger aircraft. The prototype was lost in an accident, but a second was eventually built and flown in 1997. Antonov has high hopes for the aircraft.

▲ *In a time of tightening budgets, Antonov's An-70 will have a tough time achieving sales, despite its advanced design. Political problems have clouded the development of the aircraft.*

ANTONOV AN-70

◀ **Lightweight design**
Despite the large size of the An-70, 28 per cent of its structure is composed of composite materials, allowing the airframe to be extremely light.

Powered tail ▶
The tall tail is fitted with powered upper and lower double-hinged rudders. Trimming devices are fitted to improve the An-70's low-speed handling.

◀ **Conventional design**
High-mounted wings and a large fuselage body are standard design features on current transport aircraft. The An-70 is larger than Europe's FLA.

Ample accommodation ▶
Fully pressurised, the circular-section fuselage is able to accommodate the latest Russian main battle tank or seating for 170 troops.

◀ **Advanced propulsion**
The contra-rotating propfans were developed especially for the An-70, and give the large aircraft agile performance.

FACTS AND FIGURES

➤ The first prototype crashed on 10 February 1995 after colliding with its An-72 chase plane.

➤ Antonov has proposed twin-propfan and turbojet-powered An-70 variants.

➤ Antonov's An-70 is much smaller than the American C-17A Globemaster III.

➤ Each propfan has contra-rotating propellers; the front has eight composite blades, the rear just six.

➤ The planned An-70TK will carry either 30 tonnes of cargo or 150 passengers.

➤ Antonov sees other possible An-70 roles as including firefighting and naval patrol.

Russia's revolutionary transport

On 19 August 1997, the second An-70 prototype, registered UR-NTK, was seen in public for the first time at the MAKS '97 air show at Zhukhovskii, near Moscow.

The future of the An-70 programme had been in some doubt after the tragic loss of the first prototype in February 1995, less than three months after its first flight. Funding for the design had passed from the Soviet air force to the new Ukrainian government after dissolution of the USSR. The prototype's crash was a major setback at a time when funding for the Russian aviation industry was scarce.

A STOL (Short Take-Off and Landing) design, with a large, pressurised and air conditioned fuselage, the An-70 has twice the internal capacity of either the An-12 or the Lockheed C-130 and has a maximum payload of 47 tonnes. As well as propfan engines, the aircraft features composite materials in its construction (the entire tail unit, ailerons and flaps), a modern 'glass' cockpit and an avionics fit to Western standards. The first aircraft have three flight crew, but later examples will be able to be flown by two crew.

In a joint Russian/Ukrainian programme, this promising aircraft has recently undergone a wide range of certification tests, and looks set to enter quantity production shortly, with the Russian Air Force likely to be the main recipient.

Left: Antonov's An-70 has exceptional flying characteristics, relying heavily on fly-by-wire controls and large flaps in the wings.

Above: Viewed from head-on, the unique layout of the 14 curved propeller blades fitted to each engine is clearly shown.

An-70

Type: medium-size wide-body transport

Powerplant: four 10290-kW (13,800-hp.) ZMKB Progress D-27 propfans driving SV-27 contra-rotating propellers

Cruising speed: 750 km/h (465 m.p.h.)

Range: 5530 km (3,100 mi.) with max§ payload

Service ceiling: 11000 m (33,000 ft.)

Optimum cruising height: 9000 m (29,500 ft.)

Weights: empty 72800 kg (160,160 lb.); max take-off 133000 kg (292,600 lb.)

Accommodation: 150 passengers and 4 crew

Dimensions:
span 44.06 m (40 ft. 9 in.)
length 40.73 m (133 ft. 7 in.)
height 16.38 m (53 ft. 9 in.)
wing area 200 m² (2,152 sq.ft.)

AN-70

The first aircraft to be powered only by propfans, the An-70 is a remarkable transport aircraft. Despite the abilities of Antonov's design, budget constraints put the entire programme in serious jeopardy. At the time of writing, the An-70's future looks bright, however.

The well-equipped cockpit includes a fly-by-wire control system. Operations can be undertaken with two pilots and one loadmaster.

Approximately 28 per cent of the airframe is of lightweight composite structure, including the complete tail unit, ailerons and flaps. The wings are manufactured at the Chkalov plant at Tashkent in Uzbekistan. Such delegation of construction for the aircraft is an indication of the tough times the aviation industry is facing.

The high-set tail of the An-70, coupled with the high wings, mean that the fuselage is unclutterred with any associated flight controls. Maximum space is available for cargo.

Double-slotted trailing-edge flaps in two sections are located on the wings. They are supplemented by three-section spoilers forward of each outer flap.

354
АНТОНОВ 70
UR-NTK

The large cargo door is located at the rear of the fuselage. The upper section folds up into the fuselage while the lower sections can be utilised as ramps for loading the aircraft.

ACTION DATA

CRUISING SPEED

Its four advanced propfan engines give the An-70 an exceptionally high cruising speed in comparison to the American types. The new C-17 Globemaster III – powered by four turbofans – has a poor cruising performance, only slightly better than that of the C-130J.

An-70T 750km/h (465 m.p.h.)
C-130J 645 km/h (400 m.p.h.)
C-17A GLOBEMASTER III 648 km/h (402 m.p.h.)

MAXIMUM RANGE

The ability to cover huge distances with a large payload is the key requirement for any new transport aircraft. For its class, the An-70 has the greatest range of the current crop of military transport aircraft.

An-70T 5530 km (3,100 mi.)
C-130J 5250 km (3,255 mi.)
C-17A GLOBEMASTER III 5190 km (3,218 mi.)

MAXIMUM PAYLOAD

Built on experience gained with the C-5 Galaxy and C-141 StarLifter, the C-17 Globemaster III offers the largest payload available. Able to accommodate main battle tanks as well as troops, the aircraft is unbeatable in its class.

An-70T 47000 kg (66,000 lb.)
C-130J 18955 kg (41,700 lb.)
C-17A GLOBEMASTER III 78108kg (171,850 lb.)

Russian heavyweights

An-22 'COCK': Powered by a mass of contra-rotating propellers, the 'Cock' was used extensively in Afghanistan to ferry troops and supplies to the battlefield.

An-124 'CONDOR': With a configuration similar to that of the American C-5 Galaxy, the 'Condor' is now the primary transport aircraft of the Russian armed forces.

An-225 'COSSACK': Constructed to support the Russian space shuttle programme (now grounded), the aircraft is used sporadically for cargo flights.

ANTONOV

AN-225 MRIYA 'COSSACK'

● Strategic transport ● World's largest aircraft ● Soviet shuttle carrier

Antonov's An-225 Mriya (Dream), built in the Ukraine, has been given the NATO reporting name of 'Cossack'. It is a stretched derivative of the An-124 'Condor', built for the special purpose of transporting massive 'piggyback' cargoes. This huge machine carries incredible payloads of up to 250 tonnes, and offers the unrivalled ability to move very large items of freight over respectable distances. The An-225 has not so far been used to its full potential.

▲ The An-225 restores the distinction of being the world's largest aircraft to the Antonov design bureau. However, the market for such a super-heavy cargo carrier remains open to doubt.

ANTONOV AN-225 MRIYA 'COSSACK'

▼ **Large span**
Banking gracefully, the An-225 shows off its enormous wing, equipped with almost full-span flaps, similar to those of the earlier An-12.

▲ **Buran lifter**
The An-225 was used to carry the Buran space shuttle. Britain's cancelled HOTOL space plane was another proposed cargo.

▼ **Blast off**
The astonishing thrust of the six Lotarev D-18 fan engines gives the An-225 a respectable take-off performance for such a large aircraft.

▼ **Wing on wheels**
To support its massive weight, the An-225 has seven pairs of main undercarriage wheels arranged in two units and two pairs of nosewheels. The An-225 can 'kneel' by retracting its nosewheels on the ground.

▲ **Hinged nose**
The nose section of the An-225 hinges upwards to allow outsize cargoes to be easily loaded. Even helicopters and main battle tanks can fit through this doorway.

FACTS AND FIGURES

➤ The An-225 made its first flight carrying the Buran space shuttle orbiter on 13 May 1989 from Baikonur cosmodrome.

➤ On 22 March 1989 the An-225 established 106 payload records.

➤ The Mriya is nearly twice the size of the American Lockheed C-5 Galaxy.

➤ On its record-breaking flights, the huge An-225 took off at an all-up weight of 508200 kg (1,338040 lb.).

➤ Typically, the 'Cossack' carries two pilots, two flight engineers and two navigators.

➤ Like the Su-27, the flight system incorporates fly-by-wire controls.

World's biggest aeroplane

Based on the huge An-124, but with over 50 per cent improvement in payload, the An-225 Mriya is simply the largest aircraft ever built. The An-225 added a stretched fuselage, six engines instead of four and seven pairs of wheels per side instead of five.

This flying juggernaut was developed to replace two Myasischev VM-T Atlants – converted 'Bison' bombers – used to carry outsized loads associated with the Soviet space programme's Energia rockets. The Mriya's first flight took place on 21 December 1988 and the aircraft flew with the Buran space shuttle on its back five months later.

The break-up of the USSR and the cancellation of the Soviet re-usable orbital project means that the An-225 is now reduced to working on sporadic freight jobs. For most of its life the Mriya has languished in storage and has been cannibalised for parts. Plans to use it as a launcher for Britain's HOTOL spacecraft have failed to materialise, and a second example remains uncompleted.

The An-225 appeared at a time when Soviet aviation was at its zenith and new designs were stunning Western analysts at every air show.

Below: Unlike the An-124, which has had considerable success in the heavylift cargo market, the An-225 remains unwanted. The aircraft's sheer size and operating costs make it uneconomical.

An-225 Mriya 'Cossack'

Type: very large cargo transport

Powerplant: six ZMKB Progress (Lotarev) D-18T turbofan engines each rated at 229.47 kN (51,355.4-lb.-thrust)

Maximum cruising speed: 850 km/h (527 m.p.h.)

Cruising speed: 700 km/h (434 m.p.h.)

Range: 15400 km (9,548 mi.)

Service ceiling: 11145 m (36,500 ft.)

Weights: empty 350000 kg (770,000 lb.); maximum loaded 600000 kg (1,320,000 lb.)

Accommodation: a crew of up to 12 are involved in carrying the Energia rocket; if used to carry troops it could accommodate over 600

Dimensions:
span	88.40 m	(290 ft.)
length	84.00 m	(276 ft.)
height	18.20 m	(60 ft.)
wing area	905.00 m²	(9,738 sq.ft.)

AN-225 MRIYA 'COSSACK'

The An-225 first appeared in the West at the Paris Air Show in 1989, making an unprecedented appearance by carrying the Buran space shuttle craft.

The main fuselage has a large cabin above the cargo hold, which can hold 60 to 70 passengers.

Buran was never used operationally, but made an unmanned test flight. Originally, the Russian space shuttle was to be carried by a modified 'Atlant' Mya-4 'Bison'.

The tailplane is canted upwards (known as dihedral) for added stability.

The twin-fin arrangement was a necessity for stable flight when the Buran was carried on the fuselage. A single fin would have caused unacceptable airflow problems.

As well as being the main cargo loading area, the nose contains weather radar and a downward-looking terrain avoidance and ground-mapping radar.

The wing has a leading-edge flap, trailing-edge Fowler flaps and inboard and outboard airbrakes.

The main undercarriage has seven pairs of wheels on each side.

The large Lotarev D-18 turbofan is identical to that used in the smaller An-124 'Condor'. This engine is very powerful, but there have been problems with its reliability in service.

Unlike earlier large Antonovs, for example the An-22, the An-225 has no rear cargo doors and relies on a hinged nose instead.

ACTION DATA

MAXIMUM PAYLOAD

The An-225 is capable of carrying a tonne more than its predecessor, the An-124. The huge Mriya can transport cargo equivalent to the weight of one-and-a-half empty C-5 Galaxies, and also has the ability to carry a load on top of its fuselage.

An-124 'CONDOR' 150000 kg (550,000 lb.)

An-225 MRIYA 'COSSACK' 250000 kg (330,000 lb.)

C-5 GALAXY 118387 kg (260,450 lb.)

TAKE-OFF RUN

The larger the aircraft, the longer it usually takes to get airborne. Even with its massive wing and six engines, the An-225 requires an extensive length of runway.

An-225 MRIYA 'COSSACK' 3500 m (11,480 ft.)

An-124 'CONDOR' 3000 m (9,840 ft.)

C-5 2950 m (9,676 ft.)

The world's biggest lifters

■ ANTONOV An-22 'COCK' (1965): Once the largest aircraft in the world, the An-22 remains the world's biggest turboprop. Despite its age it remains in demand, as turboprops have comparatively low operating costs. Several payload-to-height records were set by the An-22, some of which still stand.

■ LOCKHEED C-5 GALAXY (1968): Still the USAF's largest transport, the C-5 remains in service despite major problems, including structural faults with engine mountings and wing spars. The Galaxy set several records for payload delivery when it entered service, but these were all subsequently broken by the An-124.

■ ANTONOV An-124 'CONDOR' (1982): The basis of the An-225 design, the An-124 has been a commercial success. It flies with Aeroflot, Volga Dnepr and several other Russian heavylift carriers. The 'Condor' could even carry a mobile version of the SS-20 intermediate-range ballistic missile system or main battle tanks.

AVRO CANADA

C-102 JETLINER

● Jetliner prototype ● Rolls-Royce engines ● Only one built

Flown for the first time in August 1949, just two weeks after de Havilland's Comet, the C-102 was an audacious attempt by A.V. Roe Canada Limited to build a jet transport with a cruising speed twice that of contemporary piston-engined types. Canadian and American airlines showed interest in the new aircraft, but the outbreak of war in Korea and the Canadian government's demand for CF-100 fighters led to the cancellation of the project.

▲ *Rolls-Royce Avon development delays and the British reluctance to release the engine for civil use badly affected a Jetliner programme that was reliant on the new powerplant.*

AVRO CANADA C-102 JETLINER

◀ **Conservative lines**
Although a clean design, the C-102 retained the somewhat dated look of a piston-engined aircraft.

▼ **Observation ship**
After cancellation, the Jetliner spent a short time in the US before being returned to Canada for use during CF-100 tests. These included gun-pack firing and ejection seat activation.

▲ **Avro Canada products**
The prototype C-102 is seen alongside the CF-100 prototype. The Canadian government cancelled the C-102 in favour of accelerated CF-100 development.

▼ **Trans-Canada Air Lines**
After the powerplant change, TCA was released from its commitment to purchase the C-102. The re-engined aircraft needed to carry more fuel, which reduced payload.

▲ **First flight**
Upon its first flight on 10 August 1949, the C-102 became the first jet transport in North America to take to the air. The Boeing 707 prototype did not fly until 1954.

FACTS AND FIGURES

➤ After testing by the USAF, Avro Canada proposed a trainer variant with four Allison J-33 engines.

➤ Construction of a second C-102 prototype began, but was not completed.

➤ After cancellation, the C-102 was used as an observation platform for CF-100 tests.

➤ Flown for the last time on 23 November 1956, CF-EJD-X was scrapped in December, having flown about 425 hours.

➤ After flying the aircraft in 1952, Howard Hughes considered building the C-102.

➤ The C-102's nose is now in Canada's National Aeronautical Collection.

PROFILE

Canada's first and only jetliner

Only one C-102 was flown, although a second machine was close to completion when the programme was cancelled. The aircraft, registered CF-EJD-X, first flew on 10 August 1949, powered by four Rolls-Royce Derwent 5 turbojet engines.

However, these engines were not the ones originally intended for the new airliner. Avro Canada had hoped to install a pair of Rolls-Royce's new AJ 65 Avon turbojets, but the British government was not prepared to release them for civil use.

Intended to carry 30 to 50 passengers, the C-102 would have covered route stages of around 1750 km (1,085 mi.).

After an early landing accident, the prototype was repaired, demonstrated extensively and later re-engined with more powerful Derwent 8s and 9s (two of each). On one occasion the aircraft flew 587 km (400-plus mi.) from Toronto to New York in 59 minutes with a cargo of mail.

The C-102's launch customer was to be Trans-Canada Air Lines, although US firms were also impressed enough to propose a production order.

The RCAF and USAF also tested the aircraft, but ultimately performance shortcomings, the Korean War and the Canadian government's request that Avro concentrate on the CF-100 fighter led to cancellation in 1951.

Had development continued, the C-102 could have been the world's second jet airliner in service, an honour left to the Soviet Tupolev Tu-104.

The elevators and rudder were in two pieces, the rear portions being manually operated and the front section power-assisted.

Rolls-Royce Derwent turbojets were installed in nacelles designed with the aid of wartime German research.

The Jetliner's twin-spar wing was of conventional stressed-skin construction. Split flaps were fitted.

Had the British government released the Rolls-Royce Avon for civil use, the C-102 would have been fitted with two in single nacelles.

C-102 JETLINER

Although two prototypes were planned, only CF-EJD-X was completed and flown. The tail legend reads 'Designed and built by A.V. Roe Canada Limited, Malton, Ontario'.

Unswept vertical tail surfaces were a feature of many early jet types. Aerodynamic research later showed the benefits of a swept tail.

The Jetliner's flightdeck was of conventional layout with fully duplicated controls and seating for two pilots, plus a 'jump' seat between for an observer.

Pressurisation was a feature of the C-102's 3.05-m (10-ft.) diameter fuselage. Seating arrangements for between 30 and 50 passengers were proposed. During demonstration flights passengers were impressed by its low noise levels.

After its second flight the C-102 was unable to lower its main undercarriage and was forced to make a belly landing. It came to rest on its extended nose gear, the ends of its tail pipes and the rear fuselage.

While the prototype was undergoing testing, Avro worked on a production version with a 1.22-m (4-ft.) forward fuselage stretch and a rear fuselage shortened by 0.53 m (nearly 2 ft.). Alternative powerplants were suggested, including Allison J-33s and Pratt & Whitney J-42s (licence-built Rolls-Royce Nenes).

The C-102 was fitted with tricycle undercarriage, with dual mainwheels retracting into the rear of the engine nacelles.

C-102 Jetliner

Type: medium-range civil transport

Powerplant: four 16.01-kN (3,600-lb.-thrust) Rolls-Royce Derwent 5/17 turbojets

Maximum speed: 804 km/h (498 m.p.h.) at 9145 m (30,000 ft.)

Cruising speed: 692 km/h (429 m.p.h.) at 9145 m (30,000 ft.)

Initial climb rate: 561 m/min (1,840 f.p.m.)

Range: 2012 km (1,250 mi.)

Service ceiling: 11,368 m (37,300 ft.)

Weights: empty 15,050 kg (33,110 lb.); maximum take-off 29,510 kg (64,922 lb.)

Accommodation: (proposed) flight crew of two, plus 30 to 50 passengers in various seating configurations

Dimensions:
span		29.89 m (98 ft.)
length		24.61 m (80 ft. 9 in.)
height		8.06 m (26 ft. 5 in.)
wing area		107.48 m² (1,156 sq. ft.)

ACTION DATA

CRUISING SPEED

The de Havilland Comet flew two weeks before the Jetliner and was the first jet airliner to enter service. Powered by four de Havilland Ghosts, the aircraft had a 96 km/h (60 m.p.h.) speed advantage.

C-102 JETLINER	692km/h (429 m.p.h.)
COMET Mk 1	789 km/h (489 m.p.h.)
Tu-104 'CAMEL'	770 km/h (477 m.p.h.)

PASSENGERS

All three of these jetliners had similar capacity, although with 50 passengers aboard, the C-102 was at its upper limit. The Comet was later 'stretched' to increase seating.

C-102 JETLINER	50 passengers
COMET Mk 1	44 passengers
Tu-104 'CAMEL'	50 passengers

RANGE

In prototype form the C-102 demonstrated a range of just over 2000 km (1,250 mi.). When fitted with four Derwent engines, the Jetliner's fuel capacity was reduced and extra tankage was required to maintain range. Payload capability therefore suffered. Both the Comet and Tu-104 were larger aircraft, the latter having two engines.

C-102 JETLINER 2012 km (1,250 mi.)
COMET Mk 1 2816 km (1,745 mi.)
Tu-104 'CAMEL' 2650 km (1,645 mi.)

British jet transport prototypes

■ **AVRO 706 ASHTON:** Six of these large aircraft were built for the Ministry of Supply for research into jet operations. Four Rolls-Royce Nene turbojets were fitted.

■ **DE HAVILLAND DH.106 COMET:** First flown in July 1949, the de Havilland Ghost-powered Comet was to be the world's first jet airliner in service, just under three years later.

■ **VICKERS NENE-VIKING:** Rolls-Royce Nene turbojets were installed in a Viking airliner to create the world's first pure-jet transport aircraft. Flown in 1948, it was strictly a test aircraft.

■ **VICKERS VISCOUNT 663:** The second Viscount turboprop airliner prototype was rebuilt in 1950 as a flying engine testbed with two Rolls-Royce Tay turbojets.

19

AVRO CANADA

CF-105 ARROW

● High-speed interceptor ● Missile armament ● Project cancelled

▲ When unveiled, the spectacular Arrow was unfortunately overshadowed by the launch of the Soviet satellite Sputnik 1. After five Mk 1 development machines, the project was cancelled just days before the Mk 2 was scheduled to fly.

Designed to intercept Soviet bombers flying over the North Pole to launch supersonic attacks, the CF-105 was an ambitious design. It was required to have two engines, two seats, long range, a high supersonic speed and all-missile armament. The missiles were to be carried internally, which dictated a very large fighter with a high wing to make room for the missile bay in the fuselage. This resulted in the unusually long undercarriage legs.

AVRO CANADA CF-105 ARROW

Landing accidents ▶
During flight testing, the Arrow was involved in two incidents. In June 1958 the port undercarriage leg failed to extend on 25201 and took four months to repair. In November, 25202 suffered brake seizure on landing, causing an undercarriage leg to collapse. Repairs were never completed.

◀ Weapons bay
Like other ultra-high-performance interceptors of its day, the Arrow carried its weapons internally to reduce drag.

Revolutionary wing ▶
Among the CF-105's advanced features was its machined-plate wing skin with internal fuel tanks.

▼ Mission profile
The definitive Arrow was intended to fly high-speed missions, cruising at Mach 1.5, with fuel provision for five minutes of combat at 17830 metres.

▲ Public unveiling
Arrow 25201 was rolled out on 4 October 1957 at Malton, Ontario, in front of 12,000 spectators.

FACTS AND FIGURES

➤ The projected follow-on Mk 3 was to be fitted with Iroquois 3 engines, new intakes and nozzles.

➤ No fewer than 16 wind-tunnel models were used during the final design stages.

➤ The two underfuselage speed brakes could be held open during Mach 1 flights.

➤ The CF-105's advanced hydraulic system remained unique until the Rockwell B-1A strategic bomber was flown in 1974.

➤ For servicing, the Mk 2's engines could be slid out on special rails.

➤ A B-47 with a rear-mounted nacelle was used to test the Orenda Iroquois engine.

PROFILE

Canada's ill-fated Arrow

Designed with a large, thin delta wing, the Arrow prototypes used Pratt & Whitney J75 engines, although Mk 2 production aircraft were intended to use the new Orenda PS-13 Iroquois. A later version of the Iroquois was expected to give the Arrow Mk 3 a maximum speed of Mach 2.5.

The Arrow was also to have a new Astra radar and fire control system, in addition to new Sparrow II long-range missiles. Eight Falcons and four Sparrow IIs could have been carried, although the eventual cancellation of the Sparrow II led to one or two nuclear-warhead Genie missiles being specified instead.

The first of five completed prototypes initially flew in March 1958. Airborne performance was good, but landing gear failures damaged two of the prototypes on the ground. In September the radar and Sparrow II missiles were cancelled in favour of cheaper US systems.

The programme survived only a few more months. In February 1958 the government ordered all five Mk 1s and the four near-complete Mk 2 prototypes to be destroyed. The Canadian air force received F-101 Voodoos instead.

Long, slender main undercarriage struts were a feature of the CF-105. They were necessary to fit the gear into the Arrow's thin wing section.

The massive wing was cut from a single sheet, which was then machined down until just nine per cent of the metal remained.

A wing leading-edge notch was added late in development, as was an outer portion leading-edge extension. They both reduced the effect of vortex disturbance.

SPECIFICATION

CF-105 Arrow Mk 2

Type: two-seat long-range interceptor

Powerplant: two 115.66-kN (26,000-lb.-thrust) Orenda PS-13 Iroquois 2 turbojet engines

Maximum speed: 2124 km/h (1,317 m.p.h.)

Combat radius: 1143 km (710 mi.) with external fuel

Range: 2420 km (1,500 mi.) ferry range with external fuel

Service ceiling: 18290 m (60,000 ft.)

Weights: fully loaded 30006 kg (66,150 lb.)

Armament: six GAR-1A Falcon air-to-air missiles

Dimensions:
span	15.24 m (50 ft.)
length	24.38 m (78 ft.)
height	6.40 m (21 ft.)
wing area	113.8 m² (1,224 sq.ft.)

CF-105 ARROW MK 1

Avro Canada Arrow 25201 was the first to fly. Rolled out in October 1957, its first engine run followed on 4 December and the prototype, flown by Jan Zurakowski, took to the air on 25 March 1958.

CF-105s 25201 to 25205, designated Mk 1s, were purely test machines and were unarmed. The fourth and fifth aircraft had the shorter radome of the abortive Astra I radar system.

CF-105s had a crew of two seated in tandem on Martin-Baker C-5 ejection seats. Fixed air intakes were intended to be replaced on the projected Mk 2A by variable-geometry types.

The Arrow was tailless. An artificial damping system was therefore needed to give high-speed stability.

The undercarriage had to both shorten and twist to retract into the thin wing. To shorten the oleos, the wing drooped by 4°.

The RCAF demanded a highly sophisticated fire-control system. Hughes proposed the MX1179 from the Convair F-106, but RCA was given the contract to construct the Astra I, which was later abandoned.

A generous weapons bay of 5.41 m (17 ft. 9 in.) length and 2.92 m (9 ft. 7 in.) width was to carry pre-loaded packs of Sparrow 2, GAR-1A Falcon and nuclear-tipped Genie air-to-air missiles.

Several types of engine were considered, but the Orenda Iroquois was chosen for production machines. However, development aircraft like this were powered by two American Pratt & Whitney J75s.

ACTION DATA

THRUST

For its day, the CF-105 was in a class of its own in terms of the thrust produced by its twin Canadian-built Iroquois 2s. The development machines had used less powerful Pratt & Whitney engines.

CF-105 ARROW Mk 2   231.32 kN (52,000 lb.-thrust)

CF-101B VOODOO   150.4 kN (33,834 lb.-thrust)

JAVELIN FAW.Mk 7   97.9 kN (44,000 lb.-thrust)

ARMAMENT

Throughout its development there was debate about the Arrow's armament. Cannon were dispensed with, and Sparrow 2, Falcon and Genie were evaluated instead.

CF-105 ARROW Mk 2   6 x GAR-1A Falcon missiles

CF-101B VOODOO   2 x MB-1 Genie missiles, 4 x GAR-1A Falcon missiles

JAVELIN FAW.Mk 7   4 x Firestreak missiles, 2 x 30-mm cannon

SERVICE CEILING

The respectable ceiling of the CF-105 came from its design requirement: to be able to intercept high-flying Soviet turbojet bombers over Canadian territory.

CF-105 ARROW Mk 2 18290 m (60,000 ft.)

JAVELIN FAW.Mk 7 16039 m (52,600 ft.)

CF-101B VOODOO 14995 m (42,900 ft.)

Royal Canadian Air Force jet interceptors

■ **AVRO CANADA CF-100:** The CF-100 Canuck long-range interceptor was the first military aircraft to be completely designed and built in Canada. It was intended to be replaced by the CF-105.

■ **CANADAIR CF-104:** Lockheed's Starfighter was licence-built in Canada. It proved problematic, however, and reverted to strike duties before its retirement in the early 1980s.

■ **McDONNELL CF-101B:** Hastily acquired after the CF-105's cancellation, the Voodoo was a proven front-line interceptor with its Falcon and nuclear Genie air-to-air missile armament.

■ **McDONNELL DOUGLAS CF-118:** First delivered in 1982, the CF-118 is Canada's principal air defence asset. Operating a total of 98, Canada was the first Hornet export buyer.

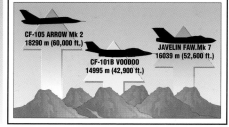

BAC

221

● High-speed ● Delta-wing research ● Concorde support

O riginally built as a pure high-speed research aircraft, the Fairey Delta 2 was the world's fastest aircraft in the mid-1950s. It set a world speed record of 1822 km/h (1,130 m.p.h.) in March 1956. In the 1960s, it found a new career in a highly modified form, as the BAC 221 aerodynamic research aircraft. Its role was to investigate the control and handling characteristics of a thin delta wing, in support of the Concorde supersonic airliner project.

▲ Having performed brilliantly as the FD 2, WG774 re-emerged as the BAC 221, in which form it provided further invaluable research data and flight experience.

BAC 221

Slender delta ▶
Press releases of the period referred to the BAC 221 as a 'slender delta research aircraft'. The thin delta wing was the principal feature of the design, as illustrated by this head-on view.

▼ With Fairey Delta 2
Only WG774 was converted to BAC 221 status; WG777 remained in Delta 2 configuration.

▲ Nose droop
Pilot visibility on landing was improved by the drooping nose. This could be set at a variety of angles, unlike that of the Delta 2.

Ogival wing planform ▶
Referred to as an ogival delta, the wing planform of the BAC 221 was very close to that of Concorde. The two-position exhaust nozzle is seen here in the closed mode.

◀ Museum piece
Both the BAC 221 and the Delta 2 survived their research programmes and are now preserved. The BAC 221 is on display at the Fleet Air Arm Museum, Yeovilton, resplendent in its blue colour scheme. The aircraft performed some early flights in bare metal.

FACTS AND FIGURES

➤ An ogival wing was chosen to give the best combination of lift, drag and stability characteristics at high Mach numbers.

➤ Fixed inlets for optimum performance at Mach 1.5-1.75 were chosen for simplicity.

➤ Some parts of the control system were based on those of the Hawker P.1127.

➤ One of the BAC 221's hydraulic systems was similar to that of the Bristol 188; the second was similar to that of the P.1127.

➤ Continuous voice transmission enabled the chase-plane to hear the 221 pilot.

➤ The blue finish was applied to make the woollen tufts stand out better on film.

PROFILE

All-blue research delta

To prepare the Delta 2 for its new role, the Filton division of the British Aircraft Corporation carried out an extensive modification programme on the former world speed record-holder.

New ogival delta wings, similar in shape to those designed for Concorde, were fitted, along with revised control surfaces and new air intakes and undercarriage. The nose droop angle was made variable, and an automatic stabilisation system, that could be used to simulate changes in the aircraft's stability

characteristics, was fitted. This enabled a variety of aerodynamic and centre-of-gravity configurations to be tested.

Now known as the BAC 221, the rebuilt aircraft flew for the first time in May 1964. Two years later, it was delivered to the Royal Aircraft Establishment at Bedford for flight trials at speeds up to Mach 1.6. The Handley Page HP 115 was used to investigate delta-winged handling at lower speeds.

Among the trials carried out were studies of the airflow and vortex formation across the

Above: In producing the 221, BAC lengthened the fuselage of the FD 2 and replaced the forward fuselage completely.

wings. Pressure transducers were fitted to record the pressure pattern on film, and woollen tufts were also used to allow the airflow pattern to be recorded. The flight data was then compared with information gathered in wind-tunnel tests.

Above: Taking-off using afterburner with the exhaust nozzle fully open, the BAC 221 demonstrates its enormously long nose undercarriage leg. The shock-absorber was modified from that of the Fairey Gannet.

BAC 221

Type: delta-winged, high-speed research aircraft

Powerplant: one 62.3-kN (14,015-lb.) thrust Rolls-Royce RA.28R Avon afterburning turbojet

Maximum speed: 1706 km/h (1,050 m.p.h.) at altitude

Service ceiling: 15240 m (50,000 ft.)

Weights: empty 6350 kg (13,970 lb.); maximum take-off 8165 kg (17,963 lb.)

Accommodation: pilot only on Martin-Baker Mk 3 FDV ejection seat

Dimensions: span 7.62 m (25 ft.)
length 17.56 m (24 ft. 9 in.)
height 3.45 m (11 ft. 2 in.)
wing area 46.5 m² (500 sq. ft.)

221

From its delivery in 1966, until it was retired on 9 June 1973, WG774 undertook a valuable programme of research flights which greatly enhanced Concorde's final configuration.

Conditions in the cockpit of the FD 2 had become increasingly cramped as more items of equipment were added. For the 221, new instrumentation was supplied, along with a revised canopy, but the layout remained unchanged.

The 221 inherited its drooping nose from the FD 2, although it had a more complex unit than the earlier type. This nose system was adopted for Concorde and the Tupolev Tu-144 'Charger'. An ogive-winged research vehicle was also constructed in the Soviet Union. It was based on the MiG-21 and known as Analog.

BAC designed the ogival (or ogive) wing in two halves, attached to either side of the fuselage. The wingroot attachments were similar to those of the FD 2. The sweep was 65° on the straight section of the leading edge, which extended forwards along the side of the fuselage to form chines.

A prominent fairing at the leading edge of the fin-tip housed a 16-mm cine camera. This was positioned to film the effects of airflow on woollen tufts connected to the starboard wing.

Unusually long undercarriage legs were a feature of the 221. Two pairs of doors were required to cover the retracted nose-wheel unit, which retained the twin wheels of the FD 2.

Components from several different aircraft were 'borrowed' for the BAC 221. These included the main undercarriage which was based on that of the Lightning. Other Lightning parts featured in the nose gear.

A total redesign of the engine air intakes was necessary, as the 221 required a sharp unbroken leading edge. The exhaust was similar to that of the FD 2 but, with a little modification, it gave increased power.

British delta-winged research

AVRO 707A: Five aircraft in the 707 series were built. The first was lost and the remainder provided much valuable data on delta-winged flight for the Vulcan project.

FAIREY DELTA 2: Designed for research into high-speed flight at a range of altitudes, using a 60° swept delta wing, the FD 2 project was extremely successful.

HANDLEY PAGE HP 115: Used to test the slow-speed handling characteristics of a delta wing, the HP 115 worked in concert with the BAC 221, flying outside the latter's envelope.

SHORT SC.1: Britain's first fixed-wing vertical/short take-off and landing (V/STOL) aircraft, the SC.1 first flew on 2 April 1957. The aircraft helped to prove the V/STOL concept.

ACTION DATA

SPEED

In producing the BAC 221, the British Aircraft Corporation lost some of the speed of the Delta 2, which had been designed purely as a supersonic research platform. The 221 was the more efficient aircraft, however, especially in cruising flight. Its specialisation in high-speed cruising made the aircraft unsuitable for low-speed delta trials, and the HP 115 was built for this purpose.

221	1706 km/h (1,058 m.p.h.)
HP 115	400 km/h (248 m.p.h)
FD 2	1805 km/h (1,119 m.p.h.)

MAXIMUM TAKE-OFF WEIGHT

A heavier aircraft than its predecessor, the BAC 221 made up for this with increased power. With no requirement for high speed, the Handley Page HP 115 could be made smaller and lighter, its less powerful engine needing less fuel. On transforming the FD 2 into the 221, BAC incorporated more modern systems and a great deal of new test and safety equipment.

221 8165 kg (17,963 lb.)
HP 115 2300 kg (5,060 lb.)
FD 2 6298 kg (13,856 lb.)

THRUST

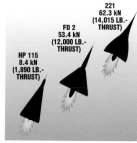

With only 8.4 kN (1,890 lb.) thrust, the Bristol Siddeley Viper 9 turbojet of the HP 115 was sufficient for its low-speed tests. The BAC 221 had basically the same engine as the FD 2, but used improved air intake design to provide large amounts of extra thrust, especially at high altitude.

221 62.3 kN (14,015 LB.-THRUST)
FD 2 53.4 kN (12,000 LB.-THRUST)
HP 115 8.4 kN (1,890 LB.-THRUST)

BAC
TSR.2

● Supersonic strike-bomber ● Advanced technology reconnaissance

BAC TSR.2

▲ **Low-speed handling**
With its large blown flaps deployed, the TSR.2 showed remarkable handling, as well as the ability to make short 'tactical' take-offs.

◄ **Final assembly**
The first TSR.2 is shown on the Weybridge assembly line. The aircraft showed its superb potential as soon as it began trials, delighting the test pilots.

▲ **Needle nose**
The head-on view of the TSR.2 shows that it was built for speed. Even today, few aircraft could match its sea-level performance.

◄ **Finished product**
The RAF never got its hands on the TSR.2, and the promised F-111s were also cancelled. Buccaneers were ordered instead.

▲ **Small wing**
The small wing with its anhedral tips was ideal for fast, low-level operations, combining low drag with a good gust response.

W ith its superb performance, state-of-the-art avionics and effective weapons load, the TSR.2 was one of the most promising warplanes ever developed in Britain, and it might have revolutionised the RAF. But even though test pilot Roland Beamont called it 'one of the most remarkable designs in aviation history', it was never to enter service, 'shot down' by rising costs and political squabbling.

▲ Had it entered service, the TSR.2 would have given Britain the most advanced combat aircraft in the world, at home in supersonic strike missions at both high and low level.

FACTS AND FIGURES

➤ The prototype TSR.2 made its first flight on 27 September 1964.

➤ The TSR.2 had a central computer, head-up display and terrain-following radar – standard in today's combat aircraft.

➤ If it had entered service, the TSR.2 would still be one of the world's best bombers.

➤ It is thought that the TSR.2 would have had better combat performance than the General Dynamics F-111.

➤ Of 49 TSR.2s planned in the first stage of the programme, only four were built.

➤ The only TSR.2 to fly logged 13 hours 9 minutes in the air before cancellation.

PROFILE

Wonder bomber that never was

The British Aircraft Corporation TSR.2 was designed to replace the Canberra bomber. Built to an extremely stiff specification, it was as fast as any fighter in the world at altitude, and at low level it promised to be nearly uncatchable.

It was equipped with terrain-following radar and infra-red sensors, and should have been able to penetrate enemy airspace and deliver weaponry with devastating accuracy.

Early test-flying confirmed that the sleek, beautiful TSR.2 would be able to deliver what had been promised, with the ability to make unrefuelled supersonic strikes at targets up to 1200 km (750 mi.) distant.

But such performance comes at a price, and costs on the project were rising as fast as the TSR.2's 15000-m/min (49,212 f.p.m.) rate of climb. In 1964 it was cancelled by the newly elected Labour government. Because of

political infighting, the RAF waited 20 years for the Tornado before they had an aircraft which could approach the performance of the TSR.2.

The TSR.2 was a superb piece of technology, let down by political argument over costs. Had it gone into service, the RAF would have had the finest long-range strike aircraft anywhere in the world.

The TSR.2 was longer and heavier than any aircraft the RAF had used during World War II.

TSR.2

The TSR.2 airframes that were built led a short and inglorious life, flying less than 14 hours in total before being scrapped or ending up in museums.

The pilot had an advanced head-up display system for weapon delivery, as well as Doppler and inertial navigation systems, radar altimeter and electronic countermeasures.

The huge fuel capacity of the TSR.2 was mostly internal. The forward fuel tank alone held over 5000 litres.

A complex air intake system included auxiliary doors in the inlet duct walls which opened and closed at different speeds to modify the engine airflow.

The wing had unusual downward-drooping wingtips.

Twin airbrakes were fitted to the rear upper fuselage. The tail was an all-moving system, with differential operation to give roll control.

Twin Olympus engines gave the TSR.2 more power than the American F-111 or F-4 Phantom.

The radar system allowed automatic terrain-following, a capability that the RAF did not have until the Tornado entered service in the 1980s.

Side-looking radar was another of the innovative ideas applied to the TSR.2. This equipment would have given the aircraft a very useful reconnaissance capability. Datalink via satellite to a ground station was planned for this system.

The long fuselage accommodated an internal weapons bay and large fuel tanks, as well as two cockpits.

A twin wheel undercarriage gave the heavy TSR.2 the ability to use rough tactical airstrips.

XR222

TSR.2

Type: two-seat attack/reconnaissance aircraft

Powerplant: two 136.16-kN (30,608-lb.) Bristol Siddeley Olympus 320 turbojets, each with a potential thrust of 147.11 kN (33,070-lb.)

Maximum speed: 2390 km/h (1,485 m.p.h.)

Ferry range: 6840 km (4,250 mi.)

Operating ceiling: 16460 m (54,000 ft.)

Weights: normal c. 36287 kg (79.831 lb.); maximum take-off c. 43500 kg (95,700 lb.)

Armament: (planned) 2722 kg (6,000 lb.) of conventional or nuclear weapons in an internal bay plus 1814 kg (3,990 lb.) of external ordnance

Dimensions:
span	11.28 m	(37ft.)
length	27.13 m	(89 ft.)
height	7.32 m	(24 ft.)
wing area	65.03 m²	(700 sq. ft.)

COMBAT DATA

SERVICE CEILING

Although the TSR.2 was an extremely capable low-level strike platform, it was also designed to have a high-level capability to maximise its reconnaissance potential. The F-111 was also intended for multiple roles, and it too had a high ceiling. The Buccaneer, by contrast, was designed from its inception to attack at very low levels, and could not climb as high.

16460 m (54,000 ft.) — TSR.2

15550 m (51,016 ft.) — F-111A

12190 m (40,000 ft.) — BUCCANEER

Strike bombers

■ **ENGLISH ELECTRIC CANBERRA:** As advanced for its time as the TSR.2, the design of the high-flying subsonic Canberra dated back to the late 1940s, and by the 1960s was long overdue for replacement. However, it has continued in service as a reconnaissance platform.

■ **GENERAL DYNAMICS F-111:** The TSR.2 was cancelled in favour of an 'off-the-shelf' purchase of the F-111 – a deal which was never completed. F-111 development was plagued by problems, but it eventually matured into a fine aircraft, which is still in service with the Australian air force.

■ **BLACKBURN BUCCANEER:** The RAF's low-level strike requirement was eventually met by the Buccaneer – which had already been in service with the Royal Navy for a decade. Although it was a fine aircraft with good low-level performance, it was still no match for the TSR.2.

BACHEM

BA 349 NATTER

● Rocket-powered ● Wooden construction ● Point defence

B y the spring of 1944 the mounting pressure placed on the Luftwaffe's fighter force by the continuous stream of Allied bombers had reached a critical point. Germany could not survive unless the effect of these raids was rapidly reduced. A radical solution was sought, and the German air ministry issued a request for a machine which combined the capabilities of an interceptor aircraft and a missile. Bachem proposed the rocket-powered Ba 349 Natter (Adder).

▲ After a number of pilotless Natter launches, the first manned flight took place on 28 February 1945. It ended fatally, but was followed by three successful tests.

BACHEM BA 349 NATTER

Museum piece ▶
One Ba 349 survived Allied evaluation after the war. It is now in the Smithsonian in Washington, DC.

▼ Fifty prototypes built in three months
Unpowered gliding trials began in November 1944. They were so successful that powered launching began the following month.

▼ On the gantry
Natters blasted off from a 6-metre (20-ft.) vertical gantry. Three channelled rails guided the wings and the lower fin.

First manned flight ▶
Oberleutnant L. Siebert died during the first manned flight. After launch the canopy blew off, probably knocking him out.

▼ Rocket armament
The Ba 349's primary weapons were the 24 Hs 217 rockets housed in the nose.

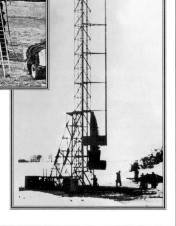

FACTS AND FIGURES

➤ Erich Bachem had first proposed his rocket-powered interceptor in 1939, but received little official encouragement.

➤ For the first unpowered flight, the Natter was carried to 5500 m (18,050 ft.) beneath an He 111.

➤ Unmanned test launches were carried out with a dummy pilot in the cockpit.

➤ The improved Ba 349B had a rocket motor of increased endurance, but only three were produced before VE Day.

➤ To fire the salvo of unguided rockets the pilot ejected the Natter's nosecone.

PROFILE

Germany's desperate defender

Four companies submitted designs to meet the German air ministry's demand for a small point interceptor and Bachem's Ba 349 was eventually chosen for evaluation. This was mainly due to the intervention of SS leader Heinrich Himmler, who was looking for ways to increase his influence in the armed forces.

With Germany's industry suffering from Allied raids it was necessary for the Natter to be built from wood and be of simple construction, allowing rapid and economical production.

The final Ba 349 design was essentially that of a manned surface-to-air missile. Launched from a vertical rail, the Natter would continue to climb vertically, controlled by an autopilot, using its main rocket engine and additional power from rocket boosters. As the aircraft reached a bomber formation, the pilot would resume control and make a firing pass using unguided rockets. The aircraft would then descend to an altitude of 1400 metres and the nose section would separate from the fuselage. The pilot would release himself

Left: A pilotless Ba 349 is prepared for the first vertical launch on 18 December 1944.

Above: This Ba 349A is mounted on a trailer which was used to transport the aircraft to the launching ramp. In the foreground is one of the Schmidding solid-fuel booster rockets, four of which were attached to the rear fuselage.

and descend, along with the fuselage, by parachute.

Of 36 airframes built, only 10 reached operational status. These never saw combat, however, but were blown up as American land forces approached their base.

Ba 349A Natter

Type: single-seat semi-expendable interceptor

Powerplant: one 19.62-kN (3,748-lb.-thrust) Walter HWK 509C-1 bi-fuel rocket motor, plus four 4.9-kN (2,640-lb.-thrust) Schmidding 109-533 solid-fuel rockets

Maximum speed: 998 km/h (619 m.p.h.)

Initial climb rate: 11400 m/min (36,415 f.p.m.)

Combat radius: 40 km (25 mi.)

Service ceiling: 14000 m (45,920 ft.)

Weights: loaded 2200 kg (4,850 lb.)

Armament: 24 73-mm Hs 217 Föhn rockets

Dimensions:
span	3.60 m (11 ft. 10 in.)
length	6.10 m (20 ft.)
wing area	2.75 m² (30 sq. ft.)

Above the nose was a ring sight for the nose-mounted rocket armament, which was covered by a jettisonable plastic fairing before launch. Twin 30-mm MK 108 cannon were proposed but never fitted.

Protection for Natter pilots was of major importance, with sandwich-type armour being fitted on all four sides. Instrumentation in the cockpit was spartan. Plans to fit an ejection seat were rejected because of space constraints.

The main engine was a variant of that fitted to the Messerschmitt Me 163 interceptor. For vertical launch four booster rockets were added, which burned during the first 10 seconds of flight.

Cruciform fins on the rear fuselage carried the control surfaces. Elevators and rudders, operating differentially, provided roll control.

COMBAT DATA

MAXIMUM SPEED

Powered by the same engine as the Messerschmitt Me 163, the Natter's lighter and more streamlined form gave it an edge in performance, pushing the aircraft close to the sound barrier. The Bolkhovitinov BI was the world's first rocket-powered fighter and had startling performance.

Ba 349B-1a NATTER	998 km/h (619 m.p.h.)
Me 163B-1a KOMET	960 km/h (595 m.p.h.)
BI	1000 km/h (620 m.p.h.)

CLIMB RATE

With its main rocket engine plus booster rockets the Natter had an amazing rate of climb from the vertical position. The g forces sustained were so great that the aircraft had to be controlled by autopilot during the ascent.

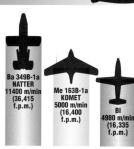

Ba 349B-1a NATTER 11400 m/min (36,415 f.p.m.)

Me 163B-1a KOMET 5000 m/min (16,400 f.p.m.)

BI 4980 m/min (16,335 f.p.m.)

The fuselage was constructed of wood. The only metal parts were control push rods, hinges and load-supporting attachment points.

Originally it was envisaged that the Natter would make ramming attacks on bomber formations once it had expended its rockets. This would have necessitated fitting an ejection seat for the pilot, but the idea was abandoned and a jettisonable nose was fitted instead.

BA 349A NATTER

This example is one of an estimated 20 Ba 349As completed by early 1945. Ten of these aircraft were set up for operations at Kirchheim, close to the Wolf Hirth production factory.

ENDURANCE

Both the Natter and the Me 163 were designed as point interceptors and had exceptionally short endurance. This meant that they were only capable of making one firing pass on an enemy formation.

Ba 349B-1a NATTER	Me 163B-1a KOMET	BI
4 min 22sec	7min 30sec	15 min

Operational Natter missions

1 LAUNCH: If the Natter had ever been used operationally it would have been launched from a vertical rail to accelerate rapidly to its operational height guided by an autopilot.

2 INTERCEPTION: On reaching the enemy bomber formation the Natter pilot would eject the nose cone and fire a salvo of unguided rockets.

3 DESCENT: When the rocket fuel was exhausted the Natter would make an unpowered descent to 1400 m (4,500 ft.).

4 TOUCHDOWN: The pilot would then jettison the nose section using explosive bolts and release himself from the fuselage. Both the pilot and the rear fuselage would then descend to the ground by parachute.

BEDE

BD-10

● Supersonic jet ● Home-built kit ● Composite structure

The Bede BD-10J is a lightweight, single-engine jet aircraft with dual controls and tandem seating. Designed by aviation genius Jim Bede, the BD-10J is meant for the civil market and offers performance characteristics which rival, and in some cases even exceed, those of military fighters. As a privately owned home-build aircraft, the BD-10J astonishingly provides brief supersonic capability at relatively little cost.

▲ Soaring to success; Jim Bede was instrumental in providing the home-built market with high performance aircraft that could be assembled by any individual relatively easily.

BEDE BD-10

◄ Bird of prey
Now called the Peregrine Falcon the BD-10 has been likened to the USAF's F-15 Eagle, both in performance characteristics and the look of the aircraft.

Man with a vision ▶
As president of Bede Aircraft Incorporated, Jim Bede has seen his company produce some of the most innovative aircraft designs ever. His vision is to make flying available to the average person.

▲ Microjet movie star
One of the first sales successes for Jim Bede was the BD-5J. Its high-speed and sparkling performance have seen the jet make numerous guest appearances in a host of films.

▲ Civilian fighter
With the collapse of the Bede Aircraft Corporation, the civil version of the BD-10 is now sold by Peregrine Flight Int.

◄ Model kit aircraft
A display of the components that go up to make the BD-5J; this simple construction is retained on the BD-10.

FACTS AND FIGURES

➤ Design of the BD-10 began in 1983 with the first flight of the aircraft being accomplished on 8 July 1992.

➤ The first kit of the aircraft was delivered in August 1993.

➤ Bede Aircraft Incorporated continues to market the military version of the BD-10.

➤ Peregrine International acquired the design and marketing rights for the civilian sports variant of the BD-10.

➤ One BD-10 was lost in a fatal crash on 30 December 1994.

➤ More than 45 examples of the BD-10 have been ordered within the United States.

PROFILE

Home-built hot rod

The Bede aviation company in St Louis, Missouri held high hopes in the early 1990s for both military and civilian use of the BD-10J, the world's first supersonic, home-built jet aircraft. The fully aerobatic BD-10J has a fighter-style tandem seating arrangement, non-boosted flight controls, and a pressurised cockpit.

Bede launched the BD-10J in 1991, believing it had strong potential for both civil and military use in the developed world and in Third World

countries. The Bede trademark of simplicity was found from one end of the aircraft to the other. It has no hydraulic flight controls and no cables, only manual controls. The flight surfaces are operated by push-rods, rod ends and ball-bearings. The BD-10J is unique in having two control sticks: a side stick and centre stick, mechanically connected, which move in sequence with each other.

Difficulties in development and the loss of the prototype have resulted in the sales of the aircraft being temporarily

suspended. Despite these set-backs huge interest remains in Bede's unique supersonic home-built jet.

Below: Providing a new dimension for the private flying enthusiast, the BD-10 was seen to offer supersonic performance for a fraction of the operating cost of other types.

Above: To reduce the overall weight of the aircraft, the BD-10 uses a composite and aluminium construction. This allows customers to construct their own aircraft in kit form, so reducing the overall purchase cost of the aircraft.

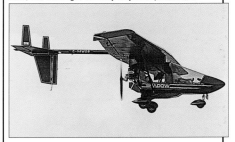

BD-10

Bringing the capabilities of a military jet fighter to the civilian home-built market, the BD-10 is the subject of an enquiry into a crash. Despite this, orders are still forthcoming.

BD-10

Type: home-build supersonic aircraft

Powerplant: one 13.12-kN (2,950-lb.-thrust) General Electric CJ-610 turbojet

Maximum speed: Mach 1.4 at high altitude

Maximum cruising speed: 957 km/h (593 m.p.h.)

Initial climb rate: 9150 m/min (30,000 f.p.m.)

Range: 2499 km (1,550 mi.)

Service ceiling: 13715 m (45,000 ft.)

Weights: maximum take-off 2014 kg (4,430 lb.)

Accommodation: two pilots seated in tandem

Dimensions:
span	6.55 m	(21 ft. 6 in.)
length	8.79 m	(28 ft. 10 in.)
height	2.46 m	(8 ft. 1 in.)
wing area	9.10 m²	(98 sq. ft.)

MILITARY LIGHTWEIGHTS

MICROLIGHT: Currently one of the most advanced microlights flying, the Shadow built by CFM was such a capable machine that military applications were soon envisaged. Equipped with a FLIR pod under its fuselage, the Shadow was to be used as a covert reconnaissance platform. Despite testing, which the Shadow passed with ease, this microlight currently only sees private use.

SAILPLANES: Schweizer has had a long history of constructing highly capable and successful sailplanes for the private market. Various models have also been used by the US military for training since World War II. The latest military application for the sailplanes have seen them being adopted by the US Navy as part of its Test Pilot School fleet.

A simple weather radar is installed within the nose of the BD-10. This provides a limited amount of data for the pilot. Options available on the aircraft are either sophisticated flight instruments or the bare necessities.

A large single piece canopy affords the tandem-seated crew excellent visibility when in flight. The cockpit is pressurised but the pilots are not equipped with ejection seats. Later military training variants were to be fitted with advanced zero-zero ejection seats.

The airframe is composed of 60 per cent metal, 40 per cent composites which include aluminium alloy and aluminium honeycomb structures. These are mounted in a sandwich construction. This has proved to be immensely strong yet incredibly light. Despite this, the fatal crash of the BD-10 was traced to the failure of a wing flap.

The only hydraulic systems used on the BD-10 are for the wheel brakes and landing gear. Positioned on either side of the fuselage are small inlets for the engine; these are electrically heated to prevent ice forming.

A single General Electric CJ-610 turbojet gives the BD-10 exceptional performance. There are five centre-fuselage fuel cells. A single refuelling point is positioned on top of the fuselage.

Breaking new ground in a Bede

■ **BD-4:** Marketed as a private utility aircraft, the BD-4 was powered by a Lycoming engine, but the design met with little success.

■ **XBD-2:** A revolutionary six-place executive aircraft, the BD-2 featured a single pusher propeller shrouded to increase thrust.

■ **BD-2:** Basically a two-seat Schweizer sailplane, this was the product of an attempt by Jim Bede to fly non-stop around the world.

■ **BD-7:** Developed from the BD-5, an increase in cockpit size allowed passengers to be carried within the small aircraft.

BELL

X-1

● Experimental rocket-plane ● Broke the sound barrier

▲ Chuck Yeager was a World War II fighter ace who became one of history's great test pilots. For security reasons, the public had to wait several weeks to learn of his feat.

On October 14, 1947, the bullet-shaped Bell X-1 took its place in aviation history when Captain Charles E. 'Chuck' Yeager penetrated the so-called sound barrier, making the world's first recorded and successful supersonic flight. Originally known as the XS-1, for experimental supersonic, the X-1 was the first in a series of rocket-powered X-planes that Yeager and his successors went on to fly at unprecedented speeds and altitudes.

BELL X-1

▲ **Record-breaker**
Chuck Yeager's name will always be associated with the X-1. Breaking the sound barrier in the original aircraft, he was to go twice as fast in the extensively modified X-1A.

▲ **Airborne launch**
The X-1 did not take off conventionally. Instead, it was carried aloft in the bomb bay of a Boeing B-29 Superfortress.

▲ **Rocket ignite**
Once the B-29 reached launch altitude, the X-1 was dropped like a huge bomb. The bullet-shaped craft fell clear of the bomber before the pilot ignited his rocket engine and the X-1 accelerated up and away.

▲ **Rocket power**
The X-1 was propelled by a Reaction Motors liquid-fueled rocket that delivered more than 26.69 kN (6,000 lb.) of thrust.

Higher and faster ▶
Bell modified the X-1 several times. In 1953, Chuck Yeager took the X-1A to a maximum speed of Mach 2.4, losing control in the process but recovering to land safely.

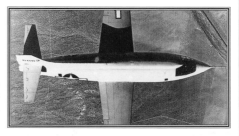

FACTS AND FIGURES

➤ First flights of the X-1 were made in Florida before tests were moved to California.

➤ On his trip through the sound barrier, Yeager reached 1078 km/h (670 m.p.h.) at an altitude of 12801 m (42,000 ft.).

➤ Captain Yeager flew the X-1 on his military salary of $275 per month.

➤ Some experts believe that the XP-86 Sabre may have gone supersonic before the X-1.

➤ The pilot of the X-1 had no throttle, although each of four rocket chambers could be fired separately.

➤ The X-1 is on display in the National Air and Space Museum in Washington, D.C.

PROFILE

Breaking the sound barrier

It didn't look like much. A small, bullet-shaped machine, painted bright orange and with the name *Glamorous Glennis* on the nose. But the Bell X-1 flown by Chuck Yeager will live forever in history because it pioneered supersonic flight.

The sound barrier was one of the great milestones of aviation, and the X-1 was specifically built to break it. Like all airplanes in the X-1 series, *Glennis* was dropped from a bomber, the test pilot strapped into its pointed nose with little ability to see outside. There was no way to bail out of the aircraft in an emergency.

In the improved X-1A with a more conventional cockpit, Yeager was eventually able to reach a speed of 2665 km/h (1,650 m.p.h.) and an altitude of 27430m (90,000 feet), faster and higher than most aircraft are able to fly today, half a century later. The X-1B, X-1D, and X-1E also contributed to exploring new realms of high-speed and high-altitude flight.

Although rocket engines have never proven practical for flying inside the Earth's atmosphere, the X-1 test program was responsible for boosting the exploration of aerodynamics, and the data collected was of immense value in the development of the first generation of supersonic jets.

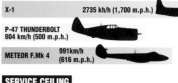

Left: Because of limited ground clearance beneath the B-29 carrier, the whole aircraft had to be jacked up in order to winch the X-1 into the bomber's modified weapons bay. The X-1's pilot then climbed down into his own aircraft just before launch.

Above: The X-1 had good handling characteristics both under power and gliding, although the small wing meant that it landed fast, at about 298 km/h (185 m.p.h.).

X-1A

Type: Rocket-propelled supersonic research aircraft.

Powerplant: One Reaction Motors XLR-11 rocket unit generating 2727 kg (6,000 lb.-thrust)

Max speed: 2735 km/h (1,700 m.p.h.)

Range: 96 km (60 mi.)

Service ceiling: Above 22,860 m (75,000 ft.)

Weights: loaded 6704 kg (14,750 lb.)

Weapons: None.

Dimensions:
Span	8.5 m (28 ft.)
Length	(9.4 m) (30 ft. 11 in.)
Height	3.3 m (10 ft. 10 in.)
Wing area	8.5 m² (92 sq. ft.)

X-1 'GLAMOROUS GLENNIS'

First flown as a glider in 1946, the Bell X-1 was the first in a series of American experimental aircraft that stretched the boundaries of aviation design and performance.

Yeager used the same name for the X-1 as he had used on his P-51 Mustang during World War II. Both were named after his wife.

The shape of the X-1 was based on that of the .50 caliber machine gun bullet, one of the few objects designers of the time knew to be stable at supersonic speeds.

Test and recording equipment was fitted in the central section of the fuselage.

Another large tank contained the second component in the X-1's fuel mixture: 1135 litres (300 gallons) of ethyl alcohol.

The original X-1 cockpit had a fixed canopy, the only access being through a small hatch in the starboard side. There was no ejection seat, and the only option a pilot had in an emergency was to try to ride the aircraft back down to the ground.

The tank immediately behind the pilot contained 1173 litres (310 US gallons) of super-cooled liquid oxygen.

The X-1's thin, razor-edged wings were designed to dissipate shock at transonic speeds.

Fuel was piped to the Reaction Motors rocket in the rear of the fuselage, where it was mixed and ignited in four combustion chambers. There was no throttle; the pilot's only engine control was in the number of chambers he had firing.

ACTION DATA

SPEED

Maximum flying speed raced ahead in the years following World War II. The P-47N was the fastest piston-engine fighter ever entered into service, but by 1945 it was easily outstripped by the new jets. The Gloster Meteor established a new speed record in the same year and surpassed it in 1946. That record was overshadowed a year later by the X-1's outstanding flight.

X-1	2735 kh/h (1,700 m.p.h.)
P-47 THUNDERBOLT	804 km/h (500 m.p.h.)
METEOR F.Mk 4	991km/h (616 m.p.h.)

SERVICE CEILING

The X-1's astonishing thrust propelled the orange bullet to unprecedented speeds as well as heights—heights that only the MiG-25 can currently approach.

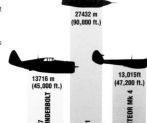

27432 m (90,000 ft.)

13716 m (45,000 ft.) P-47 THUNDERBOLT

X-1

13,015ft (47,200 ft.) METEOR Mk 4

ENDURANCE

Rockets are not the most economical of engines, and no rocket has ever been able to supply an aircraft with more than a few minutes of power. The X-1 was no exception.

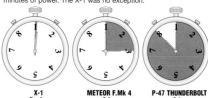

X-1 5 min.

METEOR F.Mk 4 3 hr.

P-47 THUNDERBOLT 8 hr.

To the speed of sound

1 LAUNCH HEIGHT: Climbing at 252 km/h (165 m.p.h.), the B-29 carrier rumbled up to the X-1's launch height of 7620 m (25,000 ft.).

2 FLYING SPEED: A fully fueled X-1 stalled at 379 km/h (236 m.p.h.), so the B-29 had to pick up speed in a shallow dive before the drop.

3 ROCKET IGNITION: The pilot lit his rocket once clear of the bomber. On his record run, Yeager fired all four chambers in rapid succession.

4 ACCELERATE AND CLIMB: Pulling the nose into a climb, the X-1 quickly left the B-29 and all chase planes far behind. It only carried a five-minute supply of rocket fuel, but by the time it had climbed to 12801 m (42,000 ft.), it was approaching Mach 1.

5 RECORD-BREAKER: Yeager took the X-1 past Mach 1 for the first time on the morning of October 14, 1947. Once the fuel was exhausted, aerodynamic drag quickly slowed the plane, and it glided back for a safe landing on Rogers Dry Lake.

BELL

X-1A

● High-speed research aircraft ● Mach 2 ● Rocket powerplant

▲ *Names in the X-1A/B logbook read like a hall of fame in the aviation world. They included Scott Crossfield (later to fly the X-15), Neil Armstrong, Frank Everest and, pictured above with L.D. Bell, Chuck Yeager.*

After the completion of the X-1 programme, which culminated in three aircraft built and the sound barrier successfully broken, Bell's next step was to build a plane that could fly at twice the speed of sound and at heights above 27000 metres (88,000 feet). Only one X-1A was ever completed, but it made history as the first aircraft to reach Mach 2 and paved the way for the awesome swept-wing Bell X-2 and a new generation of very fast fighters.

PHOTO FILE

BELL X-1A

▼ **Sabre chase plane**
Being a chase plane pilot was exciting work. This F-86D struggled to keep up with Yeager as he flew 'on test' preceding his record-breaking Mach 2 flight.

▲ **Through the Mach 2 barrier**
Bell's record-breaking X-1A was destined never to survive its course of flying. After a serious internal explosion the unmanned plane was dropped and destroyed.

▲ **Motherships**
The complete Bell research series from X-1 to X-2 were all launched from Boeing B-29 and B-50 four-engined piston bombers. The X-1C was cancelled before it was built.

▲ **Sister aircraft**
The X-1A and X-1B were externally similar, but the X-1B was only ever used as a training plane.

Last of the X-1s ▶
The X-1D was actually the first of the three to fly, but later it had improvements over the X-1A and X-1B.

FACTS AND FIGURES

➤ The first and only glide-flight of the X-1D took place on 24 July 1951, flown by Bell's chief test pilot Jean Ziegler.

➤ Before a flight under power on 22 August 1951, the X-1D was dropped unmanned.

➤ The training-optimised X-1B was only ever piloted by student NASA crews.

➤ The record-breaking X-1A was abandoned by its B-29 following an explosion that crippled its undercarriage.

➤ Yeager's X-1A achieved the legendary Mach 2 speed on 12 December 1953.

➤ Before its destruction the X-1A had worn orange, white and all-metal colours.

PROFILE

Twice the speed of sound

Known to Bell as the Model 58, but as X-1A to the rest of the world, this development of the classic X-1 duplicated its predecessor's record-breaking achievements, but throughout its operational life lived under a shadow of accidents. The X-1A was similar to the X-1 but had a longer fuselage, improved cockpit visibility and turbo-driven fuel pumps.

The X-1A grabbed the headlines in 1953 when veteran high-speed test-pilot Major

Charles 'Chuck' Yeager flew the rocket plane to 2560 km/h (1,650 m.p.h.) at a height of 21350 metres (70,000 feet), smashing the previous world record. Throughout its career the X-1A relied on other aircraft to lift it to around 9150 metres before being dropped for a flight of just over four minutes.

Similar to the X-1A, the X-1B was designed for research into high-speed thermal problems, but served as a crew trainer for NASA high-speed test pilots. A transonic X-1C development

Above: The X-1B's record-breaking flights were conducted over Edwards Air Force Base in California. Since then, Edwards has played host to nearly all of America's important X-plane and Space Shuttle test flights.

was cancelled, and the improved X-1D was destroyed early in its flight programme after being jettisoned unmanned following an internal explosion.

Below: The bullet-shaped X-1 was remarkable for reaching its high speeds with a straight wing. Bell finally caught up with the Messerschmitt wartime designs by fitting a swept wing on the X-2.

Bell X-1A

Type: high-altitude high-speed research aircraft

Powerplant: one 26.7-kN (6,000-lb.-thrust) (at sea level) four-chamber Reaction Motors XLR11-RM-5 rocket engine

Maximum speed: Mach 2.44 or 2655.4 km/h (1,646.35 m.p.h.)

Endurance: approximately 4 min 40 sec

Service ceiling: over 27432 m (90,000 ft.)

Weights: empty 3296 kg (7,251 lb.); loaded 7478 kg (16,452 lb.)

Armament: always unarmed

Dimensions:
span	8.53 m	(28 ft.)
length	10.90 m	(35 ft. 8 in.)
height	3.30 m	(10 ft. 10 in.)
wing area	39.60 m²	(426 sq. ft.)

BELL X-1A

Shown below is the sole Bell X-1A, whose chequered career began with Chuck Yeager's first Mach 2 flight, and ended unceremoniously when it was jettisoned to destruction after an explosion.

The nose profile was revised, giving the X-1A a slightly blunter profile than the original X-1.

Although the X-1 series of the aircraft were later painted white, the middle of the fuselage was always left unpainted because the extreme cold of the liquid oxygen tanks adversely affected the paint.

Even the aircraft that had unpainted fuselages often had white lower wing surfaces. This was thought to aid tracking from the ground in the clear-blue skies above Edwards.

Although visually similar to the X-1, the X-1A's fuselage was almost a total redesign, with increased fuel capacity, a low-pressure turbopump fuel feed and revised cockpit and canopy.

The markings on the tail consisted of an aircraft serial number and the standard USAF marking, with the national insignia on the fuselage.

The X-1A was often unpainted except for a nose logo and an anti-glare panel.

Like the X-1, the X-1A had a four-chamber XLR11 rocket engine fuelled by liquid oxygen.

ROCKET FIGHTERS

MiG I-270: This prototype rocket fighter was built and glide-flown in 1946, making a powered flight in early 1947. It was destroyed in a landing accident with test pilot A. Pakhomov at the controls. Despite being a practical design, fitted with twin cannon armament, the I-270 was abandoned in favour of jet designs.

SAUNDERS-ROE SR.53: Another mixed powerplant design, the SR.53 was a promising aircraft. It was a prototype for the SR.177 naval interceptor fighter, one of many projects killed off in the 1957 British defence review. Power was supplied by an Armstrong Siddeley Viper turbojet and a de Havilland Spectre booster rocket.

NORD GRIFFON: A highly innovative design with turbojet and ramjet propulsion, the Griffon was derived from the earlier Gerfaut. The aircraft first flew on 23 January 1957, and broke the speed of sound for the first time in May 1957 using its ramjet engine. The aircraft eventually reached Mach 2, also on ramjet power.

The Bell X-planes and their roles

■ **X-1:** The original X-1 made the all-important leap through the sound barrier, proving that flight was possible in a regime that many believed would prove impossible.

■ **X-1B:** Used primarily for research into the effects of airframe kinetic heating, the X-1B also increased scientists' knowledge of the human physiology at supersonic speeds.

■ **X-1E:** The X-1E was built to test extremely thin aerofoils and also the new engine turbopumps needed to sustain very high speeds.

■ **X-2:** Mating an X-1 fuselage with a swept wing, the X-2 was also designed to explore the effects of kinetic heating and airframe stresses on fighter aircraft designs.

BELL

X-2

● Swept-wing design ● Rocket-propelled ● High altitude

BELL X-2

Sheer elegance ▶
The vast range of duties that the X-plane series undertook led to some exotic designs, of which Bell's X-2 was one of the most attractive to grace the skies over Edwards Air Force Base.

▲ Landing problems
Accidents occurred during landing until the under-fuselage skid was enlarged.

Hitching a ride ▶
An EB-50A was used to carry the X-2 into the air for launch.

▲ No wheels
To facilitate ground movement, a special trolley was developed for the X-2 research aircraft.

The air drop ▶
Once the required height was achieved the X-2 was dropped from the adapted bomb bay of the aircraft.

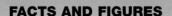

H aving gained early swept wing experience with its experimental L-39 aircraft, Bell was chosen by the USAF to design a new swept-wing research aircraft for exploration into very high-speed flight. The X-1 proved unsuitable for modification, so Bell set about the design of the all-new X-2. The aircraft went on to set unofficial world altitude and speed records, but the programme was marred by the loss of two machines and their pilots.

▲ *Pilots assigned to the X-2 test programme could reach speeds that would have been unthinkable a few years earlier but, like many cutting edge projects, this one was not without risk.*

FACTS AND FIGURES

➤ Test pilot Jean Siegler and crewman Frank Wolko died aboard the EB-50A mother ship when the first X-2 exploded.

➤ The X-2 completed its first powered flight on 18 November 1955.

➤ Captain Milburn Apt was killed in the crash of the second X-2.

➤ Apt flew the X-2 only once, on the 13th and final flight scheduled for the programme.

➤ The X-2 and X-1 were originally, and very briefly, known as the XS-2 and XS-1.

➤ Pilots were supposed to escape the X-2 via a jettisonable cockpit capsule.

Bell goes even faster

Bell began working on its X-2 in October 1945, under a USAF contract. The aircraft were rocket-powered, and designed for the analysis of structural and heating effects at speeds up to Mach 3.5 and altitudes up to 38100 m (125,000 ft.).

New metal alloys and a unique escape system were features of the X-2. The aircraft was to have a powered duration of just under 11 minutes. Captive trials beneath an EB-50A mother ship began in July 1951 and continued for some time, since technical problems delayed delivery of the XLR-25 engine.

Tests showed that the X-2 suffered landing defects, resulting in damage on every flight until a new landing skid was fitted. Tragically, with these problems solved, an aircraft exploded in captive engine tests beneath the EB-50A.

The second X-2 completed a number of amazing flights, reaching a speed of Mach 3.196 and an altitude of 38376 m (126,000 feet). This aircraft was also destroyed, on its 13th and final planned flight, when its pilot lost control at Mach 3 and unfortunately failed to bale out. Nonetheless the type paved the way for future aircraft programmes.

Above: The X-2 was planned as a successor to the X-1 series for the investigation of supersonic flight, so swept wings were fitted.

Right: The test pilot shows the small size of the cockpit. The whole nose of the X-2 was designed to be jettisoned in an emergency.

X-2

Bell's X-2 was a much improved design compared with the earlier X-1. Capable of reaching Mach 3.0, the aircraft offered numerous possibilities but two accidents ended the X-2 series' flying career.

Painted on the nose was a small black anti-glare area, which let the pilot operate the aircraft without being distracted by the sun.

The cockpit canopy was added to the aircraft once the pilot was seated. Minimal flight instruments were fitted, most being concerned with fuel tank limits.

An overall white finish was found to be much more resistant to heating at high speeds; despite this, aircraft often landed with their paintwork heavily damaged. Large photo-reference markings were also added.

In the event of an emergency the nose of the X-2 was jettisoned from the fuselage by explosive bolts; after this, a parachute was deployed from its rear.

A single nose wheel was installed on the X-2, giving the pilot some degree of directional control during landings. It retracted into a bay underneath the cockpit in flight. Because of the high operating temperatures of the fuselage, the tyre was heavily protected.

A single main skid was fitted on the fuselage, which offered a saving in both weight and space, allowing the aircraft's size to remain small. It was modified after early landing accidents.

To allow the aircraft to remain level during its landing run, bumpers were positioned on the outer wings. They also prevented the wings from being damaged during the aircraft's roll-out on Edward's dry lake bed.

US AIR FORCE 6675

Bell's X-PLANES

X-1A: The first aircraft to 'break the sound barrier', Bell's X-1 gave the company a huge lead in the experimental aircraft field. Later versions featured a revised canopy.

X-5: Using technology obtained from the Germans after World War II, this pioneering aircraft utilised a swing-wing concept to research future fighter aircraft designs.

X-14: The X-14 illustrates the diverse range of types that Bell provided for the X-series. It was used to test the handling qualities of vertical take-off and landing (VTOL) aircraft.

X-2

Type: supersonic research aircraft

Powerplant: one 66.7-kN (15,000-lb.-thrust) Curtiss-Wright XLR25-CW-1 rocket engine

Maximum speed: 3058 km/h (1,896 m.p.h.)

Endurance: 10 min 55 sec of powered flight

Fuel capacity: 2960 litres (782 gal.) of liquid oxygen; 3376 litres (892 gal.) of ethyl alcohol and water

Accommodation: one pilot

Service ceiling: 38405 m (126,000 ft.)

Weights: empty 5314 kg (11,690 lb.); maximum take-off 11299 kg (24,858 lb.)

Dimensions:
span	9.75 m (32 ft.)
length	13.41 m (44 ft.)
height	4.11 m (13 ft. 6 in.)
wing area	24.19 m² (260 sq.ft.)

ACTION DATA

MAXIMUM SPEED

It was clear from its successful first flight that the X-2 was more than capable of reaching Mach 3.0. The design that followed, the X-3, was restricted in its performance by the poor quality of its engines. The later X-15 was the fastest X-plane ever.

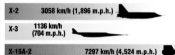

X-2	3058 km/h (1,896 m.p.h.)
X-3	1136 km/h (704 m.p.h.)
X-15A-2	7297 km/h (4,524 m.p.h.)

THRUST

Flying at the cutting edge of technology, the X-planes received a range of engines, although not all were capable of giving the anticipated performance. Most disappointing was the X-3; unable to offer the required thrust, the aircraft remained purely as a systems test research vehicle.

X-2	66.7 kN (15,000 lb.-thrust)
X-3	37.4 kN (8,415 lb.-thrust)
X-15A-2	253.6 kN (57,050 lb.-thrust)

TAKE-OFF WEIGHT

Both the X-2 and X-15 were launched in mid-air. This allowed the aircraft to operate at a higher take-off weight, most of which was made up of fuel. Additional strengthening of the fuselage saw the aircraft's weight increase.

X-2	X-3	X-15A-2
11299 kg (24,858 lb.)	10025 kg (22,055 lb.)	25461 kg (56,014 lb.)

BELL

X-5

● Single-seat experimental jet ● Swing-wing pioneer

The Bell X-5 was the world's first high-performance aircraft to fly using a variable-geometry wing – the 'swing wing' found on the modern F-14 Tomcat, F-111 and Tornado. These are set forward for low-speed flight and swept back for higher speeds at altitude. This beautiful, glossy white research aircraft was an American development of the German Messerschmitt P.1101 fighter prototype and a true pioneer of the early jet age.

▲ *The first of two Bell X-5s was flown for the first time on 20 June 1951 by Jean 'Skip' Ziegler at Edwards AFB, California. Power came from an Allison J35 turbojet engine.*

BELL X-5

▲ X-5 over Edwards
The second X-5, 50-1839, is seen here over Edwards Air Force Base, during a test flight.

◄ Messerschmitt P.1101
The wing sweep of the P.1101 was set at 40°, but it could be altered when on the ground.

No photographs ►
As a result of misunderstandings and an apparent oversight by Edwards AFB staff, no photograph of the first flight of the X-5 is believed to exist.

▼ Three sweep positions
This multiple exposure shows three wing sweep positions at 20°, 40° and 60° settings.

▲ Speed improvements
The X-5 had a maximum speed of over 1000 km/h (650 m.p.h.). Bell planned to re-engine the surviving aircraft with different jet engines and booster rockets to increase speed.

FACTS AND FIGURES

➤ The US Air Force studied a lightweight fighter version of the X-5 but did not order one to be built.

➤ Total weight of the wing sweep mechanism was 154 kg (340 lb).

➤ Armed fighter versions of both the X-5 and the P.1101 were proposed.

➤ On 13 October 1953, the second Bell X-5 crashed, killing its USAF test pilot Major Raymond Popson.

➤ The 1951-55 X-5 flight tests produced 279 reports.

➤ The last flight of 50-1838 took place on 25 October 1955.

Experimental swing wings

Two Bell X-5s flight tested the 'swing wing' in the hot California desert as a result of a discovery in the cold of Europe.

US troops occupying the town of Oberammergau, Germany, in 1945 discovered an experimental facility with the almost complete Messerschmitt P.1101 prototype. Head of the investigating team sent in to evaluate the facility was Bell's chief designer, Robert J. Woods. Intended to investigate flight with varying angles of wing sweep, the P.1101 was brought to the US, test flown and eventually reached Bell at its Buffalo, New York facility. After studying the aircraft, Bell won a contract to build two test machines based on the German design.

The two X-5s were very similar in layout to the P.1101, but considerably more complex. After taxiing trials the first aircraft was loaded aboard a C-119 transport and flown to Edwards Air Force Base, California, where it was flown extensively.

Above: The X-5 had a vicious tendency to spin. The study of this characteristic contributed to understanding the design features that induce spin. The second X-5 crashed during spin tests.

The second aircraft was lost in a mishap. Massive amounts of new data on wing design were collected before the X-5 was retired to the USAF Museum.

Below: The Bell X-5 successfully performed all the planned experimental flights laid down by the US Air Force and NACA, one of the few American research aircraft to achieve this.

X-5

Type: single-seat experimental research aircraft

Powerplant: one 21.80-kN (4,890-lb.-thrust) Allison J35-A-17 turbojet engine

Maximum speed: approximately 1046 km/h (650 m.p.h.)

Range: 1207 km (750 mi.)

Service ceiling: 13000 m (42,650 ft.)

Weights: empty 2880 kg (6,336 lb.); maximum take-off 4536 kg (9,980 lb.)

Dimensions:
span unswept	9.39 m (31 ft.)
span swept	5.66 m (19 ft.)
length	10.16 m (33 ft.)
height	3.66 m (12 ft.)
wing area	16.26 m² (175 sq. ft.)

EARLY X-PLANES

FROM X-1 TO X-4

As aircraft speeds increased in the late-1940s, the problem of the 'sound barrier' – flight at and beyond Mach 1 – loomed large. Convinced by scientists that the sound barrier could be broken, the USAAF funded a high-speed research aircraft after a Bell engineer, Robert Wolf, proposed that such a prototype be developed by the US's aviation industry, and tested by the National Advisory Committee on Aeronautics (now known as NASA).

The rocket-powered Bell X-1 broke the sound barrier on 14 October 1947. It was to be the first of a varied collection of 'X-plane' research aircraft that were to accomplish numerous other 'firsts' and continue to be produced, allowing aircraft builders, the US military and NASA to test theories and possibly apply them to production machinery.

Bell X-1

After six X-1 aircraft, which eventually took the world speed record beyond Mach 2, came the X-2. This was another rocket-powered Bell product, larger than the X-1, with swept wings. X-2s reached official speeds above Mach 2.8, set an altitude record and one unofficially achieved Mach 3.196 before crashing fatally.

The sole Douglas X-3 'Stiletto' suffered from a lack of suitably powerful turbojet engines and, although intended to explore aerodynamics during prolonged flights at over Mach 2.5, its lack of power led to its early retirement. Northrop's two X-4 'Bantams', on the other hand, successfully tested a tailless configuration at transonic speeds (up to Mach 0.94), but demonstrated that tailless swept-wing aircraft were not suitable for high-speed flight.

Bell X-2

X-5

Bell X-5 serial number 50-1838 was the first of the two examples built and the only one to survive. It is displayed at the USAF Museum, Wright-Patterson Air Force Base, Dayton, Ohio.

The pressurised and air-conditioned cockpit was fairly conventional, except for the wing sweep controls and sweep angle indicator on the instrument panel.

A hand crank was located in the cockpit in case the electric wing actuation system failed. This allowed the pilot to move the wings in case of such an emergency.

To prevent the X-5's centre of gravity moving too much the wingroot section was designed to move forward on rails when the wings were swept.

Before the X-5s were built, a full-scale wooden mock-up was produced by Bell. It was described as a 'masterpiece of the woodworker's art'. Even detail parts like the nose landing gear were made entirely of wood.

In common with all aircraft involved in experimental flight, the X-5s carried an instrumentation boom on the nose to collect flight data.

The whole wing sweep process from 20° to 60° took about 20 seconds.

The hydraulically actuated undercarriage retracted rearwards into the fuselage.

To improve the X-5's performance, Bell proposed several re-engining projects. One involved installing a Wright J65 turbojet to push top speed over the sound barrier.

The X-5's tendency to spin prompted Bell to suggest that a spin recovery parachute be fitted to the surviving aircraft. The USAF and NACA decided this was unnecessary, but agreed to a small ventral fin being fitted.

Variable-geometry wings of the X-5

The X-5 was the first 'variable-geometry' aircraft able to vary its wing sweep in flight. It provided valuable information for the 'swing wing' designers of the future. Experience gained with the X-5 was applied to such aircraft as the F-111.

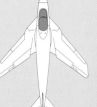

MAXIMUM SWEEP: As on other swing-wing aircraft, maximum wing sweep (60°) is used for higher speeds. The sweep mechanism used a system similar to a screw jack to move the wings and a form of discbrake to lock the wing at the desired angle.

INTERMEDIATE SWEEP: The pilot was able to select any intermediate wing sweep setting using the electrically operated actuation system. This complex equipment proved to be reliable, but could be operated manually if necessary.

MINIMUM SWEEP: The optimum wing position for take-off and landing was the fully forward (20°) position, in which the wings generated the most lift. The X-5 was unable to land safely at settings of more than 40°.

BELL

XV-15

● Experimental tilt-rotor ● Vertical take-off ● Winged flight

▲ Late in 1987 the XV-15, piloted by Dorman Cannon and Don Borge, demonstrated its capabilities in the civil transport role at locations in both Washington and Chicago.

Conceived in 1973 to follow up earlier Bell projects, the Bell XV-15 is largely unknown but very significant. This odd-looking machine was the first truly successful 'tilt rotor' – an aircraft that takes off vertically like a helicopter but flies horizontally like a fixed-wing machine. This is accomplished by transforming the rotors into propellers. The XV-15 performed invaluable research into tilt-rotor technology, making possible today's V-22 Osprey.

BELL XV-15

▲ **Early trials**
A specially built test rig and platform was constructed for early tilt rotor development trials.

▲ **Battlefield support**
The military-led research programme explored the full range of benefits that might be derived from a support aircraft that combined rotary-wing and fixed-wing flight characteristics.

▲ **Hovering**
While in its hovering configuration, the XV-15 had a span of 17.73 m (58 ft. 2 in.) between the outer edges of the arcs of each of the two 7.62-m (25-ft.) diameter rotor blades, which had a high-twist design.

▲ **Shipborne**
The XV-15 lands aboard the USS Tripoli during its initial shipboard evaluation near San Diego in August 1982.

Transition in flight ▶
After a 12-second transition, the XV-15 could go from hover to forward flight at 445 km/h (276 m.p.h.) in 30 seconds.

FACTS AND FIGURES

➤ The first XV-15 made its maiden flight on 3 May 1977, but was restricted to hovering in the helicopter mode.

➤ XV-15s were equipped with ejection seats as an additional safety feature.

➤ The XV-15 made its first transition from vertical to forward flight on 24 July 1979.

➤ Two XV-15s were built; one of them was lost in an accident towards the end of the test programme.

➤ The XV-15 was the first tilt rotor aircraft to achieve prolonged forward flight.

➤ A crew of two flew the XV-15, with up to nine passengers in the cabin.

PROFILE

Tilt-rotor testing for the V-22

Developed by the US Army and NASA (and later by the US Navy), the XV-15 was built to perform realistic flight tests of the tilt-rotor configuration.

The rotor blades of such an aircraft are shifted 90° in flight to become propellers. A successful tilt-rotor would be able to land and take off almost anywhere, while flying far faster and farther than a typical helicopter. The XV-15 was seen as the perfect tool to explore the tilt-rotor technology for both military and civil use. A civilian

tilt-rotor aircraft, as recently proposed by Bell and Boeing, would be an ideal aircraft for tasks such as oil rig support.

Bell's XV-15 demonstrated the practical benefits of tilt-rotor flight in many locations, including aboard a US Navy aircraft carrier and in front of the US Capitol building in Washington, DC.

Although unorthodox in shape and appearance, the XV-15 was dramatically successful and enabled Bell

and Boeing to overcome some of the major hurdles in designing the V-22. The US military is now proceeding with plans to acquire more than 550 V-22 Osprey tilt-rotor aircraft.

Below: From November 1987 the second XV-15 was tested with new rotor blades made by Boeing from composite materials.

Above: The XV-15s were used in a research programme to explore the limits of the flight envelope and to assess the merits of the tilt-rotor concept for future military and civilian designs.

XV-15

Type: twin-engined, tilt-rotor research aircraft

Powerplant: two 1156-kW (1,550-hp.) AVCO Lycoming LTC1K-4K turboshaft engines, each with a two-minute emergency rating of 1343 kW (1,800 hp.)

Maximum speed: 615 km/h (381 m.p.h.)

Maximum climb rate: 960 m/min (3,150 f.p.m.) at sea level

Range: 825 km (510 mi.) with maximum fuel

Service ceiling: 8840 m (29,000 ft.)

Weights: empty 4354 kg (9,579 lb.); maximum STOL take-off weight 6804 kg (14,969 lb.)

Accommodation: two crew, nine passengers

Dimensions:
rotor diameter (each)	7.62 m	(25 ft.)
wing span	10.72 m	(35 ft. 2 in.)
length	12.83 m	(42 ft. 1 in.)
height	4.67 m	(15 ft. 4 in.)
rotor disk area (each)	45.61 m	(486 sq. ft.)
wing area	15.70 m²	(169 sq. ft.)

Each of the six rotor blades was constructed from stainless steel. They were capable of withstanding the considerable twisting encountered in hovering and forwards flight.

Powered by two specially adapted Lycoming T53 turboshafts redesignated LTC1K, the XV-15 had interconnecting drive shafts for single-engine operations during such emergencies as sustaining damage in combat.

The Bell Model 301 (designated XV-15 in service) had a conventional airframe structure developed in parallel with the Bell 222 and built by Rockwell International at Tulsa.

The rear fuselage of the XV-15 could accommodate up to nine fully equipped troops.

The XV-15's tail unit incorporates a tailplane/elevator situated on top of the rear fuselage, with endplate fins and rudders.

With its useful passenger capacity, the XV-15 has returned to flight testing in connection with a new civilian project.

The XV-15 had a specially developed stability and control augmentation system, drooped ailerons and trailing-edge flaps.

The retractable tricycle undercarriage has twin wheels on each unit. The nosewheel is fully steerable.

XV-15

As a tilt-rotor aircraft, the experimental Bell XV-15 combined the best features from both helicopters and conventional fixed-wing aircraft.

ACTION DATA

PASSENGERS

Both the XV-15 and Curtiss-Wright's tilt-rotor X-19 were intended primarily to be flown as experimental machines. The Bell-Boeing V-22 Osprey, however, has a more realistic passenger and freight carrying capability.

XV-15	9
X-19	6
V-22 OSPREY	24

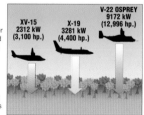

POWER

Bell's twin-engined XV-15 had less power than the four-engined X-19. However, good aerodynamics and a light overall weight afforded the former good performance. The fully-developed V-22 has nearly three times the power of its tilt-rotor forebears.

XV-15 2312 kW (3,100 hp.)
X-19 3281 kW (4,400 hp.)
V-22 OSPREY 9172 kW (12,996 hp.)

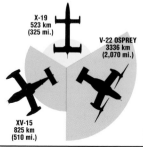

RANGE

Although in a very different class to the production-intended Bell-Boeing Osprey, the XV-15 had a fair range, enabling it to impress onlookers in realistic demonstrations around the United States, on aircraft-carriers at sea, and in a variety of other prospective military applications.

X-19 523 km (325 mi.)
V-22 OSPREY 3336 km (2,070 mi.)
XV-15 825 km (510 mi.)

XV-15 tilt-rotor operations

1 VERTICAL TAKE-OFF: For vertical take-off, the wingtip engines are rotated into the vertical axis, putting the three-bladed 7.62-m (25-feet) diameter propellers on top to act as 'helicopter' rotors, giving lift for take-off.

2 TRANSITION: The rotors are tilted forwards as airspeed builds and the wings begin to provide sufficient lift. The lift is transferred from the rotors to the wings and the engine power is used for forward, conventional flight.

3 WINGED FLIGHT: With transition complete, the XV-15 is now in conventional forward flight supported by lift from its wings, and the rotors have now become large propellers, powering the aircraft forwards.

BELL
X-22A

● **Research aircraft** ● **Vertical take-off** ● **Ducted propellers**

▲ *The unusual looks of the X-22A in no way reflected the capabilities of the design. An extremely long test programme proved the potential of the VTOL concept, and pilots found the aircraft a delight to fly.*

A bizarre vertical-lift flying machine, the Bell X-22 tested tilting ducted propellers. In the late 1960s, it was one of several revolutionary designs meant to do away with the need for long, paved runways. The X-22 looked like four rubbish bins attached to a fuselage blundering through the sky – yet it contributed tremendously to our knowledge of vertical- and short-distance take-off and landing operations.

BELL X-22A

▼ Naval helicopters
The success of the X-22 saw the aircraft used on other test programmes such as deck-landing controls for helicopters.

▲ Advanced cockpit
The complex flight controls on the X-22 were simplified through a sophisticated Variable Stability System.

Moving engines ▶
During ground operations, the engines of the X-22 could be rotated to power the aircraft along the runway for a conventional take-off.

◀ Ducted propellers
To increase lift during take-off, the propellers were surrounded by a duct, which was also meant to protect maintenance crews.

Forward flight ▶
The engines on this X-22 have begun to rotate, allowing it to operate as a conventional aircraft.

FACTS AND FIGURES

➤ The first flight of the X-22 was on 17 March 1966. The aircraft made only a short hovering flight on this occasion.

➤ A full rotation of the engines was accomplished on 1 March 1967.

➤ During the test programme, one of the X-22s was heavily damaged in a crash.

➤ A highly complex flight control system was installed on the aircraft, giving the pilots precise handling capability.

➤ An tandem-seat armed ground support variant was proposed but not built.

➤ Knowledge gained on the X-22 was applied to the later Bell V-22 Osprey.

PROFILE

Bell's ducted fan prototype

The culmination of years of work by Bell Aerospace Textron, the X-22 was one of a series of aircraft designed to explore V/STOL (vertical/short take-off and landing) characteristics. Two X-22s were built at the company's Niagara Falls, New York, facility in 1964-66. The first was destroyed in a non-fatal mishap in August 1966, but the second X-22 carried out flight tests for two and a half years. The surviving X-22 was flown first by Bell and NASA and later by its principal operator, the US Navy. On 30 July 1968, the X-22 achieved a sustained hover at a height of 2444 m (8,018 ft.) – believed to be a world record for any type of V/STOL aircraft.

The X-22's aerodynamic lift came from a variety of sources including ducts, stub wings, and from thrust generated by its special propellers. The X-22 flew well and made the transition from vertical to horizontal flight. The second X-22 continued to perform various kinds of research, flying until the early 1980s.

The box-style fuselage was manufactured from light-weight aluminium.

If any of the engines malfunctioned during flight operations, power was automatically cut to that engine and the flight controls compensated for the loss of control. Despite this, one X-22 was lost in a crash during testing.

Four General Electric turboshaft engines were mounted in pairs at the root of each rear wing. They provided additional power for the X-22 during forward flight.

The tall fin of the X-22 incorporated a large rudder to offer improved directional control of the aircraft, as conventional controls were mostly absent.

X-22A

The interest in vertical take-off aircraft saw a host of manufacturers produce designs of which the Bell X-22 was the most successful. After a long and eventful career the aircraft was retired in the 1980s.

A large glazed cockpit gave the side-by-side crew excellent visibility during flight operations. The controls of the aircraft were very similar to those of conventional aircraft, with the simple addition of levers to facilitate the operation of the tilting propellers.

The propellers were surrounded by four large ducts which were rotated at 5° a second for the transition to forward flight. All four ducts were rotated at once.

Positioned on either side of the rear ducts were two large flaps that allowed the X-22 to manoeuvre while in the hover. A loading ramp for an intended cargo-carrying variant of the X-22 design was located at the rear of the fuselage.

SPECIFICATION

X-22A

Type: tilting-duct V/STOL research aircraft

Powerplant: four 932-kW (1,250-lb.) General Electric YT-58-GE-8D turboshafts

Maximum speed: 410 km/h (255 m.p.h.) at sea level

Cruising speed: 343 km/h (213 m.p.h.)

Endurance: longest flight recorded 1 hr 20 min

Range: 716 km (445 mi.) on internal fuel

Service ceiling: 8473 m (27,798 ft.)

Weights: empty 5197 kg (11,433-lb.); maximum take-off 8172 kg (17,978-lb.)

Dimensions:
span 11.96 m (39 ft.)
length 12.06 m (40 ft.)
height 6.30 m (20 ft. 8 in.)
wing area 39.48 m² (424 sq. ft.)

With its engines rotated forward, one of the X-22s is seen in conventional forward flight mode, during one of its test sorties.

ACTION DATA

MAXIMUM SPEED

The unusual design of the X-22 meant that the aircraft was never capable of high speed. Compared to the sleek X-19, which had exceptional speed, the X-18 and X-22 were poor performers.

X-22A 410 km/h (254 m.p.h.)
X-18 407 km/h (252 m.p.h.)
X-19 730 km/h (453 m.p.h.)

MAXIMUM TAKE-OFF WEIGHT

In terms of its overall weight, the X-22A was more comparable to the Curtiss-Wright X-19, another four-propeller aircraft. The Hiller X-18 was a real heavyweight, weighing more than 13 tonnes.

X-22A 8172 kg (17,978 lb.)
X-18 13607 kg (30,000-lb.)
X-19 6196 kg (13,631-lb.)

Straight up with the X-planes

■ **HILLER X-18:** A tilt-wing design, this aircraft was considered to be a possible future transport aircraft. A full transition to forward flight was never achieved, because of problems encountered during development.

■ **CURTISS-WRIGHT X-19:** Developed as a private venture to investigate a VTOL commercial transport aircraft, the X-19 utilised the 'radial lift-force propeller' theory to fly. The programme was later cancelled.

■ **BELL XV-15:** Having proved that the concept of tilting-engine VTOL designs was viable, Bell developed the XV-15 to incorporate all the latest aviation advances. This aircraft provided much information for Boeing's Osprey.

BELL/BOEING
V-22 OSPREY

● Assault transport ● Vertical take-off ● Multiple roles

US Marines have a phrase for it: they call it 'Vertical Envelopment'. The idea is to bypass a defended coast by flying troops over the top, fast, landing them in the enemy rear before the foe can react. And nothing can move Marines as fast as the revolutionary V-22 Osprey, which flies like an aeroplane but takes off and lands like a helicopter.

▲ *The prototype V-22 Osprey is seen transitioning to horizontal flight. It is this unique ability which will revolutionise the speed of US Marine Corps amphibious assaults.*

BELL/BOEING V-22 OSPREY

Sea ▶ trials
The Osprey has shown that it can operate from any deck large enough to give sideways clearance to the twin rotors.

▲ Osprey's forerunner
The Bell XV-15 was the culmination of a long line of experimental convertiplanes, and was the direct ancestor of the V-22.

Global reach ▶
The V-22 can be refuelled in flight. It can be deployed over intercontinental distances in less than a day – which is something that no helicopter can do.

▲ High-tech
The Osprey comes equipped with a modern 'glass' cockpit, dominated by multi-function controls and computerised video displays.

Marine ◀ assault
The most enthusiastic supporters of the V-22 are the US Marines, who see the aircraft as adding greatly to the ability with which they can carry out amphibious assaults.

▲ Folding wings
The Osprey takes up a lot of space, which is at a premium aboard even the largest carrier. To make more room, the rotors fold and the wing swivels in line with the fuselage.

FACTS AND FIGURES

➤ The V-22 first flew on 19 March 1989, taking off vertically from Bell's research facility at Arlington, Texas.

➤ First transition from vertical to horizontal flight took place on 14 September 1989.

➤ The V-22 has twice the speed and twice the range of a comparable helicopter.

➤ V-22s can be deployed anywhere in the world within 36 hours.

➤ A typical helicopter needs three times as much maintenance as the V-22.

➤ Ospreys can carry a seven-tonne load slung beneath the fuselage at speeds of up to 375 km/h (235 m.p.h.).

High-speed assault

A Marine commander assaulting a defended shoreline needs to get his troops and equipment ashore fast. But landing craft are slow and make easy targets, and helicopters are horribly vulnerable to enemy fire. Until now, the only way to minimise the time the helicopters are at risk has been to launch them from as close to shore as possible, but that exposes the irreplaceable assault ships to danger from the enemy's long-range artillery and missiles.

The Osprey has changed all that. With its rotors pointing upwards, it can take off and land vertically on ship or ashore. But tilting the rotors forwards converts them into propellers, allowing the Osprey to fly twice as fast as the fastest helicopter.

Operating in conjunction with speedy air-cushion landing craft, the V-22 can deliver troops or weapons over much greater distances than a helicopter. An

The tremendous width of the Osprey's rotor blades is clear in this photo of a landing on a 'Wasp'-class assault ship.

amphibious task force commander can now launch his attack from over the horizon, and still have his troops ashore in a shorter time than would have been possible with helicopters and landing craft.

The V-22's prop-rotors are 11.58 m (38 ft.) in diameter. Immensely strong to resist combat damage, one provides enough lift to keep the aircraft in the air alone if necessary.

The wing is fitted on a pivot. Swung fore and aft and with the rotors folded, an Osprey takes up no more room than a large helicopter.

MV-22A Osprey

Type: two-crew multi-role convertiplane transport

Powerplant: two 4593-kW (6,150-hp.) Allison T406-AD-400 turboprops

Maximum speed: 556 km/h (345 mi.) at sea level

Combat radius: 1880 km (1,168 mi.) search and rescue; 1000 km (620 mi.) amphibious assault

Rate of climb: 332 m/min (1,100 f.p.m.) vertically

Service ceiling: 8000 m (26,250 ft.)

Weights: empty 14,433 kg (31,820 lb.); loaded 24,948 kg (55,000 lb.)

Payload: up to 25 fully equipped troops or 4500 kg (9,920 lb.) cargo internally, or 6800 kg (15,000 lb.) external load

Dimensions:
span (inc rotors) 25.76 m (84 ft. 6 in.)
length 17.32 m (56 ft. 10 in.)
height 6.63 m (21 ft. 9 in.)
rotor area 210 m² (2,260 sq. ft.)

XV-22 OSPREY

Although facing Congressional opposition, the V-22 has been described by senior Marine officers as 'our number one aviation priority'.

Test aircraft are often fitted with sensitive flight testing instruments to measure the aircraft's performance in all areas of the flight regime.

The Osprey is manned by a pilot and co-pilot. They control the aircraft by means of an electronic fly-by-wire system.

The Osprey's engines are immensely powerful, in order to lift the aircraft free of the ground without any aerodynamic assistance.

The huge paddle-bladed prop-rotors are a compromise between long helicopter-type rotors and much smaller aircraft-type propellers.

Osprey's twin tail is set high on a boom, in order to leave room for the rear door and loading ramp.

The extensive use of composite material means that the V-22 is about 25 per cent lighter than a metal aircraft of comparable size and lifting power.

ACTION DATA

TAKE-OFF PROCEDURE

Osprey can take off vertically or with a short take-off run. Transition from vertical flight to horizontal is automatic. As the aircraft's forward speed increases, control is switched from the aircraft's rotors (as in a helicopter) to the conventional flaps and ailerons (as in an aircraft).

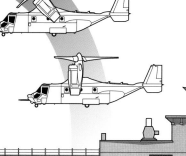

PAYLOAD EFFICIENCY

A CH-53 helicopter can carry up to 55 troops in the assault role.

Although its capacity is only 25, the V-22 can make three trips to a helicopter's one, landing 75 troops in the same time that the CH-53 lands 55.

Landing comparison

MARINE ASSAULT: An amphibious assault using Ospreys and air-cushion landing craft can stand offshore a safe distance from enemy defences, and still land troops more quickly than helicopters and landing craft.

ENEMY THREAT: Most modern artillery pieces have a range of between 17 and 30 km 10 and 20 mi.), putting at risk any vessel coming within that range.

CLOSE RANGE: Conventional assaults are limited by the slow speed of conventional landing craft. To get troops ashore in under an hour, the assault fleet has to be within a few thousand metres of the coast, well within artillery range.

LARGE ASSAULT SHIP

AIR-CUSHION LANDING CRAFT

V-22 OSPREY

ASSAULT SHIP 5 KM (3 MILES) OFFSHORE

CH-53

LANDING CRAFT

OBJECTIVE: THE BEACH

BERIEV

EKRANOPLANE/SEA MONSTER

● Surface skimmer ● Missile cruiser ● Submarine destroyer

▲ With its revolutionary ability to skim the surface of the Earth, the Ekranoplane has seen a host of applications. The Russian space shuttle resembled it in its design.

Despite the misapprehension that Russian aviation designers are heavily influenced by Western designs, in one area they are recognised as world leaders. Looking like something straight out of a science-fiction film, Ekranoplanes skim over the Earth's surface at high speed, faster than any traditional boat or land vehicle. Equipped with short stubby wings and high-mounted engines, the Ekranoplanes bring unique qualities to the world of flying.

◀ **Monino mystery**
The Bartini VVA-14 was equipped with one main engine and 14 smaller lift engines. Although it carried Aeroflot colours, it was primarily perceived as a future military aircraft.

Overland, overseas ▶
During trials, the VVA-14 was equipped with the undercarriage from a Tu-22 'Blinder' for land operations, and twin floats for overwater flights.

◀ **Flight of fantasy**
A host of designs has been proposed, including large passenger carriers, but few have seen full-scale development.

▼ **Proud heritage**
Within the next few years the VVA-14 will be fully restored by Monino's air museum.

▲ **Space skimmer**
With its blended lower body and small wings, the space shuttle had similar design characteristics to the Ekranoplanes.

FACTS AND FIGURES

➤ Ekranoplanes can be designed to any size and are able to travel five times faster than standard large marine craft.

➤ A projected civilian transport variant has yet to be completed.

➤ Sukhoi intended to develop the S-90 model with seating for 400 passengers.

➤ Designed in 1979, the A-90 'Eaglet' was able to operate in sea state 5 and could travel up a beach and over terrain.

➤ In 1980 the largest of the Ekranoplanes – the KM-04 – was lost in a crash.

➤ The KM-04 was known as the 'Caspian Sea Monster' by Western observers.

PROFILE

Soviet sea monsters

Falling somewhere between a fully-fledged flying aircraft and a hovercraft, Ekranoplanes hold a unique position within the Soviet armed forces. Utilised in the military role as assault transports and cruise missile attack platforms, Ekranoplanes will provide a unique form of commercial passenger transport in civilian applications.

Able to ride on its own cushion of air created by complex aerodynamic forces, Ekranoplanes are able to skim across the water at great speed with very little resistance.

Serious research into military development of the Ekranoplane began in the early 1960s with proposals from a multitude of Russian aviation manufacturers.

Sokolov quickly emerged as the leader in the field with its A-90 'Eaglet', which was used in the largest numbers of any Ekranoplane. Serving as an assault transport with the Soviet navy, it could be equipped with surface-to-surface missiles.

Most outstanding of all was

Above: Lack of funding has seen a host of advanced Russian aviation programmes halted.

the KM-04, known as the 'Caspian Sea Monster'. Weighing 503 tonnes (495 tons) and armed with cruise missiles, it was designed to destroy American submarines.

Above: Cuts in the Soviet air force resulted in Sukhoi's order books being drastically reduced. The company has undertaken Ekranoplane development.

A-90 Orlyonok

Type: sea-skimming assault/transport craft

Powerplant: starting, two NK-8-4K; cruise, one NK-12MK turbofan/turboprop engine

Cruise speed: 350–400 km/h (217–250 m.p.h.)

Operational range: 1000 km (621 mi.)

Range: 3000 km (1864 mi.)

Cruise height: 1–4 m

Weights: empty 86.36 tonnes (82 tons)

Armament: six 'SS-N-22 Sunburn' cruise missiles fired from retractable launchers, 76-mm cannon

Accommodation: five crew

Dimensions: span 31.50 m (103 ft. 4 in.)
length 58.00 m (190 ft. 3 in.)
wing area 304.6 m² (3,279 sq. ft.)

A-90 ORLYONOK

The first large 'wingship' to enter operational service, the A-90 Orlyonok (Eaglet) was designed in 1979. The latest variants proposed by Sokolov are a SAR model and a commercial passenger-carrying example.

Mounted on the upper fuselage was a 76-mm gun turret to provide covering fire during the final stages of the assault. Missile launchers could also be installed to attack surface ships.

Conventional stressed skin was used in the construction of the A-90. After trials, additional strengthening was added to the wings and fuselage.

Propulsion was provided by a large, tail-mounted turboprop fitted with contra-rotating AV-68N propellers. The two balanced rudders gave the A-90 exceptional manoeuvrability.

Used in the assault transport role, the A-90 'Eaglet' was equipped with a side-hinging nose. This allowed the aircraft to carry the latest Soviet main battle tanks.

The wings were mounted low on the fuselage to provide lift at high speed. Smaller skegs (which act in a similar way to tailfins) were fitted at each tip to allow the aircraft to remain stable at high speed.

Naval versions of the A-90 'Eaglet' were equipped with a pylon-mounted surveillance radar and other avionics. The crew of nine provided the Soviet navy with a rapid transport attack and assault team.

EKRANOPLANE DEVELOPMENT

PRE-1960 **1** Quickly realising the future potential in using Ekranoplanes as transports and attack platforms, a host of Russian manufacturers developed small single-seat models to test the validity of their designs.

1960s

'CASPIAN SEA MONSTER'

1970s

BARTINI

ORLYONOK

1980s

2 With unlimited funding available, the 1970s saw rapid development of a host of Ekranoplanes within the AV-MF.

3 Though intended primarily for a military role, later versions were designed with the civilian passenger market in mind.

UTKA

LUN

?

1990s

4 The collapse of the Soviet finances has resulted in the current development of Ekranoplane being temporarily suspended.

Soviet sea watchers

■ **Be-12 'MAIL':** With its design dating back to 1945, Beriev's Be-12 continues to serve in limited quantities on anti-submarine duties and rescue work.

■ **A-40 'MERMAID':** One of the biggest amphibian aircraft currently flying, the 'Mermaid' is designed to replace the Be-12 in the ASW and maritime reconnaissance role.

■ **Tu-95RT 'BEAR-D':** Following a more conventional design path, the Tupolev Tu-95 operates on extended long-range maritime reconnaissance patrols from coastal land bases.

BERIEV

A-40 ALBATROSS

● Flying amphibian ● Submarine hunter ● Search and rescue

▲ *Despite the unique advantages that the Albatross enjoys over more conventional aircraft, the present economic situation may see these test pilots as the only crew to fly the type.*

One of a rare breed of jet flying boats, the Albatross is the latest in the Beriev family and the only operational jet flying boat. Designed to fulfil such varied roles as search and rescue, anti-submarine warfare and transport, the A-40 was supposed to replace Beriev's ageing Be-12. First flown in 1986, the A-40 was a very successful design. Unfortunately the principal customers, from the Soviet Union, cannot afford the aircraft.

▲ **Sea spray**
To protect against corrosion, the engines are positioned high, above the wings.

▲ **Advanced design**
An inflight-refuelling probe is located in the nose and a large search radar is housed inside the radome.

Graceful lines ▶
The A-40 shows off its elegant swept-wing platform. ESM pods are positioned on either side of the wings.

◀ **Land operations**
Capable of operating from both land and sea, here the A-40 displays its undercarriage.

Wave rider▶
The take-off run of the A-40 Albatross is short, and is unaffected by rough sea conditions.

FACTS AND FIGURES

➤ The first flight of the A-40 Albatross took place during December 1986 amid great secrecy in Russia.

➤ The prototype made its Western debut at the Paris air show in 1991.

➤ The A-40 is the largest serving amphibian ever to enter the service.

➤ In its SAR role, the A-40 can rescue 54 survivors, and minor operations can be performed inside the aircraft.

➤ A projected passenger version called the Be-40P is awaiting financial backing.

➤ Roles foreseen for the A-40 are SAR, ASW and cargo carrying.

PROFILE

Newest jet amphibian

Beriev's long tradition of amphibious aircraft enered the jet age with the short-lived Be-10 seaplane of the 1950s. The aircraft saw limited use and was outlived by the superb Be-12 Chaika 'Mail' turboprop.

Beriev revived the jet flying boat idea with the A-40, first designed in the early 1980s. Aimed at such diverse roles as reconnaissance, rescue, anti-submarine warfare and mine laying, the A-40 was supposed to finally replace the Be-12. Featuring a swept wing and

high-mounted engines to avoid water ingestion, the A-40 displayed excellent handling in the water as well as impressive flying characteristics.

Unfortunately, the Russian military already had extensive airborne anti-submarine assets in the shape of fixed- and rotary-wing aircraft, and cash shortages have prevented the purchase of the aircraft. The unconventional nature of the design has probably put off foreign buyers; at one point, Beriev even pitched the aircraft to the RAF as a Nimrod replacement, citing its

ability to land on water as a counter to the requirement for four-engine safety over water. The Be-200 is a scaled-down version with D-436T turbofans for passenger, cargo, and SAR roles. The Be-40P was a projected 105-seat airliner.

Below: The revolutionary hull design allows the Albatross to operate in all weather, even from seas with high swells.

Above: The ungainly Albatross has proved the validity of the jet-powered flying boat, although orders for the type are scarce.

A-40 Albatross

Type: Jet-powered ASW/SAR amphibian

Powerplant: Two PNPP Soloviev D-30KPV turbofans each rated at 117,68 kN (26,473 lb.-thrust); two Klimov RD-60K turbojets each rate at 24,52 kN (5,516 lb.-thrust)

Maximum speed: 760 km/h at 6000 m (484 m.p.h. at 19,700 ft.)

Initial climb rate: 1800 m/min (5,900 f.p.m.)

Range: 5500 km (3,410 mi.) with max fuel

Service ceiling: 9700 m (31,800 ft.)

Weight: Max take-off 86 000 kg (189,200 lb.)

Weapons: None.

Dimensions: Span 41,62 m (136 ft. 6 in.)
Length 43,84 m (143 ft. 9 in.)
Height 11,07 m (36 ft. 4 in.)
Wing area 200,00 m² (2,152 sq.ft.)

A-40 ALBATROSS

A new concept in aircraft design, the A-40 offers unique abilities to the aviation world. Lack of funding has prevented the Albatross from achieving its full potential.

The fuselage can hold all the required equipment associated with the ASW role. In its SAR version, the A-40 can accommodate up to 54 survivors and give them immediate medical attenion from three onboard attendants.

The high-set wings of the A-40 are positioned to give maximum lift. They also protect the engines from ingesting any sea spray.

Two Perm/Soloviev D-30KPV turbofan engines are mounted on pylons above either wing. Situated at the wingroots within the pylons are two RD-60K turbojets. They are used during operations at sea to reduce the take-off run and to manoeuvre the A-40 once on the surface.

An IFR probe is positioned on the nose. It enables the A-40 to receive fuel from various tanker aircraft, extending the aircraft's operational range.

The single-step hull is a revolutionary design and is described as the world's first 'variable bottom' platform. The A-40 sets new standards of stability and control in the water.

Positioned at either wingtip are ESM pods which are situated above the stabilising floats. These pods protect the wings during landings and take-offs at sea.

A large non-retractable rudder is situated at the rear of the hull. When used in conjunction with the main engines' thrust reverse, the rudder allows for exceptional handling qualities during operations from sea. Due to the high position of the rudder, land operations are unaffected.

ACTION DATA

CLIMB RATE
With the unique advantage of being the only jet-powered flying boat in service, the A-40's performance is phenomenal compared to other operational types. Its climb rate is superior to that of the earlier Be-12.

A-40 ALBATROSS 1800 m/min (5,900 f.p.m.)
Be-12 'MAIL' 912 m/min (2,990 f.p.m.)
HU-16B ALBATROSS 357 m/min (1,170 f.p.m.)

SPEED
Powered by twin turbofans, the A-40 is capable of covering a large search area at high speed. Compared to earlier designs like the piston-engine HU-16B and Be-12, operational speed is significantly increased due to the introduction of the turbofans.

A-40 ALBATROSS 760 km/h (484 m.p.h.)
Be-12 'MAIL' 610 km/h (378 m.p.h.)
HU-16B ALBATROSS 383 km/h (236 m.p.h.)

RANGE
As the Albatross' role becomes less offensive, long range is becoming an increasingly important factor. During a search-and-rescue mission, range is a critical factor. The development of a civil version would be a practical venture.

A-40 ALBATROSS 5500 km (3,410 mi.)
Be-12 'MAIL' 7500 km (4,650 mi.)
HU-16B ALBATROSS 2760 km (1,147 mi.)

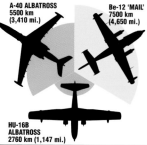

Berijev's flying boats

Be-4: Operational during World War II, the Be-4 was catapulted from warships in the role of convoy escort. Only 100 were built.

Be-6: The first large-scale flying boat to enter post-war service, over 200 examples were built. Later variants were ASW platforms.

M-10: The first jet flying boat to go into operational serice, the Be-10 first flew on July 20, 1956. It went on to set world records.

Be-12: The most successful flying boat developed by Beriev, the 'Mail' has been in service since the 1960s.

BERIEV

M-10 'MALLOW'

● Jet-powered flying-boat ● Record breaker ● Limited production

*Throughout the
Cold War the Soviet Union was keen
to demonstrate the abilities of its designs on
an international stage by attempting to break
FAI world records, and often succeeding.*

Shrouded in secrecy for many years, the M-10 was the only aircraft in its class to enter operational service. Known to NATO as 'Mallow', the M-10 (or Be-10, as it was known to the Beriev design bureau) was Beriev's second, and latest, jet flying-boat design until the Be-42 appeared in the mid-1980s. Destined to enjoy only a short service life with Soviet Naval Aviation (AV-MF), it was as a record breaker that the M-10 made its name.

PHOTO FILE

BERIEV **M-10 'MALLOW'**

Wingroot engines
At high speed and low level, the 'Mallow', with its anhedral wings, was an imposing sight. Note the engine nacelles tucked under the wingroots. The engines were attached to the fuselage and front wing spar.

Defensive armament
In common with other large Soviet military designs, including maritime patrol aircraft, bombers and transports, the M-10 featured a rear cannon turret.

Powered rudder
The M-10's large, swept fin was fitted with a powered rudder and could be used to maintain straight flight even with maximum asymmetrical power applied, for example in the event of engine failure.

Porpoising tendency
Although intended for operation in heavy seas, the M-10 was prone to 'porpoising' in bad conditions.

Beriev's first jet flying-boat
Armed with four NR-23 cannon and 1000 kg (2,000 lb.) of bombs, the R-1 was a three-man maritime patrol prototype. Experience with the R-1 was invaluable in the M-10's design.

FACTS AND FIGURES

Four M-10s flew at Tushino during the 1961 Soviet aviation day; US analysts believed it to be in squadron service.

The M-10's design was based broadly on that of the R-1 jet flying-boat of 1952.

The prototype, piloted by V. Kuryachi, first flew on 20 July 1956.

Because of the secrecy of such projects in the Soviet Union, little was known of the M-10 in the West for over 30 years.

Although the M-10 equipped two units, the exact number built is unclear.

The Be-12 turboprop flying-boat met the same requirements and remains in use.

Jet flying-boat record breaker

Beriev had already flown a jet flying-boat, a small, three-seat bomber prototype known as the R-1, in 1953. When the AV-MF requested a waterborne replacement for the Be-6 to fill the maritime reconnaissance, anti-ship and bombing roles, Beriev produced a larger, swept-wing three-seater jet with a 3300-kg (7,260-lb.) weapons load.

Strongly constructed to withstand the rigours of operations in heavy seas (an area in which it subsequently failed to perform adequately in testing), the prototype of the M-10 flew on 20 July 1956. It demonstrated a speed and ceiling performance twice that of the Be-6 'Madge', and its rate of climb was three times better than the piston-engined design.

A few M-10s joined two units of the AV-MF's Black Sea fleet, but their service use was brief. The high point of the M-10's career was establishing a number of world records for seaplanes in 1961. These included an average speed mark of 875.86 km/h (543 m.p.h.) over a 100-km (62-mile) circuit with a 5000-kg (11,000-lb.) payload, a straight line speed record of 912 km/h (565 m.p.h.) and an altitude record of 14962 metres (49,075 ft.). The last two records still stand – a remarkable achievement.

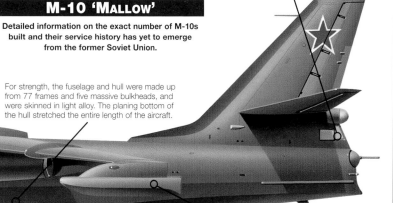

Beriev M-10s were the only jet-powered flying-boats in service during the Cold War. The US Navy had hopes for its Martin P6M SeaMaster, but it failed to proceed past prototype stage.

M-10 'MALLOW'

Detailed information on the exact number of M-10s built and their service history has yet to emerge from the former Soviet Union.

For a relatively large aircraft the M-10 had a small crew of just three: a pilot and navigator in a pressurised compartment (the former under a fighter-style canopy, and the latter in the bow of the aircraft) and a radio operator/gunner in the tail.

Two Lyul'ka AL-7PB non-afterburning turbojets powered the M-10. The AL-7 was fitted to a number of other types, including the Sukhoi Su-7 'Fitter' fighter. The engines were fed from 14 fuel tanks in the fuselage and wings.

For strength, the fuselage and hull were made up from 77 frames and five massive bulkheads, and were skinned in light alloy. The planing bottom of the hull stretched the entire length of the aircraft.

Defensive armament consisted of a twin NR-23 cannon installation in the tail turret. The radio operator/gunner's cabin was pressurised and equipped with a downward-firing ejection seat.

The wingtip floats required only small pylons, as the wings' anhedral brought them close to the water. The tailplane was constructed with dihedral and featured powered elevators.

The M-10's design was essentially an enlargement of the earlier R-1, with the engines tucked under the wingroots. Beriev conducted extensive testing to ensure that spray did not enter the engine intakes.

The underfloor area was divided into 10 watertight compartments. Immediately aft of the bottom hull 'step' was the bomb-bay with a 3300-kg (7,260-lb.) capacity. Its doors were sealed by a pneumatic tube, which was inflated at a pressure of 3 kg/cm² (42 PSI).

M-10 'Mallow'

Type: twin-jet maritime patrol flying-boat

Powerplant: two 63.75-kN (14,340-lb.-thrust) Lyul'ka AL-7PB turbojets

Maximum speed: 912 km/h (565 m.p.h.) at sea level

Cruising speed: 785 km/h (487 m.p.h.)

Initial climb rate: 7 min to 5000 m (16,400 ft.)

Weights: empty 26,500 kg (58,300 lb.); normal loaded 45,000 kg (99,000 lb.); maximum take-off 48,000 kg (105,600 lb.)

Armament: twin NR-23 23-mm cannon in rear turret, plus up to 3300 kg (7,260 lb.) of weapons, including bombs, mines and depth charges, or four torpedoes totalling 3075 kg (6,765 lb.)

Dimensions:
span	28.60 m (93 ft. 10 in.)
length	30.72 m (100 ft. 9 in.)
wing area	130 m² (1,400 sq. ft.)

COMBAT DATA

MAXIMUM SPEED

In operational guise the M-10 was designated the Be-10, and its jet engines gave it an unbeatable top speed for its type. The more recent A-40 design is not as fast, because it is optimised for range and load capacity rather than speed. Both attributes are more important for a maritime reconnaissance aircraft.

Be-10 'MALLOW'	912 km/h (565 m.p.h.)
Be-12 'MAIL'	610 km/h (378 m.p.h.)
A-40 ALBATROS 'MERMAID'	760 km/ (471 m.p.h.)h

CLIMB RATE

A modern design, the A-40 has a considerably better rate of climb than the two older designs, enabling it to take off with heavier loads and to reach operational heights quickly.

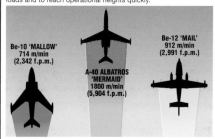

Be-10 'MALLOW' 714 m/min (2,342 f.p.m.)

A-40 ALBATROS 'MERMAID' 1800 m/min (5,904 f.p.m.)

Be-12 'MAIL' 912 m/min (2,991 f.p.m.)

WEAPONS LOAD

The installation of defensive gun armament was a feature of a number of Soviet designs in the 1950s. The Be-10's weapon load capacity was limited by the weight of the strongly-built airframe.

Be-10 'MALLOW' 2 x 23-mm cannon 3300-kg (7,260-lb.) bombload

Be-12 'MAIL' 5000-kg (11,000-lb.) bombload

A-40 ALBATROS 'MERMAID' 6500-kg (14,300-lb.) bombload

Soviet record holders

■ **ANTONOV An-124 'CONDOR':** One of Russia's giant An-124 transport aircraft set a jet-powered landplane closed circuit distance record of 20150.921 km (12,494 mi.) in 1987.

■ **MIKOYAN-GUREVICH E-266 'FOXBAT':** Early variants of the MiG-25 hold several records. In 1977 an E-266M set the current absolute world height record of 37650 metres (123,490 ft.).

■ **MIL Mi-6 'HOOK':** In August 1964 an Mi-6 broke the 100-km (62-mi.) closed-circuit speed record for helicopters. The new record was 340.15 km/h (210.89 m.p.h.) and still stands.

■ **TUPOLEV Tu-114 'CLEAT':** Derived from the Tu-95, the Tu-114 has held the turboprop closed-circuit speed record of 877.212 km/h (543.87 m.p.h.) with a 25-ton load since 1960.

BOEING/SIKORSKY

RAH-66 COMANCHE

● New-generation technology ● Stealthy airframe ● Programme cancelled

Boeing and Sikorsky combined their expertise to produce the RAH-66 Comanche, a high-tech combat aircraft designed for battle in the 21st century. The Comanche had a 'stealthy' fuselage of composite materials (making it difficult to detect on radar), the latest 'fly-by-wire' flight controls, and carried a cannon and missiles for its role as an armed scout. Only two prototypes flew before the programme was cancelled in February 2004.

▲ Combining stealth technology with highly advanced avionics, the RAH-66 would have been a huge asset to the US Army. Budget cuts and political interference proved its downfall.

BOEING/SIKORSKY RAH-66 COMANCHE

▼ **Built for stealth**
A faceted fuselage, the use of composite materials, internal weapons bays, hidden intakes and diffused, downward-pointing exhausts combined to give the RAH-66 stealth capabilities.

▲ **Eyes out**
Essential flight data was superimposed onto the electronic helmet displays worn by the crew.

▼ **Prototype construction**
Technicians work on the forward fuselage of the first Comanche.

▲ **Early impressions**
Even before its first flight, the Comanche's configuration changed several times, as can be seen from this early artist's impression.

Unique form ▶
The Comanche, with its emphasis on low observability, survivability and mission capability, was highly unusual in appearance.

FACTS AND FIGURES

➤ On 4 January 1996 the Comanche made its maiden flight at West Palm Beach, Florida, and was airborne for 36 minutes.

➤ Eight RAH-66s could be carried in a Lockheed C-5 Galaxy transport.

➤ The Comanche's gunner sat forwards, with the pilot to the rear.

➤ A competing design offered jointly by Bell and McDonnell Douglas was rejected.

➤ The US Army planned to acquire 5,000 RAH-66s, but will now purchase just 800 new helicopters and modernise another 1400.

➤ By 2004 the unit cost of each Comanche had risen to almost $60 million.

PROFILE

Stealth over the battlefield

Left: Several mock-ups of the Comanche have been built for ground testing and evaluation purposes, and the US Army hopes to procure a total of eight development airframes.

The thinking behind the RAH-66 Comanche When the fighting starts, a ground commander who does not have satellites, F-117s and other 'strategic' weapons to draw upon will be able to find and fight the enemy with the RAH-66 Comanche.

The RAH-66 was originally intended to replace the Bell AH-1, OH-58D and UH-1, along with the McDonnell Douglas OH-6, in US Army service. The RAH-66 has emerged as a scout/attack helicopter, combining the missions of the AH-1 and OH-6/OH-58D, although slow funding of the programme encouraged more roles and capabilities to be added, increasing the weight and cost. The Comanche was to be both the 'eyes' and the firepower of the modern army.

The US Army's LHX (Light Helicopter Experimental) competition was launched in the 1980s with the ambitious goal of creating a versatile helicopter able to perform many military tasks. The Boeing-Sikorsky production team was awarded the contract for the $34,000 million programme in April 1991. Extensive research was undertaken in composite structures, second-generation FLIR (forward-looking infra-red) and systems integration. However, 16 years and the expenditure of $8 billion dollars achieved little more than two flying prototypes and a partially completed test programme.

Above: Pictured on its 4 January 1996 inaugural flight, the prototype was subsequently grounded until 24 August 1996, because of transmission problems.

RAH-66 Comanche

Type: two-seat battlefield reconnaissance attack and air combat helicopter

Powerplant: two 1068-kW (1,430-hp.) LHTEC T800-LHT-800 turboshafts

Maximum speed: (estimated) 324 km/h (200 m.p.h.) 'clean' at 1220 m (4,000 ft.)

Vertical rate of climb: (estimated) 432 m/min (1,417 f.p.m.) at 1220 m (4,000 ft.)

Ferry range: 2334 km (1,447 mi.)

Weights: normal take-off 4807 kg (10,575 lb.); maximum take-off 7896 kg (17,371 lb.)

Armament: one turreted 20-mm, three-barrelled cannon with 320 rounds and up to 14 AGM-114 Hellfire anti-tank missiles or 18 AIM-28 Stinger air-to-air missiles or 56 70-mm rockets

Dimensions: main rotor diameter 11.90 m (39 ft.)
fuselage length 13.20 m (43 ft. 4 in.)
height 3.37 m (11 ft. 1 in.)
rotor area 111.22 m² (1,167 sq. ft.)

YRAH-66 COMANCHE

The YRAH-66 prototype was grounded after a poorly designed engine component failed during bench tests.

Helicopter rotors are excellent radar reflectors, producing distinctive radar flicker. The glass-skinned, graphite-sparred blades of the RAH-66 gave it a radar signature which was 1/600th of that of the Apache and 1/200th of that of the OH-58D.

Radar returns from the engine fronts and intakes were kept to a minimum by burying the engines deep in the fuselage and shrouding the intakes. This also made them less vulnerable to enemy fire.

94-0327

UNITED STATES ARMY

Lockheed Martin was responsible for the 20-mm Giat cannon. The avionics have some commonality with those of the F-22 fighter.

Weapons were stowed internally in the fuselage sides and were deployed only for launch. This kept the radar cross-section as small as possible for as long as possible.

Both T800 turboshafts had conventional exhaust systems, but they exhausted internally into large conduits which forced the efflux downward to slots beneath the tail.

A shrouded tail rotor was specified by the US Army for improved survivability, stealth and reduced noise signature.

COMBAT DATA

MAXIMUM LEVEL SPEED

In level flight the 'Hokum' has the edge in speed over all current battlefield helicopters. The Comanche's speed could be increased by retracting its undercarriage.

RAH-66 COMANCHE 324 km/h (200 m.p.h.)

Ka-50 WEREWOLF 'HOKUM-A' 350 km/h (192 m.p.h.)

AH-64D LONGBOW APACHE 295 km/h (162 m.p.h.)

ENDURANCE

The McDonnell Douglas Longbow Apache has greater endurance than the RAH-66 would have had, but is not as versatile nor able to survive as well. The Werewolf has only limited endurance.

RAH-66 COMANCHE	Ka-50 WEREWOLF 'HOKUM-A'	AH-64D LONGBOW APACHE
02:30	01:40	03:09
2 hours 30 min	1 hour 40 min	3 hours 09 min

ANTI-TANK MISSILES

Armed with 14 anti-tank missiles, the Comanche had almost the same firepower as the heavier and more powerful AH-64D. A two-seat Ka-50 is under development with new weapons systems.

RAH-66 COMANCHE	14 missiles
Ka-50 WEREWOLF 'HOKUM-A'	12 missiles
AH-64D LONGBOW APACHE	16 missiles

Facets of the Comanche

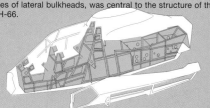

EQUIPMENT BAYS: Mission equipment was contained in three bays, one in the nose and two on the fuselage sides. The bays were pressurised and supplied with cool, filtered air.

COMPOSITE STRUCTURE: A 7.5-metre (24-foot 7-inch) long composite unit, consisting of two keel sections separated by a series of lateral bulkheads, was central to the structure of the RAH-66.

WEAPONS CARRIAGE: If additional weapons needed to be carried, a stub wing could be fitted at the expense of stealth. Here, the lower weapons rack has been deployed from the weapons bay, which is shown (right) with weapons retracted and bay closed.

BREGUET

BR.1001 TAON

● French light attack fighter prototype ● Record breaker

In the spring of 1954, NATO issued a specification for a light weight tactical strike fighter that was to become the standard aircraft in its class. Breguet responded with the Br.1001 Taon, and while NATO initially placed the aircraft first in its competition, its field performance and range were to prove deficient and the Taon lost out to the Italian-designed Fiat G91R. Breguet later used the Taon to set a world closed-circuit speed record.

▲ Breguet's Taon was one of no fewer than three French entries into a NATO competition for a light attack fighter. In spite of its good performance, handling and record-breaking speed performance, it eventually lost to the Italian G91.

BREGUET BR.1001 TAON

▼ **Quickly produced**
Construction of the Taon began in November 1956. It flew just eight months later, on July 25, 1957.

▲ **Rough landings**
Built by Messier, the Taon's undercarriage was designed for rough field operations. Low-pressure tires were fitted.

▲ **Closed-circuit speed record breaker**
A modified Taon set a new 1000-km closed-circuit world speed record in 1958, flown by Bernard Wit.

British engine ▶
Development of the Taon's British Orpheus turbojet was funded by the U.S. on behalf of NATO. This is the second Taon prototype, with a slightly larger rudder.

▲ **Light attack armament**
Four 12.7-mm (.50 calibre) guns were mounted under the lateral intakes. Air-to-ground stores were carried on four wing hardpoints.

Breguet 1100 ▶
The original Breguet 1001 (later renamed Br.1100) was the twin-engine machine from which the Br 1001B (later Br.1001) Taon was developed.

FACTS AND FIGURES

➤ Br.1002 was the designation given to a proposed missile-carrying interceptor version of the Taon.

➤ Orpheus engine development was partly funded by the U.S. on behalf of NATO.

➤ The first Taon made its first flight on July 26, 1957.

➤ In April 1958, the Taon set a new speed record of 649 m.p.h.

➤ The Taon's 1000-km (620-mi.) closed-circuit speed record was set at an average of 1073 km/h (667 m.p.h.) on July 23, 1958.

➤ During the NATO contest, the Taon was flown by French, British and U.S. pilots.

Unsuccessful NATO 'Gadfly'

Europe's aircraft manufacturers produced a range of interesting and sometimes radical design proposals in order to gain the contract for NATO's standard light strike aircraft.

Four aircraft were deemed promising enough for evaluation: the Breguet Br.1001 Taon, Dassault Etendard VI, Fiat G91R and Sud S.E.5000 Barouder. Three prototypes of each aircraft were ordered for an extensive fly-off competition involving European and

American test pilots. NATO required that the aircraft have exceptional speed performance at sea level, high maneuverability in the rolling plane, good field performance and long range.

In the first two areas the Taon excelled, but it was unable to achieve the specified 15 m (50-ft.) altitude after a 914 m (3,000-ft.) take-off run, and its range was disappointing.

In the competition the Taon therefore lost to the G91R, which was the better all-round

performer but which never became a truly standard NATO fighter. To highlight the Taon's high-speed abilities, however, Breguet modified one aircraft, using the latest advances in aerodynamics, for two successful attempts on the 1000-km (620-mi.) closed-circuit speed record. At his first attempt on April 25, 1958, test pilot Bernard Wit took the aircraft to a speed of 1044 km/h (649 m.p.h.), before breaking his own record at 1073 km/h (667 m.p.h.) on July 26, 1958.

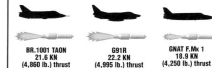

Although the Taon's handling drew praise, it had poor range and did not meet the required take-off performance.

Br.1001 Taon

Type: Single-seat lightweight strike fighter prototype.

Powerplant: One 21.5 kN (4,850-lb.)-thrust Bristol Orpheus BOr.3 turbojet.

Maximum speed: 1191 km/h (740 m.p.h.) at sea level.

Weight: Approx. takeoff 4990 kg (11,000 lb.).

Weapons: Proposed four 12.7-mm (.50 cal.) Colt-Browning machine guns or two 30-mm DEFA cannons or two MATRA rocket launchers (with 15 rockets each) internally; plus up to 454 kg (1,000 lb.) of ordnance on four wing pylons.

Dimensions: Span   6.8 m (22 ft. 4 in.)
Length   11.6 m (38 ft. 4 in.)
Height   3.7 m (12 ft. 2 in.)
Wing area 14.6 m² (158 sq. ft.)

BR.1001 TAON

Aircraft 01 was the first of three Taon prototypes. It wore this two-tone blue scheme as well as national insignia—Armée de l'Air roundels and fin flash. A 'Gadfly' artwork appears on the engine.

Conical wing-root fairings, called carenes, were added to further decrease transonic drag. This modification allowed the Taon to exceed Mach 1 at high level on the power of a non-afterburning engine.

The first Taon prototype was fitted with French equipment and instruments, while the second had an English-language, NATO-style cockpit. The pilot sat on a Martin-Baker ejection seat.

Development of the Taon took into account the latest advances in aerodynamics. The fuselage was sharply waisted to conform to the area-rule principle, which reduces transonic drag.

Rearming and refueling of both the main fuel tanks and the auxiliary carene tanks could be accomplished in under seven minutes.

Armament comprised four Browning 12.7-mm (.50 cal.) machine guns with 1,200 rounds of ammunition. The guns and ammunition were mounted on an easily interchangeable chassis for quick unloading and reloading as a pack.

The Taon (Gadfly) was named to suggest aggressiveness, while using the rearranged letters of the abbreviation NATO. The two names were combined on a badge on the intake.

Power came from a single Bristol-Siddeley Orpheus BOr.3 turbojet. The British engine manufacturer had cause to be pleased, since its engine powered all of the Taon's rivals in the NATO competition.

ACTION DATA

POWER

The winning Fiat G91 design had a slightly more powerful engine than that fitted to the Taon, though in production form the French machine was likely to have had an engine of higher thrust installed. The Gnat was an altogether smaller aircraft.

BR.1001 TAON	G91R	GNAT F.MK 1
21.6 KN (4,860 lb.) thrust	22.2 KN (4,995 lb.) thrust	18.9 KN (4,250 lb.) thrust

SPEED

Of these three lightweight fighters, the Gnat was the fastest, followed by the Taon. The production G91 was around 96.5 km/h (60 m.p.h.) slower despite its extra power, due to the weight of the operational systems carried and its less streamlined shape.

BR.1001 TAON	1190 km/h (740 m.p.h.)
G91R	1073 km/h (667 m.p.h.)
GNAT F MK1	1196 km/h (743 m.p.h.)

WEIGHT

By the time the Fiat G91 had entered service, its maximum takeoff weight (MTOW) had climbed to 12,100 pounds. The Br.1001, in prototype form, had an MTOW of 11,000 pounds, the Gnat just over four tons. The Gnat entered service in this lightweight form, but with limited combat capability.

BR.1001 TAON	G91R	GNAT F MK1
2989 KG (11,000 lb.)	5488 KG (12,100 lb.)	3967 KG (8,747 lb.)

Taon's fighter rivals

■ AERITALIA G91R: The G91 was the winner of the 1954 light tactical support aircraft contest. It failed to become the standard type, however, and was only built in Italy and West Germany.

■ DASSAULT-BREGUET ETENDARD: Later developed as a carrier-based attack aircraft (shown here), the Etendard was designed to meet the NATO shore-based requirement.

■ FOLLAND GNAT: The British-built Gnat was not officially evaluated though it was proposed as a potential contender. India, Finland and Yugoslavia took delivery of 39 production Gnats.

■ SUD-AVIATION SE.5000 BAROUDEUR: Three prototype fighters took part in the final fly-off: the Taon, G91 and Baroudeur. The latter took off from a trolley and landed on skids.

BRITISH AEROSPACE

EAP

● **Technology demonstrator** ● **Trials aircraft for Eurofighter**

God's airplane – the respectful title bestowed on the British Aerospace EAP demonstrator by test pilot Peter Orme. The Experimental Aircraft Programme aircraft was a pure research machine which pushed back the flight envelope. Test-flying this advanced, twin-engined machine produced results which enabled designers to finalise the detailed design of the Eurofighter Typhoon, now entering service.

▲ *Built at BAe's Warton plant, the EAP's airframe made extensive use of carbon-fibre composites in its construction and includes a wing skin of carbon-fibre reinforced plastic laminates.*

BRITISH AEROSPACE EAP

Airbrakes ▶
Hydraulically operated airbrakes were fitted behind the cockpit and on either side of the rear fuselage.

◀ Farnborough 1986
Only one month after its first flight the EAP aircraft was displayed at the Farnborough Air Show. Its appearance followed a number of proving flights, the 21st sortie taking it to Farnborough.

▲ Cranked arrow
The sophisticated 'cranked arrow' wing planform is the key to its manoeuvrability. Fly-by-wire technology is vital to control the aircraft.

▼ Colour scheme
ZF534 was painted a very pale semi-gloss blue with darker blue trim. The EAP logo and half of the cheat line are off-white.

▲ Air-to-air missiles
Though fitted with dummy defensive armament, the EAP aircraft was equipped to carry live missiles. The dummies were fitted to simulate the type of weapons intended for use in the Eurofighter.

FACTS AND FIGURES

➤ As the airframe contains a large amount of carbon fibre, EAP was known as 'Pete's Plastic Plane' after one of its pilots.

➤ The EAP uses 55 computers to control flight systems like fuel and hydraulics.

➤ EAP made its first flight at Warton on 8 August 1986, piloted by Dave Eagles.

➤ The EAP demonstrator was the first aircraft designed and developed entirely by British Aerospace.

➤ Test pilot Dave Eagles described the EAP as 'remarkably agile, yet very easy to fly'.

➤ The first Eurofighter 2000 used RB.199 engines; later aircraft will have EJ.200s.

PROFILE

New technology for Eurofighter

Sponsored by the United Kingdom's Ministry of Defence and aerospace industry, the BAe Experimental Aircraft Programme (EAP) demonstrator was produced to gain experience with the technology expected to be incorporated in Europe's new air-superiority fighter, the Eurofighter Typhoon.

Partners in the EAP included Italy and Germany when the type, which had been developed from the Anglo-German Agile Combat Aircraft (ACA) proposal, was originally envisaged as a pre-prototype for an operational European fighter. By 1983 Italy and Germany had pulled out of the programme. However, BAe decided to continue with the EAP aircraft, but only as a technology demonstrator as this was the only way of securing funding – the British government would not fund an all-British operational fighter.

The only aircraft produced, ZF534 first flew in August 1986.

Much experience was gained with major Eurofighter concepts, including unstable aerodynamic characteristics, 'fly-by-wire', complex avionics, multi-function cockpit displays and composite construction. Two hundred and fifty-nine sorties, totalling over 195 hours, were flown in just under five years.

The EAP's roll-out took place on 16 April 1986, with coloured lights, lasers and dry ice forming the backdrop. This high-profile launch emphasised the importance of the aircraft to the Eurofighter programme and Britain's aviation industry.

EAP Demonstrator

The Experimental Aircraft Programme (EAP) Demonstrator, serial number ZF534, was the sole example and flew for the first time on 8 August 1986. Retired on 1 May 1991 it is based at Loughborough University.

No radar or fire-control system is fitted to the aircraft, the nose being used to house flight test instrumentation.

The canard foreplanes either side of the nose can exert powerful aerodynamic forces and contribute to the high negative stability of the aircraft.

EAP's aerodynamics allow high angles of attack. At high 'alpha' the lower lip of the engine air intake hinges down to maintain air flow.

All fuel is carried internally in 14 integral fuselage tanks, giving the EAP aircraft a modest range of around 250 km (150 mi.).

Fly-by-wire controls are used throughout with no mechanical back-up. This system was developed aboard the experimental Active Control Technology Jaguar.

The single-seat cockpit is dominated by three interactive colour multi-function displays, each surrounded by input buttons allowing 'up-front' control of systems. The pilot sits on a Martin-Baker Mk 10LX 'zero-zero' ejection seat.

Dummy air-to-air missiles include four medium-range Skyflash under the fuselage and an ASRAAM on each wingtip.

The EAP aircraft is fitted with two Turbo-Union RB.199 afterburning turbofans virtually identical to those used by the RAF's Tornado F.Mk 3s, although with the thrust reversers deleted.

EAP Demonstrator

Type: single-seat technology demonstrator

Powerplant: two 75.61-kN (16,960-lb.-thrust) Turbo-Union RB.199 Mk 104D afterburning turbofan engines

Maximum speed: 2125 km/h (1,317 m.p.h.)

Range: approx. 250 km (150 mi.)

Service ceiling: approx. 12000 m (39,350 ft.)

Weights: maximum gross weight approx. 14510 kg (31,922 lb.)

Dimensions:

span	11.17 m (37 ft.)
length	17.53 m (57 ft.)
height	5.52 m (18 ft.)
wing area	50.00 m² (538 sq. ft.)

COMBAT DATA

MAXIMUM SPEED

The X-31 has a fairly modest top speed due to its single engine. This is purely a research aircraft for which speed was not particularly important. Although also a demonstrator, the EAP was originally intended to be a production aircraft.

EAP DEMONSTRATOR	2125 km/h (1,320 m.p.h.)
X-31A	1155 km/h (717 m.p.h.)
MiG-29M	2445 km/h (1,519 m.p.h.)

'G' LIMITS

Modern fighters, especially those equipped with 'fly-by-wire' controls, are capable of very tight turning manoeuvres. The MiG-29M when piloted by a skilled pilot could turn tighter than either of the other two types in a dogfight. In a combat situation, however, the ability to engage an aircraft from 'beyond visual range' (BVR) would be just as important.

EAP DEMONSTRATOR	+9/-3g
X-31A	+9/-4g
MiG-29M	+10.5/-3g

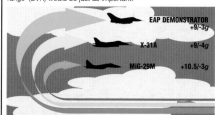

ENGINE THRUST

As an experimental aircraft the X-31 does not need the power of a combat machine, and the EAP demonstrator used readily available engines. The production Eurofighter will have engines producing over 176.53 kN of thrust.

EAP DEMONSTRATOR	151.22 kN (34,000 lb.)
X-31A	53.38 kN (12,000 lb.)
MiG-29M	172.60 kN (38,800 lb.)

From ACA to Eurofighter 2000

■ **AGILE COMBAT AIRCRAFT:** The 1982 product of Anglo-German co-operation, ACA incorporated features of MBB's TKF90 proposal.

■ **EAP:** By September 1982 ACA had become EAP, a pre-prototype for an operational fighter, with examples being built in Germany, Italy and the UK.

■ **BRITAIN GOES IT ALONE:** Italy and Germany pulled out of the project in 1983, with the sole EAP aircraft becoming a demonstrator.

■ **EUROFIGHTER 2000:** The first Eurofighter flew in March 1994. The type is now entering service with Spain, Germany, Italy and the UK.

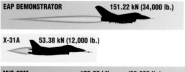

CFM

SHADOW

● Microlight family ● Range of variants ● Affordable flying

▲ Cook Flying Machines pioneered microlight production in the 1980s from a small factory in England. Unfortunately, in late 1996, the firm went into receivership.

When David Cook first fitted a go-kart engine to a hang-glider in 1977, the home-made propeller would not keep him airborne for more than a 50-metre hop. Six years later, when he flew the first Cook Flying Machines Shadow, the authorities had not even considered how to go about certifying such an aircraft. Yet today, microlights are an established route to safe, economical flying, and the Shadow remains a fine machine in its class.

CFM SHADOW

◀ STOL performance
Microlights are naturally able to use a very short take-off run. The Series B-D has a 90-m (295-ft) run on a metalled surface.

▼ Variable endurance
The Shadow has a one-hour, 45-minute endurance, and eight hours with extra fuel tanks.

▼ At the factory
CFM's headquarters and chief manufacturing facility was on an industrial estate in Suffolk. Assembly was also undertaken at Old Sarum aerodrome, near Salisbury, Wiltshire.

▼ Multi-role microlight
Suggested equipment to be fitted to the Shadow has included spray gear, cameras and thermal imagers.

◀ Military variant promoted
This Shadow variant features a British Aerospace infra-red linescan system for military use.

FACTS AND FIGURES

➤ In 1996, CFM's Streak Shadow SA microlight kit cost £10,750, exclusive of engine, propeller and sales tax.

➤ By early 1995, sales of Shadow series microlights had totalled 280.

➤ A multi-function surveillance Shadow variant features a Hasselblad camera fit.

➤ CFM entered a licence-production agreement with a firm in New Mexico.

➤ The last CFM microlight was the SA11 Starstreak, which had a 55-kW (73-hp.) engine.

➤ CFM had plans to establish a licence-production line in South Africa.

PROFILE

Popular pioneering microlight

Nearly 15 years after its first flight, the Shadow has spawned a range of derivatives. There are gliders with an optional 20-kW (27-hp.) motor for self-launching, and a version called the Wizard.

High performance is the preserve of the 48-kW (65-hp.) Streak Shadow and 63-kW (85-hp.) Star Streak. The Streak Shadow has shorter, thinner wings, while the Star Streak's extra power and reduced-chord wings give a top speed of 260 km/h (161 m.p.h.).

But flying a Shadow is mainly about safe, cheap, powered flight. The addition of wing lockers holding 5 kg (10 lb.) of baggage can make the Shadow capable of carrying enough for the pilot and a passenger to spend a weekend away. Carrying only the pilot, the Shadow has also been used for some remarkably long journeys. At least one pilot has crossed the US in such a craft, taking two and a half weeks to cover 6437 kilometres (3,990 mi.), during 69 hours aloft. Another has flown from England to China via Moscow and Siberia in the space of a month, despite thunderstorms, torrential rain and 110-km/h (68-m.p.h.) winds.

Below: In Britain, the first weekend in May sees the Microlight Trade Fair, held at Popham in Hampshire. The fair attracts microlight manufacturers from around Europe.

Above: Shadow Series C-D is the dual-control variant of the company's standard model.

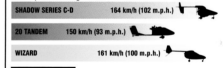

The Shadow's wings are of aluminium alloy and wood construction, with foam/glass-fibre ribs, plywood covering on the forward section and polyester fabric aft.

Wing design in the Shadow allows no 'defined stall' or spinning. Drooped wingtips increase lift on take-off. Struts are used to strengthen the wing structure.

Microlight design has advanced in leaps and bounds since the early days of the late 1970s. Today's designs feature tricycle undercarriage, enclosed cockpits in a streamlined fuselage, often with two seats, and more powerful engines. The undercarriage is non-retractable, but features brakes. Wheels may be exchanged for floats if required.

Aluminium is used in the Shadow's tailboom. The tailfin and large rudder are positioned below the boom. Finlets are fitted on the ends of the tailplane.

Fuel capacity is 23 litres (50 gallons) in a standard configuration. For long-distance flying, a 43-litre (95-gallon) auxiliary tank is optional.

The Shadow is one of many microlight designs to employ the Rotax flat-twin cylinder air-cooled engine. The Shadow B-D's engine, rated at 28 kW (38 hp.), drives a 1.3-m (4-ft. 3-in.) diameter three-bladed propeller.

G-MTSG

SHADOW

SHADOW SERIES B-D

The first Shadow flew in 1983 and was in continuous production until CFM went into receivership in 1996. G-MTSG is a dual-control Series B-D, one of a considerable number of Shadows registered in Britain.

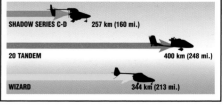
Diverse microlight designs

AEROSTRUCTURE PIPISTRELLE: Designed in France in mid-1981, this 'tail-dragging' craft had an open cockpit and vee-tail.

TIRITH FIREFLY: Two ducted propellers drove the Firefly, a design sharing its configuration with the Shadow.

TISSERAND HYDROPLUM: This unusual French amphibious design first flew in 1983 and was displayed at the 1985 Paris Air Show.

ULTRAFLIGHT LAZAIR: Canadian company, Ultraflight, offered several versions of the Lazair twin-engined design.

CHRISTEN

EAGLE

● Competition aerobatics ● Amateur construction ● 1970s design

After Frank Christensen had tried, unsuccessfully, to buy the famous Pitts Special designs, he decided to design and market a very similar aircraft, named the Christen Eagle. Available only in kit form, the original single-seat Eagle I was replaced by the Eagle II, which sold widely to amateur constructors around the world. In 1981 Christensen finally acquired the Pitts business and marketed his new acquisition alongside his well established Eagle design.

▲ With a large bubble canopy, the cockpit acts like a greenhouse in hot, sunny weather. Pilots tend to keep the canopy open, providing air to the cockpit until take-off is imminent.

PHOTO FILE

CHRISTEN EAGLE

◄ **Eagle finish**
Eagle IIs are almost exclusively finished with an eagle design extending down the fuselage side.

▼ **Bubble canopy**
A large canopy covers both occupants, giving the pilot a 360° field of vision.

▼ **Thrilling the crowds**
After helping form the 'Eagle Aerobatic Flight Team' in 1979, Gene Soucy still regularly performs at air shows in the USA.

▼ **Training or touring**
Built with equipment and comfort levels suitable for advanced aerobatic training or cross-country touring, the Eagle II appeals to a range of customers.

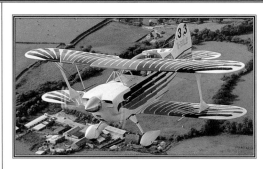

◄ **Powerful engine**
To give the Eagle II superior performance over the Pitts, a 149-kW (200-hp.) Lycoming engine was fitted, bestowing an excellent rate of climb.

FACTS AND FIGURES

➤ Construction of the prototype Eagle II began in 1975 and it flew for the first time in February 1977.

➤ The Eagle II has a maximum rate of roll of over 200° per second.

➤ The special-purpose Eagle I was not available for amateur constructors.

➤ The prototype Eagle I was built under tight security and made its debut in the 1978 US National Championships.

➤ Designed for aerobatics, the Eagle II is certified to +9/-6 g.

➤ The specially adapted fuel system allows unlimited inverted flight.

High-performance homebuild

Looking remarkably similar to the famous Pitts Special, the high-performance, aerobatic Eagle II gained a reputation in the late 1970s as a world-beating competition aerobat, despite being available only in kit form.

From its base in Wyoming, Christen marketed the Eagle II in 25 separate kits. Each kit makes a part of the aircraft and is supported by a very detailed construction manual. Christen claims that no construction experience is required and only common hand tools are needed. A typical homebuilder takes 1,400 to 1,600 hours to complete an Eagle II.

Construction of the prototype Eagle II began in 1975 and manufacture started in 1977. By this time the single-seat Eagle I was flying, and in 1978 aerobatic champion Gene Soucy flew the aircraft in the US National Championships, gaining a creditable third place.

To demonstrate the superior capabilities of the Eagle over the competing Pitts design, Christensen provided aircraft for the famous 'Red Devils' aerobatic team. The name was changed to the 'Eagles Aerobatic Flight Team' and they were soon performing at more than 60 air shows a season.

By 1986 at least 600 kits had been sold, with 250 completed and in flying condition.

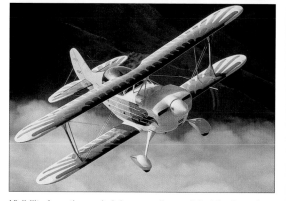

Visibility from the cockpit is generally good, but the top wing blocks out a section of the pilot's forward view. On the ground, the pilot has a restricted view over the aircraft's nose.

Eagle II

Type: two-seat homebuilt aerobatic biplane

Powerplant: one 149-kW (200-hp.) Avco Lycoming AEIO-360-A1D piston engine

Maximum speed: 296 km/h (184 m.p.h.)

Initial climb rate: 645 m/min (2,115 f.p.m.)

Range: 611 km (380 mi.) with max payload

Service ceiling: 5180 m (17,000 ft.)

Weights: empty 465 kg (1,023 lb.); max take-off 725 kg (1,595 lb.)

Dimensions:
span	6.07 m (19 ft. 11 in.)
length	5.64 m (18 ft. 6 in.)
height	1.98 m (6 ft. 6 in.)
wing area	11.61 m² (125 sq. ft.)

The Eagle II is powered by an Avco Lycoming AEIO-360-A1D piston engine driving a Hartzell constant-speed propeller. The fuel tank is situated in the fuselage and has a capacity of 98.4 litres (26 gallons), with a fuel system which allows unlimited inverted flight.

Two seats are arranged in tandem beneath the one-piece side-hinged bubble canopy. Equipment levels are fairly low, with only essential instruments and a radio fitted. A baggage hold in the turtledeck has a capacity of 13.6 kg (30 lb.).

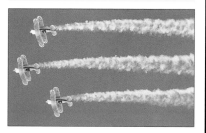

Pilots Gene Soucy, Tom Poberezny and Charlie Hillard established 'Team Eagle' and still demonstrate the aircraft's aerobatic qualities.

For simplicity, the landing gear is a fixed tail-wheel arrangement. The large spats fitted to the main wheels improve aerodynamic flow and reduce drag, giving an increase in performance.

The braced biplane wings are supported by steel tube interplane struts. Constructed from wooden spars and ribs, the lower wing has slight dihedral and ailerons are fitted to both the upper and lower wings to increase the rate of roll.

EAGLE II

Purchased as a kit from the Christen company, this Eagle II was constructed by an amateur in the UK. The number '33' was worn on the tail during participation in the Digital Schneider Trophy air race.

ACTION DATA

MAXIMUM SPEED

Fitted with a more powerful engine, and not handicapped by the drag induced by biplane wings, the Yak-50 is the fastest of these types. Although the Eagle II and Pitts S-2A are very similar, the Eagle's more powerful engine gives it an edge in performance.

EAGLE II	296 km/h (184 m.p.h.)
YAK-50	320 km/h (198 m.p.h.)
S-2A	253 km/h (157 m.p.h.)

CLIMB RATE

The Yak's powerful engine gives it excellent climb performance, which is vital for competition aerobatics. The Pitts and Christen designs have a slower rate of climb, but they compensate by having a tremendous rate of roll.

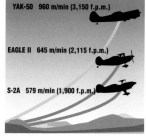

YAK-50	960 m/min (3,150 f.p.m.)
EAGLE II	645 m/min (2,115 f.p.m.)
S-2A	579 m/min (1,900 f.p.m.)

Competition aerobatic biplanes

CASA 1.131 JUNGMANN: Bücker-built Jungmanns competed in the World Aerobatic Championships in the 1960s.

DE HAVILLAND DH.82 TIGER MOTH: A number of Tiger Moths were flown in both British and World Championships in the 1950s.

PITTS S-1 SPECIAL: The Pitts Special dominated the US Championships in the late-1960s and 1970s, setting new standards.

STAMPE SV.4A: Superior to the British Tiger Moth, the Stampe dominated the European aerobatic scene in the 1950s.

CIERVA

AUTOGYROS

● Rotary-winged aircraft ● Spanish inventor ● British manufacture

G-ACIN

▲ Cierva's autogyros were among the first practical rotorcraft. However, it was not until the mid-1930s that vertical take-off in an autogyro was possible. By the end of World War II, the helicopter had demonstrated unbeatable versatility.

Juan de la Cierva was born in September 1895. He designed and built a glider when he was 15, and his first three-engined aeroplane in 1918. His true aim was to design an aircraft that would be able to maintain lift, and land safely after an engine failure. Practical helicopters were impossible with the engines and materials then available, so he turned to the concept of an aircraft using an unpowered rotor for lift and a conventional propeller for propulsion.

CIERVA AUTOGYROS

Vertically rising C.40 ▶
The C.40 of 1938 was able to make a direct vertical take-off. This was accomplished by spinning the main rotor at a high speed with the blades at zero incidence, then selecting positive pitch to create lift.

◀ First successes
With subsidies from the Spanish government, Cierva built the C.6 series, using Avro 504K fuselages. Such was its success that Cierva established a company in the UK.

Commercial successes ▶
The most commercially successful early design was the C.19, the first purpose-built autogyro. Twenty-nine were built.

G-ABUD

Air Ministry craft ▶
British Air Ministry interest in Cierva's designs began in the 1920s with the C.6. Avro was among several British companies eventually licensed to build autogyros. The RAF evaluated several prototypes, including C.6s, a C.8L and C.19s. In 1934/35, 12 C.30As were delivered.

Cierva's first autogyro ▶
Using the fuselage of a French Deperdussin monoplane, Cierva built the C.1, an aircraft that refused to fly!

FACTS AND FIGURES

➤ Twelve C.30As (designated Rota Mk I) were delivered to the RAF in the 1930s, followed by 13 civil examples after 1939.

➤ Among preserved Autogyros is a Rota Mk I (C.30A) at the RAF Museum, London.

➤ British-built C.19s were sold in countries like New Zealand, Japan and Australia.

➤ During World War II, a Jeep was fitted with a rotor and towed behind an aircraft, using the autogyro principle.

➤ Juan de la Cierva became the first autogyro passenger in a C.6D on 30 July 1927.

➤ In the late 1920s, Cierva learned to fly his own autogyros.

PROFILE

Spanish rotary-wing pioneer

Cierva patented the autogyro (or autogiro) design for his aircraft. Their key feature – a vital contribution to helicopter development – was the articulated rotor hub. Its drag and flapping hinges allowed the individual rotor blades to rise and fall and 'evened out' the lift. The first workable craft, the C.4, flew 4 km (3 miles) in January 1923. By September 1928, Cierva's C.8L Mk II design, powered by a 149-kW (200-hp.) Lynx engine and based on an Avro 504 fuselage, made a 40-km (25-mile) flight across the English Channel and on to Paris.

Cierva died in an airliner crash at Croydon in December 1936, by which time his ideas had been accepted. He had formed his own company in England, and his designs were produced in the UK, US, France and Germany. The C.40 had a newly developed tilting rotor, allowing it to take off vertically.

Below: Early autogyro flights were plagued by accidents. The first three designs failed to become airborne; it was the C.4 that finally flew in 1923.

Above: de Havilland's distinctive lines were evident in the C.24, designed and built by the company in 1931.

ROTA MK IA

One of three Cierva C.30s impressed into RAF service in World War II, this aircraft was previously G-ACWH. No. 529 Squadron employed a number of Rotas for radar calibration duties during 1943-44.

Cierva C.30A

Type: utility autogyro

Powerplant: one 104-kW (140-hp.) Armstrong Siddeley Genet Major IA radial engine

Maximum speed: 177 km/h (110 m.p.h.)

Cruising speed: 153 km/h (95 m.p.h.)

Range: 459 km (285 mi.)

Service ceiling: 5800 m (19,000 ft.)

Weights: empty 553 kg (1,217 lb.); max take-off 816 kg (1,795 lb.)

Accommodation: pilot and observer

Dimensions:
main rotor diameter	11.28 m (37 ft.)
length	6.01 m (19 ft. 9 in.)
height	3.38 m (11 ft. 1 in.)
rotor area	99.89 m² (1,075 sq.ft.)

ACTION DATA

MAXIMUM SPEED

Rota Mk Is (C.30As) had a top speed comparable to the fixed-wing Fieseler Storch. Although RAF Rotas were attached to the School of Army Co-operation, they were soon assigned a coastal radar calibration role. The Storch was a widely-used German STOL liaison aircraft.

C.30A	177 km/h (110 m.p.h.)
FI 282 V21 KOLIBRI	150 km/h (93 m.p.h.)
Fi 156C-1 STORCH	175 km/h (109 m.p.h.)

POWER

With an engine of little more power, the FI 282 search-and-rescue and spotting helicopter was able to accomplish vertical flight using two intermeshed rotors. The Storch STOL aircraft had a larger engine but none of the versatility of the rotary-winged types, relying on an airstrip from which to operate.

C.30A	FI 282 V21 KOLIBRI	Fi 156C-1 STORCH
104 kW (140 hp.)	119 kW (160 hp.)	179 kW (240 hp.)

RANGE

Cierva C.30As had a good range performance, comparable to that of the Storch. Lack of range was a shortcoming of early helicopter designs. The Kolibri was a small two-seater with little internal fuel capacity, whereas the Cierva used a larger fuselage, similar to a fixed-wing aircraft, with more tankage.

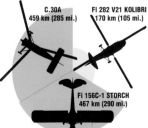

C.30A	FI 282 V21 KOLIBRI
459 km (285 mi.)	170 km (105 mi.)

Fi 156C-1 STORCH
467 km (290 mi.)

To start the main rotor spinning before take-off, the C.19 and later designs introduced a drive transmission system from the main engine. This was controlled by a rotor clutch and brake operated from the cockpit.

The C.30 was a two-seater, the pilot occupying the rear cockpit. The pilot was able to unlock and tilt (laterally, as well as fore and aft) the main rotor using the control column attached to the rotor head.

A seven-cylinder Armstrong Siddeley Genet Major IA radial rated at 104 kW (139 hp.) was installed in the C.30A. To the RAF, the engine was known as the Civet I.

For yaw stability, the C.30's vertical surfaces were of a sizeable area. A large fixed fin had a small trimmer at the extreme rear. A small ventral fin was also fitted. The horizontal fins had upturned ends for extra stability.

Although the initial Cierva designs used existing aircraft fuselages, the C.19 and subsequent models were purpose-built. Sixty-six were licence-built by A.V. Roe and Co. Ltd, all at Manchester. In France, Lioré-et-Olivier built 25 designated LeO C301, while Focke-Wulf built 40 examples.

The C.30's fuselage structure was of Duralumin tubing with a fabric skin covering. The later C.40 used wooden skinning over a metal internal frame.

Among the new features of the C.30A were folding rotor blades to allow easier hangarage, and a reverse aerofoil section on the port tailplane to counteract rotor torque.

Getting airborne in an autogyro

CIERVA'S AUTOGYRO: The term 'autogyro' was coined by Juan de la Cierva to describe his aircraft, in which the freewheeling main rotor provided lift for vertical flight.

FORWARD MOTION: With the rotor locked, the engine was started and pulled the aircraft forward. On early designs the rotor was unlocked and air flow made the rotor rotate.

TILTING ROTOR: The C.30 used a driveshaft from the engine to initiate rotor rotation. Once the rotor had reached the required number of revolutions per minute, it was tilted backwards.

LIFT FROM THE ROTOR: Combined with the aircraft's forward motion, the spinning rotor disc provided lift, much like a helicopter.

CONVAIR

B-36 FICON

● Giant strategic bomber ● Reconnaissance mother-ship

T he B-36 was the 'Big Stick' of Cold War deterrence; 383 of these stupendous bombers were the backbone of the mighty Strategic Air Command from 1948 to 1959. The largest warplanes ever to fly in the West, they carried the biggest hydrogen bombs ever built and girdled the globe on nuclear alert or highly dangerous spying missions. At one stage they even carried their own fighter aircraft.

▲ The B-36 was massive, yet its incredible weight rested on just single mainwheels. These weren't quite the biggest wheels ever carried by an aircraft, but they dwarfed ground crew.

CONVAIR B-36 FICON

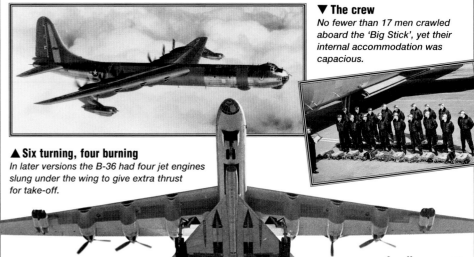

▼ The crew
No fewer than 17 men crawled aboard the 'Big Stick', yet their internal accommodation was capacious.

▲ Six turning, four burning
In later versions the B-36 had four jet engines slung under the wing to give extra thrust for take-off.

▲ Bomber testbed
This B-36 is carrying a scale model of the Convair B-58 Hustler for aerodynamic drop tests.

Loading ramp ▼
There wasn't much room under a B-36. To create the FICON combination, the bomber had to be driven on to a ramp so that the reconnaissance fighter could be squeezed underneath.

▲ Wingtip fighter
Before the FICON project, the USAF tested the B-36 with F-84 fighters towed from the wingtips using this strange attachment.

FACTS AND FIGURES

➤ A few B-36s were modified to carry a fighter in the bomb-bay.

➤ Convair developed a huge airlifter from the B-36, the experimental XC-99, but the giant transport never entered service.

➤ The B-36's radar and communications systems used 3,000 vacuum tubes.

➤ To the men who flew it, the B-36 never had a name. The nickname 'Peacemaker' was assigned to this mammoth bomber years after it went out of service.

➤ B-36 missions lasted for so long that it was said to be equipped with a calendar rather than clocks.

PROFILE

A deadly combination

Originally designed to drop bombs on Germany from bases in America, the big B-36 began as a six-engined bomber but soon had four jets added, making it a 10-engine behemoth by the time it entered service in 1948. It was tasked to rip out the heart of the Soviet Union with a retaliatory attack, using hydrogen bombs like the Mk 17, which weighed more than a DC-3 transport and was the largest bomb ever deployed by the US military.

When the B-36 flew overhead, it blotted out the sun.

In slang, it was called the 'aluminum overcast'. The bomber was so long that crewmen used a powered dolly to transport themselves through the middle of the aircraft between nose and tail.

At high altitude, the vast wings of the B-36 clawed so much air that the bomber was more manoeuvrable than jet fighters. Missions in this incredible giant lasted as long as 40 hours. No other American bomber ever approached the B-36's size, weight, and bomb-carrying capacity.

The NB-36H carried a nuclear reactor to test its effect on the aircraft. The next step would have been a nuclear-powered bomber.

GRB-36 FICON

With its enormous size, the B-36 was a natural to act as a mother-ship for a secret strategic reconnaissance programme. A small reconnaissance fighter was carried over a long distance to its target, dropped off to go in and get the pictures, and then hauled back home to the US.

The aircraft carried by the GRB-36 was the Republic GRF-84F, a special version of the USAF's main tactical camera ship.

Operational bombers had two pairs of gun turrets in the rear fuselage, operated remotely from observation posts by dedicated gunners. When not threatened by the enemy, the guns were retracted and covered by sliding panels.

To give the huge bomber an extra burst of speed over the target area, the B-36 was fitted with four J47 turbojets to augment the six huge piston engines driving the propellers.

O-492092

092 UN **U.S. AIR FORCE**

The FICON (Fighter Conveyor) combination went operational in 1955, but only a handful of missions were flown. The operating unit was the 91st Strategic Reconnaissance Squadron.

The Thunderflash fighter was held on a complicated trapeze which swung down from the bomb-bay. The doors of the bomb-bay were cut away so that the fighter could fit in snugly.

The B-36 was covered with aerials and radomes for electronic equipment and bombing radars. Many variants had huge reconnaissance cameras wedged into the bomb-bays.

B-36s were normally festooned with defensive guns, the standard bomber featuring no less than 16 20-mm cannon, including two in the tail. The FICON aircraft had them all removed to save precious weight.

U.S.AIR FORCE FS-266 F5-266

Inside the B-36
The B-36 was basically a long tube. The two crew compartments (green) were linked by a crew tunnel with a trolley on rails.

Forward crew compartment

Forward gun turrets and bombing radar

Two bomb-bays with Mk 17 thermonuclear weapons; each heavier than a small airliner of the time

Rear gun turrets

Rear crew compartment with rest bunks

B-36D Peacemaker

Type: intercontinental strategic bomber

Powerplant: six 2834-kW (3,800-hp.) Pratt & Whitney R-4360-53 piston engines and four 23.13-kN (5,200-lb.) GE J47-GE-19 turbojets

Maximum speed: 700 km/h (435 m.p.h.)

Range: 10944 km (6,800 mi.)

Service ceiling: 14780 m (48,490 ft.)

Weights: empty 77581 kg (171,036 lb.); loaded 185976 kg (410,000 lb.)

Armament: 16 20-mm cannon in nose, tail and six fuselage turrets, plus bombload of up to 39000 kg (85,980 lb.)

Dimensions:
span		70.10 m (230 ft.)
length		49.40 m (162 ft.)
height		14.22 m (46.6 ft.)
wing area		443.3 m² (4,772 sq. ft.)

COMBAT DATA

MAXIMUM SPEED

B-52 STRATOFORTRESS (1952) — 965 km/h

B-36 PEACEMAKER (1946) — 700 km/h

B-29 SUPERFORTRESS (1942) — 570 km/h

Less than a decade spanned the first flights of the Boeing B-29, the Convair B-36 and the Boeing B-52, yet in that time maximum speed almost doubled. All three bombers used their big wings and immense engine power to outperform interceptors at height.

SERVICE CEILING

Bombing from high altitude was seen as the only protection against fighters in the days before guided missiles. The B-36 FICON used another technique – its onboard fighter flew the last, most dangerous part of the mission.

9750 m — B-29 SUPERFORTRESS

14780 m — B-36 PEACEMAKER

16750 m — B-52 STRATOFORTRESS

WEIGHTS

The need for massive fuel loads for intercontinental range, and the equally pressing need for huge carrying capacity to deploy the awesome first-generation hydrogen bombs, saw the maximum weights of heavy bombers skyrocket in the decade between the B-29 and the B-52.

B-52 STRATOFORTRESS 221000 kg

B-36 PEACEMAKER 185976 kg

B-29 SUPERFORTRESS 63500 kg

Maximum take-off weights

CONVAIR

NB-36H

● Nuclear reactor carrier ● X-plane ● Only one built

Typical of the 1950s obsession with all things nuclear, the NB-36 was the prototype for the X-6 nuclear-powered bomber, which was never built. Designed to fly using a mixture of nuclear and conventional jet power, the NB-36 made 47 flights between 1955 and 1957. Impressive as it was, the whole concept was made irrelevant by advances in conventional aircraft, and the USAF later cancelled the project.

▲ The Crusader makes one of its 47 test flights in company wth a B-29/50 Superfortress formation.

CONVAIR **NB-36H**

▼ **Production line**
Convair was manufacturing B-36s as fast as it could in the 1950s, but the ill-fated X-6 never went into production. Only one NB-36H ever took to the skies.

▲ **Radiation hazard**
The large radiation hazard badge on the tail summed up what the NB-36H was all about. Much was learnt about safety shielding for aircrew, but it was all to be wasted.

Mixed power▶
Like all B-36s, the NB-36H had a mixed powerplant of R-4360 piston engines and J-47 turbojets, as well as its massive one megawatt reactor.

▼ **Last of the line**
B-36 production ended in August 1954, and the NB-36H was the last variant to fly. It was also converted for reconnaissance.

Long distance cruiser ▶
The X-6 might have been able to cruise for an unlimited distance, but the NB-36H never got further than flying trials within the USA.

FACTS AND FIGURES

➤ At the end of the test programme, the NB-36H was scrapped after the reactor was removed.

➤ The cockpit canopy's radiation-proof sections were 25 cm (10 in.) thick.

➤ No less than $469,350,000 was spent on the nuclear powered aircraft programme.

➤ The crew was protected by a 30 cm (12 in.) water window, a 5 cm (2 in.) rear lead shield and 52 cm (20 in) thick plastic.

➤ Total powerplant weight in the X-6, including the reactor, was 63.6 tonnes (70 tons).

➤ The R-1 reactor was removed and tested after each flight for research purposes.

PROFILE

Flying on nuclear power

Fascinated by the potential of endless power, the USAF began a nuclear-powered aircraft programme as early as 1944. The only suitable mount for such a project was the massive Convair B-36 bomber. Convair set to work designing the X-6, a massive test aircraft for a future nuclear-powered bomber, and the NB-36H, to test the nuclear shielding required for crew survival. The wings and engines were as for a standard B-36H. The nose, however, was not; it was an 11-tonne structure lined with lead, rubber, and a water tank radiation

shield. The liquid-sodium cooled reactor was not actually used to power the aircraft, as it would have done in the X-6, but it was winched up into the bomb bay and made critical during many of the aircraft's 47 flights. The theory was that the aircraft might cruise on nuclear power and dash to its target with added chemical energy.

The technology was indeed impressive; the X-6 would have taken off using normal jet power, but then used air heated to over 1000°C (1800°F) by the reactor to thrust the aircraft forward.

Eventually, better jets made the

Right: Everything about the NB-36H was big and impressive. While the aircraft was undoubtedly a technical success, the concept was a blind alley and no nuclear powered aircraft flew.

Above: Even without the nuclear reactor, the NB-36H was an incredible piece of engineering.

concept irrelevant and the air force stopped flying the NB-36 in 1957. Public concern about the dangers of flying nuclear reactors saw the programme discontinued in the late 1960s.

NB-36H

- **Type:** nuclear-powered strategic bomber development aircraft
- **Powerplant:** six 2834-kW (3,800-hp.) piston engines and four 23.13-kN (5,200-lb.) turbojets, one R-1 nuclear reactor rated at one megawatt
- **Maximum speed:** 616 km/h (383 m.p.h.)
- **Endurance:** theoretically unlimited
- **Crew:** five
- **Range:** theoretically unlimited
- **Weights:** empty 102272 kg (225,471 lb.) loaded 163636 kg (360,755 lb.)
- **Armament:** nuclear bombs
- **Dimensions:** span 69.60 m (228 ft. 4 in.)
  length 49.00 m (160 ft. 10 in.)
  height 14.08 m (46.2 ft. 2 in.)
  wing area 443.3 m² (4771sq.ft.)

NB-36H

The single NB-36H, number 51-5712, flew from September 1955 to March 1957. Nicknamed 'Crusader' by Convair, the aircraft had a special nose section and a nuclear reactor bay.

Crew entry was through a special cylindrical hatch in the top of the fuselage. Such was the weight of the lead shielding around it, it had to be opened mechanically.

Surprisingly, the wing of the NB-36H was completely standard, if that is an appropriate term for such a massive piece of engineering. The X-6 wings would have had a totally different structure, with heat exchange systems from the reactor passing through them.

The reactor was stored in the aircraft's rear bomb bay. To load it, the aircraft was taxied over a special pit at Convair's Fort Worth plant, and the reactor was winched into the bomb bay. The pit was covered by lead doors when the reactor was in storage.

Any doubts about the NB-36H's mission would have been dispelled by the large radioactivity symbol painted on the tailfin. Because of the small size of the test reactor, it was not actually used to power any of the aircraft's systems.

No other B-36 had a nose like the NB-36H. The crew capsule weighed no less than 11 tonnes thanks to its lead and rubber lining and protective water shield.

Located in the wings of the aircraft were six piston engines and these were supplemented by the addition of a jet pod under each wing tip. The aircraft was conventionally powered throughout the test programme and was never at any stage under nuclear power.

The fuselage was decorated with a distinctive red and blue stripe, and the 'Convair Crusader' logo on the forward fuselage. The rest of the fuselage was finished in bare metal.

The large cooling air intake on the rear fuselage was another NB-36H feature, as was the revised tailcone shape. A similar intake was mounted on the starboard side.

Strategic Air Command's Big Stick

■ **B-36A:** The first versions of the B-36 entered service in 1948, devoid of armament they served primarily as tactical training aircraft, proving the concept of ultra-long range bombing.

■ **RB-36E:** Because of the exceptional range of the B-36 reconnaissance versions were developed to undertake photographic intelligence missions around the world.

■ **B-36J:** The final version of the B-36 was developed under project Featherweight, although with an increase in performance jet bombers were soon to replace the B-36.

ACTION DATA

MAXIMUM SPEED

Despite their awesome power, the postwar B-36 variants were little faster than the wartime B-29. However, the aircraft were far heavier, and carried massive offensive and defensive armament over distances that the B-29 could not have flown even when unarmed. Extra weight made the NB-36H slower than a B-36.

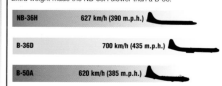

NB-36H	627 km/h (390 m.p.h.)
B-36D	700 km/h (435 m.p.h.)
B-50A	620 km/h (385 m.p.h.)

CONVAIR

R3Y TRADEWIND

● Turboprop flying-boat ● Transport tanker ● Limited US Navy service

CONVAIR R3Y TRADEWIND

▲ Solitary P5Y
The only XP5Y-1 to take to the air flew in 1950. It was the world's first turboprop-powered flying-boat.

▲ R3Y-1 maiden flight
Lacking the nose door of the R3Y-2, early Tradewinds had a large hatch in the fuselage, aft of the wing.

▼ Tanking Tradewind
In 1956 four aircraft were fitted with in-flight refuelling equipment. Fuel was carried in the wings, which left the fuselage available for cargo.

▲ Special beaching cradle
When on land P5Ys/R3Ys used an enormous 10-tonne, self-propelled cradle. Once the aircraft was in the water, the cradle was 'sailed' back to shore.

'Flying LST' ▶
The R3Y-2 was able to land Marine Corps vehicles and men at a beach head, although it was never intended that they do so under fire.

Convair's last flying-boat and the world's first turboprop seaplane was a giant that began life as a patrol aircraft, evolved into a transport and served briefly with the US Navy as both a transport and air-to-air refuelling tanker. Only one squadron operated the Tradewind, as it became known. Although the aircraft had considerable potential, it suffered from being powered by untried engines at a time when the trend was towards land-based naval aircraft.

▲ *Starting life as a maritime patrol aircraft, the P5Y always had potential as a transport. However, engine problems continued to plague the design and ultimately proved to be its downfall.*

FACTS AND FIGURES

➤ In October 1955 an R3Y flew from Hawaii to California in six hours 45 minutes at a speed of 579 km/h (359 m.p.h.).

➤ An R3Y flew across the USA at an average speed of 649 km/h (402 m.p.h.) in 1955.

➤ The entire R3Y fleet flew a total of less than 3,300 hours; one flew only 40 hours.

➤ $262 million was spent on the P5Y/R3Y; retired R3Ys had their tails cut off so that they could be hidden away from the public.

➤ The R3Y's main cabin was sound-proofed, air-conditioned and pressurised.

➤ Seven R3Ys were named after the world's oceans and seas.

PROFILE

Convair's last – the first with turbines

Left: The Tradewind's propellers were 4.6 metres (15 feet) in diameter and its underwing floats 6.4 metres (21 feet) long. The R3Y-1's gross weight was more than 79 tonnes.

Between its first flight in 1950 and the crash that ended the P5Y programme in 1953, the world's first turbine-powered seaplane became a low-altitude reconnaissance aircraft, then an anti-submarine platform and finally a mine-layer.

However, the trend towards land-based naval aircraft, plus the problems associated with the T40 twin-turbine engine and the crash of the sole XP5Y-1 stopped development. From the outset, a transport version of the Tradewind was

contemplated. The start of the Korean War in 1950 brought plans to reality. The US Navy ordered six R3Y-1 Tradewinds, which were based on the P5Y but fitted with improved, and supposedly more reliable, T40 engines.

The R3Y established several long-distance flight records. Eventually, 11 were delivered, including five of the 'Flying LST' (Landing Ship, Tank) R3Y-2 with a front-loading bow door. All of these aircraft entered service with Transport Squadron Two (VR-2), performing transport

duties between California and Hawaii from 1956 until 1958.

Four R3Ys were retro-fitted with four-point in-flight refuelling gear, which further improved their versatility. Despite plans to convert the rest of the fleet, engine problems continued, culminating in an accident in January 1958 that prompted the US Navy to ground the Tradewind fleet. By March 1958, R3Y development had ceased and within 12 months all the aircraft had been retired.

Above: The R3Y-2's T40-A-10 turboprops continued to be problematic and engine failures were routine. The Navy's VR-2 Squadron could change an engine in under 15 man-hours.

R3Y-1 Tradewind

Type: heavy transport flying-boat

Powerplant: four 4362-kW (5,850-hp.) Allison T40-A-10 turboprop engines

Maximum speed: above 579 km/h (359 m.p.h.)

Maximum range: 6437 km (3,990 mi.)

Service ceiling: 7700 m (25,250 ft.)

Weights: normal take-off 74843 kg (164,655 lb.); max take-off 79379 kg (174,634 lb.)

Dimensions:
span 44.42 m (145 ft. 8 in.)
length 42.57 m (139 ft. 7 in.)
height 13.67 m (44 ft. 9 in.)
wing area 195.18 m² (2,100 sq.ft.)

R3Y-2 TRADEWIND

South Pacific Tradewind was the 11th and last R3Y built. Here it carries the 'RA' tailcode of Navy Transport Squadron Two (VR-2), the only unit to operate the type. This example was scrapped in 1959.

The 'bridge' structure above the nose of the aircraft held the entire crew of five: two pilots, a navigator, a flight engineer and a radio operator. An extra engineer and radio operator were sometimes carried. The R3Y-2 differed primarily from the R3Y-1 in having an upward-opening bow door and hydraulic ramps for loading/unloading.

The Tradewind's very powerful, but highly unreliable, Allison T40 turboprop engines were its downfall. Each T40 was in fact two turbines driving a common gearbox and contra-rotating propellers. The gearbox was troublesome throughout the P5Y/R3Y's career, with the turbines being prone to vibration and excessive fuel consumption.

VR-2 Squadron used its 11 R3Ys to replace the Martin JRM-2 Mars flying-boats.

The P5Y's immensely strong hull was designed to leave the main deck free of obstruction and was therefore suitable for adaptation for transport roles. The main cabin could hold 103 seats or 92 stretchers, or more than 21 tonnes (20 tons) of cargo.

In order to prevent the aircraft's tail swinging during, for example, a beach landing, an anchor was deployed from the rear of the aircraft.

Convair's seaplane family

■ P4Y CORREGIDOR: Designed in the late-1930s, the P4Y maritime patrol aircraft did not proceed past the prototype stage. Shortages of the R-3350 Cyclone resulted in its cancellation.

■ PBY CATALINA: The most widely-used Allied seaplane of World War II, the 'Cat' was built at four plants in the US and Canada. It served with several air forces in offensive and rescue roles.

■ PB2Y CORONADO: This four-engined, long-range patrol-bomber suffered early handling problems, but more than 200 were built. They were not widely used operationally in World War II.

■ F2Y SEA DART: This experimental delta-winged fighter seaplane employed retractable hydroskis. It was the first seaplane to exceed Mach 1, but did not enter service.

VR-2'S OTHER BIG 'BOAT'

MARTIN JRM MARS: In its role on the resupply routes across the western Pacific, VR-2 at NAS Alameda, California, was chosen as the sole operator of the small fleet of JRM Mars transports. Like the Tradewind, the Mars, with its 75-tonne maximum take-off weight, was developed from a patrol aircraft, the XPB2M of 1943. Six JRMs were built, and the last was delivered in 1947. Two aircraft were lost in accidents, but the remaining four served until 1956.

CONVAIR

XF2Y SEA DART

● **Experimental water-based fighter** ● **First supersonic seaplane**

One of the strangest aircraft ever to fly, the Convair XF2Y Sea Dart was the abortive result of what, on the face of it, was a practical notion: if a jet fighter could operate from water, it would be able to fly and fight almost anywhere in the world. The delta-winged Sea Dart used retractable 'water skis' to lift the hull clear of the water on take-off, skimming across the surface before powering into the air.

▲ *The Sea Dart was a bold attempt to incorporate a host of new technologies into a unique airframe. The fastest seaplane ever built, it was a great aviation pioneer even though it never became operational.*

CONVAIR XF2Y SEA DART

▼ Fleet defender that wasn't
Designed to extend the defence perimeter of the US Navy, the Sea Dart's fate was to become a museum exhibit of an interesting idea that never quite made it.

▲ Hydroplanes
The Sea Dart's hydrofoil was pushed to the surface by hydrodynamic forces as the aircraft got under way, skimming across the water like a water-skier.

Flying-boat ▶
The aircraft had no conventional floats; the watertight hull and wings provided sufficient buoyancy and stability when the aircraft was in the water.

▲ Boat-shaped hull
The underside of the Sea Dart had a shallow 'V'-section profile, like a high-speed motor boat. On take-off, this was lifted clear of the water.

▲ The shaking take-off
Powering over the water on its hydroskis, the Sea Dart made for spectacular viewing. But the vibration caused by skimming across anything more than a mirror-smooth surface became almost unbearable for the pilot.

FACTS AND FIGURES

➤ The prototype Sea Dart made its initial flight on 9 May 1953.

➤ On 3 August 1954, a Sea Dart became the first supersonic seaplane, exceeding Mach 1.0 in a shallow dive.

➤ An order for 12 production F2Y Sea Dart fighters was cancelled when the test programme ran into trouble.

➤ The XF2Y was redesignated F-7A in 1962, even though no Sea Darts were still flying.

➤ The Sea Dart did not enter service, but Convair used its data in the successful F-102 and F-106 delta-winged fighters.

➤ The US Navy also tested a jet-powered patrol seaplane, the Martin P6M Seamaster.

PROFILE

Supersonic water-skier

I n 1951, the US Navy assigned Consolidated Vultee (Convair) an exciting project based on advanced aerodynamic and hydrodynamic research – the waterborne XF2Y Sea Dart.

With an eye to the post-war American role as worldwide policeman, the US Navy was looking into the possibility of using water-based fighters.

These had the potential advantage of being able to operate from any sufficiently clear stretch of water almost anywhere in the world, without the need for the long runways which so restricted land-based aircraft.

While the concept of a flying-boat fighter was reasonably practical, the Sea Dart was not the answer to the problem. It used a unique retractable hydroski system in place of floats. Taking off from the sea posed unprecedented challenges, since the hydroskis vibrated badly enough to shake the entire aircraft like a cement-mixer making control almost impossible.

There were also problems with the Westinghouse engines fitted to most Navy tactical aircraft of the period. Flown with J34 and J46 jets, the Sea Dart never had quite enough

Below: Once aloft, the Sea Dart handled well. It might have been a failure as a seaplane, but it contributed a great deal to Convair's widening database on high-performance delta-wing aircraft.

Above: Although the Sea Dart was a failure in its main aim of becoming a practical combat aircraft, it has the distinction of being the first and only supersonic flying-boat.

power for its weight, although it performed well when aloft.

Pilots had a roomy cockpit, fair forward visibility and handy controls, but the vibration problems were insurmountable, and the Sea Dart programme had to be abandoned in 1956.

The Convair company was a pioneer in exploring the properties of tailless aircraft with delta-shaped wings and control surfaces. The Sea Dart was one of the earliest aircraft to fly with this planform, and provided designers of later supersonic aircraft with a great deal of useful data.

XF2Y Sea Dart

Type: experimental seaplane fighter

Powerplant: two 26.69-kN (6,000-lb.-thrust) Westinghouse J46-WE-2 turbojets

Maximum speed: 1118 km/h (695 m.p.h.)

Range: 825 km (512 mi.)

Service ceiling: 16700 m (55,000 ft.)

Weights: empty 5739 kg (12,650 lb.); loaded 7495 kg (16,520 lb.)

Armament: up to four 20-mm cannon and two air-to-air missiles

Dimensions:
span	10.26 m (33 ft. 7 in.)
length	16.03 m (52 ft. 6 in.)
height	6.32 m (20 ft. 8 in.)
wing area	52.30 m² (563 sq.ft.)

XF2Y SEA DART

In addition to its unique method of operation, the XF2Y Sea Dart incorporated advances in construction, propulsion and aerodynamic design. It was a great technological leap forward – perhaps a leap too far.

The main engine intakes were mounted above the wing on top of the fuselage. This prevented water ingestion on take-off or landing which would destroy the powerplant.

The XF2Y was originally powered by two Westinghouse J34 jets, but these never delivered their promised performance. Even with more powerful J46s, the Sea Dart was not as fast as had been expected.

The Sea Dart had a fairly conventional cockpit, roomy and with well-thought-out controls. Pilots found it easy to work in.

The underside of the hull had a shallow boat-like section, which aided low-speed handling in the water.

Twin hydroplanes extended for beaching and for take-off, retracting into the fuselage for maximum aerodynamic efficiency.

At rest, the wings of the Sea Dart rest on the water, serving as floats to provide some measure of stability.

COMBAT DATA

MAXIMUM SPEED

XF2Y SEA DART	1118 km/h (695 m.p.h.)
F-102 DELTA DAGGER	1328 km/h (825 m.p.h.)
SRA.1	825 km/h (512 m.p.h.)

The Sea Dart's continuing engine problems meant that it never achieved the speed it might have done. Given more power, and a redesigned fuselage as had been applied to Convair's F-102 fighter, there is no reason to suppose that it might not have matched the landplane's performance. The British SRA.1 could not achieve the supersonic speeds thought necessary for a jet fighter.

ARMAMENT

Designed as a fighter, the Sea Dart would have had an effective air-to-air armament by the standards of the early 1950s, incorporating two of the newly-developed AIM-4 Falcon missiles or later AIM-9 Sidewinders, fitted inside a weapons bay in the lower fuselage.

SRA.1 — 4 x 20-mm cannon 2 x 1000-kg (2,200-lb.) bombs

XF2Y SEA DART — 4 x 20-mm cannon 2 x short-range air-to-air missiles

F-102 DELTA DAGGER — 6 x AIM-4 air-to-air missiles 12 x folding-fin unguided rockets

RANGE

The Sea Dart was an experimental aircraft, so its range was not as great as might have been expected in an operational version. It could not match the larger and slower British SRA.1 of 1947, the only other jet-powered flying-boat fighter to take to the air.

XF2Y SEA DART	F-102 DELTA DAGGER	SRA.1
825 km (812 mi.)	2175 km (1,350 mi.)	1500 km (930 mi.)

Fighters from the sea

■ **HANSA BRANDENBURG:** The German C-1 monoplane was one of the most successful fighters of World War I.

■ **CURTISS SC-1:** This single-seat scout was entering service as World War II ended. It could carry bombs in a bay in the main float.

■ **KAWANISHI N1K:** The N1K was a superb performer, but high-drag floats meant that it could not match more aerodynamic landplanes.

■ **SAUNDERS-ROE SRA.1:** Lack of airstrips in the Pacific prompted post-war Royal Navy interest in this experimental flying-boat.

CONVAIR
XFY1 'POGO'

● Experimental vertical take-off ● Turboprop power

Vertical flight has long been a dream of aviation designers, but has always been a challenge. It requires an immense amount of power to get off the ground without the benefit of wings, and it was only in the years after World War II that engines of enough power became available; it was then that some truly strange aircraft took to the skies, most notably the Convair XFY1 'Pogo'. The XFY1 was a 'tail-sitter', using the most powerful turboprop available in the Western world.

▲ *Test pilot 'Skeets' Coleman stands by the XFY1 after completing its first flight. Landing was a tough problem, undertaken by Coleman while lying on his back.*

CONVAIR XFY1 'POGO'

▲ **Tail-sitting take-off**
Getting the power settings right was very difficult with such powerful engines, and the aircraft was in constant danger of crashing.

▲ **Straight and level**
On 2 November 1954 the XFY1 made the first historic transition from vertical flight to horizontal and then back again for landing. Even in the horizontal flight phase, the aircraft showed control and handling difficulties.

◀ **Testing rig**
Prior to its first flight the XFY1 was extensively tested, dangling from this elaborate gantry.

Go-anywhere ▶ fighter
Originally intended for use from small ship decks, the XFY1 could also have been mounted on a trolley like this and towed to any place it might have been needed.

FACTS AND FIGURES

➤ The XFY1's Allison turboprop delivered almost three times the power of the biggest piston engines.

➤ Test pilot 'Skeets' Coleman made the first VTOL flight on 1 August 1954.

➤ The 'Pogo' transitioned to horizontal flight for the first time in November 1954.

➤ The pilot's seat of the XFY1 rotated forwards through 45° when the aircraft was vertically aligned.

➤ The throttle was the only control which could change altitude in hovering flight.

➤ Every non-essential item in the 'Pogo' was omitted to save weight.

PROFILE

Vertically up and down

Developed for the US Navy in the 1950s, the Convair XFY1 'Pogo' was one of two VTOL research vehicles which were built in the hope of producing an aircraft capable of 'being developed into a combat design', as the Navy specification called for.

Designed to 'pogo' up and down vertically before transitioning into horizontal flight, the XFY1 was powered by the newly developed Allison YT40-A-6 turboprop, the most powerful propeller engine of its time. Delivering more than 4101 kW (5,500 hp.), the immense power was transmitted to two contra-rotating three-bladed propellers.

Sitting on its tail, the XFY1 took off vertically on power alone before transitioning into forward, wing-borne flight. Getting into the air was relatively simple, but transitioning was difficult, since the short, stumpy machine had somewhat tricky handling.

Landing was far trickier. The pilot had to pull up vertically into a hover then, by careful manipulation of the throttle, he backed down to land. What made it even more difficult was that the pilot had to look over his shoulder to bring his awkward machine in safely.

Clawing into the sky, the XFY1 relied on the power of the enormous Allison YT40 turboprop to get it into the air.

XFY1 'Pogo'

Type: single-seat experimental tail-sitting fighter

Powerplant: one 4101-kW (5,500-hp.) Allison YT40-A-6 turboprop

Maximum speed: 980 km/h at 4500 metres (610 m.p.h. at 15,000 ft.)

Endurance: one hour at 10000 m (33,000 ft) giving an approximate range at economical cruise speed of 650 km (400 mi.)

Service ceiling: 13300 m (43,600 ft.)

Weight: empty 5325 kg (11,700 lb.); maximum gross take-off 7370 kg (16,200 lb.)

Armament: (proposed, never fitted) four cannon or unguided high-explosive rockets

Dimensions: span 8.43 m (27 ft. 6 in.)
length 10.66 m (34 ft. 11 in.)
vertical span 6.99 m (22 ft. 11 in.)
wing area 39.70 m² (427 sq. ft.)

XFY1 'POGO'

It was intended to provide a high-performance fighter able to operate from small warships. But the Convair XFY1 never lived up to its dramatic promise.

For vertical flight, the pilot's seat rotates forward through 45°. He still had to look over his shoulder to judge the distance to the ground, an awkward procedure which added considerably to the pilot's workload on landing.

Small castoring wheels on strong single-strut shock-absorbers were fitted to the wing and fin tips. These give a stable base for landing, which was eventually intended to be made on a heaving ship's deck.

The 'Pogo' could not be landed conventionally. The large delta wings were mated with huge upper and lower vertical fins to produce a cruciform layout, and a normal undercarriage would have been impossibly cumbersome.

The Allison YT40-A-6 turboprop was the most powerful engine of its type in the West, generating over 4100 kW (5,500 hp.), to which was added a small amount of jet thrust from the tailpipe.

Power from the Allison engine was delivered to two three-bladed contra-rotating propellers. These were essential, since the torque from a single propeller would have made vertical landing impossible.

Control in normal flight was provided by full-span ailerons and large rudders on both the dorsal and ventral fins. During vertical flight the propeller slipstream was deflected off these surfaces for control.

TAIL-SITTER JETS

JET POWER

The Ryan X-13 Vertijet was the first jet-powered aircraft to take off vertically, transition to horizontal flight and then return. Originally flown with a conventional undercarriage, the X-13 was adapted to hook onto a vertically mounted trapeze system. The idea was that it could be operated from small surface vessels, but it was never really a practical proposition: even experienced test pilots found the manoeuvre extremely difficult.

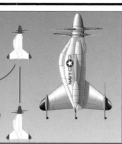

FUTURE POSSIBILITIES

The idea of tail-sitting vertical take-off aircraft is still alive, in spite of the ascendancy of much more practical vectored-thrust designs like the Harrier. In the 1970s and 1980s, the US Navy was actively looking into the possibility of a hybrid jet to operate from a revolutionary catamaran-type carrier. It would take off vertically like a tail-sitter, either landing conventionally or using vectored thrust. The concept hardly got beyond the artist's impression, but may be a possibility for the 21st century.

Transition to forward flight

1 TAKE-OFF: To take off the pilot simply ran his engine up to full power, until the aircraft began to lift off the ground on engine power alone.

2 HORIZONTAL FLIGHT: As the aircraft accelerated, the pilot pushed the nose of the 'Pogo' over. More and more lift was supplied by the wings.

3 BACK TO VERTICAL: To slow down the pilot throttled back. Bringing the nose up towards the vertical the aircraft slowed still more, until it was suspended solely by engine power.

4 LANDING: Judicious use of the throttle enabled the rate of descent to be controlled, although it took considerable pilot skill.

CURTISS-WRIGHT

X-19

● VTOL demonstrator ● Tilt-engine ● Two built, one example flown

Nothing if not innovative, the X-19 was employed to test tilting propellers as a way of achieving vertical take-off and landing (VTOL) performance. This unorthodox machine began as a private venture by the Curtiss-Wright Corporation, the one-time aircraft builder which, by the 1960s, was concentrating on engine development. As a USAF 'X-plane', the X-19 flew a two-year test programme that contributed much to knowledge of VTOL.

▲ During the course of the X-19 programme, Curtiss examined many different civil and military applications for the tilt-propeller. Not until the recent V-22 Osprey has the concept come to fruition.

CURTISS-WRIGHT **X-19**

▲ **Development aircraft**
Preceding the X-19 and X-100, the Curtiss-Wright VZ-7AP was a scaled-down model to validate the tilt-engine configuration.

▲ **Prototype airborne**
The only X-19 to fly took to the air on 20 November 1963, flown by company test pilot, Jim Ryan. This aircraft was later destroyed in a crash.

▼ **Radical powerplant arrangement**
The X-19 carried two turboprops within the fuselage. Production models would have had twin turboshafts.

▲ **Radial lift force**
Curtiss-Wright's experimental, concept-proving X-100 was the world's first VTOL aircraft to fly with the use of radial lift force propellers. It later served with NASA, based at Langley, in Virginia.

VTOL mock-up ▶
Before receiving its Air Force contract, Curtiss-Wright built a mock-up of its projected Model 200. Conceived as a transport aircraft, the Model 200 was to have been an executive aircraft with accommodation for six passengers. The programme was soon taken over by the USAF.

FACTS AND FIGURES

➤ Although it flew 50 times, the only Curtiss-Wright X-19 to fly logged just 3.85 hours in the air.

➤ The X-19 also accumulated 129.42 hours of ground running time during 269 runs.

➤ Four pilots were involved in the programme, one from the US Navy.

➤ In original design studies, this aircraft was to have been powered by four Wankel rotary engines.

➤ Curtiss-Wright built two X-19s, but the second aircraft never flew.

➤ On its 50th flight on 25 August 1965, the X-19 crashed; no serious injuries occurred.

PROFILE

Curtiss's vertical take-off prototype

Thirty years before today's Boeing/Bell V-22 Osprey multi-role 'tilt-rotor' aircraft, Curtiss-Wright paved the way for a new kind of manned flight, with the ground-breaking X-19.

The X-19 was refined for the USAF, after starting out on the drawing board as a Curtiss-Wright civil design. It was unusual to look at, but the X-19 was a new idea with its two, separate, full-sized wings and four tilting nacelles, their propellers driven by twin fuselage-mounted engines.

Like most VTOL testbeds of its day, the X-19 was a fairly small aircraft. Although equipped to carry six

passengers in the rear, it was never used as a transport. Destined to remain a test aircraft, the X-19 was used to try out a number of new features: the indirect shaft arrangement by which the engines drove the propellers; the tilting nacelles and propellers; and two sets of mainplanes. The two pilots of the X-19 were strapped into ejection seats, a situation which eventually served them well when the test programme ended in an accident.

Ironically, just when the X-19 programme was abandoned in

1965, the US was becoming involved in a new war and needed a capability for vertical take-off and landing. Although the Vietnam war never had a place for the X-19, it proved the utility of the helicopter and of the vertical flight concept, resurrected by today's V-22.

The last aircraft to be built by the once mighty Curtiss-Wright company, the X-19 was the only machine to have utilised this characteristic tandem wing and broad propeller configuration.

Unlike the XC-142A tilt propeller transport, which had provision to carry 32 troops, the X-19 had only a small payload of up to six passengers, dictated by its purely experimental status.

The tail unit comprised a fixed vertical fin and a moving rudder with trim tab. A fairing at the base of the vertical fin extended forward to form a dorsal fin.

X-19

The only X-19 to fly, 62-12197 made a total of 50 untethered flights before its disastrous crash in August 1965 in which it was destroyed after a gearbox failure. The programme was cancelled on 19 December 1965.

The three-bladed propellers were driven through a complex system of shafts and gearboxes by two Lycoming T55-L-5 free-turbine engines, mounted side-by-side in the fuselage.

Aerodynamic design of the rotor blades provided high take-off thrust and good cruise performance. Construction was of fibreglass with a strong lightweight foam plastic core.

Miscellaneous equipment included UHF and ADF receivers, a marker beacon system, two VHF navigation systems, glide slope receiver and an intercommunications control panel.

The X-19's landing gear was of conventional tricycle layout. Both retraction and extension were hydraulically actuated. The nose wheel retracted forwards.

From the outset, the aircraft was designed to make a smooth transition from vertical to level flight by mechanically tilting the engine nacelles from the vertical to the horizontal.

X-19

Type: tilt-propeller research aircraft

Powerplant: two 1640.5-kW (2,200-hp.) AVCO-Lycoming T55-L-5 turboprop engines driving four propellers

Maximum speed: 730 km/h (453 m.p.h.)

Cruising speed: 650 km/h (143 m.p.h.)

Initial climb rate: 1200 m/min (3,936 f.p.m.)

Range: 523 km (324 mi.) VTOL with payload

Service ceiling: 7254 m (23,800 ft.)

Weights: gross 6196 kg (13,633 lb.)

Accommodation: two pilots in North American LW-2B ejection seats, provision for six passengers or 454 kg (1,000 lb.) of cargo

Dimensions: span front wing 5.94 m (19 ft. 6 in.)
span rear wing 6.55 m (21 ft. 6 in.)
length 12.82 m (42 ft.)
height 5.45 m (17 ft. 10 in.)
wing area front 5.21 m² (56 sq. ft.)
wing area rear 9.15 m² (98 sq. ft.)

ACTION DATA

MAXIMUM SPEED

The Curtiss-Wright X-19 had an appreciably better performance than its two VTOL counterparts. Much of the reason for this lay in the fact that the X-19 was designed primarily as a transport aircraft, rather than just an experimental test aircraft like the other two.

X-19	730 km/h (453 m.p.h.)
X-18	400 km/h (248 m.p.h.)
X-22A	410 km/h (254 m.p.h.)

RANGE

For an experimental aircraft, the X-19 had a very impressive range. In practice, however, flights rarely lasted longer than a few minutes. The X-22 had by far the longest-running flight programme of the three, remaining in use from 1966 well into the early 1970s.

X-19 523 km (324 mi.)

X-18 360 km (223 mi.)

X-22A 716 km (444 mi.)

POWER

Both the X-18 and X-19 had twin turboprop engines, those of the X-18 producing considerable power. A rear-mounted turbojet greatly added to the aircraft's total power output, but was used for pitch control only. The X-22A was powered by four turboshafts which drove the ducted fans.

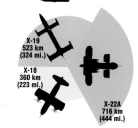

X-19 3281 kW (4,396 hp.)   X-18 8725 kW (11,691 hp.)   X-22A 3729 kW (4,997 hp.)

Different approaches to VTOL

BELL XV-3: The world's first tilt-rotor fixed-wing aircraft to achieve 100 per cent rotor tilt, the P & W piston-powered XV-3 flew in 1955 and clocked up 125 hours on more than 250 flights.

BELL-TEXTRON X-22A: An experimental transport, the X-22A had four turboshaft engines driving ducted propellers. It first flew in 1966, and flight testing continued into the early 1970s.

CANADAIR CL-84: Like the X-18, the CL-84 was a tilt-wing rather than a tilt-rotor aircraft. First flying in 1970, it completed a successful test programme, including shipboard operations.

HILLER X-18: The X-18 convertiplane of 1959 had a combined twin turboprop and J34 turbojet powerplant. The data provided was used in the development of the XC-142A and X-19.

73

DASA/EUROSPACE/NASA

SÄNGER/HERMES/X-30

● New age spacecraft ● Trans-continental interest ● Futuristic

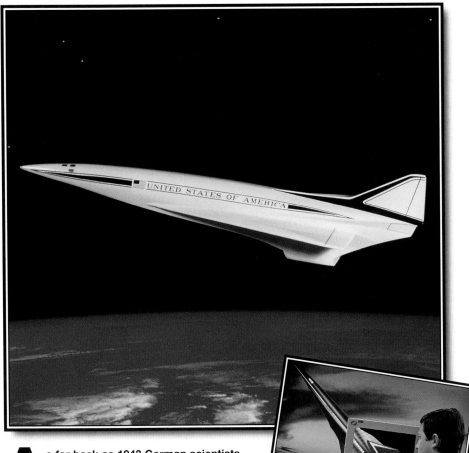

Several countries, notably France, Germany and the USA have studied the concept of Trans-Atmospheric Vehicles (TVAs), designed to operate on the fringes of space.

As far back as 1943 German scientists investigated the possibility of a rocket-launched intercontinental bomber, able to skip across the upper atmosphere to reach its target. Further research was conducted in the US and elsewhere in the 1950s and 60s leading to such aircraft as the X-20 Dyno-Soar, used in the Space Shuttle project. By the late 1980s the US X-30, the European Hermes and the Sänger were all being developed.

◀ **Definitive X-30**
After several different design proposals, this rendering of the National Aerospace Plane was selected for further development. Two machines were to be built.

Scale Model ▶
A mock-up of the now defunct Hermes illustrates the cargo bay with its characteristic double shielded doors and long loading arm.

French Space Shuttle? ▶
One of the more conventional looking trans-atmospheric vehicles, the Hermes was similar in concept to the Rockwell International 'Space Shuttle' and would have reached orbit riding on a larger booster, in this case the Ariane 5 rocket.

◀ **True spaceship**
The X-30 was to be capable of reaching orbit on its own power, taking-off from a conventional airfield. Ramjets were the intended propulsion system.

German X-30 ▶
Another ambitious European nation is Germany which has developed its own transonic re-useable space vehicle, known locally as the Sänger.

FACTS AND FIGURES

➤ Studies related to the X-30 programme have been around since the 1940s but, until 1981, were shrouded in secrecy.

➤ Both Aérospatiale and Dassault were major contractors for Hermes.

➤ Both the German and the French concepts employ a two-stage setup.

➤ Had development continued, it is estimated that more than $10 billion would have been required for the X-30.

➤ Development of such projects remains in doubt because of defence cuts.

➤ At present, the Sänger spacecraft is rumoured still to be under development.

Beyond the frontiers

The most exotic of the late 1980s space-plane projects was the NASA X-30, also known as the National Aerospace Plane (NASP) and the Orient Express. It was to use ramjet/scramjet propulsion and other new technologies enabling it to reach Mach 25, but would have needed an outlay of at least $10 billion to develop.

Hermes was designed to be launched into low earth orbit by an Ariane 5 booster. It was intended to support the European elements of the International Space Station, but was cancelled in 1993. Some of the technology may be used in a proposed crew rescue vehicle for the space station.

Sänger is a much more ambitious project. It involves a probably unmanned turbo-ramjet-powered first stage that would carry the second stage – a reusable manned vehicle or disposable cargo carrier – to a height of 30000 m (98,000 ft) and a speed of Mach 6. Then the second stage would use its rocket in order to reach orbit.

By 1997 NASA had switched its attention to the Lockheed Martin X-33 VentureStar reusable launch vehicle. The European Space Agency has continued to study concepts for future space launchers, with the Sänger being one of those projects that may still be under consideration.

Left: The Sänger would be a two-stage reusable aero-space plane configured to carry both cargo and passengers.

Above: France's Hermes was unique among the designs in having a conventional cockpit layout and fuselage, not dissimilar to that of the current Rockwell Space Shuttle.

Hermes

Payload: up to 4.5 tonnes

Crew: 2 to 6

Weights: launch 29000 kg (63,800 lb.), re-entry 15000 kg (33,000 lb.)

Dimensions:
span	9 m (29 ft. 6 in.)
length	13 m (43 ft.)

Sänger

Powerplant: six 400-kN (90,000-lb.-thrust) turbo-ramjets, one 1280-kN (287,950-lb.-thrust) liquid-fuelled ATCRE rocket

Weights: empty 188000 kg (413,600 lb.), max take-off 366000 kg (805,200 lb.)

Dimensions:
span	41.04 m (134 ft. 8 in.)
length	84.05 m (275 ft. 8 in.)

X-30

Powerplant: one 1372.9-kN (308,850-lb.-thrust) scramjet

Weights: empty 60000 kg (132,000 lb.), max take-off 140000 kg (308,000 lb.)

Dimensions:
span	36 m (118 ft. 1 in.)
length	80 m (262 ft. 5 in.)

The tail surfaces resemble those of current high tech combat aircraft, such as the F/A-18, with large canted fins and conventional style rudders.

Mounted on top of the stage one craft is the smaller, rocket-powered manned cargo carrier, which is similar in concept to the Space Shuttle. It has been designed as a manned craft, and would return to earth once the mission was complete.

Extensive research into such craft has resulted in a clean, integrated delta wing configuration being the most popular, in order to achieve greatest aerodynamic efficiency. Not surprisingly, the Sänger resembles something out of a science fiction film.

SÄNGER

Deutsche Aerospace has so far made considerable progress with the Sänger Trans Atmospheric Vehicle and a 1:8 scale mock-up was unveiled to the public. The future of this project remains uncertain.

Some illustrations depict the stage one booster as an unmanned device, though a scale mock-up was fitted with some sort of cockpit windows perhaps indicating otherwise.

For such a machine to be capable of reaching orbit, powerful ramjet/scramjet motors would be required. Developing such a powerplant would be hideously expensive and it would be difficult to produce using current technology.

As it is designed to return to earth once the second stage has separated, the booster features a retractable undercarriage very similar to that of a normal airliner. On the mock-up, this comprised twin nosewheels on a single oleo and twin main legs, each fitted with twelve wheels and tyres to help distribute the incredible weight of this machine.

Besides its role as a Low Earth Orbit (LEO) vehicle, the Sänger was conceived as a conventional airliner, albeit one which could fly at much greater speeds and over even greater distances than commercial jets. Because the performance envelope will be so large, with huge differences between landing and and orbit speeds, very advanced materials and construction techniques will be needed.

ACTION DATA

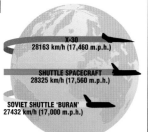

ORBITAL SPEED

Only the Rockwell International Space Shuttle is in use at present. This incredible machine has an orbital speed of 28325 km/h (17,560 m.p.h.). Had the X-30 been built, it would have flown at more or less the same velocity, but directly from the airfield without the aid of a booster.

X-30	28163 km/h (17,460 m.p.h.)
SHUTTLE SPACECRAFT	28325 km/h (17,560 m.p.h.)
SOVIET SHUTTLE 'BURAN'	27432 km/h (17,000 m.p.h.)

LANDING SPEED

To design a craft which can fly at 25000 km/h (17,000 m.p.h.) in orbit and yet still land at around 300 km/h (220 m.p.h.) is difficult. A disadvantage with the shuttle craft is that it cannot land under its own power and only one landing attempt can be made. The X-30 would have been able to make several attempts if required.

X-30	346 km/h (215 m.p.h.)
SHUTTLE SPACECRAFT	363 km/h (225 m.p.h.)
SOVIET SHUTTLE 'BURAN'	340 km/h (211 m.p.h.)

Ambitious ideas

BRITISH AEROSPACE HOTOL: Conceived in the heady days of the 1980s this was one attempt to rival US dominance in the space race.

DASSAULT STAR-H: Incorporating the Hermes, this French project was to have been an element of the International Space Station.

LOCKHEED TAV: An early study for the US Air Force was this combined spacecraft/conventional air transport design.

NASA SHUTTLE BOOSTER: The differences between concept and reality are evident in this 1970 impression of the booster.

DASSAULT-BREGUET

MIRAGE 4000

● Interceptor and attack prototype ● Mach 2 performance

Built as a private venture experimental prototype by Dassault-Breguet, the twin-engined Super Mirage 4000 drew on the experience gained in the development of the single-engined Mirage 2000 fighter. Capable of a speed exceeding Mach 2, it had the potential to be a worldbeater in its class. Budgetary cutbacks and the very high price tag of the new Mirage meant that it was not placed in production, despite its capability.

▲ Powered by two SNECMA M.53 engines, as fitted to the smaller Mirage 2000, the 4000 prototype attained a speed of Mach 2.2 with ease on its sixth flight in April 1979.

DASSAULT-BREGUET MIRAGE 4000

▼ **Composite construction**
In order to save weight, extensive use was made of carbon fibre and boron composites in structures including the fin, rudder, elevons and foreplanes.

▲ **Mirage 2000 and 4000 prototypes**
The prototypes of the Mirage 2000 and 4000 flew within a year of each other, the former in March 1978.

▲ **Mock-up first**
Prior to assembly of the prototype, a full-scale mock-up was built. It was unveiled in December 1977.

▼ **Eight-tonne bombload**
The Mirage 4000 was able to carry over 8000 kg (17,600 lb.) of bombs, missiles and other equipment.

▲ **Delta wings**
The third-generation Mirages returned to the delta-wing design pioneered in the Mirage III/5 family of the 1960s.

FACTS AND FIGURES

➤ The Mirage 4000 design was heavily influenced by the cancelled Mirage F2 low-level attack aircraft.

➤ As many as 14 air-to-air missiles could be carried at once by the Mirage 4000.

➤ The prototype broke the speed of sound on its first flight, achieving Mach 1.2.

➤ Although a very capable aircraft, the 4000 offered little more than the smaller 2000, at considerably greater cost.

➤ Despite funding from Saudi Arabia, the type lost out to the F-15 and Tornado.

➤ Airbrakes are fitted above each wingroot leading edge.

Dassault's big delta prototype

Flying for the first time on 9 March 1979, the Mirage 4000 was a twin-engined interceptor and low-altitude attack prototype in the 20-tonne class. With a delta wing planform and canard foreplanes the Mirage 4000 employed fly-by-wire controls, but was a comparatively simple design with ease of maintenance on forward airfields in mind.

Its overall dimensions put it midway between the size of the F-14 Tomcat and the F/A-18 Hornet. The aircraft's twin engines provided a thrust-to-weight ratio greater than 1:1 in its original interceptor form.

The generous nose profile enabled the installation of a 80-cm (31-in.) radar dish which offered an effective range of 120 km (75 mi.).

Computer projection placed this apparently outstanding performance ahead of any other fighter in its class. Indeed, when the project was first announced in December 1975 the makers boldly assured potential export customers of the Mirage 4000's superiority over any similar aircraft in production or under development.

Although an operational version was envisaged, Dassault hoped to sell the type in export markets as well as to the Armée de l'Air as a replacement for the Mirage IV bomber, but orders did not materialise. What was destined to be the sole prototype has been used as a 'chase plane' during flight tests of the new Dassault Rafale advanced combat aircraft, the successor to the Mirage family.

Above: At an early stage of development the Mirage 4000 was known as the Super Mirage Delta.

Above: The prototype featured desert camouflage while flying in the Middle East. Despite the success of earlier Mirages in that region, the price tag of the 4000 deterred buyers.

Mirage 4000

Type: single-seat multi-role combat aircraft

Powerplant: two 95.13-kN (21,400-lb. thrust) SNECMA M.53 afterburning turbofans

Maximum speed: 2655 km/h (1,650 m.p.h.)

Initial climb rate: 18,300 m/min (60,039 f.p.m.)

Combat radius: 1850 km (1,150 mi.)

Service ceiling: 20,000 m (65,600 ft.)

Weights: combat 16,100 kg (35,494 lb.)

Armament: over 8000 kg (17,630 lb.) of external stores including bombs, rockets, air-to-air and air-to-surface missiles and cluster munitions

Dimensions:
span	12.00 m (39 ft. 4 in.)
length	18.70 m (61 ft. 4 in.)
wing area	73 m² (786 sq. ft.)

MIRAGE 4000

The prototype Mirage 4000 took to the air for the first time in early 1979. Despite an aggressive sales campaign by the makers, the prototype remains the sole example.

A two-seat version of the Mirage 4000 was under study by Dassault-Breguet, but was not built.

Dassault-Breguet hoped for sales of the 4000 in the Middle East. For sales tours in the region it therefore carried a 'desert' camouflage.

To provide extra fuel capacity, the tailfin of the 4000 contains a fuel tank; other tanks are found in the wings and fuselage. External tanks can also be carried.

The powerful 80-cm (31-in.) RDM multi-mode radar is the same as that fitted to the Mirage 2000C interceptor.

The Mirage 4000's flight-control system has been used as a technology demonstrator for the Rafale combat aircraft.

Provision was made for two DEFA 30-mm cannon and up to 11 pylons for external stores, including weapons and fuel tanks.

MATRA Magic missiles were among the variety of air-to-air weapons which the 4000 could carry for self-defence.

Power was provided by two SNECMA M.53 turbofan engines, which gave the 4000 a thrust-to-weight ratio in the same class as that of the F-15 or Sukhoi Su-27.

MAXIMUM SPEED

A top speed of over Mach 2 is a necessity for a modern, long-range, high-altitude interceptor designed to defeat waves of bombers or cruise missiles. The F-15 and Su-27 represent the most capable interceptors in service.

MIRAGE 4000	2655 km/h (1,650 m.p.h.)	
F-15C EAGLE	2655 km/h (1,650 m.p.h.)	
Su-27 'FLANKER'	2350 km/h (1,460 m.p.h.)	

RANGE

The range of the Sukhoi Su-27 reflects the size and fuel-carrying capacity of an aircraft designed to defend the vast area of the Soviet Union. The first export customer for the Su-27, China, has similarly large areas to patrol. The F-15 and Mirage 4000 carry the same fuel load, with tanks, as an Su-27 carries internally.

F-15C EAGLE 1967 km (1,222 mi.)

MIRAGE 4000 3700 km (2,299 mi.)

Su-27 'FLANKER' 3000 km (1,864 mi.)

CLIMB RATE

Interceptors need to be able to climb quickly to the altitude of attacking aircraft. A power-to-weight ratio better than 1:1 allows excellent rates of climb. All three types have twin engines which give the aircraft exceptional power.

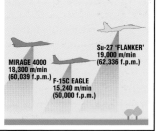

Su-27 'FLANKER' 19,000 m/min (62,336 f.p.m.)

MIRAGE 4000 18,300 m/min (60,039 f.p.m.)

F-15C EAGLE 15,240 m/min (50,000 f.p.m.)

The Dassault Mirage family

■ **MIRAGE III/5:** This Mach 2 delta-wing fighter and fighter-bomber provided the core of the French air forces in the 1960s and 1970s and won large foreign orders.

■ **MIRAGE IV:** This was a scaled-up, twin-engined bomber version of the Mirage delta, designed with a nuclear capability. The prototype first flew in 1959.

■ **MIRAGE F1:** The second-generation Mirage multi-role aircraft intended to replace the Mirage III and 5, the F1 discarded the delta wing for a more conventional layout.

■ **MIRAGE 2000:** Fly-by-wire controls solved the handling problems found in delta-winged aircraft. The prototype flew in 1978, and fighter, attack and reconnaissance versions followed.

DE HAVILLAND
DH.108 SWALLOW

● Tailless configuration ● Airliner research ● Three prototypes

▲ *Although it used components of the Vampire, the DH.108 was radically different from any other British jet flying at the time, and considerably faster.*

Anxious to claim a place in the forefront of post-war aviation, de Havilland began preliminary studies for its DH.106 Comet, the world's first jet airliner, during the later stages of World War II. A tailless aircraft was envisaged and in order to investigate the characteristics of such a design, three DH.108s were built. All three were involved in fatal crashes, and the tailless airliner concept had been abandoned before the Comet's first flight.

DE HAVILLAND **DH.108 SWALLOW**

▼ **Handley Page slots**
TG283, the first DH.108 prototype, demonstrates the large-area swept wing design of the type. Fixed leading-edge slots are prominent on each wing, having been installed on the advice of the Royal Aircraft Establishment (RAE).

▲ **Vampire features**
In its original, unmodified form, the DH.108 was very Vampire-like in the forward fuselage area. Later, with an altered cockpit line and longer nose, the similarity was not so apparent.

▼ **Faster Swallow**
In the quest for ever more speed, a new longer nose section was tested on a Vampire. Fitted to a DH.108 airframe, this produced the third prototype, VW120.

▼ **Record breaker**
On 12 April 1948, VW120 set a new 100-km (60-mi.) closed circuit record with 974.02 km/h (605 m.p.h.).

▲ **Second prototype**
A revised canopy was used on TG306. This had considerably less glazed area and was backed by a metal fairing, but its Vampire origins were readily apparent.

FACTS AND FIGURES

➤ English Electric's production line supplied the Vampire fuselages for the DH.108 programme.

➤ TG283 was taken from Hatfield by road to Woodbridge for its first flight.

➤ Anti-spin parachutes were fitted to the wingtips of TG283.

➤ Though it did not contribute to the DH.106 Comet design, the DH.108 provided data for the DH.110 project.

➤ TG306 featured a lowered seat and pointed nose for increased speed.

➤ De Havilland never adopted the Swallow name used by the Ministry of Supply.

PROFILE

Testing the Swallow

Using the fuselage and engine of a Vampire, mated to a longer tailpipe and new wings, TG283, destined for low-speed trials, flew for the first time on 15 May 1946. Wind tunnel tests had suggested serious handling problems with the tailless configuration, but none was detected. Test pilot Geoffrey de Havilland flew at low speeds with a Percival Procter for air-to-air photography and later tried out dog-fighting with a Mosquito. Several flights were performed by the aircraft until

it crashed, killing its pilot, during stall trials in 1950.

Meanwhile, on 23 August 1946, de Havilland had flown a modified, more powerful DH.108. TG306 soon showed its ability to exceed the world absolute speed record and plans were laid for an attempt. Tragically, de Havilland was killed during practice for the record attempt, his aircraft breaking up over the Thames Estuary after a dive from 3050 m (10,000 ft.). A speed in the region of Mach 0.9 was achieved.

A third DH.108, more powerful than TG306, was also intended for high-speed research and was flown on 24 July 1947. Having set a closed circuit speed record, VW120 became the first aircraft to go supersonic in Britain and performed a stunning aerobatic routine at Farnborough in 1949. Unfortunately, a faulty oxygen system claimed VW120 and the life of its pilot in February 1951.

Having taken third place in the Society of British Aircraft Constructors Challenge Trophy Air Race in 1949, the third aircraft was handed over to the Ministry of Supply and test flown from RAE Farnborough.

DH.108 Swallow

Specifications apply to TG283

Type: single-seat tailless research aircraft

Powerplant: one 13.35-kN (3,000-lb.-thrust) de Havilland Goblin 2 turbojet

Maximum speed: 1030 km/h (640 m.p.h)

Weights: maximum take-off 3992 kg (8,800 lb.)

Dimensions: span 11.89 m (280 m.p.h.)
length 7.87 m (26 ft.)
wing area 30.47 m² (328 sq. ft.)

A tall fin was required to provide the necessary directional stability. The behaviour of the tailless configuration was largely unpredictable, especially at the high speeds which had been little explored by conventional aircraft.

DH.108

VW120 was flown for the first time on 24 July 1947 with John Cunningham at the controls. On 9 September 1947 the aircraft exceeded the speed of sound in a barely controlled dive.

With its Goblin 4 engine, VW120 was the fastest of the DH.108s. De Havilland's Goblin engine performed well throughout the DH.108 programme.

Both the second and third prototypes were designed for high-speed flight and featured a streamlined forward fuselage. The canopy was lowered and more cleanly faired into the fuselage.

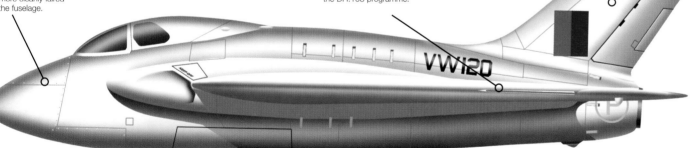

VW120

ACTION DATA

THRUST

TG306 used the Goblin 3 engine of the Vampire FB.Mk 6, although in its DH.108 application the engine produced less thrust. Compared to the Gloster Meteor F.Mk 4, the DH.108 had considerably less thrust but was able to offer far superior performance.

DH.108 SWALLOW
14.68 kN
(3,300- lb.-thrust)

VAMPIRE FB.Mk 6
14.90 kN
3,349- lb.-thrust)

METEOR F.Mk 4
31.10 kN
(6,991- lb.-thrust)

MAXIMUM SPEED

With its new wing design, the Swallow was much faster than either of these contemporary British jet fighters. The aircraft was purely a testbed aimed at airliner research, however, with no provision for weapons or military systems.

DH.108 SWALLOW   1030 km/h (640 m.p.h.)

VAMPIRE FB.Mk 6 882 km/h (548 m.p.h.)

METEOR F.Mk 4   933 km/h (578 m.p.h.)

WING AREA

Based on several Vampire components, the DH.108 exhibited a wing of considerably greater area. The wing attachment points were based on those of the Vampire. With its large, straight wings, the Meteor F.Mk 4 had only slightly more wing area than the DH.108. The Meteor's heavier weight made it less manoeuvrable.

DH.108 SWALLOW
30.47 m²
(327 sq. ft.)

VAMPIRE FB.Mk 6
24.33 m²
(262 sq. ft.)

METEOR F.Mk 4
32.50 m²
(349 sq. ft.)

Sub-scale research prototypes

AVRO 707: A series of 707 prototypes was constructed to perform research and support duties during development of the Avro Vulcan.

HANDLEY PAGE H.P. 88: With a tragic history like that of the DH.108, the H.P. 88 tested a small-scale version of the Victor wing.

SAAB 210 LILL-DRAKEN: A 7/10-scale prototype for the J 35 Draken fighter, the 210 was the first double-delta winged aircraft to fly.

SHORT S.31: An aerodynamically perfect, 1/2-scale model of the Stirling, the S.31 was used to test several features of the bomber.

DEPERDUSSIN

MONOCOQUE RACER

● Advanced construction ● Schneider Trophy winner ● Early monoplane

DEPERDUSSIN MONOCOQUE RACER

Powerful start ▶
Like most fast aircraft, the Monocoque owed much of its success to its powerful engine. The Gnome was a 14-cylinder two-row rotary and was quite superior to almost any other engine.

▲ Streamlined
Compared to most of the ungainly aircraft of the era, the Monocoque flew like a bullet.

Ready to race ▶
With an assistant holding the fuselage as the pilot revved the engine, the Deperdussin made a rapid start when racing.

▲ Snapped tail
Not everything went smoothly at Monaco, with the Monocoque's slender, rear fuselage being damaged during taxiing. But after being repaired it went on to beat the rival Nieuport and Morane-Saulnier aircraft.

▼ Still going
This Deperdussin was flown by Wing Commander Kent at the Royal Aeronautical Society's party in 1949.

▲ Pylon turn
When racing, the pilots flew tightly around large marker pylons at the turning points.

Deperdussin's SPAD company went on to produce some of the best fighters of World War I, but during the last months of peace racing planes carrying the name of Armand Deperdussin were the fastest in the world. With the help of designer Louis Bechereau and pilot Maurice Prévost, his machines dominated the air races and set nine world speed records.

▲ The company started by a former silk merchant made winning aeroplanes. Most of the famous names in French aviation, like Garros and Blériot, were eventually associated with the firm.

FACTS AND FIGURES

➤ A Deperdussin, flown by Eugene Gilbert, won the Henry Deutsch de la Meurthe race around Paris in 1913.

➤ Armand Deperdussin was imprisoned for embezzlement in 1913.

➤ The land-based racers of 1913 often had clipped wings for reduced drag.

➤ Maurice Prévost almost failed to complete the course at Monaco when he initially forgot to fly across the finishing line.

➤ After Deperdussin's arrest, Louis Blériot renamed the company SPAD.

➤ One of the 1913 racers featured unusual reverse tapering on the trailing edge.

PROFILE

Schneider winner

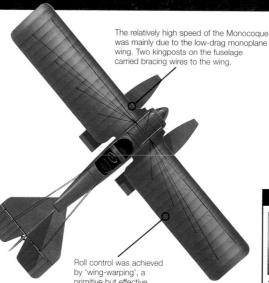

O ne of the key factors of the Deperdussin aircraft's extraordinary performance was the powerplant. The rotary engine, with its cylinders rotating around a central shaft for cooling, was difficult to control but light and powerful. Another factor was the method of construction. Instead of building the fuselage around an internal frame, Deperdussin's designer saved weight and increased strength by using monocoque – literally, single

eggshell – construction. Three 1.5-mm layers of tulipwood were glued, one on top of the other, around a cigar-shaped mould to produce a fuselage whose skin needed no internal bracing.

The aircraft took first and second places in the 1912 James Gordon-Bennett Cup Race at Chicago. The following year Prévost won the Schneider Trophy Air Race at Monaco, for which the aircraft was equipped with floats.

At Reims in September 1913

Monoplanes were a radical design in 1913 and many designers would not consider building them. The success of the Fokker Eindeker showed just how good the concept was.

Prévost did even better. With the racer fitted with smaller wings, he completed the 200-km (124-mile) race in just under an hour, as well as pushing the world speed record over a 1 km distance above 200 km/h (125 m.p.h.) for the first time.

The relatively high speed of the Monocoque was mainly due to the low-drag monoplane wing. Two kingposts on the fuselage carried bracing wires to the wing.

Roll control was achieved by 'wing-warping', a primitive but effective solution before ailerons were invented.

Monocoque

Type: rotary engine monoplane racing aircraft with monocoque fuselage

Powerplant: one 119-kW (160-hp.) Gnome 14-cylinder twin-row rotary engine

Maximum speed: 203.85 km/h (126 m.p.h.)

Weights: maximum take-off 450 kg (990 lb.)

Dimensions:
span	6.55 m (21 ft.)
length	6.10 m (20 ft.)
height	2.30 m (8 ft.)
wing area	9.66 m² (104 sq. ft.)

HISTORY OF DEPERDUSSIN

1912 Deperdussin TT observation and patrol monoplane.

Armand Deperdussin was a wealthy French silk merchant who founded the Société Pour les Appareils Deperdussin, or SPAD, in 1910, at Bethernay, near Reims. After Deperdussin was imprisoned in 1913, two talented employees, André Herbemont and Louis Bechereau, carried on where he had left off. They designed a number of successful high-speed lightweight monocoque Gnome-powered monoplanes. On 9 September 1912 a Monocoque flown by Jules Véderines won the fourth James Gordon-Bennett Aviation Cup Race at Chicago, Illinois, and further successes followed.

The record-breaking Deperdussin Monocoque Gordon-Bennett Racer.

On 16 April 1913 Maurice Prévost won the first ever Schneider Trophy Air Race at Monaco. He won the Reims Gordon-Bennett race on 29 September, setting a new absolute speed record of 203.85 km/h (126 m.p.h.). A successful year was completed when Eugène Gilbert won the Henry Deutsch de la Meurthe Air Race around Paris on 27 October. In just a few months Herbemont and Bechereau had built the world's fastest aircraft and given prestige to the Deperdussin name. By 1914 the company had been taken over by premier aviation pioneer Louis Blériot and named Société Pour L'Aviation Dérives (also SPAD).

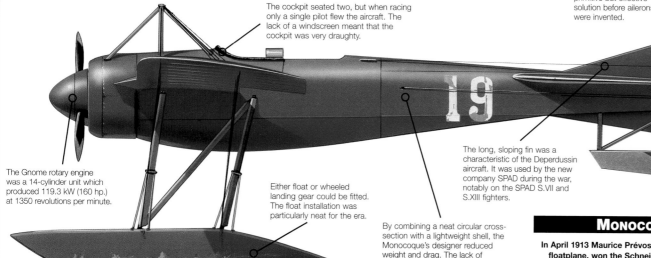

The cockpit seated two, but when racing only a single pilot flew the aircraft. The lack of a windscreen meant that the cockpit was very draughty.

The Gnome rotary engine was a 14-cylinder unit which produced 119.3 kW (160 hp.) at 1350 revolutions per minute.

Either float or wheeled landing gear could be fitted. The float installation was particularly neat for the era.

By combining a neat circular cross-section with a lightweight shell, the Monocoque's designer reduced weight and drag. The lack of internal bracing made it easier to fit control cables and fuel lines.

The long, sloping fin was a characteristic of the Deperdussin aircraft. It was used by the new company SPAD during the war, notably on the SPAD S.VII and S.XIII fighters.

MONOCOQUE

In April 1913 Maurice Prévost, flying a Monocoque floatplane, won the Schneider Trophy Air Race in Monaco, ensuring that France would host the next Schneider race.

A SPAD S.VII C.1 of 'Lafayette' Escadrille, French army, during World War I.

First-generation floatplanes and flying-boats

■ **CURTISS A-SERIES 'HYDROPLANES':** Exhibited to the US Navy by Curtiss himself, the A-1 and A-2 paved the way for a series of successful production aircraft. They flew in 1911, and undertook aircraft-carrier deck trials.

■ **OERTZ W6:** Oertz's W6 Flugschoner of 1917 was an innovative design for the German navy. Powered by two 179-kW (240-hp.) Maybach engines, the aircraft had twin sets of biplane wings mounted onto a boat's wooden hull.

■ **SHORT TYPE 74:** One of Short's Admiralty Class floatplanes, this aircraft entered RNAS service in 1914 when Type 74s took part in the historic Christmas Day raid on Cuxhaven, flying from the carriers *Arthusa*, *Engadine* and *Riviera*.

■ **SOPWITH BAT BOAT:** Britain's first flying-boat, the Bat Boat served with the No. 118 Naval Wing from 1913, performing Scapa Flow patrol duties until late 1914. It had an Austro-Daimler, or Green, 75-kW (100-hp.) engine.

DORNIER
Do X

● Pioneering flying-boat ● Largest aircraft of its time

Today, it is the haunt of holidaying sailors and windsurfers. But in 1929 Lake Constance was the home of the world's largest aeroplane. Created by the legendary designer Dr Claudius Dornier as a trans-Atlantic passenger carrier, the huge 12-engined Dornier Do X was a marginal performer which was never to be a commercial proposition. But it pushed back the boundaries of aviation.

▲ The appropriately-named Richard Wagner, Dornier's chief test pilot, was behind the huge control wheel of the titanic flying-boat for its first flight.

PHOTO FILE

DORNIER Do X

The main attraction ▶
The Do X drew great crowds wherever and whenever it appeared.

▲ Innovation
Claudius Dornier was one of aviation's great pioneers. He had many successful flying-boats in the early 1920s, refining the design features that would eventually appear on the Do X.

▲ Luxury accommodation
Flying in the 1920s and 1930s was only for the rich, and the sumptuous interior of the Do X reflects the luxury which they would have expected.

▲ Power
Twelve radial engines made the Do X the most powerful aircraft of its day.

At home on water ▶
The Do X was a boat that could fly, rather than an aeroplane that could float.

FACTS AND FIGURES

➤ The Do X's record passenger load stood at a crew of 10, 150 invited passengers, and nine stowaways.

➤ In its initial form, the Do X took a snail-like 20 minutes to reach a height of 600 m (2,000 ft.).

➤ The wings were thick enough to allow an engineer access to the engines.

➤ On one attempted flight, the Do X ran for 13 km (8 miles) without being able to lift off.

➤ Even with more powerful engines, the Do X cruised at a leisurely 175 km/h (110 m.p.h.).

➤ The Do X was in the air for a total of 211 hours on its maiden transatlantic voyage – spread over a period of 19 months!

PROFILE

Transatlantic Titan

The only revolutionary thing about the massive Dornier Do X was its size. But this alone represented a huge leap into the unknown.

At 56 tons all-up weight, it was by far the largest aircraft in the world. But in spite of having more power than any aircraft of its time, the Do X was never more than a marginal performer. The huge flying-boat was painfully slow, and took an age to reach its meagre operating height of less than 1250 metres (3,300 ft.).

But the Do X represented Germany's reappearance on the world aviation stage, only a decade after its industry had been dismantled at the end of World War I. And that rebirth was celebrated by an epoch-making maiden voyage, from Europe to Africa, across the Atlantic to South America, and on to New York and back.

The Do X lifts majestically from the surface of Lake Constance on the morning of 12 July 1929.

The huge machine was eventually handed over to Lufthansa, but the airliner was not commercially viable, and never took any fare-paying passengers. It was to end its days in a Berlin museum and was destroyed in an air raid in 1945.

The Do X's successful, if delayed, flight to New York gave a great boost to the German aircraft industry, which was recovering from the crippling blow of World War I.

Do X

Type: experimental passenger flying-boat

Powerplant: 12 450-kW (660-hp.) Curtiss Conqueror nine-cylinder radial engines

Maximum speed: 210 km/h (130 m.p.h.); cruising speed 175 km/h (110 m.p.h.)

Time to height: 14 minutes to 1000 m (3,280 ft.)

Maximum range: 2200 km (1,370 mi.)

Service ceiling: 1250 m (4,100 ft.)

Weights: empty 32,675 kg (72,040 lb.); loaded 56,000 kg (123,406 lb.)

Payload: 15,325 kg (33,790 lb.), comprising 14 crew, 66 passengers; record flight from Lake Constance, 10 crew, 150 passengers and nine stowaways – a total of 169 people

Dimensions: span 48.00 m (157 ft. 5 in.)
length 40.05 m (131 ft. 2 in.)
height 10.10 m (33 ft. 1 in.)
wing area 250 m² (2,690 sq. ft.)

DO X 'MONSTER OF THE SEA'

Dornier's huge flying-boat was an attempt to revolutionise air transport. Unfortunately ambition outstripped available technology, and it was not a success.

The pilot of the Do X sat at the front of the upper deck, behind a large steering-wheel. Smaller wheels controlled trim in flight and the rudder in the water.

The Do X had 12 engines in six nacelles above the wing. The wing was thick enough for a crawlspace, which led to ladders up to each nacelle, allowing engineers free access to the engines, even in flight.

The upper deck was occupied by the flight engineer, navigators, maintenance technicians and radio operators.

The Do X was originally powered by 12 British-designed Bristol Jupiter radial engines, but for the Atlantic crossing they were replaced by 12 slightly more powerful Curtiss Conquerors.

D-1929

Passengers were carried in two cabins fore and aft of the wing leading edge. The bar and smoking room were in the bow, and the galley was at the rear. Baggage was stowed aft of the galley.

The Do X was fitted with a rudder at the rear of the keel to enable the aircraft to be steered while on the water.

The hull and wing of the Do X was of all-metal construction, but the heavy weight and lack of power meant that it could never reach its designed operating altitude.

Large tail surfaces gave the Do X fair stability. For added control, an extra horizontal tailplane was attached to the fuselage.

With the Do X across the Atlantic

DEPARTURE: The trip was made in easy stages, with calls at seaplane bases at Amsterdam (left) and Calshott in the south of England. Wherever the Do X went, it drew sightseeing crowds.

WEST AFRICA: In spite of its huge fuel load the Do X had limited range, so the Atlantic crossing had to be made at its narrowest point. On 3 June 1931 the Do X set off from Portuguese Guinea.

FLYING DOWN TO RIO: Seventeen days later, the Do X reached Rio de Janeiro. The widest part of the crossing, from the Cape Verde Islands to Fernando Noronha, took 13 hours.

WELCOME TO NEW YORK: Over the next eight weeks, the Do X worked its way up South and North America via the Caribbean. The huge plane caused a sensation on reaching New York.

HOME AGAIN: After wintering in America, the Do X crossed the North Atlantic via Newfoundland and the Azores. On 24 May 1932 it landed on Berlin's Müggelsee to a tumultuous welcome.

DORNIER

Do 29

● **Research aircraft** ● **Pivoting propellers** ● **Vertical take-off**

Built for research into short and vertical take-off and landing (STOL and VTOL) flight, the Do 29 flew for the first time in December 1958. It was powered by twin GO-480 engines driving three-bladed pusher propellers which could be pivoted downward at angles of up to 90° for maximum VTOL performance. There was never any intention to build a production version of the aircraft, which was financed as a research project by the German defence ministry.

▲ A master designer of structures, Professor Claude Dornier influenced German aircraft design for decades. He produced some of the most innovative aircraft ever built.

DORNIER Do 29

▼ **Pivoting propellers**
Making a rapid take-off with the aid of its two Lycoming engines, the Do 29 proved to have a remarkably short take-off run.

▲ **Future fighter**
Despite its ungainly looks, the Do 29 was developed to investigate the potential of a vertical take-off fighter and a transport aircraft for the German air force, though both projects were later cancelled.

Proven design ▶
The basic airframe of the Do 29 used the fuselage of a Do 27, which allowed the costs of the programme to be kept to a minimum with modification required only to the wings.

◀ **Test flights**
German test-pilots found that they could quickly adapt to the techniques required to fly the revolutionary aircraft.

Unimpaired view ▶
The pilot was seated under a bulbous canopy and had excellent visibility from the nose of the aircraft. A Martin-Baker ejection seat was provided in case of a mishap. Though the type was extensively flown, no major problems ever occurred.

FACTS AND FIGURES

➤ The first prototype Do 29 flew in December 1958, quickly followed into the air by two other examples.

➤ The propellers could be pivoted through a maximum of 90°.

➤ Power was provided by two American Avco Lycoming piston engines.

➤ German interest in vertical take-off aircraft stemmed from World War II, and continued with post-war designs.

➤ Sections of the aircraft were adopted from the Do 27 to reduce costs.

➤ One preserved Do 29 is in the Helicopter Museum at Buckeburg in Germany.

Dornier's rising success

Much useful information on STOL and VSTOL flight was gathered by the Do 29 programme. The data was needed for the development of a planned military transport aircraft. Germany was also working on a vertical take-off fighter and applied the data to this concept also.

Three aircraft were built. Compared with the original Do 27, the Do 29 had a bigger fin and rudder, plus an additional fin below the tail, to improve low-speed control. The wings also had to be modified

for the engine mountings, and their span and area were increased. The single pilot had an ejection seat in the redesigned forward fuselage.

The propellers rotated in opposite directions so that their torque would be cancelled-out. The structure also had to be strengthened by stiffeners along the sides and bottom of the fuselage, partly to cope with the increased loading and partly to protect the fuselage sides from the propeller tip vortices.

Dornier went on to build prototypes of the Do 31

Below: With a test boom projecting from its nose, a Do.29 takes off at the start of another experimental flight. The engines are positioned in the fully deflected position.

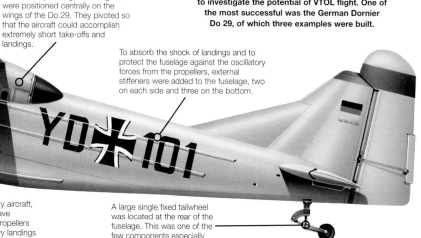

Above: 'A room with a view'; the pilot of the Dornier Do.29 enjoyed excellent visibility.

STOL/VTOL transport aircraft, which used two jet engines for propulsion and another eight for lift, but the excessive complexity of the powerplant arrangement meant planned production versions were never built.

Do 29

Numerous experimental aircraft were developed to investigate the potential of VTOL flight. One of the most successful was the German Dornier Do 29, of which three examples were built.

Do 29

Type: short take-off and vertical landing research aircraft

Powerplant: two 201-kW (270-hp.) Avco Lycoming GO-480-B1A6 piston engines, driving opposite-rotating three-bladed Hartzell propellers

Maximum speed: 290 km/h (180 m.p.h.) at optimum altitude

Stalling speed: 75 km/h (47 m.p.h.)

Take-off distance: 15 m (50 ft.)

Weights: maximum take-off 2500 kg (5,500 lb.)

Accommodation: one pilot

Dimensions: span 13.20 m (43 ft. 4 in.)
length 9.50 m (31 ft. 2 in.)
wing area 21.80 m² (235 sq. ft.)

Two Avco Lycoming radial engines were positioned centrally on the wings of the Do.29. They pivoted so that the aircraft could accomplish extremely short take-offs and landings.

To absorb the shock of landings and to protect the fuselage against the oscillatory forces from the propellers, external stiffeners were added to the fuselage, two on each side and three on the bottom.

The cockpit was built around a single pilot and was equipped with a Martin-Baker ejection seat. The excellent visibility allowed the pilot to observe the rotation of the engines.

Adopted from the Do 27 utility aircraft, the high-set undercarriage gave adequate clearance for the propellers and was able to absorb heavy landings during the early stages of test flying.

A large single fixed tailwheel was located at the rear of the fuselage. This was one of the few components especially designed for the aircraft.

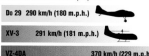

MAXIMUM SPEED

Experimental aircraft were never designed to fly quickly but the Do 29's speed was nonetheless still relatively poor compared to other convertiplanes. Fastest of these was the Doak VZ-4DA, which used two ducted propellers.

Do 29	290 km/h (180 m.p.h.)
XV-3	291 km/h (181 m.p.h.)
VZ-4DA	370 km/h (229 m.p.h.)

POWER

Designed later, the Doak VZ-4DA used a bigger powerplant than the Do 29, so it was a more stable aircraft while in the hover. Although fitted with two engines, the power available to the Do 29 was surprisingly small, but this was compensated for by the small dimensions of the aircraft. The XV-3 had a very modest power output.

Do 29 — 402 kW (540 hp.)
XV-3 — 336 kW (450 hp.)
VZ-4DA — 626 kW (625 hp.)

TAKE-OFF WEIGHT

Though they were experimental designs, the take-off weights of these aircraft were of vital importance if they were to be viable. Despite its having a small fuselage, the Do 29's take-off weight was surprisingly large compared to the other types.

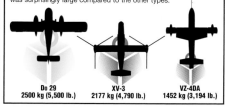

Do 29 2500 kg (5,500 lb.) — XV-3 2177 kg (4,790 lb.) — VZ-4DA 1452 kg (3,194 lb.)

Unconventional convertiplanes

VERTOL VZ-2A: This was one of the first convertiplanes to be developed for the US Army and Navy. First flying in August 1957, the aircraft completed several hundred test flights before being retired.

HILLER X-18: One of the real pioneers in the convertiplane field, the large X-18 was tested as a future transport aircraft for the US military. A turbojet gave additional power for improved take-off performance.

RYAN VZ-3RY: First flying in December 1958, the little Ryan played a vital role in exploring the field of vertical flight. Eventually passing to NASA, the aircraft continued to fly into the 1960s.

DOUGLAS

D-558 SKYSTREAK/SKYROCKET

● Record breaker ● Rocket/jet power ● Supersonic research

I t looked like a bullet with small wings and flew like its name – Skyrocket. The gleaming-white Douglas D-558-II was part of the family of experimental airplanes that pushed beyond the sound barrier just after World War II. Using rocket power to explore supersonic speed and the effects of high-speed flight on its swept-back wings, the Skyrocket broke several records in a series of stunning flights.

▲ Although it was too late to capture the glory of being the first supersonic aircraft, the Skystreak pushed back the frontiers of aeronautical knowledge and high-speed design.

DOUGLAS D-558 SKYSTREAK/SKYROCKET

▲ Straight lines
The Skyrocket had much more conventional aerodynamics than the racy Skyrocket, with a straight wing and tail that would have looked at home on a World War II design. The cockpit was tiny.

◀ Sabre chase
An F-86 chase plane was often used to follow the Skyrocket in test flights. Much of the F-86's success was owed to eearly high-speed aircraft.

▲ Swept wing
The Skyrocket was extensively redesigned with a swept wing and new mixed rocket/jet powerplant, becoming the Skyrocket.

▼ Futuristic
Although the Skyrocket looked amazing in the 1950s, its similarity to fighters of 10 years after shows the pace of aircraft design.

▲ Drop launch
A Navy P2B model of the B-29 carried the Skyrocket aloft for later flights, giving the aircraft more power to develop higher speeds, as it used up much of it short fuel supply in climbing to altitude.

FACTS AND FIGURES

➤ The first of three D-558-II Skyrockets made its maiden flight in California on 4 February 1948.

➤ The last Skystreak flew 82 research flights before it was retired in 1953.

➤ The third Skystreak was kept flying with spare parts from the first one.

➤ Designer Ed Heinemann was given the 1951 Sylvanus Albert Reed aeronautical award for his work on the D-558-II.

➤ Lt Col M Carl set an unofficial altitude record of 25,364 m (83,214 ft.) in the D-588-II.

➤ The final flight by a Skyrocket was made on 20 December 1956.

PROFIL

Twice the speed of sound

Douglas designed the Skystreak and then the Skyrocket in response to a National Advisory Committee for Aeronautics (NACA) requirement for high-speed research aircraft. The first Skystreak flew in 1947, and broke the world speed record in August of that year. The supersonic D-558-II Skyrocket, with a swept wing, was also designed by the great Ed Heinemann. its fuselage contained the pilot's jettisonable compartment, turbojet, rocket engine, landing gear and fuel.

The original clamshell canopy was changed to a raised cockpit to improve visibility. The three Skyrockets initially took off from land with combined jet/rocket power for their research flights. Later, they were air-launched from a Navy P2B-1S.

From 1950 through 1956, courageous test pilots – especially William B. Bridgeman and Scott Crossfield – made rocket flights that pushed the airplane to the edge of the envelope and yielded a wealth of new aeronautical knowledge.

Below: A Skystreak attracted a lot of attention with its orange colour scheme wherever it appeared, especially after the world speed record had been broken twice in one week.

The Skyrocket became the first aircraft to fly twice the speed of sound when Crossfield took it to Mach 2.005 on 20 November, 1953.

Above: Rocket-assisted take-offs were spectacular affairs, and pilots enjoyed the enormous thrust of the rocket engine. Despite the trials of rocket assistance with jets such as the Mirage III and MiG-21, rocket engines were generally more trouble than they were worth.

D-558-II Skyrocket

Type: Swept-wing research aircraft

Powerplant: One 13.61 kN (3.059-lb.-thrust) Westinghouse J34-W-22 plus one 27.2 kN (6,117-lb.-thrust) Reaction Motors XLR-8 rocket motor

Max speed: (turbojet only) 941 km/h (583 m.p.h.); (mixed power) 1159 km/h (718 m.p.h.); (rocket power only) 2012 km/h (1,247 m.p.h.)

Weight: Max take-off 6925 kg (15,267 lb.) (turbojet). (mixed powerplant) 7171 kg (15,800 lb.)

Accommodation: Pilot, powerplant and fuel

Dimensions:
Span:	7,62 m (25 ft.)
Length:	13,79 m (45 ft.)
Height:	3,51 m (11 ft.)
Wing area:	16,26 m² (125 sq.ft.)

D-558-I SKYSTREAK

The Douglas Skystreak flew a series of high-speed test flights between May 1947 and June 1953, setting a new world record of 1031 km/h (639 m.p.h.) in August 1947, subsequently surpassed five days later to 1047 km/h (649 m.p.h.).

The 'V'-shaped canopy fitted for high-speed flights reduced cockpit size so much that pilots wore soft helmets.

The second Skystreak was destroyed after the compressor of the J35 engine disintegrated.

The tube-shaped fuselage was of conventional alloy construction. Strain gauges were fitted in various parts of the wings and tail to assess the stresses of high-speed flight.

Perhaps the most unusual feature of the Skystreak was the escape system in which the nose section fell away from the main airframe, allowing the pilot to escape by bailing out once the nose had slowed down enough to allow it.

The nose undercarriage retracted forward, and the mainwheels inward.

Intended for high subsonic speeds, the Skystreak had a straight wing as did the supersonic Bell X-1. The knowledge gained from the Skystreak of airflow at transonic speeds helped develop the swept-wing Skyrocket and later fighter designs.

The Skystreak was powered by an Allison J35A-11 turbojet of 22.68 kN (4,990-lb.-thrust). This engine was also used in prototype Boeing B-47s and Douglas F4D Skyrays.

Getting the X-Planes airborne

■ **GROUND LAUNCHED:** Using its rocket motor, the Skyrocket could be ground launched. In this respect, it was ahead of the Bell X-1, which could only be air-launched. Designers were drawn to the concept of rocket-assisted interceptors because of the high-level bomber threat in the 1950s, but none ever entered service. They were, however, useful in generating massive thrust for high-speed research flying.

■ **AIR LAUNCHED:** Like its great rival, the Bell X-1, the Skyrocket was dropped from a B-29 variant. This had the advantage of starting the Skyrocket off at around 320 km/h (200 m.p.h.) even before it had ignited its rocket and jet engines, and saved fuel normally used in take-off and climbing. Unlike the X-1, the pilot remained in the Skyrocket during the entire flight and did not climb into the aircraft before it was launched.

ACTION DATA

SPEED

The Skyrocket was more powerful than the DH.108 or Yak-50, due to rocket engine assistance. Using the turbine only, it could reach 941 km/h (583 m.p.h.). With the rocket only, and aircraft launching, speeds of around 2012 km/h (1,247 m.p.h.) were possible. The Yak-50 was almost as fast with just a VK-1 jet engine.

DH.108	1030 km/h (639 m.p.h.)
D-558 SKYROCKET	1159 km/h (718 m.p.h.)
YAK-50	1135 km/h (704 m.p.h.)

THRUST

With rocket assistance, the Skyrocket was almost as powerful as a Yak-50 and DH.108 combined. Rocket engines have low endurance, and even the Skyrocket could only use its rocket engine for limited periods. The DH.108 was powered by a single Goblin engine and was a much smaller airplane, though still fast.

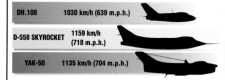

DH.108 14,97 kN (3,293 lb.)
D-558 SKYROCKET
YAK-50 27 kW (5,940 lb.)
13,61 kN + 27,22 kN = 40,83 kN (8,982 lb.)

FIRST SUPERSONIC FLIGHT

In the race to be supersonic, the USA was ahead, and the Skyrocket was supersonic before either the DH.108 or the Yak. The DH.108 crashed while making a supersonic flight attempt in 1946. By 1953, the Skyrocket was flying at twice the speed of sound. The Yak-50 flew supersonically before the rival MiG-15.

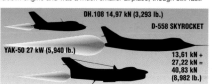

	MACH 1:
DH.108	1948
YAK-50	1949
D-558 SKYROCKET	1948

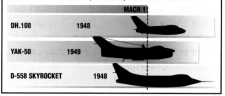

DOUGLAS

X-3

● High speed ● Titanium construction ● Research aircraft

▲ Douglas had expected the X-3 to reach speeds in excess of Mach 2, but it became clear at an early stage to both the manufacturer and the USAF that this would not happen.

Visually one of the most striking aircraft ever, the Douglas X-3 was dubbed 'Stiletto'. A product of the post-war pioneering days of experimental 'X-planes' tested over the Californian desert in the 1940s and 1950s, the X-3 appeared ready to pave the way for new discoveries at the outer edge of the performance envelope. Unfortunately, although it provided some useful research data, the X-3's performance did not live up to expectations.

DOUGLAS X-3

◄ **Futuristic design**
Contemporary engine technology could not match the potential of the advanced airframe design.

▼ **White 'Stiletto'**
The gloss white fuselage and tail surfaces contrasted with the highly polished aluminium wings.

▲ **X-3 survives**
After completing its test duties the X-3 was handed over to the US Air Force Museum, in Ohio, where it can still be seen.

▼ **Experimental Douglas jets**
Even in the company of the D-558-1 Skystreak (to the left) and D-558-2 Skyrocket, the 'Stiletto' looks futuristic. The two earlier Douglas aircraft enjoyed far greater success than the X-3.

▼ **Fine lines**
Douglas used a long, slender fuselage with low-aspect ratio straight wings for the X-3.

FACTS AND FIGURES

➤ On 15 October 1952 the X-3 made an unscheduled, but brief, trip aloft and an official first flight five days later.

➤ In its fastest flight on 28 July 1953 the X-3 was clocked at Mach 1.21 in a dive.

➤ The X-3 is on display at the US Air Force Museum, Wright-Patterson AFB, Ohio.

➤ The X-3 used 850 pinholes, spread over its structure, to record pressures and 185 strain gauges to record air loads.

➤ There were 150 temperature recording points spread across the X-3 airframe.

➤ The X-3 had one of the fastest take-off speeds in history – 418 km/h (260 m.p.h.).

Distinctive Douglas design

Intended for research into the extreme temperatures and stresses encountered during high-altitude, high-speed flight, the X-3 began life on the designers' drawing boards in 1945. The programme was so complex that three years elapsed before construction of a mock-up was approved, in August 1948. In June 1949 Douglas won a contract for two aircraft plus a static-test example but, in the end, only one prototype was built, with the second partly completed machine providing spare parts for the first.

Flying for the first time in 1952, the X-3 looked weird. The pilot sat in a pressurised cabin on a downwards-firing ejection seat, which also served as an electric lift to provide access from the ground. The X-3 was difficult to handle when taxiing, tricky on take-off and very difficult to fly.

Design of the X-3 was of unprecedented complexity because of the use of titanium and other advanced materials. Unfortunately, despite its rakish appearance and revolutionary construction, the X-3 was underpowered and offered little

to researchers. The USAF flew the aircraft only six times, Douglas 25 times and the NACA (National Advisory Committee for Aeronautics) funded 20 flights before retiring the X-3 in 1956.

Above: Experts realised that aircraft such as the X-1 and X-2 would be capable of reaching very high speeds only briefly, and so the X-3 was designed for sustained high-speed flight.

Above: Shoulder-mounted air intakes fed the Westinghouse turbojets. The intakes had fixed ramps but were optimised for maximum efficiency at Mach 2.

X-3

Type: single-seat research aircraft

Powerplant: two 21.6-kN (4,860-lb.-thrust) Westinghouse J34-WE-17 turbojet engines

Maximum speed: 1136 km/h (704 m.p.h.)

Take-off speed: 418 km/h (260 m.p.h.)

Endurance: 1 hour

Range: 805 km (500 mi.)

Service ceiling: 11580 m (38,000 ft.)

Weights: empty 7312 kg (16,086 lb.); maximum take-off 10813 kg (23,788 lb.)

Dimensions:
span	6.91 m (22 ft. 8 in.)
length	20.35 m (66 ft. 9 in.)
height	3.81 m (12 ft. 6 in.)
wing area	15.47 m² (166 sq. ft.)

ACTION DATA

MAXIMUM SPEED

Even though it was designed for high-speed flight, the X-3 was rapidly outpaced by the new generation of fighters that soon entered service. The F-104A, in particular, far outperformed the 'Stiletto'.

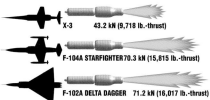

X-3 1136 km/h (704 m.p.h.)

F-104A STARFIGHTER 1850 km/h (1,147 m.p.h.)

F-102A DELTA DAGGER 1266 km/h (785 m.p.h.)

THRUST

One of the main reasons for the poor performance of the X-3 was the low power available from its engines. Aircraft weight was also a problem and although various methods of water or liquid ammonia injection were proposed, none was tried.

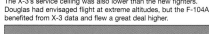

X-3 43.2 kN (9,718 lb.-thrust)

F-104A STARFIGHTER 70.3 kN (15,815 lb.-thrust)

F-102A DELTA DAGGER 71.2 kN (16,017 lb.-thrust)

SERVICE CEILING

The X-3's service ceiling was also lower than the new fighters. Douglas had envisaged flight at extreme altitudes, but the F-104A benefited from X-3 data and flew a great deal higher.

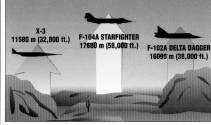

X-3 11580 m (32,800 ft.)

F-104A STARFIGHTER 17680 m (58,000 ft.)

F-102A DELTA DAGGER 16095 m (38,000 ft.)

X-3

Only one X-3 flew, providing little data for researchers into high-speed flight. It did, however, provide some useful data and gave Douglas experience in the use of titanium and other exotic production techniques.

An air data boom extended ahead of the long nose. All details of every flight could be recorded and analysed by the large numbers of sensors incorporated in the airframe.

Douglas developed a special flight suit and helmet for the pilot, allowing a supersonic ejection. The cockpit was pressurised and air-conditioned, which was particularly important since cockpit temperatures were expected to be high.

Internally the fuselage had aluminium framing covered with heavy-gauge aluminium skinning. In all, 544 kg (1200 lb.) of test equipment was carried, but all data had to be analysed after landing.

Westinghouse continually revised its estimates of the thrust available from the J46 (which was never used) and J34 turbojets. As power ratings were falling, Douglas designers found that airframe weight was increasing. Schemes to use rocket assistance were abandoned when it became clear that the F-104 would offer far superior performance.

The very long nose provided extra space for test equipment and allowed Douglas to keep the aircraft's frontal area to a minimum.

The unusual shape of the X-3's glazing was yet another result of the need to keep the aircraft as thin and aerodynamically clean as possible. In flight, the windscreen was expected to get very hot.

Lockheed's 'Kelly' Johnson used data relating to the low aspect ratio wing of the X-3 when finalising his F-104 design.

The underside of the tailboom, where heat from the engine exhaust was expected to be greatest, was covered by a sheet of titanium and was left unpainted. The slab tailplanes also had titanium skins.

X-jets at Edwards Air Force Base

■ **NORTH AMERICAN X-10:** This remotely controlled, unmanned drone was used to test the aerodynamic concepts to be used in the upper stage of the Navaho missile. In spite of accidents, the programme was a success and the Mach 2-capable X-10s were used for further research.

■ **RYAN X-13 VERTIJET:** A programme of highly successful flights using the two X-13s was undertaken in the 1950s. The aircraft demonstrated transitions from vertical to horizontal flight and when 'landing' from vertical flight, it 'docked' on a special gantry.

■ **BELL X-14:** Intended to investigate the unique qualities and problems of vectored thrust vertical/short take-off and landing aircraft, the X-14 went on to serve for almost 25 years. It was used to simulate the characteristics of other V/STOL types and to give pilots vital experience.

EUROFIGHTER

TYPHOON

● Agile fighter ● Ground attacker ● Multinational

Embodying everything that aeronautical science has learned in the 20th century, the Typhoon is destined to be the Top Gun of the 21st century. Developed by four nations, it will be one of the cornerstones of European air defence over the next 25 years. This is the fighter of tomorrow, bristling with the products of advanced science, relying on new technology for hi-tech victory in aerial combat.

▲ *Fast, agile and highly potent, the Eurofighter Typhoon uses extremely advanced technology to provide Europe with one of the most flexible of the latest generation of superfighters.*

PHOTO FILE

EUROFIGHTER TYPHOON

▲ Euro-power
The Eurofighter's EJ200 engines are produced by a highly experienced consortium led by Rolls-Royce and MTU.

▼ Forward control
The rear-mounted delta wing and 'canard' foreplanes give the Typhoon incredible manoeuvrability at low and high speeds.

▲ Europe's defender
Launched in a media spectacular, the Eurofighter will provide the backbone of European air defence as well as deadly-accurate strike capability for the next 30 years.

▲ High-tech warrior
It doesn't look exotic, but the Eurofighter incorporates the latest advances in airframe and engine design with new avionics, stealth and weapons technology.

◀ Multi-role, multinational fighter
Designed to meet exacting British, German, Italian and Spanish air force requirements, the Typhoon will be a true multi-purpose fighter.

FACTS AND FIGURES

➤ The Eurofighter flies twice as fast as a 9-mm pistol bullet.

➤ Not only fast and high-flying, the Typhoon performs high-angle manoeuvres for victory in a close-up dogfight.

➤ Eurofighter simultaneously tracks a dozen targets, and engages six at once.

➤ Eurofighter design features were tested on British Aerospace's Experimental Aircraft Programme (EAP) demonstrator in the late 1980s.

➤ In common with most new-generation fighters, the Eurofighter uses canards – small wings near the nose – to improve performance.

PROFILE

Defender of Europe's skies

Hard proof that Europe has a vision and that its nations can co-operate to produce the ultimate fighter for common defence, this purposeful, high-performance delta-winged jet offers significant advances in engines, radar, combat systems and weaponry. From nose to tail, the Eurofighter is one of the most advanced fighters in the skies today, equally at home as a highly agile interceptor and as a precision ground attacker.

It has not been easy for experts in Britain, Germany, Italy and Spain to develop their new warplane. The original Eurofighter was even more capable than that now being built, but following considerable German opposition to the original price tag the consortium agreed to build a much less costly design now known as the Eurofighter Typhoon.

Even so, the Typhoon's advanced new radar, infra-red sensors and avionics mean that it is the best multi-role fighter flying today, which will form the backbone of Europe's fighter resources for many years.

The EAP trials confirmed that the canard layout and fly-by-wire controls would produce a superb fighter.

'Canard' foreplanes are primarily used to provide increased lift on take-off and at low speeds. This translates into greatly increased agility in dogfights.

Fuel-efficient EJ200 turbofan engines will allow the Eurofighter to cruise supersonically without the need for afterburning, greatly enhancing the fighter's range at high speed.

The Typhoon's delta wing is very effective at high speeds and high altitudes, but slow-speed performance is equally good, thanks to computer-controlled fly-by-wire technology.

EF 2000

No single aircraft can perform every military role, but the EF 2000 will come closer than most. Agile, with good radar and a heavy weapons load, it will be called on to fight enemies both in the air and on the ground.

The advanced cockpit has been designed to reduce pilot workload. High-technology features include multi-function video displays, and some non-essential functions will be voice-activated.

The Eurofighter has no conventional tailplanes, climbing and diving being controlled by a combination of the aircraft's foreplanes and the control surfaces at the wing trailing edge.

ZH588

Eurofighter will enter service with the Marconi-developed ECR-90 radar. This will have lookup/lookdown air-to-air capability, and will be able to search for, track and engage multiple targets.

A passive infra-red search-and-track sensor mounted just to the left of the cockpit can detect and track multiple targets without any give-away radar signals.

Although weighing less than 10 tons, a Typhoon can carry more than six tons of weapons or fuel on nine hardpoints.

Eurofighter is designed to be armed with fire-and-forget active radar AMRAAM missiles and heat-seeking ASRAAM dogfight weapons, but will also be able to carry earlier-generation missiles such as the AIM-7 Sparrow and AIM-9 Sidewinder.

EF 2000

Type: high-performance jet fighter

Powerplant: two 60.02-kN (13,500-lb. thrust) Eurojet EJ200 engines, increased to 90.03 kN (20,257-lb. thrust) with afterburning

Maximum speed: Mach 2.0+, or 2125 km/h (1320 m.p.h.) at 6096 m (20,000 ft.)

Combat radius: up to 556 km (345 mi.) with full weapons load

Weights: empty 9750 kg (21,495 lb.); loaded 21,000 kg (46,297 lb.)

Armament: 6500 kg (14,330 lb.) of ordnance including up to eight missiles such as Sky Flash, ASRAAM, AMRAAM or Sidewinder, plus a 27-mm rapid-fire cannon

Dimensions:
span	10.50 m (34 ft. 5 in.)
length	14.50 m (47 ft. 7 in.)
height	4.00 m (13 ft. 1 in.)
wing area	50 m² (538 sq. ft.)

COMBAT DATA

MAXIMUM SPEED

The Eurofighter is one of the fastest of the latest generation of combat jets. However, although the phenomenally expensive American F-22 is slower, it can maintain supersonic speeds for longer periods.

TYPHOON	Mach 2.0
JAS 39 GRIPEN	Mach 1.8
F-22 RAPIER	Mach 1.7

COMBAT RADIUS

Typhoon is at a disadvantage in terms of combat radius. The single-engined Gripen is smaller and less fuel-hungry, and the F-22 is much larger and carries a bigger fuel load. But for most tactical purposes the EFA has enough range for its missions.

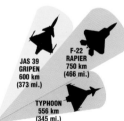

JAS 39 GRIPEN 600 km (373 mi.)

F-22 RAPIER 750 km (466 mi.)

TYPHOON 556 km (345 mi.)

ARMAMENT

Most modern fighters carry a very large weapons load. Both the Typhoon and the Gripen have been designed to be dual air-to-air and air-to-ground capable. The F-22 has the capability, but is more dedicated to the air-superiority role.

TYPHOON
27-mm cannon
8–10 short- and medium-range AAM
6500 kg (14,330 lb.) of weapons and stores

JAS 39 GRIPEN
27-mm cannon
6-8 short- and medium-range AAM
6500 kg (14,330 lb.) of weapons and stores

F-22 RAPTOR
20-mm cannon
AIM-120 AMRAAM and AIM-9 Sidewinders carried internally
10,000 kg (22,046 lb.) of air-to-surface weapons

Tomorrow's fighters today

■ **SUKHOI Su-27 'FLANKER'**
This is arguably the best fighter currently in service. The Eurofighter was designed to outperform advanced versions currently under development.

■ **DASSAULT RAFALE**
Developed after the French withdrew from the Eurofighter programme, the Rafale is a French national project. It is similar in design to the EFA, but is somewhat lighter.

■ **SAAB JAS 39 GRIPEN**
A product of Sweden's highly respected Saab concern, the Gripen is also a tail-less delta with canard foreplanes but is much smaller, and is powered by a single engine.

■ **LOCKHEED F-22 RAPTOR**
The F-22 incorporates a great deal of stealth technology, and is the most capable of the new batch of fighter designs. But that performance comes at phenomenal cost.

FAIREY

LONG-RANGE MONOPLANE

● Two-seat long-range aircraft ● Record-breaking flights to Cape Town

O n its second attempt at breaking the world nonstop distance record in December 1929, the original Fairey Long-range Monoplane crashed in Tunisia, killing the two pilots. The aircraft was trying to fly from the RAF base at Cranwell, England to Cape Town, South Africa, but crashed into a mountainside in bad weather. The RAF commissioned a new aircraft for another attempt at the record; by July 1931, that distance stood at 8066 kilometres (5,000 miles).

▲ *Before the flight to South Africa, a flight to Bangalore was attempted. At Karachi, the crew realised that there was insufficient fuel for the whole flight.*

▼ **Wing tanks**
The Monoplane's massive cantilever wings contained fuel tanks.

▲ **Triumphant return**
K1991, the second Monoplane, taxis in at a wet Farnborough on 2 May, 1933 for the official reception after the record-breaking flight to southern Africa completed in February.

Reliable Napier Lion ▶
Both Monoplanes had 12-cylinder Napier Lion engines. In 1934, thought was given to re-engining K1991 with a 447-kw (600-hp.) Junkers Jumo diesel engine. Expected to give a range of over 13000 kilometres (8,060 miles), nothing came of the idea.

▼ **Long-Range Monoplane II**
Built to replace J9479, which was destroyed in a crash en route to South Africa, K1991 embodied a number of improvements, including wheel fairings to reduce drag, a new fuel system and an autopilot.

▲ **Massive wing**
After extensive wind tunnel testing of several configurations, the cantilever high wing was chosen for the aircraft.

FACT AND FIGURES

➤ In order to placate a cost-conscious Treasury and Parliament, the Monoplanes were called 'Postal Aircraft'.

➤ Plans to equip K 1991 with an economical Phoenix diesel engine were scrapped.

➤ The agreed price for the construction of the first Monoplane was £15,000.

➤ K1991's distance record stood until August, when a French Bleriot-Zapata flew from New York to Syria.

➤ RAF Cranwell was used for long-distance flights because it had the longest runway.

➤ Initially, J9479 was unable to take off at its maximum take-off weight.

Long-range records for Britain

First flown in June 1931, the second aircraft was similar to the high-winged original. It had a more streamlined undercarriage, however, and was equipped with an autopilot to control the aircraft in roll and heading. It also carried four compasses, three altimeters, two airspeed indicators and other instruments to help the crew maintain the planned course in darkness or poor visibility.

After a test flight to Egypt in October 1931, the aircraft was damaged on landing when it returned to England. A full moon and winter winds were needed to give it the best chance of reaching South Africa, and, after several delays due to bad weather, the aircraft finally took off from Cranwell early on the morning of 6 February, 1933.

The autopilot failed over central Africa, but Squadron Leader Gayford and Flight Lieutenant Nicholetts flew on. After 57 hours and 25 minutes, the aircraft landed in Walvis Bay, 8577 kilometres (5,330 miles) from England.

The record stood for six months until Bleriot raised it to 9084 kilometres (5,645 miles). Plans to modify the Fairey for an even longer range by fitting new engines were defeated by difficulties and cost constraints.

J9479 was the first Monoplane and was flown successfully to Karachi in late April 1929 (though Bangalore was the intended destination). En route to Cape Town in July, it crashed fatally in Tunisia.

The Napier Lion engine drove a fixed-pitch two-blade propeller engine.

Long-Range Monoplane II

Type: Two-seat long-range monoplane

Powerplant: One 425-kw (570-hp.) Napier Lion IXA liquid-cooled piston engine

Cruising speed: 177 km/h (110 m.p.h.)

Range: 8932 km (5,540 mi.)

Weight: Max take-off 7938 kg (17,464 lb.)

Accommodation: Pilot and navigator

Dimensions:
Span:	24,99 m (82 ft.)	
Length:	14,78 m (48 ft. 6 in.)	
Height:	3,66 m (12 ft.)	
Wing area:	78,97 m² (828 sq. ft.)	

A high cantilever wing was chosen for the Monoplane largely to satisfy the need for a fuel system gravity-fed from tanks that were, by necessity, situated in the vast wing space. The gravity system fed a collector tank, from which a mechanical pump fed the engine. In case of pump failure, an emergency pump powered by a small propeller extended into the airstream could be used.

Wooden spars were employed in the Monoplane's cantilever wing; torsioned rigidity was maintained by a steel pyramid bracing system developed by Fairey especially for the aircraft.

Both Monoplanes carried this silver finish with standard RAF markings of the day, including wing roundels, fin flash and serial numbers.

LONG-RANGE MONOPLANE II

K1991 first flew on 30 June, 1931, in the hands of Fairey test pilot C. S. Staniland. It was delivered to the RAF on 29 July. Eighteen months elapsed before the flight to Cape Town was attempted.

Despite its position, the cockpit provided reasonable visibility thanks to the extra windows below the leading edge of the wing.

K1991 had a larger fuel capacity of 5228 litres (1,381 gallons) and a new fuel system that minimised fuel loss due to surging and evaporation.

The Monoplanes' Napier Lion IXA engine was a 12-cylinder, three-bank, 'broad-arrow' design. Also employed in the Fairey IIIF and Vickers Victoria, it proved troublesome in RAF aircraft serving in the Middle East.

The radiator for the Lion engine was situated below the fuselage in the air flow. It was one of the few externally fitted features of an otherwise aerodynamically clean design.

Long-range flights

Four major flights: Over a three-year period, the two Fairey Monoplanes made a number of long-distance flights. The most impressive of these was the one made in K1991 in February 1933.

J9479 24–25 April 1929
J9479 16 Dec 1929
K1991 27–28 Oct 1931
K1991 6–8 Feb 1933

RAF Cranwell
Tunis
Abu Sueir
Karachi
Bangalore
Walvis Bay
Cape Town

Flight to Cape Town, 1933: Since July 1931 the world non-stop distance record had been held by an US crew who had flown 8066 kilometres (5,000 miles) from New York to Istanbul in a Bellanca aircraft. Squadron Leader Gayford and Flight Lieutenant Nicholetts needed to fly at least as far as Zesfontain in Southwest Africa to beat this. Leaving RAF Cranwell on 6 February in K1991, Gayford and Nicholetts landed at Walvis Bay on 8 February after flying 8597 kilometres (5,330 miles). The triumphant crew flew on to Cape Town and then completed a 14,805-kilometre (9,180-mile) tour of Africa, before returning to Farnborough and an official reception on 2 May.

Distance record holders of the 1920 and '30s

BREGUET 19: French crews in breguet 19s increased the world record distance five separate times during the 1920s. By 1929 they had doubled the mark they themselves had set in 1925.

SAVOIA-MARCHETTI S.64: In July 1928, an Italian crew took an S.64 (a modified version of the S.55 with wheeled undercarriage) the 7188 kilometres (4,457 miles) from Italy to Brazil.

VICKERS WELLESLEY: Equipped with Wellesleys, the RAF Long-Range Development Flight flew 11,526 kilometres (7,146 miles) from Ismailia, Egypt to Darwin, Australia in November 1938.

FAIREY

DELTA 2

● High-speed research aircraft ● Delta wing ● Record breaker

Iain Wyllie

The Fairey Delta 2 was one of many record-breaking aircraft to emerge in the rapidly developing post-war aviation scene. It was Britain's first supersonic delta, and the first aircraft with a nose that could be dropped to improve visibility at low speed, a feature later adopted by the Concorde. Two Delta 2s began a programme of research flights from 1954, generating an immense amount of data for future military and civil aircraft.

▲ The Delta 2 was an aircraft ahead of its time. It flew at almost twice the speed of contemporary fighters and showed the way for the designs of the following decade with its delta wing and supersonic speed.

PHOTO FILE

FAIREY DELTA 2

Supersonic ►
Unlike earlier supersonic record breakers, the Delta and BAC.221 experienced no control problems when going through Mach 1.

Lasting record ►
Britain's Fairey Delta 2 surpassed the previous speed record by a huge 499 km/h (310 m.p.h.). It was the biggest jump in speed for conventional aircraft ever recorded.

▲ Nose high
Like most deltas, the Delta 2's handling at low speed was not perfect. It had a notably high nose attitude on landing.

▼ Accident
An engine failure caused this crash, but the Delta 2 was repaired and soon flew again. The pilot, Peter Twiss, escaped injury.

▲ Pure delta
The lure of high airspeeds attracted designers to the delta wing shape.

FACTS AND FIGURES

➤ The Delta 2 was the first aircraft to attain supersonic flight at low altitude, flying at Mach 1.04 (1250 km/h) at 928 metres.

➤ On 28 October 1955 the Delta 2 made its first supersonic flight.

➤ The second Fairey Delta 2 flew for the first time on 15 February 1956.

➤ The Delta 2 was delayed because of the priority enjoyed by the Fairey Gannet, a naval anti-submarine aircraft.

➤ The first Delta 2 was rebuilt as the BAC 221 with a Concorde wing shape.

➤ Concorde owed much of its wing design to the Delta 2.

PROFILE

Britain's last record breaker

Although it never became a long-range interceptor, as was contemplated after it flew, the Delta 2 was a great success in achieving its original purpose – investigating control and other problems experienced when breaking the 'sound barrier'. The Delta 2 also gave the world advanced features, including its famous hinged nose, a tailless layout, ultra-thin wing, and fully powered flight controls.

This fine research aircraft was almost lost; on its 14th flight in 1954, pilot Peter Twiss had an engine and hydraulic failure and made a masterly dead-stick landing at 426 km/h (265 m.p.h.) with only the nosewheel extended.

Other flights were successful, and paved the way for generations of supersonic aircraft to follow. On 10 March 1956 the Delta 2 captured the world air speed record for Britain, becoming the first conventional take-off aircraft to fly faster than 1000 miles per hour (1610 km/h), flying at Mach 1.731.

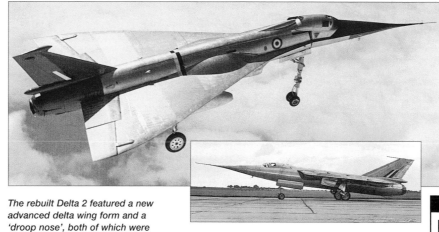

The rebuilt Delta 2 featured a new advanced delta wing form and a 'droop nose', both of which were to reappear when the Anglo-French Concorde made its maiden flight a decade later.

The Delta 2 was the last fixed-wing type to be built by Fairey. It was also the last British aeroplane to achieve an absolute world airspeed record.

Delta 2

- **Type:** single-seat supersonic research aircraft
- **Powerplant:** one 44.48-kN (10,000 lb.) Rolls-Royce RA.28 Avon 200 turbojet
- **Maximum speed:** over 2092 km/h (1,300 m.p.h.) at 11580 m (38,000 ft.)
- **Range:** 1335 km (829 mi.)
- **Service ceiling:** 14640 m (48,000 ft.)
- **Weights:** empty 4990 kg (11,000 lb.); loaded 6298 kg (13,884 lb.)
- **Dimensions:**
  span 8,18 m (26 ft. 10 in.)
  length 15,74 m (51 ft. 7 in.)
  height 3,35 m (11 ft.)
  wing area 33.44 m² (360 sq.ft.)

ACTION DATA

MAXIMUM SPEED

The Fairey Delta 2 comfortably exeeded the maximum speed of the original Bell X-1, although later versions of the American rocket were faster. The Dessault Mirage first flew in the late 1950s, and was one of the first production fighters capable of exceeding Mach 2.

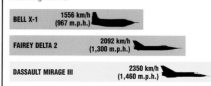

BELL X-1	1556 km/h (967 m.p.h.)
FAIREY DELTA 2	2092 km/h (1,300 m.p.h.)
DASSAULT MIRAGE III	2350 km/h (1,460 m.p.h.)

DELTA 2

WG 774, the first of two Delta 2 aircraft, broke the world airspeed record on 10 March 1956, with Lieutenant Commander Peter Twiss at the controls. The Delta 2 reached 1822 km/h (1,132 m.p.h.) on this occasion, flying at 11580 metres (38,000 ft.).

Small fences were fitted to the upper surface of the wing to control spanwise airflow during transonic flight. All flying controls were hydraulic, with no manual reversion.

The delta wing had probably the lowest thickness-to-chord ratio that had ever been seen up to that time. The fuel tanks were contained within the wings.

The Rolls-Royce Avon turbojet was also used in the Lightning fighter, and in non-afterburning form it powered the Caravelle airliner and the Canberra bomber.

In order to reduce glare for the pilot, the area in front of the cockpit was painted matt black.

The cockpit was pressurised and air-conditioned and fitted with a Martin Baker ejection seat. It was as small as possible to reduce frontal area.

To give the pilot a better view on landing, the nose and cockpit area could be 'drooped' by 10° using hydraulic power.

Wing-mounted air inlets were designed to be the minimum size for supersonic flight, but proved able to sustain flight at higher than envisaged speeds.

The tailpipe was a variable 'eyelid' type. The engine was a very tight fit inside the fuselage, with hardly any clearance between it and the aircraft's skin.

SERVICE CEILING

The X-1 used its rocket power to fly to record heights – although it had a flying start, since it was launched from the bomb-bay of a modified Boeing B-29 bomber flighing at around 10000 m (33,000 ft.). The Fairey's delta wing gave it a high-altitude performance at least as good as contemporary fighters, and the Mirage III used a similar wing, making it one of the highest flying warplanes of its time.

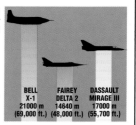

BELL X-1 21000 m (69,000 ft.)	FAIREY DELTA 2 14640 m (48,000 ft.)	DASSAULT MIRAGE III 17000 m (55,700 ft.)

RANGE

The X-1 only carried fuel for about 150 seconds of thrust, so it was never a practical long-distance aircraft. The Delta 2 had a reasonable reange by the standards of previous jets, and many thought that it formed the basis of quite a good fighter, which would probably have had Mirage-like performance.

FAIREY DELTA 2 1335 km (830 mi.)

DASSAULT MIRAGE III 2400 km (1,491 mi.)

BELL X-1 65 km (40 mi.)

Beyond the sound barrier

■ **BELL X-1:** Dropped from a B-29 bomber and flown by Chuck Yeager on 14 October 1947, the rocket-powered X-1 was the first aircraft to exceed the speed of sound.

■ **DOUGLAS SKYROCKET:** The combination jet- and rocket-powered Skyrocket was the first conventional take-off aircraft to break the sound barrier, a year after the X-1.

■ **MIKOYAN-GUREVICH MIG-19:** The world's first production supersonic fighter, the prototype MiG-19 first flew late in 1952 and exceeded Mach 1 in level flight early in 1953.

■ **NORD GERFAUT:** This was France's first supersonic aircraft, and the first pure jet to exceed Mach 1 in level flight without boost, achieving the feat on 3 August 1954.

■ **ENGLISH ELECTRIC P.1:** Britain's first supersonic aircraft broke the sound barrier on its maiden flight, one day after the Gerfaut. It was developed into the highly successful Lightning.

95

FAIREY
ROTODYNE

● 'Compound' helicopter/fixed wing ● Heli-liner and cargo-lifter

I t has always been a dream – an airliner able to leap into the sky from the middle of the big city, traverse great distances and carry passengers direct to their destination. Fairey, Britain's Ministry of Supply and British European Airways became three-way partners in 1948 in pursuing this vision. The ambitious Rotodyne compound helicopter, or convertiplane, could have succeeded if boardroom politics by its manufacturer had not prevented it from entering production.

▲ Nothing before or since has been built like the Rotodyne. Basically an airliner with rotors and wings, it was a technical success which avoided many of the problems of today's 'tilt rotor' designs.

FAIREY ROTODYNE

▲ Casualty evacuation
A 1960 mock-up made for exercise 'White Swan' demonstrated that the Rotodyne could have made a highly effective flying ambulance.

▲ Freight loader
The Rotodyne could carry loads far beyond the capacity of most helicopters of the late 1950s.

Distinctive profile ▶
Like the huge Soviet Mil Mi-6, the Rotodyne featured wings and rotors, but no other aircraft featured twin turboprops as well.

Building a beast ▶
Because of the huge size of the Rotodyne, some very unusual construction techniques were required by Fairey. Only one example of this unique machine was ever completed despite its success.

▲ Heavy lifter
Thanks to its powered rotor, the Rotodyne could hover even with a girder slung underneath it.

FACTS AND FIGURES

➤ The Gyrodyne tested the concepts used on the Rotodyne and took a 200-km/h (124 m.p.h.) speed record in June 1948.

➤ In April 1958 the Rotodyne made its first transition to level flight.

➤ The production Rotodyne would have used Rolls-Royce Tyne engines.

➤ On 5 January 1959, the Rotodyne set a speed record in the convertiplane class by flying at 307.2 km/h (190 m.p.h.).

➤ Okanagan Helicopters and Japan Air Lines were interested in Rotodynes.

➤ British and American forces studied a possible military Rotodyne.

The ultimate helicopter

The Fairey Rotodyne was a bold attempt to build and sell a practical vertical take-off airliner. When it first flew on 6 November 1957, the Rotodyne was breathtaking – a new concept in aviation which could take off and land like a helicopter, but fly with almost the same performance as a conventional aircraft.

The Rotodyne's large, four-blade rotor for vertical flight was driven by tip jets which received compressed air from the two

Eland turbine engines. These also drove propellers for horizontal flight.

The Rotodyne had the potential to transform city-to-city travel. Kaman wanted to manufacture it in the US; New York Airways pledged to purchase five aircraft – then backed out. When Fairey merged with Westland in 1960 and numerous corporate changes took place quickly, the once-promising Rotodyne was suddenly deemed no longer

A huge chance was missed when the Rotodyne was cancelled. The potential for heavylift helicopters was shown by the subsequent success of the Boeing Chinook.

worth the investment it required.

Though the aircraft flew well and its technical problems could have been solved, the Rotodyne could not defeat Westland's cost accountants, and the project was cancelled in February 1962.

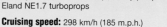

The prototype Rotodyne could carry two crew and 40 passengers, but production machines would have seated as many as 70 in a one-class configuration.

Because the main rotor was located above the centre of gravity, unlike a normal helicopter, the main cabin could be fully filled with cargo.

The blade tip jets were known as Fairey High Pressure Combustion Chambers.

Rotodyne 'Y' prototype

Type: experimental compound helicopter

Powerplant: two 2088-kW (2,800 hp.) Napier Eland NE1.7 turboprops

Cruising speed: 298 km/h (185 m.p.h.)

Service ceiling: 4000 m (1,219 ft.) estimated

Range: 725 km (450 mi.)

Weights: empty (estimated) 10000 kg (22,000-lb.); loaded 15000 kg (33,000-lb.)

Accommodation: production Rotodyne Z would have had two pilots, two flight attendants and between 54 and 70 passengers

Dimensions:
span	14.17 m	(46 ft. 4 in.)
rotor diameter	27.43 m	(90 ft.)
length	17.88 m	(58 ft. 7 in.)
height	6.76 m	(22 ft. 1in.)
rotor area	591.00 m²	(6,359 ft.)

ROTODYNE

XE 521 was the only Fairey Rotodyne ever built. Flying between 1957 and 1960, it proved the potential of the convertiplane, but the aircraft was too costly to put into production.

The cockpit was fitted with fairly limited equipment, but gave the pilots a superb view. The controls included a cyclic and collective pitch lever, as in a conventional helicopter.

The Napier Eland engines drove large four-metre Rotol propellers. Production Rotodynes were to have had the more powerful and reliable Rolls-Royce Tyne engine. A separate compressor generated high-pressure air which drove jets at the rotor tips.

The stubby wings provided lift in forward flight. They were equipped with trim tabs but no ailerons, roll control being effected through the rotor head.

FAIREY ROTODYNE

XE 521

The Rotodyne's great weight required twin nosewheels to be fitted.

Fixed main gear was chosen in the prototype because of possible resonance problems.

The tail structure was similar to a conventional aeroplane, with fins, tabbed elevators, rudders and tailplane.

ACTION DATA

MAXIMUM SPEED

Although the Rotodyne was faster than any helicopter of the late 1950s, its rotary wing was less efficient than a conventional wing. The X-18's wing and engines tilted forward for normal flight, while the Dornier Do 31 was powered by two Rolls-Royce Pegasus turbojets, each delivering 7 tonnes of thrust.

ROTODYNE	307 km/h (190 m.p.h.)
X-18	400 km/h (250 m.p.h.)
Do 31	640 km/h (397 m.p.h.)

RANGE

The Rotodyne's range made it suitable for commuter airline operations, particularly with its ability to operate out of city centre heliports. The two experimental aircraft programmes had not addressed the problems of range before they were cancelled.

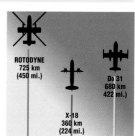

ROTODYNE 725 km (450 mi.)

Do 31 680 km (422 mi.)

X-18 360 km (224 mi.)

PAYLOAD

ROTODYNE	X-18	Do 31
40 passengers or 4800 kg (10,560-lb.)	capable of c. 2500 kg (5,500-lb.) lift	34 troops or 5000 kg (11,000-lb.)

The production Rotodyne would have had the passenger capacity of a medium-sized airliner, and its rear loading doors would have given it a significant cargo handling ability. The Dornier could have carried a similar payload far faster, but at much greater cost and, with its eight lift engines and two thrust engines, with many more parts to cause problems.

Vertical take-off load-lifters

■ **HELICOPTERS: (Mi-6)** The only practical vertical take-off lifters have been outsize conventional helicopters such as the giant Mil Mi-6 and Mi-26.

■ **COMPOUND HELICOPTERS: (Fairey Gyrodyne)** Combining a rotor with wings and engines for forward flight increases flying efficiency.

■ **CONVERTIPLANES: (Curtiss-Wright X-19)** These tilt the wing and engines through 90° for lift and forward flight.

■ **TILTING DUCTED FANS: (Bell X-22A)** This is a special variant of the convertiplane, with the propellers inside cowlings.

■ **LIFT AND THRUST: (Dornier Do 31)** Separate lift and thrust engines are the simplest solution, but they are bulky and add complexity.

GLOSTER
METEOR

● RAF's first jet fighter ● Flying bomb interceptor ● Single squadron

Even before Britain's first jet aircraft, the E.28/39, proved the practicality of this radical power source, Gloster was planning a new fighter to use the jet engine. After convincing the Air Ministry to draw up a specification (F.9/40) around their design, Gloster built a number of prototypes and by mid-1944 had equipped the first RAF jet unit, No. 616 Squadron. The intention was that the new jet would be pitted against Germany's jet fighter, the Me 262.

Entering service in 1944, the Meteor scored most of its victories against the high-speed V-1 flying bombs that plagued the British Isles towards the end of the war.

GLOSTER METEOR

▲ Meteor F.Mk 1s in colour
Contemporary colour images of wartime Meteors are rare. This photograph was taken in June 1944, at Farnborough, prior to a flight to Manston.

▲ No. 616 re-equips
No. 616 Squadron, RAF, was flying Spitfire Mk VIIs when it was announced that the unit was to become the RAF's first jet squadron. Here, Mk 1s and Mk 3s can be seen at RAF Manston.

▲ Short service life
Issued to No. 616 Squadron in July 1944, this Meteor F.Mk 1 was written off one month later after suffering a forced landing.

▼ Clear-view canopy
Unlike the F.9/40, the Meteor had a clear-view canopy to allow the pilot to see the rear of his aircraft.

▲ Three different engines
Of the three engine types fitted to F.9/40s, the Rover W.2B and Halford H.1 were centrifugal flow designs, while the Metropolitan-Vickers F.2 had an axial-flow compressor. One aircraft flew with the Metro-Vickers engines installed, but soon crashed.

FACTS AND FIGURES

➤ Among the other names suggested for the Meteor were Ace, Reaper, Scourge, Terrific, Thunderbolt and Wildfire.

➤ F.Mk 1s took part in trials to give USAAF crews experience of jet fighter tactics.

➤ When first deployed in Europe, Meteors were forbidden from flying over Germany.

➤ F.9/40 prototype, DG202/G, was later used for deck handling trials aboard HMS *Pretoria Castle*.

➤ The Halford H.1 engine was developed as the Goblin for the Vampire jet fighter.

➤ DG202, the first F.9/40, is displayed at the Aerospace Museum, Cosford.

PROFILE

RAF jet pioneer at war

Below: A Meteor F.Mk 3 is seen here just prior to touch-down. The Meteor Mk 3 benefitted from improved Rolls-Royce Derwent engines.

Above: EE214/G was the fifth F.Mk 1 and was used to test a ventral fuel tank. It was scrapped in 1949.

As the first jet engines produced little thrust, Gloster was forced to design a twin-engined aircraft. As this allowed the installation of different engine types with relative ease, it was decided to test three different engines in the F.9/40 prototypes, eight of which were built.

Delays with the Rover W.2B engine (based on Frank Whittle's engine for the E.28/39 aircraft) resulted in prototype DG206/G, powered by two Halford H.1s, taking to the air first on 5 March 1943. As the other prototypes

were flown, testing revealed a lack of directional stability, though these teething problems were corrected by modifications to the aircraft's tail.

On 12 January 1944, the Meteor F.Mk 1 made its first flight. This was effectively an F.9/40 powered by Rolls-Royce W.2B/23C Welland engines (Rolls having taken over development of the W.2B from Rover) and fitted with four 20-mm (0.79-in.) nose-mounted cannon.

Twelve F.Mk 1s were handed to No. 616 Squadron in July 1944 and the following month

Flying Officer Dean scored the RAF's first jet 'kill', when he downed a V-1 flying bomb.

In December, No. 616 re-equipped with the improved F.Mk 3. In 1945 the unit moved to Holland to make armed reconnaissance flights over Germany, but no Messerschmitt Me 262s were ever encountered.

Meteor F.Mk 1

Type: single-seat day fighter

Powerplant: two 7.56-kN (17,000-lb.-thrust) Rolls-Royce W.2B/23C Welland Series 1 turbojets

Maximum speed: 675 km/h (419 m.p.h.) at 3048 m (10,000 ft.)

Service ceiling: 12,192 m (40,000 ft.)

Weights: empty 3737 kg (8,221 lb.); loaded 6258 kg (13,768 lb.)

Fuel capacity: 1363 litres (360 gal.)

Armament: four Hispano 20-mm (0.79-in.) cannon in the nose

Dimensions:	span	13.10 m (42 ft. 11 in.)
	length	12.50 m (41 ft.)
	height	3.90 m (12 ft. 9 in.)
	wing area	34.70 m² (373 sq. ft.)

F.9/40

DG205/G was the fourth F.9/40 prototype and the second to fly, on 12 June 1943. It was therefore the first example to fly with W.2 engines fitted, but had only a short life, being written off in April 1944.

Among the improvements introduced in the Meteor F.Mk 3 were a sliding cockpit canopy, increased fuel capacity, new Derwent I engines, slotted air brakes and a strengthened airframe.

Like many of the Meteor variants that followed it, the F.9/40 was an all-metal, stressed-skin design. The fuselage was constructed in three sections: the front fuselage with cockpit and armament; the centre-section with the fuel tank, main landing gear, engines and air brakes; and the rear fuselage and lower fin.

To correct the directional stability problems exhibited by the F.9/40, an enlarged fin and rudder, test flown on DG 208/G, were fitted, along with flat-sided rudders and an 'acorn' fairing at the intersection of the fin and tailplane.

Though not fitted to the F.9/40 prototypes, four Hispano 20-mm (0.79-in.) cannon were installed in the F.Mk 1 and F.Mk 3 service variants. These were prone to jamming in early production aircraft.

DG205/G was powered by W.2 engines derived from Frank Whittle's original design for the E.28/39 pioneer jet. Five of the eight F.9/40s were so-equipped; two others had Halford H.1s, the eighth having Metro-Vickers F.2s.

Standard Fighter Command day-fighter camouflage was applied to the upper surfaces of the F.9/40s, with prototype yellow on the undersides to aid recognition. The 'P' marking in a yellow circle indicated a prototype aircraft.

The aircraft had a 'G' suffix added to its serial number to indicate that it was to have an armed guard at all times when on the ground. This was a reflection of the secret nature of jet-powered aircraft at the time of their appearance.

ACTION DATA

MAXIMUM SPEED

With its Derwent engines, the Meteor F.Mk 3 was able to exceed the top speed of the RAF's fastest piston-engined fighter, the Hawker Tempest Mk V (and tropicalised Mk VI). The Luftwaffe's Messerschmitt Me 262 was faster than both aircraft, but suffered serious engine reliability problems.

METEOR F.Mk 3	793 km/h (492 m.p.h.)
TEMPEST Mk V	
Me 262A-1a SCHWALBE	869 km/h (539 m.p.h.)

OPERATIONAL RANGE

An area in which the Meteor very comfortably out-performed the Me 262 was its range. It was able to fly almost as far as the Tempest Mk V, nearly three times the German jet's range. Later Meteors carried ventral fuel tanks to increase range even further.

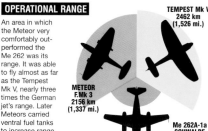

TEMPEST Mk V 2462 km (1,526 mi.)

METEOR F.Mk 3 2156 km (1,337 mi.)

Me 262A-1a SCHWALBE 844 km (523 mi.)

MAXIMUM TAKE-OFF WEIGHT

Though heavier than the Hawker Tempest, the Gloster Meteor had a lower maximum take-off weight than the Messerschmitt Me 262. Unlike the other two types, the Meteor was also limited to gun armament and carried no air-to-surface weapons. The Luftwaffe was forced to use its Me 262s in the ground-attack role.

METEOR F.Mk III 6033 kg (13,272 lb.)

TEMPEST Mk V 5897 kg (12,973 lb.)

Me 262A-1a SCHWALBE 6400 kg (14,080 lb.)

Early Meteor variations

■ **METEOR F.Mk 3:** For service in Europe in the final weeks before VE-Day, No. 616 Squadron's Meteor F.Mk 3s wore this overall white paint scheme during a harsh winter.

■ **'TRENT METEOR':** EE227, the eighth Meteor F.Mk 1 completed 80 hours of trials fitted with two Rolls-Royce Trents – the world's first turboprop engines.

■ **'CAMERA NOSE' Mk 3:** During planning for the still-born photo-reconnaissance version of the post-war Meteor Mk 4, Gloster fitted Mk 3 EE338 with a nose-mounted camera.

■ **'HOOKED' F.Mk 3:** With EE387, EE337 was fitted with an arrester hook for deck-landing trials aboard HMS *Implacable*. Thirty-two highly successful landings were made in all.

GLOSTER

METEOR MK 8 (PRONE PILOT)

● Meteor fighter ● Extended nose ● Experimental jet

As part of an RAF research programme in the mid-1950s, the last Gloster Meteor F.Mk 8 was given an elongated nose housing a second cockpit. It was not a conventional cockpit, however. Instead, it required the pilot to assume a front-down prone position. Its objective was to assess the ability of pilots to fly the aircraft from such a cockpit, the sort planned for the projected Bristol Type 185 rocket-powered interceptor.

▲ As the speed of jet fighters increased, the search was on for a way of increasing the pilot's tolerance to high g forces. One method investigated was to have the pilot lie down.

GLOSTER METEOR MK 8

▼ Few changes
Little was changed from the Meteor fighter apart from the nose and the necessary installation of a larger rudder to compensate for the loss of stability caused by the nose modification.

▲ Lying down
The prone pilot was equipped with a couch and a full set of controls for the aircraft. They were hydraulically boosted so that he needed to make only minimum movements.

▼ Two cockpits
A feature of the Prone Pilot Meteor was the adoption of twin canopies. One was a conventional fighter type while the forward canopy was especially constructed for the aircraft.

▲ Extended length
The nose modification greatly increased the overall length of the Meteor.

▼ Pilots' report
Pilots found that the modified aircraft had similar handling qualities to the fighter variants of the Meteor, despite the huge nose extension.

FACTS AND FIGURES

➤ Armstrong Whitworth undertook the conversion of the Gloster Meteor F.Mk 8 (WK935) for the prone pilot programme.

➤ A larger Meteor Mk 12 rudder was fitted to the aircraft.

➤ A second pilot was always carried in the rear cockpit for safety reasons.

➤ The Meteor made its first flight on 10 February 1954 from Baginton, Warwickshire.

➤ Prone pilots complained that they became cold and numb during flights.

➤ In February 1977 the aircraft was donated to Cosford Aerospace Museum.

PROFILE

Lying down on the job

Although the Wright brothers had adopted the prone position for pilots of their early aircraft, they did not fly at the same sort of speeds as the Meteor. The need to intercept high-flying Soviet bombers meant novel solutions had to be investigated, however, and the converted Meteor fighter was one.

The prone position did reduce the effects of high-g manoeuvres. Increasing g tends to reduce the flow of blood to the brain, an effect that is reduced substantially if the pilot is lying down. Subsequent research has shown that a recline angle of at least 65° is needed to provide a worthwhile increase in g tolerance for pilots.

On the other hand, the limited degree of arm movement made the controls difficult to manipulate. The pilot rested on padded supports adjustable by jacks, but could only move his forearms, which meant the controls were hard to reach and there was little leverage to handle them.

The most serious drawback, though, was the lack of visibility for the pilot. Being unable to look anywhere but forward is simply not acceptable in a fighter mission, when scanning for hostile aircraft is the main priority.

Above: The Meteor (PP) was based on an F.Mk 8 airframe. This mark was in widespread RAF service during the 1950s.

Right: The sole example of the Prone Pilot Meteor is now preserved, having been used as an instructional airframe for engineers at RAF Colerne.

Meteor Mk 8

Type: single-seat day fighter

Powerplant: two 15.56-kN (3,500-lb.-thrust) Rolls-Royce Derwent Series 8 turbojet engines

Maximum speed: 962 km/h (596 m.p.h.) at 3048 m (12,000 ft.)

Endurance: 3 hr maximum

Initial climb rate: 2133 m per min (7,000 f.p.m.)

Range: 1931 km (1,200 mi.) with max fuel load

Service ceiling: 13106 m (43,000 ft.)

Weights: empty 4846 kg (10,661 lb.); maximum take-off 7121 kg (15,666 lb.)

Armament: four 20-mm Hispano cannon

Dimensions:
span	11.30 m	(37 ft. 1 in.)
length	13.50 m	(44 ft. 3 in.)
height	3.90 m	(12 ft. 9 in.)
wing area	32.50 m²	(350 sq. ft.)

METEOR F.MK 8 PRONE PILOT

Post-war aviation manufacturers produced a host of aircraft to test various concepts. One of the most unusual was the prone-pilot attempt to give fighter pilots a greater tolerance of high g manoeuvres.

Standard flight controls were retained in the rear cockpit, the only modification being a switch that let control of the aircraft be passed to the forward cockpit. Only the rear pilot was supplied with an ejection seat.

In its overall silver colour scheme the aircraft was easily distinguished from service machines during flight testing and at the various air bases from where flights were made.

A larger rudder from a Meteor NF.Mk 12 was installed to keep the aircraft stable.

A couch in the forward cockpit allowed the pilot to lie down and fly the Meteor.

The nose extension was unpressurised. Test pilots often complained about the limited movement available and the lack of heating.

WK935

Positioned on the rear fuselage was a tail bumper that protected the rear fuselage from damage, which was a particular problem during landings. Pilots had to be reminded of this before each test flight.

ACTION DATA

BRITISH EXPERIMENTS: One of the options examined for fast flying in the early post-war years was that of a prone position for the pilot. In September 1948 Reid & Sigrist proposed to test the theory on a specially developed aircraft. Flying for the first time on 13 June 1951, the Reid & Sigrist Bobsleigh (pictured below) proved that aircraft could be operated safely from the prone position. This provided enough information for the development of the Prone Pilot Meteor. Eventually, the Bobsleigh was sold to a civilian film company which used it for photographic work. After years of neglect the aircraft was later restored to airworthy condition.

FLYING WINGS: Northrop's Flying Wings broke all conventions when they were unveiled to the world. Incorporating numerous technological innovations, the 'wings' required an extremely thin cross-section. To accomplish this, the pilot was placed in a prone position at the front of the aircraft. Although not as successful as envisaged, the rocket-powered MX-324 (pictured below) proved to American designers that aircraft could be operated in this way. No other manufacturers adopted this method for their fighter designs, for a number of reasons. One was the overall advance in the design of fighter aircraft; another was persuading pilots to adopt this position when flying combat missions that would involve dogfights and bombing duties.

Testing times for Gloster

■ **METEOR T.Mk 7:** As a demonstration aircraft, *The Reaper*, as it was known, was used to test a number of innovations that were later incorporated into front-line service aircraft.

■ **METEOR U.Mk 16:** Still serving in the late 1990s, the Meteors of the Royal Aircraft Establishment are used as practice target aircraft for RAF fighter squadrons.

■ **METEOR NF.Mk 11:** The first true prototype of the night-fighter Meteors, the NF.11 allowed the RAF to undertake intercept missions in total darkness thanks to its advanced radar.

GOTHA

GO 229 (HORTEN HO IX)

- Jet-powered, flying-wing fighter-bomber ● Flown in 1945

One of the most remarkable of Germany's many advanced aircraft designs of the late 1930s and '40s, the Gotha Go 229 was the culmination of more than 10 years of research by Reimar and Walter Horten. Their Ho I sailplane of 1931 was the first of a dozen designs exploring the flying-wing concept; some were powered aircraft. Their jet-powered Ho IX, which Gotha was to mass produce as the Go 229, was intended for combat.

▲ Ho IX V2 was the world's first jet-powered, flying-wing aircraft. Parallel research by Northrop in the U.S. produced a rocket-powered flying wing, which flew in 1944.

GOTHA GO 229 (HORTEN HO IX)

▲ Captured by the Allies
Ho IX V3 was nearly complete when U.S. troops arrived at Gotha's Friedrichsroda plant. Notice the sturdy construction of the undercarriage.

▲ Junkers turbojets
Ho IX V2's Junkers engines exhausted over the wing. Metal skins protected the wing's surface.

▲ Ho IX V1 glider
There was no official recognition of the Ho IX programme until after Ho IX V1 had flown. The RLM soon ordered powered trials to begin.

◄ Ho IIIB, classic flying wing
The Horten brothers designed a number of flying wing gliders during the 1930s. The Ho IIIB was a classic example.

Ho IX V1 plan view ▶
This view from above shows the 32° leading edge sweep of the Ho IX V1.

FACTS AND FIGURES

- ➤ Among other Horten flying-wing proposals was the Ho VIII, a transport with a 262-foot span and six engines.

- ➤ The elimination of parasitic drag was the primary aim of flying-wing research.

- ➤ Gothaer Waggonfabrik was founded in 1898 as a builder of railway locomotives.

- ➤ The Horten brothers were attached to the Luftwaffe's Sonderkommando (Special Detachment) 9 during World War II.

- ➤ Gotha was one of the few manufacturers that built aircraft for World War I and II.

- ➤ Postwar, Reimar Horten designed an aircraft for production in Argentina.

PROFILE

Luftwaffe's fighting flying wing

Despite intelligence reports that Northrop was conducting similar research in the U.S., official interest in the Horten flying wings was fading in 1943. An order for 20 Ho VIIs, officially two-seat research and communications aircraft (which were in fact trainers for the Hortens' projected Ho IX fighter) had been cancelled after just two had been completed.

Undaunted, the Hortens continued unauthorized work on their fighter, constructing Ho IX V1 as a glider to test the aircraft's

flight characteristics. When the RLM (Air Ministry) became aware of the Hortens' work in early 1944, the brothers' reputation was enough to gain official sanction from the Luftwaffe commander Reichsmarschall Göring. Successful gliding trials with Ho IX V1 led to the construction of a second aircraft, V2, with two Junkers turbojets installed. The RLM ordered seven more prototypes and 20 preproduction aircraft in the summer of 1944.

V2 flew in January 1945 and in March reached 798 km/h (496

Above: It is not known whether the Ho IX V1 was ever intended to carry engines; it was completed as a glider and flew in 1944.

m.p.h.) in level flight. It suffered engine failure and crashed shortly afterward. Meanwhile, Gotha had begun construction of the first Go 229, V3. This aircraft was nearing completion at Gotha's Friedrichsroda plant when, in May, it was overrun by troops from the U.S. Third Army.

Above: Horten Ho IX V2, the second example and the first with engines, is seen at Oranienburg near Berlin for test flying. It was destroyed in a landing accident in March 1944, after reaching a speed of 798 km/h (496 m.p.h.).

Go 229A-0

Type: Single-seat, jet-powered, flying-wing fighter-bomber

Powerplant: Two 8.73 kN (1,965-lb.-thrust) Junkers 004B-1, -2 or -3 axial-flow turbojet engines

Maximum speed: 962 km/h (598 m.p.h.) at normal loaded weight; 974 km/h (605 m.p.h.) at 11887 m (39,000 ft.)

Range: 1896 km (1,178 mi.) with max internal fuel at 631 km/h (392 m.p.h.) average speed

Maximum ceiling: 16,000 m (52,500 ft)

Weights: Empty equipped 4590 kg (10,120 lb.); normal loaded 7484 kg (16,500 lb.); max takeoff 8981 kg (19,800 lb.)

Weapons: Four 30-mm MK103 or MK108 cannon; plus two 1000-kg (2,200-lb.) bombs

Dimensions:
Span	16,76m (54 ft. 11in.)
Length	7,5 m (24 ft. 6 in.)
Height	2,7 m (9 ft. 2 in.)
Wing area	52,49 m² (565 sq. ft.)

The pilot of the Ho IX/Go 229 sat in a conventional cockpit with a spring-operated ejection seat. The control column could be raised vertically to increase leverage at high speeds.

Originally intended to have BMW 003 turbojets, Ho IX V2 had two of the more reliable Junkers 004s installed. They were fed by intakes in the leading edge of the wing and exhausted over the top side of the wing.

Go 229 V1 (Ho IX V3)

Had the first Go 229 (Ho IX V3) been completed and flown, it would have looked, finished in standard camouflage and national markings.

ACTION DATA

SPEED

Had it entered service, the Go 229A-0 would have had a greater top speed than the rocket-powered Messerschmitt Me 163 Komet and the Heinkel He 162. The latter was a more basic aircraft than the Gotha.

Go 229A-0	977 km/h (598 m.p.h.)
Me 163B KOMET	965 km/h (595 m.p.h.)
He 162 SALAMANDER	890 km/h (553 m.p.h.)

RANGE

To be a viable fighter-bomber, the Go 229 would have required good range performance. The Gotha's range was much better than that of the Salamander and the short-ranged Komet interceptor. Long range is easily accomplished with flying-wing designs.

Go 229A-0 1900 km (1,178 mi.)

Me 163B KOMET 100 km (60 mi.)

He 162 SALAMANDER 620 km (384 mi.)

Four 30-mm cannon were mounted in the leading edge of the wing, outboard of the engine intakes. Hardpoints along the center section carried two 1000 kg (2,200-lb) bombs or two long-range fuel tanks. A night-fighter version, the Go 229B, was planned. It would have been a two-seater with radar antenna in front of the cockpit.

The Go 229 had a tricycle undercarriage. The large nose leg retracted rearward while the main gears retracted inward. A braking parachute was installed to assist deceleration on landing. Elevons and plain flaps on the trailing edge of the outer wing panels, and glide control spoiler flaps on the undersurface of the wing, provided lateral and logitudinal control.

Coventional welded steel tube construction was used in the center section of the aircraft. Apart from metal tips, the rest of the wing was wooden. The Go 229's outer wing sections each held five fuel tanks. The surface coating is said to be radar-absorbent.

Horten flying-wing family

1 Ho I: Development of the Ho I glider began in 1931. The aircraft had a 24° wing leading-edge sweep. The pilot flew the Ho I from a prone position.

2 Ho II: Dissatisfied, the Hortens burned the Ho I in 1934, and built the Ho II later that year. Again they used wood and fabric construction. Four gliders were built, followed by a powered version with a 60 kW (80-hp.) engine.

3 Ho III: In 1938, the Hortens built the Ho III, with official backing. Essentially an enlarged Ho II, the Ho III was built in four different versions, the last of which had an engine. During gliding flight, its propeller blades were folded away.

4 Ho V: The first of the Horten flying wings designed from the outset as a powered aircraft, the Ho V of the late 1930s used bonded plastics in its construction and had two engines.

5 Ho IX: With everything they had learned during the 1930s, the Hortens designed the Ho IX using a mixture of steel and wooden construction. It had jet engines and the top speed of nearly 800 km/h (500 m.p.h.).

GRUMMAN
X-29

● Forward-swept wing ● Ultra-manoeuvrable research plane

Grumman's X-29 looks like a strange apparition, but it is an 'X-plane' with a purpose. Germany's wartime Junkers Ju 287 bomber proved that a forward-swept wing (FSW) can improve performance at high speeds. But the FSW was largely ignored until structural problems associated with the concept could be solved by advanced composite materials, enabling the X-29 to test this wing shape and to bring a wealth of new knowledge to aviation.

▲ The advantage of a forward-swept wing is that the root of the wing stalls before the tip, which prevents aileron control loss and can also prevent spins occurring in certain flight parameters.

PHOTO FILE

GRUMMAN X-29

▼ Low and slow
The forward-swept wing gives very good handling characteristics at low airspeed and high angle of attack, making landings very simple. The undercarriage was from the F-16, but as the X-29 did not need a tactical 'rough field' capability it used small wheels and narrow tyres, retaining the anti-skid system and carbon brakes.

▲ Fun to fly
The X-29 proved a delight to fly, so much so that test pilot Chuck Sewell could not resist the temptation to roll the aircraft on one of its first flights, before it was cleared to do so.

Plastic plane ▼
It was not just the aerodynamics of the X-29 that were revolutionary. The aircraft had a very high percentage of carbon fibre and composites in its variable camber wings.

Nose strakes ▶
One of the features that became common in many later fighters was the small nose strakes just behind the pitot tube. These devices improved directional stability at high angles of attack.

◀ Spin free
The first X-29 was not equipped with a spin recovery parachute, as it was not expected to go into a spin. The second X-29 was given such a parachute.

FACTS AND FIGURES

➤ The wings of the X-29, made partly of graphite epoxy, were swept at more than 33° forward.

➤ The first X-29 was taken aloft by test pilot Chuck Sewell on 14 December 1984.

➤ The X-29 began a NASA test programme only four months after its first flight.

➤ The X-29 proved very reliable, and by August 1986 was flying research missions lasting more than three hours.

➤ The second X-29 was used in a high angle-of-attack research programme.

➤ By the time the first X-29 was retired in 1989, it had been flown 242 times.

PROFILE

Forward-swept flying

The benefits of forward-swept wings have been known since World War II, offering enhanced agility, virtually spin-proof handling, lower drag, better low-speed flight and lower stalling speeds.

But early efforts were defeated by aeroelasticity – the tendency of wings to twist under normal flight loads. Practical designs had to wait until the strength of available structural materials caught up with theory.

After years of work on FSW design, Grumman won a 1981 contract to build two X-29 research planes. The company slashed manufacturing costs by using parts from many aircraft:

F-5 fuselage and nosewheel, F/A-18 Hornet engine and F-16 main undercarriage.

The result was more than the sum of its parts. In several years of experiments, the X-29 demonstrated an ability to manoeuvre at angles of attack as high as 67°, and showed that the FSW configuration can result in large fuel savings.

Test pilots found the X-29 exciting to fly. With its wing shape and agility, it gave meaning to the motto on a sign at Edwards Air Force Base: 'Toward the Unknown'. Today the X-29 has been retired, but its contribution to aviation is very much alive.

Forward-swept wings have not yet arrived on front-line fighters, but canards, strakes and relaxed stability are now commonplace.

The data from the X-29 has been of great use to NASA, as the ceaseless quest for greater agility continues.

X-29A

Type: single-seat forward-swept-wing high-agility research aircraft

Powerplant: one 71.17-kN (15,965-lb.-thrust) General Electric F404-GE-400 turbofan

Maximum speed: Mach 1.87 or 1900 km/h at 10000 m (1,178 m.p.h. at 33,000 ft.)

Range: 560 km (347 mi.)

Service ceiling: 15300 m (50,000 ft.)

Weights: empty 6260 kg (13,772 lb.); maximum 8074 kg (17,763 lb.)

Dimensions:
span	8.29 m	(27 ft.)
length	16.44 m	(54 ft.)
height	4.26 m	(14 ft.)
wing area	188.80 m²	(2,031 sq.ft.)

The variable-incidence canards could be rotated as much as 60° around their axis.

The wing sub-structure is built of titanium and aluminium. The wing is extremely thin, and is fitted with leading- and trailing-edge flaps.

The rear fuselage strakes are a very unusual feature. Each strake has a flap on its trailing edge actuated by a single Moog servo actuator.

X-29A

Two Grumman X-29 aircraft were built, flying from 1984 to 1991. Both aircraft are now in storage at the Dryden Flight Research Facility of NASA in California.

The cockpit of the X-29 is surprisingly simple, with traditional dials and switches. Apart from the large amount of telemetry gear, the only advanced systems were a Litton altitude/heading reference system and the Martin-Baker ejection seat.

The forward fuselage was based on the Northrop F-5A, using parts taken from ex-Norwegian and USAF aircraft.

The small ram air inlet under the tail houses a heat exchanger unit.

The engine intakes were of simple rectangular design with splitter plates and fixed ramp intakes.

The composite materials of the wing were laid in carefully calculated patterns to avoid the aerodynamic twisting effect of the forward-swept wing.

The General Electric F-404 engine is a low-bypass ratio turbofan, also used in the F/A-18 Hornet.

THE HIGH FRONTIER

NASA IN ACTION

There can be few places in the world where the term NASA is not recognised as being synonymous with space flight. Indeed, after the Apollo moon programme and the ongoing Space Shuttle missions, many people have come to regard NASA as America's 'space agency'. But the initials actually stand for the National Aeronautics and Space Administration, and while the exploration of the cosmos is an important part of the agency's brief, so too is its work with aeronautics. Indeed, NASA is the world's leading aviation research organisation, which since the 1940s has blazed a trail in virtually every field of military, civil and commercial flight, designing and testing new concepts which push back the frontiers of aviation. Today's aeronautics programme is conducted at three principal research centres. Ames, in California, which also controls the NASA facility at the famous Edwards Air Force Base, is the primary flight test centre, but important work is also carried out at Langley in Virginia and at Lewis, near Cleveland, in Ohio.

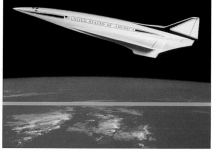

Making swept-wings work better

■ **JUNKERS PIONEER:** The Ju 287 was the first FSW jet, proving the many advantages of the concept. But 1940s engineering was never able to overcome the structural challenges.

■ **SUPERCRITICAL CRUSADER:** A Vought F-8 Crusader was fitted with a 'supercritical' laminar-flow wing, designed to reduce the turbulence between air flow and wing surface.

■ **TRANSONIC FLOW:** A Mach 2-capable F-111 bomber was fitted with supercritical strips on its wing to study laminar flow and drag reduction at the speed of sound and beyond.

■ **HINGELESS FLAPS:** The Mission Adaptive Wing has flexible leading and trailing edges, allowing it to adopt the optimum aerofoil profile for all speeds, greatly reducing drag.

■ **SLEW WING:** The Ames AD-1 has a rigid wing that is at right-angles for take-off but at speed is slewed to provide one forward and one aft wingtip. It proved surprisingly effective.

HANDLEY PAGE
H.P.75/88/115

● Radical designs ● British research projects ● New technology

▲ *Handley Page was at the forefront of research and new technology, but when the UK aerospace industry was rationalised it no longer remained an independent company.*

As a top manufacturer working at the cutting edge of technology, Britain's Handley Page produced a number of advanced research aircraft. Principal among these were three aircraft: the H.P.75 Manx for research into tailless aircraft, the H.P.88 which tested the crescent-shaped wing of the Victor bomber, and the H.P.115 which performed invaluable work for the Concorde project, exploring the slow-speed handling characteristics of delta-winged aircraft.

HANDLEY PAGE H.P.75/88/115

▼ Problematic Manx
Delays and technical problems were encountered throughout the H.P.75 programme, including the death of a technician who walked into one of the propellers.

◄ Perfect H.P.115
Unlike the H.P.75, the H.P.115 achieved all of its design goals and proved to be capable of far greater performance than had been predicted.

▼ Hybrid H.P.88
An odd mix of features taken from other designs distinguished the H.P.88 during its tragically short career.

Limited ▶ potential
Having displayed numerous handling and powerplant shortcomings, the Manx taught Handley Page more about the problems of tailless aircraft than about their practicality.

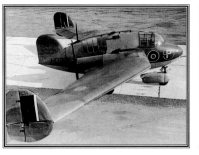

▲ Distinctly Victor
The wing of the Victor clearly owed much to that of the H.P.88.

FACTS AND FIGURES

➤ During the first flight of the H.P.75 on 25 June 1943, its cockpit canopy blew off at an altitude of 33 metres (108 ft.).

➤ In 1952 the Manx was burned as scrap after flying for just 16 hours 53 minutes.

➤ Although design of the H.P.88 was approved in 1947, it did not fly until 1951.

➤ By the time of its maiden flight, the H.P.88 consisted of a Victor-type wing, Attacker fuselage and Swift wingroots.

➤ The top speed of the H.P.115 was only limited by the low power of its engine.

➤ The H.P.115 was flown for the last time on 1 February 1974.

PROFILE

Handley Page – heralding new eras

Gustav Lachmann was a key figure in the history of Handley Page and served in a number of roles, including that of chief designer. During the late 1930s he became convinced that a successful aircraft could be built without a conventional tail unit, which would result in considerable savings in weight and structural complexity.

A period of protracted development resulted in the tailless H.P.75, an aircraft which inadvertently flew for the first

time in December 1942 and was christened Manx when revealed to the press in 1945. The project was unsuccessful and ended when the H.P.75's regular crew was killed in the prototype Hermes in late 1945.

In 1947 the company returned to testing unusual configurations with the H.P.88. This machine combined the fuselage of a Supermarine Attacker with a wing similar in design to that of the Victor 'V-Bomber'. The aircraft proved tricky to handle, but was cleared to progressively

higher Mach numbers until it broke up in the air in 1951, and its pilot was killed.

Experience gained with the flight control system of the Manx was useful in producing the H.P.115 in 1961. The aircraft proved to be extremely pleasant to fly and was flown well beyond its design envelope. The H.P.115 contributed greatly to the development of Concorde and survives in the Fleet Air Arm Museum at RNAS Yeovilton.

Above: The H.P.88 was due to appear at the 1951 Society of British Aircraft Constructors (SBAC) air show at Farnborough, but the aircraft broke up in the air on 26 August.

Left: Coloured smoke and woollen tufts attached to the airframe allowed aerodynamicists to monitor airflow over the H.P.115.

H.P.115

Type: research aircraft designed to test the handling of delta wings at low speed

Powerplant: one 8.45-kN (1,900-lb.-thrust) Bristol Siddeley BSV.9 turbojet engine

Maximum speed: 400 km/h (248 m.p.h.)

Endurance: 40 min

Weights: empty 1668 kg (3,667 lb.); maximum take-off 2300 kg (5070 lb.)

Accommodation: pilot only

Dimensions: span 6.10 m (20 ft.)
length 13.72 m (45 ft)
wing area 39.95 m² (430 sq. ft.)

H.P.115

Only one H.P.115 was completed and was initially flown by Squadron Leader J. M. Henderson, who had trained extensively in a simulator before the first flight. The aircraft was never painted.

Most of the cockpit nacelle was located beneath the leading edge of the delta wing. It accommodated a single pilot on an ejection seat which allowed escape at zero altitude but was never required since the H.P.115 programme was entirely successful and accident-free. Cockpit instrumentation was minimal and included no provision for lighting; battery power was required only for the glide-slip indicator.

A rectangular girder ran the length of the aircraft's centreline, forming the mid-rib of the delta wing. At its forward end it supported the cockpit, and to the rear there was a nacelle for the Viper turbojet.

Most of the H.P.115's structure was of aluminium alloy, except for the wing leading edges which were made from plywood. This allowed their removal for testing alternative configurations.

Large perforated airbrakes were mounted above and below each wing in a half-chord position. They were actuated by compressed air and functioned as infinitely variable split flaps. Three tanks, located inside the wing structure at its centreline, held 682 litres (180 US gallons) of fuel.

Since it was only required to investigate slow-speed handling, there was no requirement to fit the H.P.115 with a retractable undercarriage, which would have added extra weight and complexity to the design. Performance proved to be so good, however, that a more powerful engine and retractable landing gear may have allowed expansion of the programme.

ACTION DATA

POWER

In the pre- and early-war years, Britain produced a number of highly unusual aircraft, each of which tested radical new aerodynamic features. The H.P.75 had exactly the same power as the Miles M.39B Libellula, but had disappointing performance.

H.P.75 MANX	M.39B LIBELLULA	PTERODACTYL Mk V
208 kW (278 hp.)	208 kW (278 hp.)	459 kW (615 hp.)

MAXIMUM SPEED

Handley Page hoped for great improvements from the Manx, but it performed no better than aircraft with the same power produced 20 years earlier. The Westland Pterodactyl Mk V was the culmination of a series of experimental fighter designs.

H.P.75 MANX 235 km/h (146 m.p.h.)
M.39B LIBELLULA 264 km/h (164 m.p.h.)
PTERODACTYL Mk V 266 km/h (165 m.p.h.)

MAXIMUM TAKE-OFF WEIGHT

Although heavier than the Libellula, the Manx's take-off weight was disappointing and the aircraft had less development potential than the Miles machine. The Pterodactyl was much heavier and was the only one of the three aircraft to regularly fly with machine-gun armament. It was the most representative of a service type.

H.P.75 MANX 1814 kg (4,000 lb.)
M.39B LIBELLULA 1270 kg (2,800 lb.)
PTERODACTYL Mk V 2313 kg (5,100 lb.)

Handley Page prototypes

TYPE C7 HANDCROSS: First flown in 1924 as a bomber prototype, the Handcross was used for a number of trials programmes until 1928.

TYPE E HARROW II: Having failed as a torpedo-bomber prototype, the Type E flew trials with wing leading-edge slats.

H.P.43: Produced to satisfy an RAF requirement for a bomber-transport, the H.P.43 was never ordered into production.

H.P.47: Dr Lachmann was deeply involved in the design of the cantilever-winged H.P.47, which owed much to German technology.

HAWKER SIDDELEY

P.1127 KESTREL

● Vertical take-off research aircraft ● Ancestor of the Harrier

▲ The P.1127 was one of the most productive research projects of the post-war period. It was run on a very small budget, but with very few problems it opened up a whole new area of aviation.

Hawker Siddeley's P.1127 is one of history's great trailblazing aviation designs. Developed from the late 1950s and flown in the early 1960s, the Kestrel introduced thrust-vectoring, the first practical system for vertical take-off and landing. In the process it paved the way for the Harrier 'jump jet', still a unique combat aircraft after a quarter of a century of combat-tested military service.

HAWKER SIDDELEY P.1127 KESTREL

Blast-off ▶
The P.1127 showed its mettle in vertical take-offs from day one, despite the lack of power of the first series of Rolls-Royce Pegasus turbofans. These engines were much improved for later aircraft.

◀ Rubber lips
The intake design caused a lot of headaches for the Kestrel designers. To experiment with different configurations, an adjustable rubber boot was fitted around the intake.

Harrier shape ▶
The Kestrel evolved into the Harrier with relatively few changes in shape. The basic profile lasted until the AV-8B of the late 1980s.

▲ Sea trials
The Royal Navy took the Kestrel to sea for trials, which proved the concept for the later Sea Harrier.

NATO trials ▶
The Kestrel programme included weapon tests, including short take-offs with SNEB rocket pods.

FACTS AND FIGURES

➤ The P.1127 flew on 21 October 1960, and first transitioned to horizontal flight on 12 September 1961.

➤ The nine Kestrels were larger and flew better than the six original P.1127s.

➤ The Kestrel's success led the USA to abandon 'tail-sitter' VTOL experiments.

➤ The cancelled P.1154, designed using P.1127 data, would have been a Mach 2 VTOL fighter for the Royal Navy.

➤ The Kestrel was trouble-free in vertical flight, but needed wing modifications.

➤ A P.1127 can still be seen at the Royal Air Force Museum, Hendon.

PROFILE

Vertical take-off becomes a reality

The Harrier is one of world's most well-known aircraft, and the everyday miracle of vertical take-off and landing has become commonplace. But it took a brilliant designer, a magnificent engine and years of testing by the Hawker Siddeley Kestrel before the Harrier could make the leap from dream to reality.

Searching for a new approach to vertical flight aviation, the great Sir Sydney Camm chose the Kestrel's shape and engine. With four legs of hot air holding the

Kestrel aloft in 'vectored flight', the engine was inevitably named Pegasus after the mythological winged horse. From 1960, when the P.1127 took to the air, six prototypes showed that vertical flight was practical.

A second generation of nine P.1127 prototypes, the first to bear the Kestrel name, took this new concept to the limit. The RAF had formed a 'Tripartite' squadron in which the Kestrel explored new techniques at the hands of pilots from Britain, Germany and the US. Germany

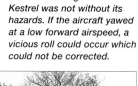
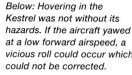

Below: Hovering in the Kestrel was not without its hazards. If the aircraft yawed at a low forward airspeed, a vicious roll could occur which could not be corrected.

Above: Although the P.1127 project was a success, it failed to convince many sceptics about the value of vertical take-off. Even so, the Kestrel paved the way for the Harrier.

dropped out of the programme, but the US Air Force and Marine Corps were fiercely interested and flew Kestrels designated XV-6A. The Tripartite squadron operated until late 1965, by which time the Harrier was well on its way to production.

P.1127 Kestrel

Type: single-seat research aircraft

Powerplant: one 48.94-kN (10,991-lb.-thrust) Rolls-Royce (Bristol Siddeley) B.E.53/3 Pegasus 2 vectored-thrust turbofan

Maximum speed: 1166 km/h (725 m.p.h.) at sea level

Range: 1125 km (699 mi.)

Service ceiling: 15480 m (16,929 ft.)

Weights: empty 4040 kg (8,899 lb.); loaded 7031 kg (15,487 lb.)

Armament: none, but larger 'Tripartite' Kestrels had provision for operational equipment

Dimensions:
span	7.43 m	(24 ft.)
length	12.55 m	(41 ft.)
height	3.32 m	(11 ft.)
wing area	17.37 m²	(187 sq.ft.)

ACTION DATA

TAIL-SITTERS

The first attempt to produce a winged aircraft that could take off and land vertically were the tail-sitters, like the XFY-1 Pogo pictured below. These were, as the name suggests, aircraft which pointed upwards and took off like helicopters, converting to forward flight once in the air. They required immense skill on the part of the pilot, however, and were never really practical propositions.

P.1127 KESTREL

Six first generation P.1127s were constructed, of which two were lost in non-fatal accidents. In 1963, nine military models known as P.1127 Kestrels were evaluated by an Anglo/American/German 'Tripartite' squadron.

The P.1127 wing was redesigned for the Kestrels; it was a simple design with conventional ailerons and flaps. Harrier wings were to be modified, enlarged and improved many times over the next three decades.

The tailplane was extensively redesigned as the project progressed, with reduced sweepback and increased span.

To control the aircraft in pitch in the hover, the projecting tailboom contained a rear 'puffer jet'.

The cockpit was small but well laid out, and not cluttered with the mass of operational equipment fitted to the Harrier. The pilot sat in a Martin Baker ejection seat, which two pilots used for real in the P.1127 trials flights.

The Pegasus engine delivered thrust through four moving nozzles, the front pair delivering low-pressure air and the rear pair high-pressure air.

Wingtip outriggers were used to stabilise the Kestrel on landing, folding to the rear in flight. Despite the worries of the design team, the fragile-looking wheels proved to be quite durable.

LIFT AND THRUST

Dassault's Mirage III-V Balzac used separate engines for vertical lift and for thrust. Although the design worked technically it never led to an operational machine, since the extra engines took up space that could have carried fuel, avionics and weaponry.

Evolving operational techniques

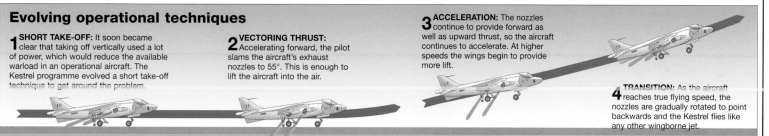

1 SHORT TAKE-OFF: It soon became clear that taking off vertically used a lot of power, which would reduce the available warload in an operational aircraft. The Kestrel programme evolved a short take-off technique to get around the problem.

2 VECTORING THRUST: Accelerating forward, the pilot slams the aircraft's exhaust nozzles to 55°. This is enough to lift the aircraft into the air.

3 ACCELERATION: The nozzles continue to provide forward as well as upward thrust, so the aircraft continues to accelerate. At higher speeds the wings begin to provide more lift.

4 TRANSITION: As the aircraft reaches true flying speed, the nozzles are gradually rotated to point backwards and the Kestrel flies like any other wingborne jet.

HEINKEL

HE 162 SALAMANDER

● Wooden construction ● Single-seat 'Volksjäger'

▲ Novice pilots, with training only on gliders, were to have flown the He 162, and would have completed their training in combat. The Salamander was an interesting concept, but it was doomed to fail.

Heinkel rushed the design of the He 162 Salamander in an attempt to develop a mass-produced fighter that would stem the tide of Allied bombers over the Reich. One of the first operational jet aircraft, the He 162 was a sound concept but suffered from structural and aerodynamic problems as a result of its hasty introduction. This was a tricky and difficult aircraft to fly, and few saw any combat action before the end of hostilities.

PHOTO FILE

HEINKEL HE 162 SALAMANDER

▲ **Underground production**
US units advancing on Magdeburg found a massive production facility for the He 162 in abandoned salt mines. Several of the jets were near completion.

▲ **Post-war testing**
Large numbers of former Luftwaffe aircraft, including He 162s, were captured by the Allies and tested in Britain and the United States.

▼ **Narrow track**
A very narrow undercarriage, combined with the heavy, dorsally mounted engine, would have made ground handling tricky.

▲ **Perfectly preserved**
Several He 162s survive in museums. This aircraft is finished in the colours of II/Jagdgeschwader 1, which became part of Einsatz-Gruppe I/JG 1.

Tail prop ▶
Parked aircraft, especially those with their guns removed, tended to fall back onto their tails, and therefore a tail prop was used to prevent damage.

FACTS AND FIGURES

➤ The prototype He 162 made its first flight on 6 December 1944 but was lost in a mishap four days later.

➤ A Gruppe equipped with 50 He 162 fighters was formed at Leck on 4 May 1945.

➤ More than 270 He 162s were completed and 800 unfinished aircraft were captured.

➤ Heinkel's jet was one of the first aircraft to use an ejection seat for emergency escape by the pilot.

➤ Plans were in existence to build 5000 He 162s per month.

➤ Loss of the prototype in December 1944 was due to the break-up of the right wing.

PROFILE

Luftwaffe's last line of defence

Designed, developed and built in an extraordinarily short time, the Heinkel He 162 was first flown as the pressures of war closed in on Germany. The prototype was in the air just 38 days after detail drawings were issued to the factory.

An attractive and potentially useful fighter, the He 162 was plagued by problems resulting from its over-hasty development. This single-seat, single-engined warplane was supposed to be a

'people's fighter', devoid of frills, inexpensive to manufacture and easy to use. In fact it proved to be extremely difficult to fly. Wartime leaders had hoped that pilots with little or no experience could be recruited and trained quickly to fly the aircraft, but the He 162 could be fatally difficult, even in the hands of experienced fighter aces with hundreds of hours in the Messerschmitt Bf 109 or Focke-Wulf Fw 190. One pilot called the He 162 'totally unforgiving',

but spoke of the jet as a pleasure to fly in favourable circumstances.

The programme, and not the aircraft, was called the Salamander and designer Ernst Heinkel called the jet the 'Swallow'. The He 162 became operational but no reports of actual combat were ever confirmed.

Photographed during a high-speed pass, this He 162 underwent tests in Britain. One aircraft was destroyed in a fatal crash.

Mounting the BMW 003 engine above the fuselage made the aircraft unstable in pitch, which made it very difficult to fly.

A cartridge-actuated ejection seat provided an escape route for the pilot. Leaving the aircraft by the conventional means of bailing out with a parachute would have been impossible with the jet intake behind and above the cockpit.

He 162A-2

Type: single-seat jet fighter

Powerplant: one BMW 003E-1 axial-flow turbojet engine rated at 7.80 kN (1,755 lb. thrust) for take-off and 9.02 kN (2,030 lb. thrust) for maximum bursts of up to 30 seconds

Maximum speed: 890 km/h (490 m.p.h.) at sea level

Range: 620 km (384 mi.)

Service ceiling: 12,010 m (39,400 ft.)

Weights: empty 1663 kg (3,659 lb.); empty equipped 1758 kg (3,868 lb.); loaded 2805 kg (6,171 lb.)

Armament: two 20-mm (0.79-in.) MG 151 cannon in forward fuselage

Dimensions:
span 7.20 m (23 ft. 7 in.)
length 9.05 m (29 ft. 8 in.)
height 2.60 m (8 ft. 6 in.)
wing area 11.20 m² (121 sq. ft.)

HE 162A-2

This aircraft was captured by the British at Leck. It had previously served with 3. Staffel, Einsatz-Gruppe I/JG 1 and was the personal aircraft of the Staffelkapitän.

A one-piece canopy and windscreen glazing gave the pilot an exceptional view. The raised position of the cockpit glazing was similar to that of modern fighters.

An unusually narrow main undercarriage was fitted to the He 162. This resulted from there being no room for the structure in the wings, and therefore all systems had to be accommodated in the narrow, cramped fuselage.

Oberleutnant Erich Demuth had 16 kill markings on the tail of his He 162, all gained in other types.

A single MG 151 cannon was mounted in a recess on either side of the lower forward fuselage. By good fortune, Heinkel had chosen a configuration which avoided engine gun-gas ingestion problems.

Aerodynamic problems led to the adoption of turned down wingtips. The small wings were mostly of wood, with light alloy flaps. Much of the wooden wing, tail and undercarriage door structure was of adhesively bonded wood and after an undercarriage door had broken away in flight, it was discovered that acid in the adhesive was corroding the wood.

COMBAT DATA

THRUST

Both the Meteor and Me 262 employed twin engines to overcome the low thrust available from early turbojets. Fitted with only one engine the He 162 was a much simpler, lighter design.

He 162A-2	METEOR F.Mk 1	Me 262A-1A
9.02 kN (2,030 lb. thrust)	15.1 kN (3,397 lb. thrust)	17.66 kN (3,973 lb. thrust)

MAXIMUM SPEED

Due to its streamlined fuselage and small size the He 162 was a fast aircraft, especially compared to Britain's first operational jet fighter, the Gloster Meteor. The speed shown is for maximum engine power.

He 162A-2	890 km/h (521 m.p.h.)
METEOR F.Mk 1	668 km/h (414 m.p.h.)
Me 262A-1A	869 km/h (540 m.p.h.)

ARMAMENT

Early jets relied on their speed for surprise attacks, with armament limited by the need to save weight to maintain performance. The Me 262 was the most successful design and had powerful weapons.

He 162A-2	METEOR F.Mk 1	Me 262A-1A
2 x 20-mm (0.79-in.) cannon	4 x 20-mm (0.79-in.) cannon	4 x 30-mm (1.18-in.) cannon 12 x rockets

German jet developments

■ **ARADO Ar 234 BLITZ:** Ar 234s saw some operational service, mostly in the reconnaissance role, and proved to be immune to interception by Allied fighters. However, they suffered from short engine life and servicibility problems.

■ **GOTHA Go 229 (HORTEN Ho IX):** Gotha developed the radical Ho IX tailless glider as the Go 229 jet-powered fighter. Tests showed the aircraft had exceptional handling, but the war ended before production aircraft were completed.

■ **HEINKEL He 280:** Having lost out in the competition with the exceptional Me 262, examples of this single-seat, twin-jet interceptor were used as research aircraft and included a version with a V-tail.

■ **MESSERSCHMITT P.1101:** Although failing to fly before the end of the war, the P.1101 was a highly advanced aircraft which indicated Germany's lead in jet aircraft design. It was used by the US as the basis of the Bell X-5.

HUGHES

H-4 'SPRUCE GOOSE'

● Largest aircraft ● Wooden construction ● Strategic transport

For more than three decades the Hughes HFB-1 (H-4) Hercules was the biggest flying machine ever built. It was a towering achievement of entrepreneurial spirit and aviation pioneering, all the more remarkable because the behemoth was built without essential wartime materials. Popularly called the 'Spruce Goose' because of its wooden construction, Hughes' flying-boat was an incredible sight, which flew just once.

▲ Variously known as the HFB-1, H-4 or HK-1, the monster flying-boat designed by Howard Hughes was a giant in every way. Even the flight deck had more space than the passenger cabins of many airliners of the period.

PHOTO FILE

HUGHES H-4 'SPRUCE GOOSE'

◀ The monster rises
At the end of the taxi trials, all of the guests left the aircraft. Hughes then took the 'Goose' out into the harbour for its one and only flight.

▼ Launch day
'Spruce Goose' was launched from its 88.4-m (290-ft.) dry dock into Long Beach Harbor on 1 November 1947.

◀ Eight-engine power
Propelled by eight huge Pratt & Whitney 28-cylinder radial engines, Hughes' flying-boat had more than twice the power of a Boeing B-29 Superfortress heavy bomber.

▼ Gathering dust
After its one flight, the mighty flying-boat was left in storage for 35 years, gathering dust and attracting fascinated tourists.

◀ Taxi trials
The HK-1 moved under its own power for the first time on 2 November. Hughes undertook a taxi trial with 18 crew, five officials and nine invited guests aboard before flying the H-4 himself.

FACTS AND FIGURES

➤ Hughes wrecked a Sikorsky S-43 while experimenting with centre-of-gravity and power settings for the HK-1.

➤ 'Spruce Goose' was flown just once, over Los Angeles harbour on 2 November 1947.

➤ The HK-1 was built in the world's largest wooden building at Culver Field.

➤ The huge flying-boat was taxi-tested with its eight engines controlled by four throttles harnessed in pairs.

➤ Hughes planned a larger flying-boat, the HFB-2, which was never built.

➤ 'Spruce Goose' was transported by barge to its present owners in Oregon.

PROFILE

The 'Spruce Goose' flies

In 1944, when Howard Hughes unveiled plans for the HFB-1 (Hughes Flying Boat First Design) or HK-1 (Hughes-Kaiser First Design) Hercules flying-boat, no one believed he was serious. He intended to build a seaborne giant that could carry up to 750 troops, without using steel or aluminium except in the engines. The airframe would be manufactured of non-strategic wood products. At that time, the Allies still thought that a large-scale invasion of Japan would be needed to bring the Pacific War to an end, and the H-4 would have been much in demand as a flying troopship.

Everything about the HK-1 flying-boat was big. When it was built, it was the largest aircraft in the world. Today, the Ukrainian Antonov An-225 is larger, but the Hughes flying-boat still has a greater wing span.

Hughes and his experts saw the flying-boat as a great, globe-girdling craft which would change the way people and cargo were moved across vast distances.

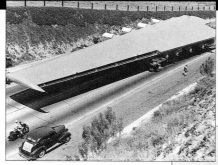

Left: The huge wingspan of the 'Spruce Goose' was as long as a soccer pitch. Street lighting had to be dismantled at great expense to allow the road transportation of such a huge aircraft for final assembly in Los Angeles.

In a sense, this is what was accomplished decades later by the Boeing 747 jetliner.

Unfortunately, the very promising Hughes flying-boat was flown only once. Though it was a true pioneer, its potential was never fulfilled despite the genius of its design.

Above: The flight of the 'Spruce Goose' attracted great media interest, and Los Angeles harbour was packed with a flotilla of small boats. Little did they know that they would be the only people to see this great beast fly.

H-4 'Spruce Goose'

Type: very large long-range flying-boat transport

Powerplant: eight 2240-kW (3,000-hp.) Pratt & Whitney R-4360-4A 28-cylinder four-row radial engines

Maximum speed: 377 km/h (175 m.p.h.) at 1525 m (5,000 ft.)

Range: 4825 km (3,500 mi.)

Weights: empty estimated 90,000 kg (198,000 lb.); loaded 181,437 kg (400,000 lb.)

Accommodation: the Hughes flying-boat was built to carry up to 750 troops or more than 70,000 kg (154,000 lb.) of freight or cargo

Dimensions:
span	97.54 m (320 ft.)
length	66.75 m (219 ft.)
height	15.32 m (79 ft.)
wing area	1029 m² (11,072 sq. ft.)

H-4 'SPRUCE GOOSE'

The massive aircraft gained its popular name from the derogatory comment of a senator investigating what he saw as a waste of public money. 'It's a Spruce Goose,' he said, 'it'll never fly.'

'Spruce Goose' was powered by eight Pratt & Whitney Wasp Major R-4360 radial engines, each delivering some 2240 kW (3,000 hp.). These were the most powerful conventional piston-driven engines ever built.

The leading edge of the massive wings housed a catwalk which allowed inflight access to the engine nacelles.

Tailplanes and fin were of wood construction, though the rudder and elevators were fabric covered. The massive tailplane was longer than the wing of a Lancaster bomber.

The reason that such a large aircraft could be built from wood was that the Hughes Corporation had recently developed the Duramold process, which laminated plywood and epoxy resin into a lightweight but very strong building material.

NX37602

The 'Spruce Goose' was designed to be flown by two pilots. On its only flight the aircraft carried 18 working personnel, including flight engineers and flight test observers. There were also 15 airline-type seats on the upper deck for use by reporters and invited guests.

Although the nose of the aircraft was solid, its structure was designed to be easily fitted with clamshell doors to allow the loading of outsize cargo.

Up to 53,000 litres (14,000 gal.) of fuel were carried in 14 underfloor tanks.

The only flight of the Hercules

1 TAXI TO TAKE OFF: Hughes was supposed to keep the flying-boat on the surface, but to engineer Dave Grant's surprise the multi-millionaire ordered 15° of flap – which was the take-off setting.

2 LIFT OFF: Accelerating through 150 km/h (93 m.p.h.), the huge boat began skimming across the surface. Then, to the delight of thousands of people watching from the shore, it lifted slowly and gracefully into the air.

3 TOUCHDOWN: Hughes eased his huge machine back onto the water. The flight had lasted less than a minute, never more than 25 m (80 ft.) above the water and covering less than 1.6 km (one mile).

ACTION DATA

COMPARATIVE SIZE

When steel and shipping magnate Henry J. Kaiser proposed that Howard Hughes should build a giant transport flying-boat for use in the vast expanses of the Pacific, he could not have foreseen that the eccentric millionaire would produce the world's largest plane. Twice the size and more than four times the weight of a four-engined bomber or long-distance airliner, and as long as nine five-ton trucks, the H-4 flying-boat would have carried 750 troops or more than 60 tons of cargo. Its potential would not be matched for more than two decades, until the era of the 'Jumbo' jet.

H-4 'SPRUCE GOOSE'   66.75 m (219 ft.)

C-130   35 m (115 ft.)

HUGHES
XF-11

● Reconnaissance prototypes ● 98 ordered ● Contraprops

▲ Howard Hughes
based the design of the XF-11 on his earlier D-2, an aircraft with a wooden hull designed to the same specification as the all-metal Lockheed P-38 Lightning.

A beautiful aircraft caused a bad day for the famous billionaire and aviation pioneer Howard Hughes on 7 July 1946. That day, Hughes crashed in Los Angeles in a graceful and potent high-speed reconnaissance aircraft that might have made an indelible mark on its era. The Hughes XF-11 was a great aircraft. But the end of World War II, the crash, and the advent of the jet age prevented the XF-11 from becoming an operational warplane.

HUGHES **XF-11**

◀ **Prototype's crash**
After one of the XF-11's propellers went into reverse pitch, Hughes lost control and crashed.

▼ **Production cancelled**
Plans to build 98 production F-11s were cancelled post-war.

▼ **Second prototype**
The surviving XF-11 (44-70156, known as the XR-11 after 1947) was evaluated by the USAF's Reconnaissance Section, but the advent of the jet rendered the design obsolete almost overnight.

▼ **Wreckage**
The XF-11's crash demolished a house, destroying the aircraft and injuring Hughes.

▲ **Contraprops**
The ill-fated first prototype was distinguishable by its highly complex contra-rotating propeller system.

FACTS AND FIGURES

➤ The first fateful flight of the XF-11 took place on 7 July 1946, with Howard Hughes himself as the test pilot.

➤ After Hughes' crash, the second XF-11 made its maiden flight on 5 April 1947.

➤ The second prototype was fitted with conventional propeller blades.

➤ Howard Hughes was pulled to safety from the XF-11 crash by a passer-by, Marine Sgt William Durkin.

➤ A grey filler was applied to the aircraft's fuselage to increase the airspeed.

➤ Design features used on the XF-11 appeared later on the P-80 and XP-84.

PROFILE

Howard Hughes' ill-fated high flyer

The twin-boom Hughes XF-11 was designed in 1943 as the heaviest and fastest twin-engined aircraft in the world. Based on the Hughes D-2 wartime fighter, the XF-11 was described as 'massive and mean' by ground crew members at Hughes' California factory. The XF-11 was intended as a fast, long-range, photo-reconnaissance craft but could also have doubled as a fighter.

The giant, shark-like XF-11 was viewed as the ideal photo platform for the anticipated 1946 invasion of Japan. When the war ended without an invasion, the future of the XF-11 became doubtful. The US Army at one point had plans to order 98 aircraft, but construction was shelved in the post-war era.

Although the first aircraft was destroyed on its only flight, the second flying version (with Curtiss-Wright propellers) was evaluated in flight tests for several years. Legend has it that Hughes masterminded the engine modifications from his hospital bed and eventually recovered sufficiently to fly the redesigned machine. The aircraft was praised for its performance – particularly its gentle stall characteristics. However, the onset of jet powered aircraft prevented the XF-11 from ever reaching production and the only flyable XF-11 was eventually scrapped.

Left: Hughes' XF-11 was designed for a top speed of 724 km/h (450 m.p.h.) and an 8000-km (5,000-mile) range.

SXF-11

Type: two-seat, long-range, high-altitude reconnaissance platform

Powerplant: two 2237-kW (3,000-hp.) Pratt & Whitney R-4360-31 Wasp Major radial piston engines

Maximum speed: 724 km/h (449 m.p.h.)

Range: approximately 8000 km (5,000 mi.)

Service ceiling: 13411 m (44,000 ft.)

Weights: empty 16830 kg (37,026 lb.); maximum take-off 26672 kg (58,678 lb.)

Dimensions: span 30.91 m (101 ft. 5 in.)
length 19.94 m (65 ft. 5 in.)
height 7.09 m (23 ft. 3 in.)
wing area 91.32 m² (983 sq.ft.)

Left: Pratt & Whitney's 28-cylinder R-4360 radial provided the XF-11 with its speed at altitude. The engine's appearance earned it the 'corn cob' nickname.

The central pod housing the cockpit and camera operator's position also held the camera fit. Up to eight cameras could be carried, but they proved difficult and time-consuming to load and unload. Republic's XR-12 differed from the Hughes design in having on-board photo processing facilities.

The F-11 was originally intended to replace the Lockheed F-5, a reconnaissance version of the the P-38 Lightning. The sudden end of World War II led to the cancellation of a production order, but the second XR-11 was nevertheless evaluated alongside the Republic XF-12 Rainbow.

In its configuration the XF-11 closely resembled the Hughes D-2 bomber and long-range fighter design which had flown in 1943. Howard Hughes was convinced that Kelly Johnson 'stole' this design for his own XP-38.

Duramold, a resin impregnated plywood, had been used to build the D-2, but for the D-5 (XF-11) conventional aluminium construction was specified.

470156

XF-11

Two of Pratt & Whitney's new R-4360-31 'corn cob' Wasp Major radials powered the first XF-11. These drove eight-bladed Hamilton Standard contraprops, one of which malfunctioned causing its destruction.

The second XF-11 had two R-4360-37 engines powering conventional Curtiss-Wright four-bladed propellers. Fuel for these thirsty engines was held mainly in the aircraft's long tail booms.

44-70156 was the second of the two XF-11s built and was redesignated XR-11 in 1947. After evaluation at Eglin AFB, Florida, in 1948, this aircraft was passed to a ground instruction school at Sheppard AFB.

ACTION DATA

MAXIMUM SPEED

The high speed of the XF-11 was achieved by its precise design. The aircraft's smooth twin-boom layout offered a major advantage over the F-15A Reporter which was a development of the P-61 Black Widow night-fighter.

XF-11 **724 km/h (449 m.p.h.)**
F-15A 'REPORTER' 708 km/h (438 m.p.h.)
XF-12 'RAINBOW' **743 km/h (461 m.p.h.)**

SERVICE CEILING

The large wing span of the XF-11 allowed the aircraft to attain a phenomenal operating altitude. Compared to the four-engined XF-12 Rainbow, the Hughes design proved to have a major advantage.

XF-11 13411 m (44,000 ft.)
F-15A 'REPORTER' 12497 m (41,000 ft.)
XF-12 'RAINBOW' 12800 m (42,000 ft.)

RANGE

The XF-11 was designed with long range as a major consideration. It was intended to use the aircraft from Pacific bases for reconnaissance over Japan. Neither the F-15 or XF-12 could match the XF-11's exceptional range.

XF-11 8000 km (5,000 mi.)
F-15A 'REPORTER' 6437 km (4,000 mi.)
XF-12 'RAINBOW' 5552 km (3,440 mi.)

Powered by P&W's R-4360 'Corn Cob'

■ **BOEING B-50:** This development of the B-29 was ordered before the end of World War II, but the first example did not fly until 1947. Many were converted for tanker duty.

■ **BOEING XF8B:** Boeing's last fighter was this fighter-bomber intended for use from US Navy carriers during the planned invasion of Japan. Flown in 1944, only three were built.

■ **REPUBLIC XF-12 RAINBOW:** Designed to fill the same need as the XF-11, the XF-12 was faster but had a shorter range. Two were built; both crashed. An airliner version was planned.

■ **VOUGHT F2G:** Developed by Goodyear, which had built large numbers of F4Us, this was a land-based, low-altitude variant. Three prototypes and 15 production aircraft were built.

HUNTING

126

● 'Jet-flap' demonstrator ● Sole prototype ● STOL performance

▲ *After an exhaustive series of test flights in England and wind-tunnel testing in the US, 'jet-flap' research was sidelined by Hunting's new owners, the British Aircraft Corporation.*

T his ungainly machine was built to prove the concept of the 'jet-flap' – a means of using the thrust of a turbine engine to increase the lift generated by an aircraft's wing. The system's benefits were reduced take-off and landing speeds and distances. Hunting's 126 was used for years of testing, which showed that the idea worked, but the 'jet-flap' was abandoned because of the lack of obvious applications and official interest.

HUNTING 126

Airflow research ▶
On an early flight from the Royal Aircraft Establishment's Bedford airfield, XN714 had wool 'tufts' attached to the fuselage to indicate how the air flowed over the aircraft.

▼ To the United States
After its appearance at the 1965 Paris air show, XN714 returned to Bedford for further experimental flights. In 1969 it was transported to America for wind-tunnel testing by NASA at a naval facility in California.

▲ Maiden flight
XN714 was accompanied on its first flight, on 26 March 1963, by two RAE Gloster Meteor chase aircraft.

▼ Nose-down attitude
The Hunting 126 had a characteristic nose-down attitude in flight.

▲ On display
On its return from the United States in 1970, XN714 was not uncrated. In 1974 it was allocated to the Aerospace Museum at RAF Cosford.

FACTS AND FIGURES

➤ Although BAC decided to abandon the 'jet-flap' idea, Hunting proposed a 'jet-flap' attack version of the Jet Provost.

➤ Jet thrust meant wing nozzles could reach temperatures of 600°C (1,112°F).

➤ For shipping to the US, XN714 was carried aboard an RAF Belfast transport.

➤ For safety reasons flight testing was carried out at Bedford because of Luton's proximity to Heathrow airport.

➤ With full power selected the 126 was prone to stalling without warning.

➤ On its maiden flight the 126 had a take-off run of about 550 m (1,800 ft).

Pioneering 'jet-flap' demonstrator

In the early 1950s Britain's National Gas Turbine Establishment (NGTE) carried out research into a new way of using the power of the jet engine. Originally it was proposed to duct all exhaust gases through the trailing edge of the main wing to create a 'jet-flap'. This would increase lift with flaps and ailerons lowered, thus reducing take-off and landing speeds and distances.

However, it was soon realised that only a proportion of the exhaust gases was

required, and the rest was available for propulsion. To test the idea for possible application in a production aircraft, Hunting produced a number of designs. The H.126/50 was chosen after a formal specification was issued in 1959.

Two aircraft, XN714 and XN719, were ordered, although only the former was completed. Powered by one of the most advanced medium-thrust turbojets of the day, the Orpheus, it took to the air in March 1963. For the next five years XN714 was used

for exhaustive tests of the 'jet-flap' concept. But after Hunting was absorbed by the British Aircraft Corporation this unique technology demonstrator became a museum exhibit.

Above: Rolled out in August 1962 from what was, by then, the British Aircraft Corporation's Luton factory, XN714 carried out taxiing trials before being trucked to Bedford.

Below: Unfavourable weather conditions meant the XN714 did not make its first flight until March 1963. It was flown by Hunting's chief test pilot, Stanley Oliver, and no problems were encountered.

126

Type: single-seat 'jet-flap' technology demonstrator

Powerplant: one derated 21.57-kN (4,850-lb.-thrust) Bristol Siddeley Orpheus 805 turbojet engine

Designed maximum speed: 463 km/h (287 m.p.h.)

Weight: all-up 4749 kg (10,450 lb.)

Dimensions: span 13.84 m (45 ft. 5 in.)
length 13.54 m (44 ft. 5 in.)
height 4.72 m (15 ft. 6 in.)
wheel track 3.30 m (10 ft. 10 in.)

EARLY TESTBEDS

DE HAVILLAND CANADA DHC-3 OTTER: After the NGTE's research into jet thrust applications in the early 1950s, the next logical step was to build a testbed for its ideas. Original plans involved fitting a DHC-3 Otter, like the one below, with two Rolls-Royce RB.108 turbines in the fuselage to power the 'jet-flap'. The aircraft's Twin Wasp piston engine would have been retained for propulsion. However, by 1957 the need for a new, pure research aircraft was clear. Specification ER.189D was raised in 1959 and Hunting was awarded a contract.

PERCIVAL P.74: Hunting's involvement in 'jet-flap' research had its origins in the work of a company that joined the Hunting Group in 1944. Percival Aircraft, and engine builders Napier, had examined the possibilities of a ducted thrust helicopter. The resulting P.74 was a 10-seat aircraft powered by two Napier Oryx turbine engines, the exhaust gases of which were released at the blade tips to turn the main rotor. Despite the fact that the P.74 never left the ground, Hunting now had a nucleus of personnel for the H.126 project.

126

XN714 was the only Hunting 126 to be completed. Rolled out in August 1962, it made numerous flights before it went to the Aerospace Museum, RAF Cosford, Shropshire, in 1974.

Using an elaborate ducting system from the engine, approximately 55 per cent of its thrust was ejected through 16 fishtail nozzles (eight per wing) on the trailing edge to produce a 'jet-flap'. The remaining 45 per cent was used for propulsion and flight control.

The pilot's control column and rudder bar, in addition to operating the normal control surfaces, also operated the jet nozzles in the tail of the aircraft to control pitch and yaw at low speeds. Ailerons still provided roll control when giving 'jet-flap' lift. The roll nozzles on the wing tips were operated by an autostabiliser and were not coupled to the pilot's control column.

With the exception of the wing, the 126 was basically of conventional design and construction. It was an all-metal aircraft with a fixed tricycle undercarriage.

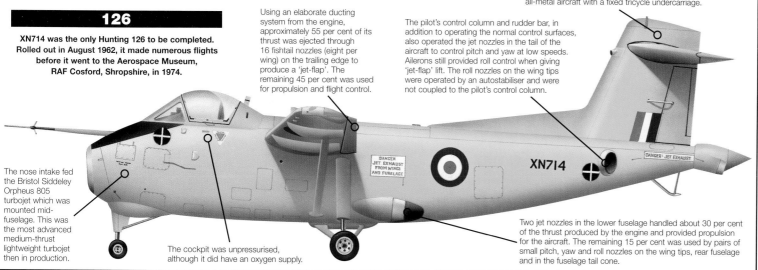

The nose intake fed the Bristol Siddeley Orpheus 805 turbojet which was mounted mid-fuselage. This was the most advanced medium-thrust lightweight turbojet then in production.

The cockpit was unpressurised, although it did have an oxygen supply.

Two jet nozzles in the lower fuselage handled about 30 per cent of the thrust produced by the engine and provided propulsion for the aircraft. The remaining 15 per cent was used by pairs of small pitch, yaw and roll nozzles on the wing tips, rear fuselage and in the fuselage tail cone.

'Jet-flap' evolution

BASIC AEROFOIL: The lift produced by a wing increases with angle of attack (raising of the leading edge) until the air flow slows down too much and a stall occurs. Stalling can happen gradually or suddenly, depending on wing thickness.

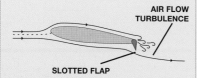

MECHANICAL FLAP: A basic trailing-edge flap changes air flow by altering wing camber and area in such a way that the lift and drag generated by the wing are increased. Slotted flaps are common now.

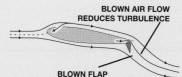

BLOWN FLAP: Air bled from the compressor of a turbine-type engine and ducted over a flap has much greater energy. This allows greater flap angles which, in turn, produce more lift. In addition, smaller, lighter flaps can be used.

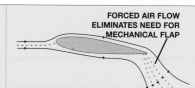

IDEAL 'JET-FLAP': When originally conceived, the 'jet-flap' idea consisted of a jet sheet blown from the trailing edge of the wing. However, the problem of engineering such a system proved to be too difficult.

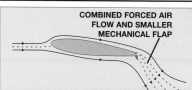

PRACTICAL JET-FLAP: To solve this problem, a small mechanical flap utilises the Coanda effect to turn the jet sheet downwards. This effect describes the way a jet of air adheres to a solid wall even if it curves away from the jet axis.

JUNKERS

Ju 287

● Jet-powered bomber ● Forward-swept wing ● Only two built

Among a number of far-sighted designs initiated by the Luftwaffe during World War II, the Junkers Ju 287 was one of the most radical. It featured not only turbojet propulsion, but also a forward-swept wing. The wing was intended to alleviate the low-speed handling problems inherent in conventionally swept designs. The Luftwaffe wanted a high-speed bomber immune from Allied interception, but the Ju 287 came too late.

▲ *Again German engineers had demonstrated their innovation during the 1940s with an unorthodox aircraft. Captured in 1945, the new technology was tested in the USSR post-war.*

JUNKERS Ju 287

▼ **In flight**
Seen here during trials in 1944, Ju 287 V1 was a highly unconventional aircraft for its day and remained unique as an FSW aircraft with podded engines.

▲ **Ungainly prototype**
Constructed from the components of a number of different aircraft types and fitted with a fixed undercarriage, Ju 287 V1 lacked finesse.

▼ **Under construction**
Ju 187 V1 nears completion at the Dessau factory in the early summer of 1944.

▼ **Forward-facing camera**
A camera was fitted to a tripod in front of the tail fin to record the aircraft's behaviour.

◄ **Rocket boosters**
A Walter 501 jettisonable rocket booster was fitted beneath each turbojet engine nacelle to assist take-off. The low power of early jet engines hampered development.

FACTS AND FIGURES

➤ Post-war, Hans Wocke designed the HFB 320 Hansa business jet with forward-swept wings.

➤ A low-speed test aircraft, Ju 287 V1 still achieved speeds of 650 km/h (400 m.p.h.).

➤ Ju 287 V1 was badly damaged by Allied bombing in late 1944 or early 1945.

➤ After VE-Day, Ju 287s V1 and V2 were shipped to the Soviet Union, where the latter flew in 1947.

➤ Successive Ju 287 models were to have more, less powerful engines.

➤ Some sources say that Ju 287 V2 flew in the USSR with conventional swept wings.

PROFILE

Junkers' unorthodox jet bomber

Only one Ju 287 was completed and flown before the end of World War II – a prototype designated Ju 287 V1. Originally, Junkers designer Hans Wocke intended to build a conventional swept-wing jet, of the the type that would become a common sight from the 1950s, but he found undesirable low-speed handling characteristics that appeared insurmountable.

Wocke then proposed to reverse the wing configuration. This presented its own problems (including impaired control responses at higher speeds), but Wocke felt sure that they could be resolved. Ju 287 V1 first flew on 16 August 1944, powered by four 8.82-kN (1,984-lb.-thrust) Jumo 004B-1 turbojets. A testbed for the new wing, it consisted of a Heinkel He 177A fuselage with a Junkers Ju 388 tail and fixed tricycle undercarriage.

A further 16 flights were made, the aircraft exhibiting good flying characteristics. A high-speed prototype, Ju 287 V2, was ordered, but, as Germany urgently needed fighters, work was suspended.

However, a production prototype (Ju 287 V3) was ordered in early 1945. This and the second aircraft featured six BMW engines and retractable undercarriage. In addition, Ju 287 V3 would have had a pressure cabin and a bomb bay for 4000 kg (8,800 lb.) of bombs. The Junkers factory was overrun before either V2 or V3 had ever flown.

Two of the prototype's four engines were unusually mounted either side of the forward fuselage. Ju 287 V2 and V3 were to be powered by six wing-mounted BMW engines.

Delays in the development of the intended engines meant that Ju 287 V2 and V3 were to have their six smaller engines, attached in two groups of three under the wings.

Defensive armament for Ju 287 V1 was restricted to a pair of remotely-controlled MG 131 13-mm machine-guns in the tail barbette.

Ju 287 V3

Type: advanced, three-seat, jet-powered heavy bomber

Powerplant: six 7.83-kN (1761-lb.-thrust) BMW 003A-1 Sturm axial-flow turbojets

Maximum speed: 864 km/h (536 m.p.h.) at 5000 m (16,400 ft.) and 16057 kg (35,325 lb.) all-up weight

Initial climb rate: 10.5 min to 6005 m (19,700 ft.)

Range: 1585 km (983 mi.) with max bomb load

Weights: empty equipped 11919 kg (26,222 lb.); maximum loaded 21500 kg (47,300 lb.)

Armament: (defensive) twin 13-mm MG 131 machine-guns in tail barbette; (offensive) 4000 kg (8,800 lb.) of bombs in internal bay

Dimensions: span 20.11 m (66 ft.); length 18.60 m (61 ft.); wing area 61.00 m² (656 sq. ft.)

Ju 287 V1

On 16 August 1944 the Ju 287 prototype (RS+RA) took to the air for the first time. Another 16 flights were made from Brandis before it was moved to Rechlin, where it was damaged in an Allied air raid.

Like the V1 prototype, the Ju 287A-0 (as the first production examples were to be known) would have featured a fully glazed nose for the crew of three.

The need for wing structural integrity during testing led to the use of fixed undercarriage on Ju 287 V1. Ju 287 V3 and subsequent aircraft were to have retractable gear.

Construction of production prototype V3 had begun by the time the war in Europe had ended. Its fuselage was essentially that of the aborted Ju 388 bomber, with a pressurised cabin and a more up-swept tail.

Fixed nose gear on the Ju 287 V1 was supported by nose wheels salvaged from a USAAF Consolidated B-24 Liberator and enclosed in a large fairing.

The main gear was fixed and shrouded in large fairings. Braced to the forward wing spars, it employed wheels designed for the Ju 352 transport.

A recessed wheel in the rear fuselage was a feature of Ju 287 V1. It was designed to prevent damage to the aircraft should the tail touch the ground during rotation.

COMBAT DATA

MAXIMUM SPEED

Compared to the Arado Ar 234, a jet bomber design that was to enter Luftwaffe service in the closing stages of the war, and the piston-engined Boeing B-29 Superfortress, Ju 287 V3 would have been very fast indeed.

Ju 287 V3 — 864 km/h (536 m.p.h.)
Ar 234B-2 — 741 km/h (459 m.p.h.)
B-29 — 576 km/h (357 m.p.h.)

RANGE

Range was an area in which the early jet bombers could not compete with piston-engined bombers. The USAAF's B-29 had a range more than three times that of the Ju 287 and almost five times that of the Ar 234. B-29s were also able to lift heavier loads – just over 9000 kg.

B-29 5230 km (3,243 mi.)
Ju 287 V3 1585 km (983 mi.)
Ar 234B-2 1101 km (683 mi.)

SERVICE CEILING

Both the jet types had service ceilings of around 10000 m (33,000 ft.), around 1000 m (2,000 ft.) more than that of the B-29. Flying at higher altitudes allowed bombers to evade anti-aircraft fire and enemy fighters more easily. But the Arado's missions tended to be tactical and held at low altitudes.

Ju 287 V3 9997 m (33,000 ft.)
Ar 234B-2 10000 m (33,000 ft.)
B-29 9170 m (31,000 ft.)

World War II Junkers projects

■ **Ju 252:** Designed for Deutsche Lufthansa in 1939, the Ju 252 was intended to replace the Ju 52/3m. A few were built for the Luftwaffe.

■ **Ju 288:** Though nominally related to the Ju 88, the Ju 288 was a new medium bomber design. Development snags led to cancellation.

■ **Ju 290:** The Ju 290 can trace its origins to the pre-war Ju 89 bomber. Derived from the Ju 90 airliner, it was adapted for maritime patrol.

■ **Ju 388:** Derived from the Ju 188, the Ju 388 was a produced in small numbers as a high-altitude reconnaissance aircraft.

JUNKERS

JU 322 MAMMUT

● Giant glider ● Flying wing ● Only one flown

A mong the transport aircraft types to enter Luftwaffe service during World War II, the Ju 52/3m was the best known. Other Junkers transport designs to see service included the Ju 160 single-engined, high-speed airliner, the Ju 252 pressurised tri-motored airliner and the even bigger Ju 352. The Ju 352 was built mainly of wood, a feature shared with the most bizarre of the Junkers wartime transports, the Ju 322 Mammut glider.

▲ The Junkers Ju 49 monoplane was developed in 1927-28 for high altitude experiments. It claimed the world height record in 1929, reaching an altitude of 12735 m (41,770 ft.).

JUNKERS JU 322 MAMMUT

▼ High-altitude testplane
In 1936 Junkers developed the EF 61 research aircraft. It provided valuable data for the Ju 86P and Ju 86R reconnaissance aircraft.

▲ Parasol design
Developed from the H.21 of the early 1920s, the Junkers H.22 was a single-seat parasol design with unusual undercarriage fairings.

◄ Rare bird
Only one Ju 322 flew and it made just a few flights. This is believed to be the only existing picture of the Ju 322.

Wartime trainer ►
Developed in 1933-34 from the Ju 60 high-speed airliner, the Ju 160 was used by the Luftwaffe for communication/training.

▼ Tri-engined transporter
The Ju 252 was built to replace the Ju 52/3m in Lufthansa service; 15 were used by the Luftwaffe for transport duties.

FACTS AND FIGURES

➤ Intended loads for the Ju 322 included 100 fully-equipped troops, a PzKw IV tank, or a towed 8.8-cm gun with crew.

➤ Two Ju 322s were completed; 98 production examples had been ordered.

➤ In all, 45 million Reichsmarks were spent on the unsuccessful Mammut project.

➤ For its first flight, Ju 322 V1 was towed aloft on an 8000-kg (17,600-lb.) trolley. When released, it disintegrated on impact.

➤ After cancellation, Ju 322s were used as fuel for wood-burning vehicles.

➤ The Ju 322 was based on the earlier Junkers G.38 and EF 94 designs.

Junkers' mighty Mammoth

The Mammut (Mammoth) was built to the same specification as the Me 321, but was of all-wood construction. Both designs were required to deliver a 20-tonne load during the planned airborne assault on Britain.

The Ju 322 was effectively a 'flying wing' design. Its short fuselage supported only the tailplane, the bulk of the glider's payload being carried inside the wing. The use of wood caused a number of problems, not least of which was Junkers' inexperience with the material.

Sub-standard and rotten timber and defective glue meant that the airframe lacked sufficient strength; by the time the Ju 322 V1 prototype flew in April 1941, its design payload had slipped to 16 tonnes, then 11. The second payload reduction was necessitated by the need to strengthen the aircraft's cargo floor after a PzKw IV tank fell through it during loading trials.

On its first flight, towed by a Ju 90, the Mammut was unstable and began to climb above the tug aircraft. As the climbing Mammut began to pull the Ju 90's tail alarmingly upwards, the glider's pilot was fortunately able quickly to release the tow line and avert disaster. Though the Ju 322 made a perfect landing, modifications were carried out and further trials flown, the overwhelming weaknesses of the design led to development being abandoned in May 1941.

The Mammut was basically a 'flying wing' with a rear fuselage section to carry the tail surfaces. The wing was of multi-spar wooden construction.

The cargo hold was to carry a payload of 20000 kg (40,000 lb.). After a weakness in the main spar was recognised, this was reduced to 11000 kg (22,000 lb.).

The outer panels of the wing had dihedral on their undersides. The swollen centre-section formed the cargo hold and had a detachable leading edge for the loading of cargo.

The pilot's cockpit was a raised, glazed gondola which was offset to the port side. The pilot had excellent forward vision from this raised position which would have been vital for landing in small fields.

Ju 322 V1 Mammut

Type: high-capacity experimental transport glider

Glide angle: 1:50

Payload: 11000 kg (22,000 lb.)

Armament: production versions were to receive three turrets each mounting a single 7.9-mm MG 15 machine gun

Dimensions:
span 62.00 m (203 ft. 4 in.)
length 30.25 m (99 ft. 3 in.)
wing area 925 m² (9,953 sq. ft.)

EF 94

The Junkers Ju 322 was largely based on the EF 94 project which never reached flying status, but would have looked something like this in service. The Ju 322 featured a revised armament.

The EF 94, like the Ju 322, was fitted with three turrets, each containing a single 7.9-mm machine gun. The turrets fitted to the wings of the EF 94 were moved forward to the front of the fuselage section on the Ju 322.

Although the tail surfaces on the EF 94 appear large, the surfaces on the final Ju 322 were actually quite small for an aircraft of this size. After the near-disastrous first flight the vertical tail surfaces were enlarged to improve stability.

Above: Two prototypes of the EF 61 were constructed and were used in the development of pressurised cabins and turrets. They were powered by two Daimler-Benz DB 600 engines.

For take-off a large jettisonable trolley constructed of lattice girders with eight pairs of wheels was to be used. Beneath the centre-section were four steel-sprung landing skids.

COMBAT DATA

PAYLOAD

Designed to the same specification, the Me 321 and the Ju 322 were to have had similar payloads. However, structural deficiencies with the Ju 322 reduced the payload by 45 per cent. British gliders such as the Horsa were much smaller and carried far less.

Ju 322 MAMMUT 11000 kg (22,000 lb.)
Me 321 GIGANT 21000 kg (46,200 lb.)
AS 58 HORSA 3200 kg (7,040 lb.)

WINGSPAN

With its 'flying wing' layout, the Ju 322 had a massive wingspan and wing area. This provided a tremendous amount of lift, allowing large loads to be carried. The Horsa with its smaller dimensions was able to use smaller landing grounds than the larger German gliders.

Ju 322 MAMMUT 62.00 m (203 ft. 4 in.)
Me 321 GIGANT 55.00 m (180 ft. 5 in.)
AS 58 HORSA 26.82 m (87 ft. 11 in.)

German gliders of World War II

■ **BLOHM UND VOSS BV 40:** With a pilot in the prone position and heavy cockpit armour, the BV 40 was designed as a fighter and intended to make diving head-on attacks.

■ **DFS 331:** Designed during 1940, only one example of this cargo glider was flown. The cockpit was positioned on a raised platform to allow a large cargo door on the port side.

■ **GOTHA Go 242:** The only aircraft produced by Gotha to see large-scale service in World War II, the Go 242 was a successful assault glider. In all, 1528 examples were produced.

■ **MESSERSCHMITT Me 321 GIGANT:** This high-capacity, high-wing transport glider was usually towed by either a single Junkers Ju 290A-1 or a trio of Messerschmitt Bf 110Cs.

LEDUC

O.21/O.22

● Research aircraft ● Ramjet-powered design ● Air-launched initially

Frenchman René Leduc had his first success with ramjet propulsion in 1935, when he ran a practical engine producing 0.039 kN (9 lb.) of thrust. After World War II his experiments resumed, and in 1949 the first O.10 ramjet-powered aircraft was flown from the back of a Languedoc airliner. Development continued into the 1950s and culminated in the O.22 Mach 2 interceptor prototype, which, although flown, was ultimately crippled by a lack of funding.

▲ A test pilot enters the cockpit of the Leduc in preparation for a test flight. The unusual seating position required a certain amount of courage during those early days.

LEDUC **O.21/O.22**

Airborne departure ▶
To keep the weight of the aircraft to a minimum and save fuel, the Leduc was carried aloft on a Languedoc transport.

▼ Flying powerplant
Essentially a flying engine perched on a delicate undercarriage, with control surfaces added, the Leduc was a revolutionary aircraft for its day.

▲ Bail out problems solved
Sited in the middle of the engine intake, the whole nose could be jettisoned in an emergency.

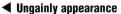

◀ Ungainly appearance
Despite the unusual impression that the Leduc presented on the ground, once airborne the aircraft took on a beauty all of its own. This example is fitted with extra wing-tip fuel tanks to extend flight duration.

Proud history ▶
Both examples of the O.21 Leduc are seen on display at a French aeronautics exhibition in the 1950s. Although neither aircraft was developed into a fighter, the French aviation industry took immense pride in the design.

FACTS AND FIGURES

➤ René Leduc first became interested in ramjet engines in 1933 and presented numerous proposals to his government.

➤ The first Leduc was completed in 1953, with flight trials starting on 16 May.

➤ Gliding trials were performed first to establish handling characteristics.

➤ The pilot was seated ahead of the intake in a semi-reclined cabin which was completely sealed and air-conditioned.

➤ The O.10 was initially flown as glider in 1946 and later under power.

➤ Features of the design were later incorporated in front-line fighters.

PROFILE

René Leduc's experimental ramjets

Known technically as an aero-thermodynamic-duct, or athodyd, the ramjet has no major rotating parts. It relies on air being forced into an intake designed to ensure that this air loses kinetic energy but gains pressure. The air enters, via a diverging duct, a combustion chamber where burning fuel is added. The expanding gases are then exhausted, producing considerable thrust.

The O.10 aircraft reached 680 km/h (422 m.p.h.) on its 12-minute flight in 1949. On half power during a later flight it topped 805 km/h (500 m.p.h.). Two more examples were built; the second was known as the O.16 and differed from the first aircraft in having wingtip-mounted turbojets to accelerate the machine up to ramjet ignition speed.

Two O.21s followed in 1953, reaching Mach 0.87 at 20000 m (65,616 ft.). By then, there was official interest in an interceptor variant, the Mach 2-capable O.22. It featured a single auxiliary turbojet within its ramjet main engine. In the

event, all 30 flights made by the single prototype (the first in 1956) were powered by the turbojet only. Funding cuts saw the project scrapped in 1958/9.

Above: During landing the engine was cut and a parachute deployed to reduce the landing run.

Right: Trailing its outrigger wheels, a Leduc O.22 returns from a supersonic test flight.

O.21

Aircraft '01' was the first of two examples. Between them, 160 test flights were made from the back of a specially-configured SE.161 Languedoc transport.

A conical, jettisonable cockpit housed the O.21's pilot, who sat in a semi-reclined seat. Radio equipment, oxygen bottles and the parachute for the cabin were fitted in a compartment behind the cockpit.

The two O.21s had an internally-mounted Turboméca Artouste turbojet to provide thrust to accelerate the craft to a sufficient speed to ignite the ramjet. This allowed the aircraft to be launched from the ground, rather than from the back of a 'mother ship', as during testing. Plans to install turbojets in the wingtips were never carried through.

Effectively 'flying engines', Leduc ramjet aircraft would have been hampered by their lack of fuel capacity and therefore endurance had they entered service.

A tandem main undercarriage assembly supported the O.21 and retracted into a bay between the cockpit section and the outer skin. It was covered by a louvred door when retracted. The wings were supported by the wingtip outrigger wheels.

Large fairings on each wingtip housed the retracted outrigger wheels and, in the proposed interceptor version, the armament of two 20-mm cannon.

The O.21's fuselage was made up of six concentric stainless steel skins which were joined by perforated 'burner crowns', making up the ramjet. The turbine engine was mounted at the cockpit end of the aircraft.

ACTION DATA

MAXIMUM SPEED

Because of its unique design the Leduc was capable of high speed, but the ramjet engine limited duration. The speed potential of the Leduc ramjets was never fully realised.

LEDUC O.21	1000 km/h (621 m.p.h.)	
GRIFFON II	1500 km/h (932 m.p.h.)	
GERFAUT IA	1593 km/h (956 m.p.h.)	

THRUST

As with any ramjet, the thrust was considerable, but for only a short time. Most experimental aircraft of the period employed jet engines such as those in the Griffon.

LEDUC O.21
59 kN
(1,326-lb.-thrust)

GRIFFON II
34.32 kN
(7,715-lb.-thrust)

GERFAUT 1A
39.23 kN
(973-lb.-thrust)

Pioneering Nord aircraft

■ **500:** This aircraft was constructed to investigate the tilting-ducted fan concept. The first tethered flight occurred in July 1968 and hover and transition trials commenced later. However, the programme was cancelled before full flight trials began.

■ **GERFAUT IA:** This small delta-winged aircraft was operated to explore the high speed regions of flight using a delta wing platform. Despite its small size, the Gerfaut was the first European aircraft to exceed Mach 1 in level flight without afterburner.

■ **GRIFFON II:** Though originally intended to enter service as an interceptor, the Griffon remained only a research aircraft used to test various turbojet engines that French companies were producing. Two configurations of the design were tested.

LOCKHEED

A-12 BLACKBIRD

● Mach 3 flight ● Reconnaissance aircraft ● Covert over-flights

I n the 1960s a secret Central Intelligence Agency (CIA) aircraft flew 'Black Shield' spy missions over China, Korea and Vietnam – thumbing its nose at attempts to shoot it down. The Lockheed A-12 was developed in the hush-hush 'Oxcart' programme, and was one of only a handful of aircraft developed specifically for civil espionage operations. It later evolved into the military SR-71 Blackbird.

▲ Wearing spacesuits, the crew of a YF-12 (the fighter derivative of the A-12) prepare for a test flight that will involve flying three times faster than the speed of sound.

LOCKHEED A-12 BLACKBIRD

▼ Covert airfield
These A-12s are lined up on the hardstanding at Groom Lake. The air base was concealed within the Nellis bombing range in Nevada.

▲ High-speed office
Despite the advanced design of the Blackbird, the cockpit was equipped with conventional dial-type instruments.

▼ 'Titanium goose'
The two-seat trainer version of the A-12, with its raised second cockpit, was dubbed the 'titanium goose' because of its looks.

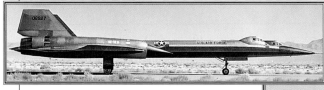

▼ Eject, eject
Ejecting from an aircraft flying at three times the speed of sound required some unorthodox testing. Here the rig is towed by a Ford car.

▼ The interceptor
Early models of the Blackbird were flown in a bare metal and black colour scheme, although an overall black scheme was later adopted.

FACTS AND FIGURES

➤ All A-12s were initially operated by America's Central Intelligence Agency amid great secrecy.

➤ The first flight of the A-12 took place on 26 January 1962.

➤ Later models were equipped with more powerful J58 engines.

➤ A-12 were active in the Far East and over North Vietnam; these operational deployments still remain classified.

➤ Total production of the A-12 amounted to 15 examples, all for the CIA.

➤ The A-12 was eventually replaced by the two-seat SR-71 Blackbird.

PROFILE

Lockheed's covert observer

Sometimes called the 'Oxcart' after the programme which produced it, the Lockheed A-12 was a revolutionary aircraft designed to replace the Lockheed U-2, alias the 'Dragon Lady,' as the CIA's principal reconnaissance aircraft. Today, the A-12 is recognised as the civilian predecessor of the better-known SR-71 Blackbird.

Initially tested at a secret US air base at Groom Lake in Nevada (now also known as 'Area 51'), the A-12 became fully operational in great secrecy. The Blackbird flew faster and higher than any machine of its era. Pilots of the A-12 experienced the 'adrenaline high' of flying at the very edge of the envelope

while doing so in absolute secrecy, in the interests of national security.

In a major US policy change in 1968, however, the strategic reconnaissance mission was taken over by the military. Although this ended further development of the A-12, the aircraft continued to undertake spy missions for several years after.

The A-12 was also developed into the M-21 and used as a flying launch platform for the D-21 hypersonic ramjet-powered reconnaissance drone, although this was not revealed until 1976. A few launches took place, but the project was halted by a mid-air collision.

Above: Before launching the drone numerous 'captive' flights were undertaken to test the D-21's systems.

The A-12 was the first aircraft to use stealth technology, with its blended fuselage shape and small frontal cross-section.

Positioned behind the pilot was an area known as the Q-bay, which could hold either a second crew-member or a large camera.

Because of a fatal mid-air collision during the launch of a drone on a test flight, the project was abandoned in favour of a B-52 launch platform.

The bat-like GTD-21A reconnaissance drone resembled an A-12 engine nacelle. The Lockheed engineers used similar aerodynamics in its development.

The most significant modification made to the M-21 was the addition of an extra crew-member, the Launch Control Officer (LCO), who was positioned immediately behind the pilot. Tasked with managing the systems of the D-21, the LCO separated the drone from the M-21 while the pilot controlled the main aircraft.

As the speed increased, two enormous inlet spikes moved backwards to correctly position the shockwave inside the inlet throat. The spikes were canted inward and downward to counteract wind flow over the chines.

The A-12 carried its sensors in a Q-bay and in the chine sections. The later SR-71 introduced a wider frontal area, with detachable nose sections, for sensors and cameras.

This aircraft has only some parts painted in the familiar black scheme. The paint was designed to reduce radar cross-section and was consequently only applied, as seen here, to the reflective leading-edge surfaces of the M-21.

The Goodrich tyres were protected during high-speed flight by impregnating them with aluminium powder to reflect any thermodynamic heat from the airframe.

M-21 'MOTHER GOOSE'

After CIA U-2 pilot Gary Powers was shot down in his U-2A in May 1960, the CIA requested that an A-12 be converted to launch a hypersonic reconnaissance drone in mid-air.

A-12 Blackbird

Type: high-speed reconnaissance aircraft

Powerplant: two 144.6-kN (32,500-lb.-thrust) Pratt & Whitney J58 high-bypass ratio turbojets with afterburner; D-21 Drone 6.6kN (1,484-lb.-thrust) Marquardt RJ43-MA-11 ramjet

Maximum speed: Mach 3.35 at 24384 m (80,000 ft.)

Range: 4023 km (2,500 mi.); D-21 reconnaissance drone 5555 km (3451 mi.)

Service ceiling: 28 956 m (95,000 ft.)

Weights: empty 27546 kg (60,728 lb.); maximum take-off 57605 kg (126,997 lb.); D-21 drone take-off weight 9071 kg (20,000 lb.)

Accommodation: one pilot, plus a Launch Control Officer in the M-21 variant

Dimensions:
span	16.94 m	(55 ft. 7 in.)
length	31.08 m	(102 ft.)
height	5.64 m	(18 ft. 6 in.)
wing area	167.30 m²	(1800 sq. ft.)

ACTION DATA

MAXIMUM CRUISING SPEED

With its exceptionally high cruising speed, the A-12 was able to cover vast distances without the risk of interception by fighters or surface-to-air missiles.

A-12 BLACKBIRD   4000 km/h (2,485 m.p.h.)

U-2C   740 km/h (460 m.p.h.)

RB-57F   761 km/h (472 m.p.h.)

MAXIMUM RANGE

Acting like powered gliders because of their huge wingspan, the Lockheed U-2 and Martin RB-57F could cover vast distances but at a relatively slow speed. For successful operations the A-12 had to rely on an extensive network of waiting Boeing KC-135 tankers.

A-12 BLACKBIRD 4023 km (2,500 mi.)

U-2C 6440 km (4,000 mil.)

RB-57F 5133 km (3,189 mi.)

SERVICE CEILING

Flying at high altitude allows reconnaissance aircraft to photograph a wider field of view. When operating along nations' borders it enables the aircraft to peer at the target installations without risk.

A-12 BLACKBIRD 28 956 m (95,000 ft)

U-2B 24200 m (79,396 ft)

RB-57F 19507 m (64,000 ft)

Legendary Lockheeds

C-5 GALAXY: Currently the largest aircraft in the United States inventory, the Galaxy is capable of airlifting the latest main battle tanks and AH-64 Apache attack helicopters.

C-130 HERCULES: The mainstay of the USAF transport fleet, the C-130 has been used in every major recent conflict as wells as for numerous humanitarian relief operations.

F-104 STARFIGHTER: Unfairly referred to as 'The Widow Maker', the Starfighter served as an interceptor within America's Air Defence Command during the 1950s and 1960s.

P-38 LIGHTNING: With its unique twin-boom layout the P-38 gained an enviable reputation as a ground attack aircraft during the later stages of World War II.

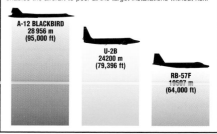

LOCKHEED

AH-56 CHEYENNE

● High-speed gunship ● Two-seat aircraft ● Cancelled after 375 ordered

▲ The specifically designed gunship helicopter was a novel idea in the 1960s. With the end of the Cheyenne programme, the US Army was forced to wait more than 10 years for the AH-64 Apache.

Helicopters proved their worth once-and-for-all during the Vietnam War as troop carriers without equal. However, a pressing need for a specialised escort helicopter was soon apparent. Armed UH-1 'Hueys' were used in the meantime and Bell's AH-1 provided another interim solution, but the answer lay in the Cheyenne. However, this high-speed, heavily-armed weapons system was plagued by problems.

PHOTO FILE

LOCKHEED AH-56 CHEYENNE

▲ **STOL take-off**
Intended to make short rolling take-offs when loaded, the AH-56 had a wheeled undercarriage.

▲ **Ahead of its time**
The cancellation of the Cheyenne forced the US Army to soldier on with the 'interim' Bell AH-1 HueyCobra for many years. The purpose-built AH-64 Apache was finally ordered in 1982.

▲ **Ground clearance**
To provide sufficient ground clearance for the ventral gun pack, tall landing gear was used.

▲ **Pusher rotor and wings**
For high-speed flight small wings produced most of the lift, while much of the engine power went to the pusher propeller and provided forward thrust.

Gunship layout ▶
Lockheed set the now-established formula for gunship helicopters. The gunner sat forward, taking responsibility for the weapons systems.

FACTS AND FIGURES

➤ Since the Cheyenne project, Lockheed has not put a military or civil helicopter into production.

➤ Power of the T64 engine was increased to 2927 kW (3,922 hp.) during testing.

➤ Cancellation, in May 1969, came just six months before production began.

➤ In common with other US Army helicopters, the Cheyenne was named after a native American tribe.

➤ The highly manoeuvrable AH-56 was found to be a stable weapons platform.

➤ The other short-listed AAFSS prototype was the Sikorsky S-66.

PROFILE

Fast and formidable

A top speed of 407 km/h (252 m.p.h.), a 4650-km (2,889-mi.) ferry range and good hover performance in hot-and-high conditions were among the US Army's Advanced Aerial Fire Support System's (AAFSS) requirements.

Twelve companies submitted proposals, with Lockheed being chosen to build 10 prototypes of their CL-840 compound helicopter. The first example flew on 21 September 1967. Initial testing was promising and the Army ordered 375 AH-56As.

On 7 January 1968 the US Department of Defense ordered 375 AH-56As for the US Army. In May 1969 the order was cancelled, although testing continued until 1972.

Then disaster struck. High-speed flight (over 320 km/h [200 m.p.h.]) revealed stability problems. A cure proved difficult to find, and when a Cheyenne crashed in 1969 the rest of the aircraft were grounded and the production order was cancelled. Despite further testing, the controversy surrounding the project and the strain placed on the defence budget by the Vietnam War saw all development cease in 1972.

Production Cheyennes would have had six underwing attachment points for missiles and rockets. The inboard pair were able to carry fuel tanks.

Cockpit systems included a weapon sighting system with night-vision equipment and a helmet-mounted gunsight.

The small, low-set cantilever wings, which have no control surfaces, almost entirely 'offload' the main rotor (provide lift) during high-speed flight. Two pylons are provided under each one.

AH-56A CHEYENNE

66-8827 was the second prototype to be built. Two were destroyed in accidents and one (66-8830) has survived to be displayed at the US Army Aviation Museum at Fort Rucker.

The first Cheyenne crash on 12 March 1969 was a result of the main rotor hitting the aft fuselage during high-speed flight. A second aircraft was badly damaged in similar circumstances in a NASA wind tunnel in September of that year.

During high-speed flight most of the engine output is directed to the tail-mounted propeller, with only 223 kW for the feathered main rotor. This prevents drag induced by 'windmilling'.

Pratt & Whitney's T64 turboshaft engine also powered Sikorsky's S-65 heavylift helicopter which entered US Marine Corps service as the CH-53 in mid-1966.

Unlike more modern combat helicopters, the AH-56 was a dual-control machine. The pilot was in the rear position with the gunner/co-pilot in the front on a seat able to swivel through 360°.

The main undercarriage retracted rearwards into wingroot fairings. The rear of the helicopter was supported by a wheel in the ventral fin. Two turrets were to be fitted to service aircraft: one in the nose able to swing through 180° and another (detachable) under the fuselage.

AH-56A Cheyenne

Type: two-seat all-weather compound combat helicopter

Powerplant: one 2561-kW (7,354-hp.) Pratt & Whitney T64-GE-16 turboshaft

Max speed: 407 km/h (252 m.p.h.) at sea level

Range: 1400 km (868 mi.) at max take-off weight with external fuel

Service ceiling: 7925 m (26,000 ft.)

Weights: empty 5320 kg (11,704 lb.); design take-off 7710 kg (16,962 lb.)

Armament: in nose turret, either one XM129 40-mm grenade-launcher or one 7.62-mm Minigun; in belly turret, XM140 30-mm cannon; two pylons under each wing for TOW anti-tank missiles or 70-mm rocket pods

Dimensions:
main rotor diameter	15.36 m (50 ft.)
length	18.31 m (60 ft.)
height	4,18 m (14 ft.)
rotor disc area	12.07 m² (130 sq. ft.)

COMBAT DATA

MAXIMUM SPEED

Speed was an important consideration in the Cheyenne's design. The AH-56 was almost twice as fast as the contemporary AH-1.

AH-56A CHEYENNE	407 km/h (252 m.p.h.)
AH-1S HUEYCOBRA	227 km/h (141m.p.h.)
AH-64A APACHE	365 km/h (226 m.p.h.)

FERRY RANGE

The Cheyenne compound helicopter's wings gave it a remarkable ferry range, which was unattainable in a standard helicopter.

AH-56A CHEYENNE	4650 km (2,883 mi.)
AH-1S HUEYCOBRA	507 km (314 mi.)
AH-64A APACHE	1701 km (1,054 mi.)

The Cheyenne/TOW weapon system

■ **TOW MISSILES:** Hughes' Tube-launched, Optically-tracked, Wire-guided (TOW) missile was to be a key element of the Cheyenne 'weapon system'. This sequence shows a TOW launch at the Yuma missile test site in Arizona in 1970.

■ **TANK KILLER:** Designed to destroy tanks and ground fortifications, the TOW missile has a nose-mounted camera which relays an image to a screen in the gunner's cockpit. This allows him to steer the missile with a small joystick.

■ **WIRE-GUIDED:** A wire trailed behind the missile carries control commands from the helicopter's gunner. Cruciform 'pop-out' fins on the missile guide it to the target. TOW is powered by a small solid propellant rocket motor.

■ **WARHEAD:** The first Hughes BGM-71A TOW missiles (operational from 1975 aboard AH-1 HueyCobras) had a high-explosive shaped charge warhead (seen here destroying an old M4 tank hull) and a range of 4 km.

LOCKHEED

P-80 SHOOTING STAR

● Jet fighter ● European deployment ● Test flying

In 1944 the US Army Air Force began gunnery trials in Nevada with the Lockheed P-80 Shooting Star; this design promised to revolutionise air warfare. The P-80 was the first fully operational type in the US to have a jet engine – an innovation already familiar to German and British scientists. The US rushed four P-80s to Europe – two each to England and Italy – and they were hours from entering combat when World War II ended.

▲ Proudly wearing the Lockheed emblem on its nose, the P-80 Shooting Star was equipped with six forward-firing machine-guns, a typical armament fit for fighters of the era.

LOCKHEED P-80 SHOOTING STAR

▼ Graceful lines
Before the addition of wingtip tanks and essential service equipment, the Shooting Star was one of the most elegant aircraft ever produced by Lockheed. Pilots marvelled at the design.

▲ Fighter testing
Known as Lulu Belle, this P-80 was flown against the conventionally powered fighters of the period to explore jet tactics.

▲ Future potential
With large test markings displayed on its fuselage, this particular P-80 undertook a series of developmental flights to try out future jet fighter equipment.

▲ Service entry
Seen high over California's foothills, this P-80A was assigned to the 412th Fighter Group at March Field in late 1945.

◄ Lakebed landings
Early flights were performed from the Muroc range in California, and made use of the many dry lakebeds.

FACTS AND FIGURES

➤ The Shooting Star was designed from the start to be the United States Army Air Force's first operational jet fighter.

➤ One of the first examples of the P-80 was completed in just 143 days.

➤ Early aircraft were given names like The Grey Ghost and Silver Ghost.

➤ Lockheed hoped to deliver 450 Shooting Stars per month during World War II, but this was never accomplished.

➤ Richard Ira Bong, America's highest-scoring ace, was killed testing a P-80.

➤ Many pilots found it hard to adjust to the new demands of jet flying.

PROFILE

Shooting for success

Below: Having just completed another test flight, an early P-80 is seen parked on one of Muroc's dry lakebeds. A major debrief followed each flight.

Work on the P-80 began in 1943 when famous engineer Clarence L. ('Kelly') Johnson persuaded his bosses at Lockheed to attempt to build the USAAF's first operational jet fighter in just 180 days. They actually completed the pace-setting first P-80 in 143 days.

The P-80 was a clean design with straight wings and tail surfaces, and a tricycle landing gear. Air intakes positioned on the lower fuselage forward of the wing leading edge fed the British-designed de Havilland H.1B turbojet, which was replaced in production examples by the Allison/General Electric I-40 (J33).

Many pilots with propeller experience took to the jet-powered P-80 with enormous enthusiasm. An ambitious programme progressed toward the goal of getting the Shooting Star into combat. Several P-80s were lost in tragic mishaps, but the aircraft performed well, and the USAAF moved rapidly to finalise the configuration of this

Above: After completing extensive test work, this Shooting Star was restored by ex-Lockheed employees.

fighter and to develop a photo-reconnaissance version. Had World War II lasted weeks longer, it is certain that the P-80 Shooting Star would have done battle with the top fighters developed by the Axis, including Germany's much-vaunted Messerschmitt Me 262.

XP-80 Shooting Star

Type: single-seat jet fighter

Powerplant: one 10.9-kN (2,450-lb.-thrust) de Havilland H.1B Goblin turbojet

Maximum speed: 808 km/h (502 m.p.h.); cruising speed 692 km/h (430 m.p.h.)

Initial climb rate: 914 m/min (3,000 ft. min.) from sea level

Range: 1609 km (1,000 mi.)

Service ceiling: 12497 m (41,000ft.)

Weights: empty 2852 kg (6,274 lb.); maximum take-off 4498 kg (9,895 lb.)

Armament: six 12.7-mm nose-mounted machine-guns

Dimensions: span 11.27 m (37 ft.)
length 10.00 m (32 ft.)
height 3.12 m (10 ft. 3 in.)
wing area 22.29 m² (240 sq. ft.)

RF-80A SHOOTING STAR

Many early model Shooting Stars were built for, or converted to, the photo-reconnaissance role. This example saw service in Korea, where the aircraft operated with an escort of fighters.

The pilot enjoyed exceptional visibility through a teardrop sliding canopy. The cockpits of reconnaissance versions differed very little from fighter variants. The only additions were camera switches, film counters and blinker lights to replace the K-14 gunsight.

Despite the early success of the Shooting Star, it was quickly overshadowed by more advanced designs from rival manufacturers. The type was retained for second-line duties, in which the Shooting Stars remained for a number of years until fatigue problems caused their withdrawal.

Though the aircraft were initially flown in their peacetime natural colour scheme, some RF-80s adopted olive-drab upper surfaces when they went to war in Korea. Despite this the retention of the large 'buzz' numbers compromised the end result.

An enlarged forward section housed the reconnaissance camera suite. Access to the camera bay installation was by way of an upward-hinging nose section. Camera film could be replaced in a few minutes by experienced personnel.

Mounted low on either side of the fuselage were the small intakes. They were prone to ingesting foreign objects when the aircraft operated from semi-prepared runways.

To answer requests from USAF pilots for additional range, wingtip tanks were installed on the Shooting Star. They varied in size, and later models were fitted with additional fuel tanks under the wings.

A red fuselage band was painted on all early Shooting Stars. This denoted the turbine position within the engine. At this point the rear fuselage could be removed to allow maintenance personnel access to the engine.

FIGHTING JETS

BRITISH FIGHTERS: Entering service with the Royal Air Force in late 1944, the Gloster Meteor (pictured above) saw limited use, often on ground attack duties. After the end of World War II, a host of specialised variants were introduced into service, such as night-fighters, target-tugs and tactical photo-reconnaissance models. Widely exported to European and Middle Eastern countries, the Meteor remained in limited service until the late 1970s when it was finally replaced by more modern types. The Meteor had the distinction of being the first jet fighter in RAF service.

GERMAN GENESIS: Widely regarded as the best fighter of World War II, the Messerschmitt Me 262 was introduced into (limited) operational service before its rivals. Allied pilots found the Me 262 had remarkable agility and was able to outperform anything the Americans or British could offer. Hampered by a dwindling fuel supply, the Germans initially used the aircraft as a light bomber before pilots saw the full potential of the fighter. After the end of hostilities, Allied pilots flight-tested the aircraft and were thoroughly impressed. It had only limited post-war service, but the aircraft's design influenced fighter design for years to come. Other variants constructed were two-seat trainers, night-fighters, and precision attack bombers which were equipped with a glazed nose-section for an additional crew member.

Lockheed's adaptable lady

T-33 SHOOTING STAR: Developed into a highly successful trainer, the T-33 operated by a number of countries. It provides the first experience of jet flight for many pilots.

XF-90: Offered to the USAF as a potential long-range bomber escort, the XF-90 was not successful and eventually lost out to the two-seat McDonnell F-101 Voodoo.

F-94C STARFIRE: A specialised variant of the T-33 was developed to intercept intruders at night. Fitted with an improved radar, the aircraft saw much service with the USAF.

LOCKHEED

ER-2

● Research ● Ecological monitoring ● Sensor platform

N ASA's ER-2 (ER for Earth Resources) is a peaceful version of the Cold War's U-2 spyplane. The nuclear stand-off between the West and the Soviet Union made it necessary to use high-flying reconnaissance aircraft, but the airframe became a less sinister tool when NASA began using it. ER-2s have been vital in recent years for monitoring the hole in the ozone layer, and for performing tasks that would otherwise be carried out by satellites.

▲ NASA operates just three ER-2 survey platforms, and all are based at NASA's experimental facility at Moffett Field. NASA-Ames has also operated civilian versions of the earlier U-2 aircraft.

LOCKHEED ER-2

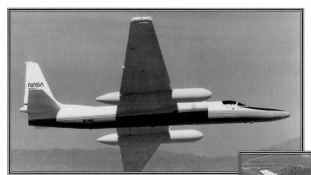

▲ **Narrow body**
The TR-1 fuselage assembly is a narrow structure, a shape optimised for low drag in high-altitude flight.

▲ **NASA's special missions master**
The ER-2 is operated specifically by a unit of NASA known as the High Altitude Missions Branch.

▲ **Training variant**
Prospective NASA research pilots become accustomed to the unusual handling characteristics of the ER-2 in the USAF's tandem two-seat Lockheed U-2RTs of the the 9th Reconnaissance Wing.

▲ **Multi-mission cockpit**
Essentially similar to the military TR-1A, the ER-2's cockpit contains various sensor displays.

Foreign detachments ▶
As well as operating in the USA, NASA U-2s and ER-2s were often detached to Norway.

FACTS AND FIGURES

➤ One of NASA's three original U-2 pilots was a Briton, Ivor Webster, who trained for spy flight missions in the RAF.

➤ In 1980 an ER-2 studied volcanic eruptions from Mount St. Helens.

➤ Two TR-1s were originally given to NASA and redesignated ER-2.

➤ Extra cameras used by NASA included Wild-Heerbrug RC-10 s with 15.2- and 30.5-cm (six- and 12-inch) focal lengths.

➤ A third ER-2 (formerly a TR-1A of the 9th SRW) is now in service with NASA.

➤ The military TR-1 was used as a precision electronic reconnaissance aircraft.

PROFILE

NASA's civilian spyplanes

To most of the world the Lockheed U-2, manufactured at the top-secret 'Skunk Works', is remembered for being the spyplane shot down over Russia in 1960.

Originally, NASA (National Aeronautics and Space Administration) and its predecessor had only one connection with this Cold War spook, also called the 'Black Lady': NASA's civilian research was originally the 'cover story' for CIA spy flights in the U-2. But with the 1971 Earth Resources Satellite Technology programme (later called Landsat), NASA began operating

two U-2Cs (joined by the improved ER-2 model in 1983) for genuine, peaceful research using sensors and infra-red cameras. The U-2s complemented the satellite in providing a better understanding of the planet we live on, for example, measuring the chlorophyll content of vegetation. The ER-2 model carried most of its sensors in two 'superpods', one under each wing.

Although the U-2 is a difficult aircraft to fly, pilots appreciate this type of work because they are using a one-time clandestine weapon of war for a purpose that benefits mankind.

Above: ER-2s wear NASA's standard civilian-style paint scheme of upper surface gloss white with pale grey undersides and lateral blue stripe. The white paint scheme helps to prevent the systems overheating in strong sunlight.

Above: Lockheed ER-2s are useful to NASA because of their high ceiling. ER-2s regularly fly at heights of up to 24,000 m (78,740 ft.) and have a range of nearly 5000 km (3,100 mi.).

U-2R

Type: single-seat high-altitude strategic reconnaissance aircraft

Powerplant: one 75.02-kN (16,880 lb.-thrust) Pratt & Whitney J75-P-13B turbojet engine

Cruising speed: 740 km/h (460 m.p.h.) at 19,810 m (65,000 ft.)

Operating altitude: 19,810 to 21,335 m (65,000 to 70,000 ft.)

Maximum altitude: 24,000 m (78,740 ft.)

Range: 4365 km (2,712 mi.)

Weight: maximum take-off 18,733 kg (41,300 lb.)

Payload: (NASA U-2C) 658 kg (1,450 lb.) of sensors; (ER-2) 1361 kg (3,000 lb.) of optical, thermal and electronic sensors

Dimensions:
span	31.39 m (103 ft.)
length	19.13 m (62 ft. 9 in.)
height	4.88 m (16 ft.)
wing area	92.90 m² (1,000 sq. ft.)

ER-2

Shown below is one of NASA's three ER-2 single-seat high-altitude earth resources aircraft, based at Moffett Field in the United States and detached to Bodø in Norway.

The ER-2's ultra-high-aspect ratio wings are similar to those of a glider, enabling the aircraft to act almost as a powered sailplane when at high altitude. They also make the aircraft probably the most difficult aircraft in the world to land, and several U-2 and TR-1 pilots have died in crashes after losing control just before touchdown.

The long nose is hollow and can hold whatever equipment is suitable for the ER-2's particular mission profile. Further space is provided by the 'Q-bay' behind the pilot.

On take off the ER-2 jettisons its wing-mounted outrigger wheels, later coming in to land gently on one of its wingtip skids.

The Lockheed U-2 series are the world's largest single-engined production aircraft, propelled by an enormous Pratt & Whitney J75 engine.

The cockpit is fully pressurised to withstand high-altitude missions and contains a single space-suited pilot.

Long, detachable 'superpods' are built under the wings and contain various different missions sensors.

A small composite tailwheel is housed in the rear fuselage, and outrigger wheels on the wings are used for extra balance.

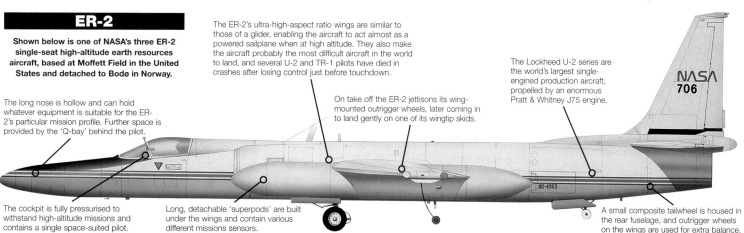

Environmental missions

OZONE RESEARCH: When detached to Norway, the ER-2's prime task is the continued monitoring of the upper atmosphere's ozone levels.

BIOLOGICAL RECONNAISSANCE: NASA has employed the sophisticated monitoring gear of its ER-2s to record a population boom in a species of moth which was destroying crops on the American coast.

VOLCANIC MONITORING: The ER-2 was also successfully used to monitor the activity of Washington State's Mount St Helens during a period of eruptions in 1980.

ACTION DATA

SERVICE CEILING

In their assigned roles, whether it be ozone research or monitoring, these aircraft operate on the fringes of the atmosphere. The pilots all wear suits very similar to those used by astronauts in space.

ER-2 21,335 m (70,000 ft.)	M-55 GEOFIZICA 21,500 m (70,540 ft.)
	MiG-25R 'FOXBAT' 21,000 m (69,000 ft.)

RANGE

Long range is useful in a survey aircraft (and in spyplanes), as data needs to be collected over large areas. The MiG-25 is designed to evade defences by flying at high speed over the target. This means shorter range and much higher fuel consumption.

ER-2 4365 km (2,712 mi.)

M-55 GEOFIZICA 4965 km (3,085 mi.)

MiG-25R 'FOXBAT' 1865 km (1,159 mi.)

ENDURANCE

Long wings mean large fuel tanks can be incorporated, and with a single engine running at low power settings both the ER-2 and M-55 can cruise for hours. The MiG-25R was designed to fly very fast but not to stay in the air for long periods.

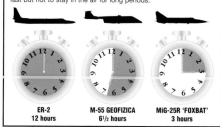

ER-2 12 hours	M-55 GEOFIZICA 6½ hours	MiG-25R 'FOXBAT' 3 hours

LOCKHEED

QT-2/Q-STAR/YO-3

● Advanced technology ● Quiet covert ● Observation aircraft

▲ The QT-2 'Quiet Thrust', the Q-Star (above) and the more developed YO-3 light observation aircraft (main picture), were produced for the US Army by the Lockheed Missiles and Space division.

Many years before the word 'stealth' earned its place in the vocabulary of aviation, Lockheed's QT-2, Q-Star and YO-3 were pioneering deception. This family of fine aircraft was developed to fly in almost total silence over the enemy, carrying reconnaissance sensors on an efficient airframe and powered by a silencer-equipped engine driving a slow propeller. These 'quiet flyers' had an important role in Vietnam.

PHOTO FILE

LOCKHEED **QT-2/Q-STAR/YO-3**

◀ **Sailplane origins**
Although the Lockheed QT-2 differs quite markedly in appearance from the YO-3, both aircraft were based on the Schweizer SGS 2-32 sailplane. The main differences on the YO-3 are a nose-mounted engine, two-seat cockpit, low wings and fully retractable undercarriage.

▼ **Service tests**
The YO-3A underwent extensive pre-service testing for the US Army in May and June 1970, during which time the tenth pre-production aircraft was destroyed in a crash.

▲ **Glider wings**
With its high aspect ratio wings and a very light loading wing, the YO-3A climbed at 187 m/min (613 f.p.m.) to 4265 metres (14,000 ft.).

▼ **Powered X-26A**
The two Lockheed QT-2s were 75-kW Continental-powered conversions of X-26A gliders.

▲ **Q-Star**
A third glider was converted in 1969 as the Q-Star. It subsequently had a de-rated Wankel rotary engine, cooled by an automobile radiator, fitted in the nose.

FACTS AND FIGURES

➤ The QT-2 was first tested in great secrecy at a remote civil airstrip in the Mojave Desert from July 1967.

➤ The YO-3A had a nose-mounted engine and fully retractable landing gear.

➤ The Q-Star was a 'one-off' testbed that was flown with two types of engines.

➤ These stealthy observation aircraft carried sensors, listening devices, cameras and infra-red detectors.

➤ Lockheed's Missiles and Space division produced only these aircraft.

➤ Nine YO-3As flew 1,116 missions in Vietnam without the loss of any aircraft.

Silent spies over the battlefield

The Lockheed QT-2, Q-Star and YO-3 combined a Schweizer sailplane fuselage with the quietest engines that had ever been developed for a military aircraft. These were almost totally silent reconnaissance aircraft that flew directly over the enemy without being detected.

After the first two QT-2s were evaluated in Vietnam, Lockheed proceeded with the YO-3A version of these stealthy powered gliders for the US Army. Thirteen YO-3As

went to Vietnam in 1970 for operational evaluation.

Proven in war, they were retired in 1972 and used for military research though some went to civil operators. One was used by fisheries authorities to stalk poachers, and two further aircraft were operated by the Federal Bureau of Investigation for law enforcement work. Another was used by NASA as a microphone-carrying vehicle to measure rotor blade noise in a helicopter test programme.

The small, versatile, virtually

silent observation aircraft has great value in both peacetime and war. These planes showed the way for a new kind of practical flying, but no modern-day equivalent of them has been developed.

Above: Various types and sizes of propellers were fitted to the YO-3A's Continental engine, including this six-bladed unit.

LOCKHEED YO-3A

This quiet, single-engined observation aircraft was converted from Schweizer's SGS 2-32 sailplane. A specially silenced Continental IO-360D engine was fitted with a variety of airborne sensors.

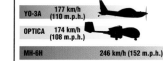

Above: The civil-registered Q-Star was re-engined in 1969 with a Wright RC2-60 liquid-cooled rotary engine. This was the first time that a Wankel-type powerplant was used in an aircraft.

Sensors, including an infra-red illuminator and infra-red designator were fitted beneath the nose and rear fuselage. A night viewing aerial periscope was fitted in the front cockpit.

The modified tandem, two-seat cockpit was covered by a large, single-piece, upward-hinged bubble canopy with a separate front windscreen.

Production YO-3As were fitted with a nose-mounted Teledyne Continental IO-360D six-cylinder, air-cooled piston engine. Early aircraft had a six-bladed fixed-pitch propeller, but later a three-bladed variable-pitch unit was fitted.

The long-span, all-metal wings had a trailing-edge extension to the inner section from mid-span, giving a total wing area of 19.05 m² (205 sq. ft.).

The basic Schweizer SGS2-32 all-metal structure was retained for the wings and fuselage. A normal tailwheel undercarriage had the main legs retracting inwards into the wings.

U.S. ARMY 18001

Vietnam spy in the sky

1 ENEMY OBSERVATION: Flying quietly at low level, using the lie of the land to remain covert, the YO-3A used its onboard sensors to track an enemy convoy. It then transmitted details to a patrolling Hercules gunship.

2 TARGET PINPOINTED: Using information radioed from the spyplane, the heavily armed AC-130 swooped down to make its attack.

YO-3A

Type: two-seat single-engined 'quiet' observation aircraft

Powerplant: one 158-kW (210-hp.) Continental IO-360D six-cylinder air-cooled piston engine

Maximum speed: 222 km/h (138 m.p.h.) at sea level

Cruising speed: 177 km/h (110 m.p.h.) at sea level

Initial climb rate: 187 m/min (613 ft./min.)

Service ceiling: 4265 m (14,000 ft.)

Endurance: 4 hours 25 min at sea level

Weights: empty 1419 kg (3,122 lb.); loaded 1596 kg (3,518 lb.); max 1724 kg (3,800 lb.)

Dimensions:
span	17.37 m (56 ft. 11 in.)
length	8.94 m (29 ft. 4 in.)
height	2.77 m (9 ft. 1 in.)
wing area	19.05 m² (205 sq. ft.)

ACTION DATA

CRUISING SPEED

Although they represent designs separated by several years, the YO-3A and Optica were intended to fulfil similar roles and offered very similar performance. Cruising at low speeds over the operational area, these aircraft offered long endurance and low noise for tasks normally undertaken by helicopters.

YO-3A	177 km/h (110 m.p.h.)
OPTICA	174 km/h (108 m.p.h.)
MH-6H	246 km/h (152 m.p.h.)

INITIAL CLIMB RATE

McDonnell Douglas' specially modified MH-6H for use by US Special Forces offers the low noise of the other types in addition to impressive climb performance. The helicopter cannot compete in terms of range, endurance or cost-effectiveness, however.

YO-3A 187 m/min (613 f.p.m.)
OPTICA 219 m/min (718 f.p.m.)
MH-6H 631 m/min (2,070 f.p.m.)

SERVICE CEILING

Both the YO-3A and Optica were built with prolonged flight at very low altitudes as their main area of operation. Vulnerability to small-arms fire and the modern generation of high-performance attack/escort helicopters mean that pilots seek the safety of higher altitudes in combat.

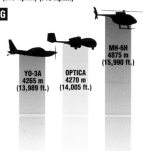

YO-3A 4265 m (13,989 ft.)
OPTICA 4270 m (14,005 ft.)
MH-6H 4875 m (15,990 ft.)

LOCKHEED
XFV-1 SALMON

● Experimental fighter ● Vertical take-off and landing ● Turboprop power

Lockheed employees gave the XFV-1 the nickname 'Pogo Stick' when this bizarre aircraft was revealed in 1955. The XFV-1 was one of two designs (the other being the Convair XFY-1) developed as a tail-sitting air defence fighter for vertical take-off and landing from small sites or naval warships. The XFV-1 was expected to land in the vertical position, but failed because it did not have a sufficiently powerful engine to do so.

▲ Extensive wind tunnel tests and subsequent flight tests proved the validity of the concept of transitioning from vertical to horizontal flight, but engine problems effectively killed the XFV-1.

LOCKHEED XFV-1 SALMON

Preserved Salmon ▶
Two XFV-1s were built, but only the first took part in flight tests. The second was passed to NAS Los Alamitos and used as a gate guardian.

▼ Attaching the cradle
Having been equipped for horizontal take-off, the Salmon was placed in the vertical position by using a special cradle.

Reaching the cockpit ▶
When resting vertically on its tail, the Salmon's cockpit was high above the ground and the pilot had to climb a long ladder to reach it.

▼ Unique configuration
With its cruciform tail, huge spinner and contra-rotating propellers, the XFV-1 was made even more ungainly by the addition of spindly landing gear.

▼ Nearing the vertical
Several photographs show the XFV-1 as though it was about to launch in the vertical mode. Unfortunately, although it made horizontal-vertical transitions and hovered at altitude, it was never able to take off vertically without the intended YT40-A-14 engine.

FACTS AND FIGURES

➤ On 23 December 1953, during taxi tests, the XFV-1 inadvertently became airborne for the first time.

➤ Two XFV-1 prototypes were built but the second aircraft never flew.

➤ The US Navy cancelled further tests of the XFV-1 on 16 June 1955.

➤ Lockheed's Clarence L. (Kelly) Johnson acknowledged that test pilots were 'afraid to fly' the XFV-1 in final tests.

➤ The US Navy had hoped to carry the XFV-1 aboard destroyers and frigates.

➤ The second XFV-1 is now on display at the US Naval Aviation Museum in Pensacola.

PROFILE

Vertical take-off fighter dream

In an attempt to exploit new areas of air power and spurred on by competition with the USAF, the US Navy began studies of vertical take-off and landing (VTOL) fighters in the 1950s. Lockheed's XFV-1, together with the competing Convair XFY-1, were interesting concepts which would have

permitted naval aviators to go into combat from just about anywhere, without the need for an airfield or an aircraft-carrier. The concept may have been inspired, in part, by the speed with which Chinese troops overran US airbases in Korea in January 1951.

Even if it had not been underpowered, it is questionable whether the 'Pogo Stick' would ever have entered service or have been a practical

aircraft. Unlike the competing Convair fighter, it never made a successful vertical take-off or landing. When tests were stopped, the Navy continued to develop conventional fighters.

Above: Several flights were completed using the conventional undercarriage.

Above: The large size of the XFV-1 can be seen in comparison to its T-33 chase plane. By the time the Salmon flew, its performance was already inadequate for a fighter.

XFV-1 SALMON

Herman 'Fish' Salmon took this aircraft aloft for the first time on 23 December 1953. It made several other flights before the programme was cancelled in 1955.

XFV-1 Salmon

Type: single-seat experimental VTOL fighter

Powerplant: (for flight tests) one 4362-kW (5,849 lb.) Allison XT40-A-6 turboprop engine driving contra-rotating propellers; (planned) one 5294-kW (7,099 lb.) Allison YT40-A-14

Maximum speed: 933 km/h (579 m.p.h.)

Endurance: 1 hour 10 min

Range: estimated 600 km (373 mi.)

Service ceiling: 13200 m (43,300 ft.)

Weights: empty 5261 kg (11,574 lb.); maximum take-off 7358 kg (16,187 lb.)

Armament: (planned FV-2) four 20-mm Mk 12 cannon or 48 70-mm 'Mighty Mouse' folding-fin aircraft rocket projectiles

Dimensions: span 9.40 m (30 ft. 10 in.)
length 11.40 m (37 ft. 4 in.)
height (est.) 8.00 m (26 ft. 3 in.)
wing area 22.85 m² (256 sq. ft.)

A production version of the XFV-1 was proposed by Lockheed, known as the FV-2, fitted with spinner-mounted radar.

A bulletproof windscreen and armour were to have been added to the cockpit of any operational aircraft. Pilot workload would have been very high, with the possibility of a night-time deck landing in poor weather at the end of a combat mission.

Although the Allison XT40-A-6 turboprop produced 4362 kW, this was insufficient power as it did not allow the XFV-1 to achieve the 1.2:1 power-to-weight ratio necessary for vertical take-off. The engine consisted of twin T38 turbines and drove three-bladed contra-rotating propellers. In its YT40-A-14 form the engine would have produced 5294 kW (8,000 hp.), but this engine never became available.

In the FV-2, the tip-tanks would have accommodated fuel and either four 20-mm cannon or 48 folding-fin aircraft rockets of 70-mm calibre.

Having decided to carry out initial tests in the conventional flight mode, Lockheed fitted this make-shift undercarriage and delivered the aircraft to Edwards Air Force Base by truck. Taxiing trials began in November 1953.

Wheels were added to the tailfins for conventional operations, while the tip of each fin also held a wheel for vertical operations. The XFV-1 pilot would have landed vertically while hanging in his gimbal-mounted ejection seat and looking vertically downwards over his shoulder. In reality, this would have been impossible on the moving deck of a ship.

ACTION DATA

MAXIMUM TAKE-OFF WEIGHT

The XFV-1 and the Convair XFY-1 Pogo were designed to satisfy the same requirement. The only comparable tail-sitting vertical take-off aircraft was the Ryan X-13 Vertijet, which was also considered as the basis for a fighter.

XFV-1 SALMON 7358 kg (16,187 lb.)
XFY-1 POGO 7371 kg 16,216 lb.)
X-13 VERTIJET 3317 kg (7,297 lb.)

MAXIMUM SPEED

Delays with the Allison engine caused the entire XFV-1 programme to slip. Any operational fighter based on either the XFV-1 or XFY-1 would have been hopelessly outperformed.

XFV-1 SALMON 933 km/h (580 m.p.h.)
X-13 VERTIJET 777 km/h (483 m.p.h.)
XFY-1 POGO 982 km/h (610 m.p.h.)

SERVICE CEILING

If the concept had proved successful, these aircraft would have displayed exceptional climb capabilities, allowing them to reach high altitudes very quickly. They could act as point-interceptors or gain the advantage in combat by reaching their ceiling quickly.

XFV-1 SALMON 13200 m (43,300 ft.)
X-13 VERTIJET 9144 m (30,000 ft.)
XFY-1 POGO 13320 m (43,700 ft.)

Salmon in action

VERTICAL TAKE-OFF: The XFV-1 was designed to be launched vertically from the deck of a ship or a dispersed field landing-pad. Missions would be flown in the horizontal position, however.

VERTICAL LANDING: Having completed the mission, the pilot would not be restricted to a fixed airfield which might be prone to attack. The XFV-1 would be flown slowly into the vertical position and could be landed as power was decreased.

FLIGHT TESTS: Flights were performed with the fixed undercarriage, taking off and landing in the conventional manner. A cradle was necessary for the transfer to the vertical position on the ground.

TAIL SITTING: There was insufficient power from the XT40-A-6 engine for the XFV-1 to perform vertical take-offs or landings.

LOCKHEED MARTIN

F-16XL

● Cranked-arrow wing ● Long-range fighter ● Research prototype

▲ If the XL had entered service, the single-seat aircraft would have been the F-16E, with the F-16F being the two-seat version. Both prototypes now serve with NASA on high-speed research tests.

A design exercise aimed at extending the first-line service life of the F-16, the delta-winged XL was mainly the victim of the end of the Cold War and the resulting budgetary cutbacks rather than a lack of performance. The F-16XL was one of a number of 'life-extension' options for the Fighting Falcon explored by a consortium of US manufacturers. The test airframes continue to expand the flight envelope for future fighters in this class.

PHOTO FILE

LOCKHEED MARTIN F-16XL

▲ Low-drag missiles
The service F-16E/F would have carried four AMRAAM missiles nestling in bays under the wingroots.

▲ Agile fighter
Although at low speeds the large-wing XL was outmanoeuvred by the standard F-16, at high speeds it retained a great deal of the Falcon's legendary turning capability.

◄ Short take-off
The huge wing of the F-16XL allowed it to take off in very short distances, even with a heavy bombload.

▼ Airliner tests
NASA uses the F-16XLs on supersonic drag-reduction tests for future high-speed airliners.

▲ Stretched Falcon
While the front and back portions of the XL were unmistakably F-16, the central fuselage was dramatically lengthened. This allowed the carriage of much more fuel for greater range.

FACTS AND FIGURES

➤ The F-16XL was initially known as the SCAMP – Supersonic Cruise and Maneuvering Prototype.

➤ The F-16E/F lost to the F-15E Strike Eagle in a competition for a new strike fighter.

➤ Another F-16 was used to test multi-axis thrust vectoring with moving tail nozzle.

➤ No less than 17 stores stations were allowed for under the XL's big 'cranked-delta' wing.

➤ The second F-16XL had a more powerful General Electric F110 powerplant.

➤ The F-16XL airframe was designed to withstand more than 9g during turns.

PROFILE

Cranked-arrow Falcon

Before a modern combat aircraft even enters service, the manufacturers have invariably explored numerous ways to modify the basic concept to increase capability and undertake new roles. The revised configuration of the General Dynamics F-16XL was one of a number of design options tested by the parent company in partnership with other manufacturers within the development programme for one of the world's most successful combat aircraft.

Fitted with a cranked-arrow

wing planform distinctly different to that of production F-16s, two XL test vehicles were built during the 1980s, primarily for studies into the practicality of wing skins made entirely of composite materials. Both began life as single-seat F-16 airframes.

Hundreds of test flights were made by the F-16XLs, to prove that a new wing could enhance the Fighting Falcon's already impressive performance in both air-to-air and air-to-surface combat missions. Both aircraft went into storage after completion of the initial test programme, although in 1989

one was passed to NASA for research into laminar flow wings and had hundreds of tiny holes drilled into a section its wing. The second machine, which had been previously fitted with a two-seat cockpit and designated F-16XL-2, participated in a programme to test vortex flaps for high-speed civil transports.

Single examples of a single-seat and a two-seat XL were produced. Both flew many times during the competition for a new strike fighter, but the design lost out to the cheaper but more conventional F-15E Eagle.

The cranked-arrow wing shape consisted of a compound 50°/70° sweepback on the leading edge. The outer portion of the wing had powerful leading-edge flaps.

To optimise airflow and preserve the area ruling (which gives the best supersonic performance), the F-16XLs had large 'carrot' fairings on the wing trailing edges.

F-16XL

Type: lightweight fighter research aircraft

Powerplant: one Pratt & Whitney F100-P-100 turbofan engine rated at 65.39-kN (14,700-lb.-thrust) dry power or 106.22 kN (23,878-lb.-thrust) with afterburner

Maximum speed: 2126 km/h (1,321 m.p.h.)

Initial climb rate: above 15240 m/min (50,589 f.p.m.)

Ferry range: 4630 km (2,877 mi.)

Service ceiling: beyond 15000 m (49,212 ft.)

Weights: max take-off 21773 kg (47,900 lb.)

Armament: max ordnance 6804 kg (14,968 lb.)

Dimensions:
span	10.43 m (34 ft. 2 in.)
length	16.51 m (54 ft. 2 in.)
height	5.36 m (17 ft. 7 in.)
wing area	61.59 m² (663 sq. ft.)

F-16XL-1

With Jim McKinney at the controls, the first F-16XL prototype took to the air on 15 July 1982, followed by the F-16XL-2 two-seater in October. Both had been produced by General Dynamics to fight a competition against the strike version of the mighty McDonnell Douglas Eagle.

For night attack the F-16XL could have carried LANTIRN infra-red and laser designation pods on hardpoints under the engine intake. A production variant may have carried such sensors buried in the leading edge of the wings.

The first F-16XL was powered by the Pratt & Whitney F100, while the second had a General Electric F110.

In several flights the F-16XLs demonstrated the ability to carry large bombloads. In addition to fuselage hardpoints, the XL had six under each wing arranged in a triangular pattern to keep drag to a minimum.

GENERAL DYNAMICS
F-16XL
745

The two F-16XLs carried the standard F-16's APG-66 radar. This is a very versatile multi-mode unit offering excellent capability in both air-to-air and air-to-ground modes.

For the air-to-air role the F-16XL could carry four AIM-120 AMRAAMs under the wingroots and a pair of AIM-9 Sidewinders on the wingtip launch rails. A gun was also carried in the port wingroot.

There were airbrakes on either side of the engine jetpipes, which split to open above and below the aircraft. The long, box-like projection at the base of the fin housed a braking parachute.

COMBAT DATA

MAXIMUM SPEED

The XL had the same top speed as the standard F-16, but both were slower than the MiG-29. However, modern combat aircraft rarely fight at anything like their full maximum high-altitude speed potential, giving the MiG-29 no real significant advantage in this area.

F-16XL	2126 km/h (1,321 m.p.h.)
F-16C FIGHTING FALCON	2126 km/h (1,321 m.p.h.)
MiG-29 'FULCRUM'	2445 km/h (1,519 m.p.h.)

PAYLOAD

The standard F-16 was developed to carry a significant weapons load, whereas the MiG-29 was intended to have more of a pure fighter role. One key advantage of the XL design was the significant increase in weapons-carrying ability, lifting it out of the light-fighter class and enabling it to compete (eventually without success) with the much heavier F-15E Eagle.

F-16XL	F-16C FIGHTING FALCON	MiG-29 'FULCRUM'
6804 kg (14,968 lb.)	5421 kg (11,926 lb.)	3000 kg (6,600 lb.)

RANGE

Another area where the XL scored highly was range, achieved by a combination of extra internal fuel capacity and a more efficient wing design. Nevertheless, today's standard F-16 has a respectable combat radius, while the MiG-29 in its basic form is very much a short-range warplane. Later versions of the Russian aircraft have attempted to remedy this shortfall to some degree, but the 'Fulcrum' remains inferior to the F-16's range/load capabilities.

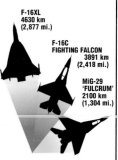

F-16XL	4630 km (2,877 mi.)
F-16C FIGHTING FALCON	3891 km (2,418 mi.)
MiG-29 'FULCRUM'	2100 km (1,304 mi.)

F-16 wing shapes

■ **F-16XL:** The cranked-arrow wing offered outstanding range and performance with only a small penalty in manoeuvrability. It also introduced a greater number of pylons for low-drag weapons carriage.

■ **F-16C:** This is the standard F-16 configuration, an excellent compromise between speed/range performance and manoeuvrability. There are two pylons per wing, plus the wingtip missile rails.

■ **F-16 FSW:** This was intended to win a contract for a forward-swept wing (FSW) demonstrator, but was never actually flown. The contract was won by the Grumman X-29, of which two were built.

LOCKHEED MARTIN

X-35/F-35 JSF

● Single-seat strike fighter ● Multi-service ● Service entry 2008

▲ US Congressional pressure produced the JSF: an amalgamation of the CALF (Common Affordable Lightweight Fighter) and JAST (Joint Advanced Strike Technology) programmes. The USN, USAF and USMC require 2852 examples.

The X-35, Lockheed Martin's winning contender in the Joint Strike Fighter contest, is the product of the biggest military aircraft procurement programme in history. The aircraft embodies a wide range of capabilities that will fulfil the requirements of the US Air Force, US Navy, US Marine Corps and the British armed forces well into the twenty-first century. Twenty-two development aircraft are currently in production.

LOCKHEED MARTIN X-35/F-35 JSF

▲ **Conventional demonstrator**
The first version of the X-35 to fly was the conventional X-35A, which validated the basic handling characteristics.

Colour cockpit ▶
The F-35C cockpit will have full-colour displays and a sidestick.

▼ **Lift fan and vectoring nozzle**
To provide vertical lift (required in the naval JSF variant), the X-35 has a lift fan shaft-driven from the main engine – behind the cockpit – which means a separate lift engine is not required.

▲ **Ultra-manoeuvrable**
A vectored engine nozzle and computer-controlled power-by-wire flight controls make the JSF virtually spin-proof.

▲ **Flexible refuelling options**
The X-35 prototypes had a USAF-style boom and receptacle refuelling system, but British, US Navy and Marine Corps F-35s will have a retractable probe.

FACTS AND FIGURES

➤ Lockheed Martin's proposal used design data purchased from the Russian builder of V/STOL aircraft, Yakovlev.

➤ Boeing's unsuccessful design for the JSF was designated X-32.

➤ Export potential for the JSF has been identified in several countries, including Australia, Canada, Germany and Spain.

➤ General Electric/Rolls-Royce and Pratt & Whitney are both developing interchangeable engines for the JSF under a unique arrangement.

➤ By 2011 the JSF production rate is expected to reach 122 per year, with manufacturers in the UK producing various elements.

PROFILE

21st century strike-fighter

The Joint Strike Fighter (JSF) will replace Harriers and Hornets, F-16s and A-10s within the US services and will likely equal the F-16 for export sales. More than 3000 are to be built for the US and UK alone, but this may eventually reach more than 6000 examples, with many nations almost certain to select it as their next fighter.

The JSF programme began in 1994, and by 1997 two manufacturers had been selected to produce two demonstrators each to prove their designs. Boeing's X-32

used a similar propulsion system to the Harrier, in a tailless delta configuration with a huge air intake under the nose. Lockheed Martin's X-35 looked more conventional, but the X-35B variant featured a 'lift fan' arrangement, a thrust-vectoring jet pipe and roll-control ducts. The winning X-35 design was the first ever aircraft to perform a short take-off, level supersonic dash, and vertical landing, all in a single flight.

The details of the actual F-35 will differ considerably from the

X-35s, as will the performance specifications. An estimate of the relative costs puts the USAF's conventional F-35A at $40 million, while the lift-fan and roll-control X-35B and C will be $50 million apiece. So far costs have been kept in check, but the most complicated, risky part of the programme has yet to be undertaken.

Left: One of the specific features of the X-35C is a stronger undercarriage able to take the added stresses of catapult take-offs and arrested landings.

The pilot's full-colour helmet-mounted display (HMD) will give him a 'through-the-floor' simulated display provided by three focal plane array sensors arranged to give a spherical field of view. This information is particularly useful during a vertical landing.

F-35B JSF

This is an artist's impression of the carrier version (CV) of the F-35. It will have larger wings and tail surfaces, strengthened undercarriage, arrester hook and other naval features for deck operations.

The use of a vectoring exhaust and a shaft-driven lift fan rather than a direct lift system avoids many of the problems associated with jet engines reingesting hot exhaust gases. Operations from carrier decks are also less hazardous for deck crew when using the lift fan system.

The variant produced for the US Navy will have a larger wing area, 57.6 m² (620 sq ft) rather than 42.7 m² (460 sq ft), to allow greater range and better low-speed handling around the carrier.

ACTION DATA

JSF REQUIREMENTS

The USAF currently has the largest initial requirement for JSF aircraft, as the type will replace the large fleet of F-16s amassed by Air Combat Command during the 1980s. The JSF also represents the US Navy's long-awaited A-6 replacement, while the STOVL version will take over from Harriers in both the USMC and Royal Navy.

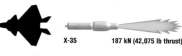

RAF/RN 150
US NAVY 480
US MARINE CORPS 609
US AIR FORCE 1763

The F-35 has a noticeable bulge in its fuselage just in front of the air intakes. This works in conjunction with the swept-forward inlet lip to provide stealth.

Unlike other STOVL aircraft like the Harrier, the entire powered lift and propulsion system is controlled by computers, making the F-35 much easier to fly. As the aircraft transitions from wing-borne to jet-borne flight, the throttle and stick functions change automatically.

MAXIMUM THRUST

Few figures have been released regarding the JSF's final specification. The X-35 prototype had an engine which developed around 187-kN (42,075-lb-thrust); production aircraft are likely to be a little more powerful. The X-35 falls between the thrust figures of the Harrier and higher performance types such as the F-15.

X-35   187 kN (42,075 lb thrust)

SEA HARRIER F/A.Mk 2   95.6 kN (21,510 lb thrust)

F-15E EAGLE   212.0 kN (47,700 lb thrust)

Replaced by the Joint Strike Fighter?

■ **HARRIER II:** The US Marine Corps will use the JSF to replace the AV-8B Harrier II. The RAF is also a potential customer.

■ **SEA HARRIER:** The Royal Navy is hoping to purchase up to 60 JSFs to operate from its aircraft-carriers.

■ **F-16 FIGHTING FALCON:** The largest single order for JSFs will come from the USAF, which requires 2036 to replace its large F-16 fleet.

■ **F/A-18 HORNET:** Marine Corps F/A-18s and Navy A-6s and F-14s will be replaced by a conventional carrier-based form of the JSF.

MacCready

GOSSAMER ALBATROSS

● Unorthodox design ● Repeated success ● Advanced technology

Dr Paul MacCready ventured into the world of sailplanes in the 1970s when he began construction of the Condor, in response to a challenge laid down by industrialist Henry Kremer. In 1977, the Condor set a world record, flying in a figure of eight over a distance of 1.6 km (one mile). Two years later, another challenge was offered, to cross the English Channel by man-powered sailplane.

▲ *On 12 June 1979, a historic event took place. Bryan Allen, flying the MacCready Gossamer Albatross, became the first person to fly over the English Channel in a man-powered craft.*

MacCready GOSSAMER ALBATROSS

▼ **Anatomy of the Albatros**
Even today, the Albatross remains one of the most bizarre looking creations ever to take to the skies. It features a high-mounted wing and a pusher layout, with extremely large propellers for the greatest amount of thrust possible. It weighs only 97.5 kg (215 lb.) fully loaded.

▲ **Rudimentary flying**
This type of craft represents manned flight in one of its purest forms. Note the wing construction and the location of the spars on this Liverpuffin.

◀ **Relying on solar energy**
Similar in design to the Gossamer Albatross was the later Solar Challenger. As the name implied, this little contraption relied on energy from the sun, using no fewer than 16,218 photo-volatic cells to generate 2.2 kW (2.95 hp) of power.

▼ **Scale aircraft technology**
Looking like an experimental aircraft from the World War II period, this unidentified machine sports a slightly swept wing and pusher layout.

▲ **Large span**
This photograph of a Liverpuffin illustrates the extremely long-span wings common to sailplanes. Note the dihedral of the outer wings.

FACTS AND FIGURES

➤ Pilot Bryan Allen had broken a record in 1977 for flying in a figure-of-eight over a distance of 1.6 km (one mile).

➤ No batteries or energy storage devices were employed on the Solar Challenger.

➤ Allen won a total of £150,000 in prizes for his achievements.

➤ After the record-breaking Channel crossing, MacCready did it again in 1981, this time in the Solar Challenger.

➤ A British machine, Solar One, made the first solar/electric-powered flight in 1978.

➤ The first man to cross the English Channel by hang-glider was David Cook, in May 1978.

PROFILE

Across the Channel by pedal power

Unlike just about any other flying craft, the machines that emerged from MacCready's workshop near Los Angeles were built with one aim in mind: to break records.

The first of these, the Condor, had a wingspan of 29.26 m and was a pusher design, with a large two-bladed propeller mounted at the back and an auxiliary aerofoil placed well forward. The pilot sat in an enclosed cabin directly below the main wing. For the record-breaking flight which took place at Shafter, California, championship cyclist Bryan Allen was chosen as the pilot. On the

hot August day in 1977, he flew the strange-looking Condor between the two pylons in 7 minutes 2.5 seconds.

Two years later, the industrialist Henry Kremer sponsored another challenge. This time it was more ambitious – to fly a pedal-powered sailplane across the English Channel. At MacCready, Vernon Oldershaw and his team built an improved version of the Condor, the Albatross. In many respects it was identical to the Condor and Bryan Allen once again piloted it on the journey. He landed at Cap Gris-Nez, near Boulogne, after pedalling 37 km (23 miles) over water.

Above: MacCready's man-powered sailplanes became household names during the late 1970s.

Gossamer Albatross

Type: single-seat man-powered sailplane

Powerplant: one human via bicycle pedals

Maximum speed: 11 km/h (6.8 m.p.h.)

Endurance: 2 hours 49 minutes

Range: 37 km (23 mi.)

Weights: empty 31.8 kg (70 lb.); maximum take-off (including pilot) 97.5 kg (215 lb.)

Propeller RPM: 115

Dimensions:
span	28.60 m	(93 ft. 9 in.)
length (est)	18.00 m	(59 ft.)
height (est)	7.00 m	(23 ft.)
wing area (est)	73 m²	(785 sq. ft.)

Left: This little craft is a Jupiter MPA. It was built by RAF apprentices at Halton.

To make the Albatross as light as possible, materials used included balsa wood (for the propeller), Mylar (for the fuselage covering, aerofoil and wing sections), plus alloy and foam sheet for the leading edge of the wing.

Protruding rearward from the wing was another outrigger pole, which doubled as a ballast weight to help maintain stability while in flight.

Ahead of the main wing, mounted at the end of of a long cylindrical pole, was the auxiliary aerofoil section. It was designed to pivot universally on the outrigger pole.

Centrally located above the main outrigger spar was the air speed indicator. Although rudimentary, it was a vital piece of equipment, helping the pilot ensure that the speed of the Albatross was sufficient to keep the craft airborne.

To sustain level flight, the Albatross required at least 0.25 kW of power to the propeller. This factor alone ensured that the pilot had to be at peak fitness in order to complete the cross-Channel trip successfully, For turning, 20 per cent more power was required.

GOSSAMER ALBATROSS

Using technology from the preceding Condor, a single Gossamer Albatross was built. It was remarkably successful on its flight across the Channel, and inspired the solar-powered Penguin.

The pilot sat on a bicycle-type frame and power was by means of peddling. A chain drive and sprocket provided a direct link to the two-bladed balsa wood propeller. In flight, a maximum of 115 revolutions per minute was achieved.

For landing, twin bicycle tyres mounted in tandem could be fitted. They were non-retractable and protruded slightly from the floor of the Mylar-covered cabin. Contrary to popular belief, they were not pedal-powered, but purely freewheeling items.

FLIGHT OF THE ALBATROSS

1 MAKING HISTORY: Having established a world record in the USA for flying a man-powered sailplane in a figure of eight between two pylons spaced 1.6 km (1 mile) apart, pilot Bryan Allen realised another ambition: to be the first man to cross the English Channel in a man-powered sailplane. The journey would begin from Folkestone in Kent and finish at Cap Gris-Nez in France.

FOLKESTONE

ENGLISH CHANNEL

2 ENDURANCE TEST: On 12 June 1979, at 05.51, Allen set off, easing the odd-looking craft into the air. Flying across the Channel can present many problems, especially in a craft as flimsy as the Albatross. Luckily, no problems were encountered during the journey and Allen arrived safely at the Cap in just 2 hours and 49 minutes. He won a £100,000 prize for the trip, presented by British industrialist, Henry Kremer.

37 km (23 miles)

CAP GRIS-NEZ

02:49:00

Modern-day pioneers in aviation

■ **BEDE BD.5:** Jim Bede has made his reputation on marketing ultra-small and light homebuilt aircraft. The BD.5, a small pusher machine made its first flight in 1972 and made speeds of up to 322 km/h (200 m.p.h.).

■ **ROBINSON R.22 BETA:** After working for Hughes, engineer Frank Robinson began developing a low-cost two-seat helicopter. Since its 1973 launch, the R.22 has become an extremely popular little machine.

■ **RUTAN DEFIANT:** Burt Rutan has been a pioneer in building small, low-cost aircraft, making extensive use of lightweight materials and advanced aerodynamics. The Defiant is one such machine.

MARTIN
XB-48

● Six engines ● Early jet bomber ● Bicycle undercarriage

MARTIN **XB-48**

◀ **Bicycle undercarriage**
With its tandem-style undercarriage on the fuselage and two small 'outrigger' wheels beneath the engine nacelles, the XB-48 had an extremely unusual appearance when taxiing at airfields.

▲ **Slow approach**
As a straight-winged, high-lift design, the XB-48 offered a very slow and safe landing speed.

High lift ▶
Test pilots reported that the XB-48 had exceptional lift in part because of the shape of its engine pods.

▲ **Smoky departure**
Plumes of exhaust smoke were a common sight during the take-off thanks to the six engines, each producing enough smoke to alarm people new to the aircraft.

Clean design ▶
Despite the strong competition the XB-48 faced, the design was one of the most graceful of the period, with a 'clean' fuselage and excellent visibilit for the pilot.

A heavy jet-bomber of the post-World War II era, the Martin XB-48 was not advanced enough to win a production contract. Although designed from the beginning for six jet engines, the XB-48 had the look of a propeller-driven aircraft: it was neat but rather boxy and straight-winged. The aircraft performed well but was outclassed – and beaten in competition – by the sleek, swept-wing Boeing B-47 Stratojet.

▲ *The first generation of jet bombers for the USAAF was of immense size, as illustrated here by ground crew working on the undercarriage of the unsuccessful Martin XB-48.*

FACTS AND FIGURES

➤ The first generation of US jet bombers was requested in April 1944, with an order placed to four companies.

➤ A bicycle undercarriage was first tested on a converted B-26 Marauder.

➤ Martin established a dedicated company to construct the first XB-48.

➤ First flight of the XB-48 was on 22 June 1947 with a short 37-minute hop to the Patuxent River test facility in Maryland.

➤ Top speed of the Martin XB-48 was a very poor 830 km/h (515 m.p.h.).

➤ The last surviving XB-48 was used as a ground target for the US Army.

Bombers in competition

Coming from the Glenn L. Martin Company of Baltimore, Maryland, the XB-48 followed Martin's famous B-26 Marauder bomber. A Marauder was used to test the bicycle landing gear of the XB-48, which consisted of two main wheels in the fuselage and two outrigger wheels extending from the side of the engine nacelles. In 1944, the US Army Air Force called for a heavy bomber to replace the Boeing B-29 Superfortress, and the XB-48 was Martin's candidate.

The XB-48 was exceedingly conventional in appearance, not unlike early jet bombers from the German wartime firm, Arado.

Its engine nacelles, which held three engines on each side of the aircraft, were really 'lifting bodies' that improved flying performance – but there was little else that was innovative in the XB-48 and Air Force officers quickly realised that the Boeing B-47 Stratojet was superior. Ironically, by the time the second XB-48 took to the air in late 1948 it was useful only as a test aircraft to carry equipment intended for use in its rival, the B-47.

The aircraft ended its day as a ground target for the US Army at the Aberdeen Proving Ground, where it was destroyed before being used for scrap.

Above: Seen landing at the Martin Company airfield, the XB-48 was the largest multi-engined conventional bomber built for the USAAF.

Right: Martin employees tow the XB-48 into place. It was vigorously marketed during the competition.

XB-48

Type: land-based bomber

Powerplant: six 17.8-kN 3,750-lb.-thrust) Allison/General Electric J35-A-5 turbojets

Maximum speed: 830 km/h (515 m.p.h.)

Initial climb rate: 991 m/min (3,250 f.p.m.)

Range: 4023 km (2,494 mi.)

Service ceiling: 11948 m (39,200 ft.)

Weights: empty 23705 kg (52,152 lb.); maximum take-off 46538 kg (102,384 lb.)

Armament: 9979 kg (21,950 lb.) bombload, plus two radar-directed 12.7-mm (.50 cal.) machine-guns in the tail turret

Dimensions: span 33.00 m (108 ft. 3 in.)
length 26.15 m (85 ft. 9 in.)
height 7.92 m (25 ft. 11 in.)
wing area 123.56 m² (1,330sq. ft.)

XB-48

Designed for the first USAAF jet bomber competition, the Martin XB-48 followed a conventional layout. The aircraft failed to win because of its poor performance when compared to the Boeing B-47 Stratojet.

The cockpit was positioned high on the fuselage, affording the pilot excellent all-round visibility. The crew was seated in single file, with the second pilot facing to the rear behind the first.

The six jet engines were installed in two sets of three under each wing. Martin opted for lifting-body style engine nacelles, while Boeing went for more conventional podded engines on the B-47.

The second prototype of the XB-48 went through a weight reduction programme to increase the performance of the aircraft, but this proved unsuccessful. A large tail incorporating a huge rudder the gave the aircraft good directional control.

The glazed nose of the aircraft allowed the bombardier to view the target from his position. Two small side windows were fitted either side of the nose.

Installing the main undercarriage beneath the fuselage enabled Martin to keep the wing free of complicated undercarriage members.

A single gun turret was installed in the tail of the XB-48 and controlled by radar. On the first prototype the fairing for the turret was found to be too small and was subsequently enlarged.

559585

COMBAT DATA

MAXIMUM SPEED

Despite its six Allison turbojets, the straight-winged XB-48 was still considerably slower than the smaller three-engined XB-51. In addition, the XB-51 could call upon 14 seconds of external rocket power. The B-47 was also a faster machine.

XB-48	830 km/h (515 m.p.h.)	
B-47E-11	975 km/h (605 m.p.h.)	
XB-51	1038 km/h (644 m.p.h.)	

SERVICE CEILING

Although the designers did not know it at the time, both the XB-48 and XB-47 were intended to carry nuclear weapons, so a high ceiling was vital. Surprisingly, the radical XB-51 was meant for lower-level ground support operations, though the USAF preferred the B-57 Canberra.

XB-48 11948 m (39,200 ft.)
B-47E-11 12345 m (40,500 ft.)
XB-51 12344 m (40,500 ft.)

MAXIMUM TAKE-OFF WEIGHT

Both the XB-48 and the B-47 Stratojet were six-engined bicycle-undercarriage types, although the successful B-47 – with superior aerodynamics and powerplants – could operate at nearly twice the weight of the XB-48. The smaller XB-51 was much lighter.

XB-48 46538 kg (102,384 lb.)
B-47E-11 89893 kg (197,765 lb.)
XB-51 26973 kg (59,341 lb.)

Martin's jet-powered designs

B-61 MATADOR: A large battlefield guided missile, the Matador came at a time when unmanned projects were the focus of attention. Here an example is prepared for an experimental launch at Holloman Air Force Base's range, New Mexico, in April 1951.

XP6M-1 SEAMASTER: Although a small number of highly advanced Seamaster jet-powered record-breaking flying-boats were delivered to the US Navy, none became fully operational.

XB-51: Conceived as a close-air support platform and attack aircraft, the revolutionary three-engined XB-51 was a delight to fly and performed well. It lost out in production orders in favour of smaller, more flexible multi-role fighter-bombers.

MARTIN
XB-51

● Tri-jet close support bomber ● Two prototypes ● Advanced features

U S Air Force units could have been equipped with the Martin B-51 bomber in the 1950s, were it not for changes to requirements that saw a British design chosen in its place. The XB-51 was fast and effective, but somewhat unorthodox in appearance. It was the world's first tri-jet, appearing long before the Boeing 727 jetliner, and it performed well in trials. However, the onset of war in Korea led to the building of the Canberra, albeit by Martin, as the B-57.

▲ One of a number of aircraft to have been cancelled after its design requirement was changed, the XB-51 introduced a number of novel aerodynamic features.

MARTIN XB-51

▲ First close-support jet
The first jet designed for close-support tasks, the XB-51 was destined to remain a prototype when USAF needs changed.

▲ Elegant thin wing
The XB-51 was an elegant aircraft, lacking the nacelles, tanks, landing gear wells and weapons pylons often seen on the wings of other designs.

▼ Early T-tail application
In order to keep the tailplane free from the rear jet's exhaust, the XB-51 used the T-tail design.

▲ Rocket-assisted take-off
Four 4.24-kN (954-lb.-thrust) RATO bottles with a 14-second burn duration could be attached to the rear fuselage of the XB-51 to improve take-off.

Drag 'chute deployed ▶
A common sight on 1950s jet bomber designs, the drag 'chute slowed an aircraft on landing, reducing wheel brake wear.

FACTS AND FIGURES

➤ *Toward the Unknown*, a film starring William Holden, featured an XB-51 known as the 'Gilmore fighter'.

➤ XB-51 46-685 made its first flight on 28 October 1949 at Baltimore, Maryland.

➤ Although Martin failed to secure an XB-51 contract, it went on to build 300 B-57s.

➤ XB-51s employed a bicycle-type landing gear which was evaluated on a Martin XB-26H Marauder named *Stump Jumper*.

➤ The two XB-51 prototypes cost the US government $12.5 million.

➤ The XB-51 did not receive a name, although 'Panther' was suggested.

PROFILE

Martin's radical close supporter

Everything about the Martin XB-51 was advanced, from nose to tail. The swept-wing, tri-jet XB-51 incorporated a rotary weapons bay that enabled it to deliver bombs while flying at high speed. In fact, speed was its trademark: the XB-51 would have been able to outrun most fighter aircraft of the early 1950s.

The bomber had a crew of two. The pilot sat beneath a fighter-style 'bubble' canopy. The second crew member, a radio-operator/navigator, had only a small observation window. Both men sat in

pressurised, air-conditioned comfort, strapped into upward-firing ejection seats.

The XB-51 programme originated in a 1946 USAAF competition for a close-support design to replace the Douglas A-26 Invader. After the air force dropped the A-for-Attack designation for these aircraft, the requirement was redrawn to specify a jet-powered machine.

Two prototypes flew just before the Korean War, the new type being an obvious candidate for night-time attacks on enemy supply lines. However, it was

soon realised that the aircraft's speed was better suited to daytime missions in Europe; MiGs had not yet appeared in the skies over Korea. Thus, after a number of alternative designs had been considered, the English Electric Canberra was chosen and, in 1952, the XB-51 was cancelled.

Above: General Electric's J47 turbojet powered the XB-51s to a top speed of 1038 km/h (645 m.p.h.). J47s were also fitted to aircraft such as the F-86 Sabre fighter.

Above: Under pressure from the Army, the USAF was forced to consider other types for the night intruder role, including a version of the Navy's AJ Savage, a modernised B-45, Avro Canada's CF-100 fighter and the British Canberra bomber.

An aerodynamically clean, if unorthodox, design, the XB-51 carried as much equipment as possible on the inside of the aircraft. All fuel was carried internally, and the only external features were the fuselage-mounted engines. The design had a 26-m (85-foot) fuselage, unusually long compared with its 16-m (52-foot) wing span.

XB-51

Type: two-seat close-support bomber

Powerplant: three 23.13-kN (5,200-lb.-thrust) General Electric J47 turbojet engines, plus, if required, four 4.24-kN (954-lb.-thrust) RATO bottles

Maximum speed: 1038 km/h (644 m.p.h.)

Cruising speed: 856 km/h (530 m.p.h.)

Initial climb rate: 2128 m/min (6,980 f.p.m.)

Range: 2575 km (1,600 mi.)

Service ceiling: 12344 m (40,500 ft.)

Weights: loaded 26974 kg (59,344 lb.)

Armament: eight 20-mm cannon in the nose with 1,280 rounds of ammunition, plus provision for up to 4760 kg (10,500 lb.) of bombs

Dimensions:
span	15.88 m (52 ft. 1 in.)
length	25.94 m (85 ft.1 in.)
height	5.28 m (17 ft. 4 in.)
wing area	50.91 m² (548 sq.ft.)

XB-51

46-686 was the second of the two Martin Model 234 XB-51s built, and flew for the first time in 1950. After the project was cancelled, both aircraft continued to undertake aerodynamic and weapons-handling trials until they were written off in accidents.

Two crew manned the XB-51, a pilot and a SHORAN operator. The pilot sat under a fighter-style 'bubble' canopy, while the navigator/bombardier occupied a compartment behind and to the rear of the cockpit.

The wing was the first variable-incidence wing fitted to a bomber, enabling the pilot to adjust the angle at which the leading edge met the air and thus shorten the aircraft's take-off run. Advanced spoiler ailerons and slotted flaps were also fitted.

The heart of the XB-51's weapons delivery system was the SHORAN short-range navigation and bombing system, which had a 322-km (200 mile) range, and was judged more suitable for high-speed daytime missions in Europe.

The XB-51's rotary bomb bay was an innovative feature. Lacking drag-inducing bomb doors, it allowed the delivery of 4760 kg (10,500 lb.) of bombs at high speed. Eight 20-mm cannon were to be installed in the nose of production aircraft.

General Electric supplied the three 23.13-kN (5,200-lb.-thrust) J47 turbojets for the XB-51s. To improve take-off performance, four rocket-assisted take-off (RATO) bottles could be fitted to the rear fuselage.

ACTION DATA

MAXIMUM SPEED

The XB-51 was a fast machine compared to the straight-winged B-45, the USAF's first jet bomber. The Stratojet was not as fast, but had a much longer range.

XB-51	1038 km/h (644 m.p.h.)
B-45C TORNADO	932 km/h (578 m.p.h.)
B-47E-II STRATOJET	975 km/h (605 m.p.h.)

ARMAMENT

XB-51s were to be fitted with a formidable armament of eight 20-mm cannon for ground strafing. The Tornado and Stratojet were lightly armed, but carried much greater bombloads.

XB-51	8 x 20-mm cannon 4760-kg (10,500-lb.) bombload
B-45C TORNADO	2 x 12.7-mm machine-guns 9979-kg (22,000-lb.) bombload
B-47E-II STRATOJET	2 x 20-mm cannon 9071-kg (20,000-lb.) bombload

RANGE

As a close-support design, the XB-51 lacked the range of larger types like the B-47. Its range even fell short of that of the B-45. The Canberra, which was built in preference to the XB-51, had better range and superior agility at low speeds.

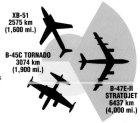

XB-51	2575 km (1,600 mi.)
B-45C TORNADO	3074 km (1,900 mi.)
B-47E-II STRATOJET	6437 km (4,000 mi.)

Martin's USAAF/USAF bomber dynasty

■ **B-10/B-12:** The USAAF's first all-metal monoplane bomber, the B-10 entered service in 1934 and was faster than contemporary fighters.

■ **B-26 MARAUDER:** Built to meet a 1939 USAAF need for a high-speed medium bomber, the B-26s saw extensive service in World War II.

■ **B-48:** Two of these six-engined bombers were built in competition with Boeing's B-47 Stratojet, a far more advanced design.

■ **B-57 CANBERRA:** Martin licence-built and went on to develop this night-intruder bomber, which was to serve in the Vietnam War.

MARTIN

P6M SEAMASTER

● Jet maritime seaplane ● Martin's last warplane ● Minelayer

Seaplane Striking Force was the name given to the US Navy's proposed units of minelaying maritime patrol aircraft equipped with the new generation of flying-boat, the Martin SeaMaster. However, the P6M was, in fact, a strategic, medium bomber. Inter-service rivalry had forced the Navy to disguise the real role of this seaplane from the Martin stable. Promising, but ultimately ill-conceived and accident-prone, the SeaMaster never entered squadron service.

▲ The SeaMaster was
an immensely strong aircraft designed to fly at high speed and low level to deliver its war load. It was to be Martin's last flying-boat. Only in Japan and Russia have military flying-boat designs been pursued since then.

MARTIN **P6M SEAMASTER**

▲ Into the sunset
Pilots noted that the SeaMaster handled more like a fighter than a bomber, being very responsive and capable of supersonic speeds.

▲ Overtaken by events
The over-budget P6M ultimately fell victim to the funding requirements of nuclear submarines and their Polaris missiles. Its minelaying role was performed by other types.

▲ First prototype
Aircraft 138821 was the first P6M and was tragically lost with all crew on 7 December 1955.

◀ Seaplane bases
The US Navy began building a shore base and converting a seaplane tender for production P6Ms.

Strongly constructed ▶
To provide the strength required for high-speed flight at low level a thick aluminium wing skin was used. The skin at the root of the upper wing surface was up to 25.4-mm (1-in.) thick.

FACTS AND FIGURES

➤ The ejection of four crew from the second XP6M-1 was the first American multiple ejection.

➤ The P6M broke world altitude and speed records in its category on early flights.

➤ The P6M's hull design was tested on a modified XP5M Marlin prototype.

➤ The SeaMaster was more than 25 tonnes heavier than the giant wartime Martin PB2M Mars flying-boat.

➤ The SeaMaster was designed to operate in 1.8- to 2.75-metre (6- to 9-foot) seas.

➤ World War II seaplane tender USS Albemarle was modified for use by P6Ms.

PROFILE

Last of the Martin seaplanes

Although deprived of the supercarrier *United States* by a Congress keen to cut peacetime defence budgets after 1945, the US Navy was eager to gain a nuclear capability to match that of the USAF. Martin was contracted to develop its flying-boat, the P6M SeaMaster.

Inter-service rivalry (the newly independent USAF tried to eliminate fixed-wing aircraft from the Army and Navy) was such that the nuclear role was played down so the Seaplane Strike Force (SSF) was devised to disguise the strategic bombing capability. SSF P6Ms would be deployed to lay mines in the sea

lanes around Soviet naval bases.

Refuelling en route if necessary, these craft were required to carry a 13·6-tonne payload over 2400 km (1,500 miles) and produce a dash speed of 1100 km/h (682 m.p.h.) over a 185-km (115-mile) leg running-in to the target.

Two prototypes were built, but after encouraging initial flights both were lost in accidents, knocking confidence and increasing costs. Further funding pressures meant that orders for this highly specialised machine were cancelled after just three P6M-2s had been delivered.

Above: An important part of the SeaMaster system was its automatic beaching gear. The P6M simply taxied into the unit, electrical and hydraulic connections were made (for brakes and steering) and the aircraft went ashore.

Below: On the hull below the 'Navy' legend is the starboard hydroflap, which was used as a rudder (one deployed) or brake (two deployed) on the water, or as a divebrake in the air.

YP6M-1 SeaMaster

Type: mine-laying and maritime reconnaissance aircraft

Powerplant: four 57.8-kN (13,001-lb.-thrust) Allison J71-A-6 afterburning turbojets

Maximum speed: 1107 km/h (686 m.p.h.)

Combat radius: 2270 km (1,407 mi.)

Service ceiling: 10668 m (34,991 ft.)

Weights: empty 38412 kg (17,439 lb.); maximum take-off 72574 kg (32,949 lb.) (rough waters), 86182 kg (39,127 lb.) (sheltered waters)

Armament: two 20-mm cannon in tail turret and up to 13607 kg (6.178 lb.) of mines and/or bombs

Dimensions:
span	31.30 m (102 ft. 8 in.)
length	40.93 m (134 ft. 3 in.)
height	10.33 m (33 ft. 11 in.)
wing area	176.51 m² (1,759 sq. ft.)

P6M-2 SeaMaster

Initially 30 P6M-2s were ordered, but this figure was progressively cut back until only three were delivered to the Navy. The programme was cancelled in August 1959.

The four crew (pilot, co-pilot, navigator/mine-layer and radio/armament defence operator) were seated in ejection seats, although these were not fitted to the first XP6M-1. Ahead of the cockpit was a nose radome for the main radar scanner.

The door of the watertight mine bay behind the cockpit rotated to open. The stores were attached to the inside of the door and were dropped when the door had rotated 180°. The SeaMaster sat low in the water – its wing floats were attached to the wingtips.

The SeaMaster did not perform to specification until the P6M-2 was fitted with 70.3-kN (15,747-lb.-thrust) J75 engines. Two prototypes and four pre-production P6Ms used afterburning Allison J71s, mounted parallel to the fuselage on the first two aircraft. After the afterburners caused damage to the fuselage skin, the engines were canted 5° outwards.

Compared to the USAF's contemporary B-47 Stratojet, the P6M had a 4.27-metre (14-ft.) longer wing span and a wing area some 46 m² (458 sq. ft.) greater. The entire structure was stressed to 3.8g, although the second P6M-2 was looped at 6g without sustaining damage.

After two accidents involving the prototypes (the first of which was fatal), the tailplane and its control surfaces were redesigned. The hull of the aircraft was designed to keep spray off the 'T-tail'.

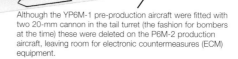

Although the YP6M-1 pre-production aircraft were fitted with two 20-mm cannon in the tail turret (the fashion for bombers at the time) these were deleted on the P6M-2 production aircraft, leaving room for electronic countermeasures (ECM) equipment.

ACTION DATA

MAXIMUM LOW-LEVEL SPEED

The P6M was designed as a high-speed, low-level attack aircraft and thus possessed a good top speed. Search-and-rescue machines tend to patrol at more modest speeds.

XP6M-1 SEAMASTER	960 km/h (595 m.p.h.)
Be-10 'MALLOW'	912 km/h (565 m.p.h.)
Be-42 ALBATROS	760 km/h (471 m.p.h.)

MAXIMUM THRUST

Even with afterburning turbojets the SeaMaster was underpowered. It was not until the production standard P6M-2 was available that the required performance was possible.

XP6M-1 SEAMASTER	231.2 kN (52,033 lb.)
Be-10 'MALLOW'	127.5 kN (28,682 lb.)
Be-42 ALBATROS	284.4 kN (63,979 lb.)

RANGE

The Be-10 was an advanced aircraft in its day and set speed, distance and altitude records. However, its limited operational usefulness led to its early retirement. For its intended role the SeaMaster needed good range. The Albatros also has good range, which is essential for maritime patrol and search-and-rescue roles.

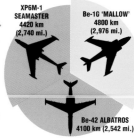

XP6M-1 SEAMASTER 4420 km (2,740 mi.)

Be-10 'MALLOW' 4800 km (2,976 mi.)

Be-42 ALBATROS 4100 km (2,542 mi.)

Jet-powered military flying-boats

■ **BERIEV Be-10 'MALLOW':** Little known in the West and the only aircraft of its class ever to go into operational service, the Be-10 was used in the Black Sea area from the early-1960s.

■ **BERIEV Be-42 ALBATROS:** Intended to replace the Be-12 turboprop in military maritime roles, the Be-42 flew in 1986. The status of Russian orders remains uncertain.

■ **CONVAIR XF2Y SEA DART:** The product of advanced research, the first of four Sea Dart jet seaplane fighter prototypes flew in 1953. Poor performance saw its cancellation in 1956.

■ **SARO SR.A/1:** With a top speed of 824-km/h (511- m.p.h.), this twin-engined, pressurised and ejection seat-equipped fighter still lacked official support. The first of three flew in 1947.

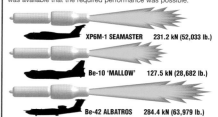

MCDONNELL

XP-67

- Long-range, high-altitude fighter ● First flown in 1944 ● Only one built

▲ McDonnell engineers designed the twin-engined XP-67 using the latest aircraft technology, combining an advanced airframe with a pair of unfortunately unproven, turbo-charged Continental I-1430 engines. The engines proved to be the weakest aspect of the design.

USAAC specification R-40, calling for a long-range fighter, was answered by McDonnell in 1940 with an unorthodox single-engined, twin-prop design. This was rejected but, undaunted, McDonnell tried again in 1941. This time they produced a more conventional, but aerodynamically advanced, machine. It was to be the first McDonnell-designed aircraft ordered by the US forces, but was plagued by problems with its new turbo-charged engines.

MCDONNELL XP-67

▼ Early flights disappointing
With engine problems at least temporarily solved, Edward E. Elliott took the XP-67 into the air for the first time on 6 January 1944. The de-rated engines failed to produce the power needed to reach the intended top speed.

▲ Tricycle landing gear
The forward strut of the undercarriage retracted rearwards into the fuselage, while the main gear retracted to the rear into the engine nacelles.

▲ Low profile design
The XP-67 was undoubtedly a sleek aircraft, but its performance did not match its looks.

▲ Well-armed interceptor
The sole XP-67 to be completed was unarmed. After initial proposals for 10-gun armament, in was decided that production aircraft should be fitted with six powerful 37-mm cannon, mounted in the inner wings. There was also a proposal for a single 75-mm cannon installation.

◄ Nicknames
'Bat' and 'Moonbat' were nicknames given to the XP-67 on account of its blended wing and fuselage. Its intended role as a high-altitude interceptor also gave rise to the name 'Bomber destroyer'. None was adopted officially.

FACTS AND FIGURES

➤ Although McDonnell manufactured the Fairchild AT-21 trainer, the XP-67 was the first USAAF aircraft of its own design.

➤ The troubled Continental XI-1430 engine was also fitted in the Lockheed XP-49.

➤ The XP-67 made its maiden flight at Scott Field, Illinois on 6 January 1944.

➤ On 6 September 1944, after just 43 hours flying, the XP-67 caught fire; it landed safely, but was burnt-out on the ground.

➤ Seven weeks after the first aircraft was lost the XP-67 programme was halted.

➤ Almost three years elapsed between the USAAF's order and the XP-67's first flight.

PROFILE

'Moonbat' bomber-destroyer prototype

Under the leadership of Garrett C. Covington, McDonnell's design team had been working on a new long-range interceptor since July 1939. The first proposal, with a single engine driving two pusher propellers via two extension shafts and angled gear drive, was rejected.

The next design was more favourably received, and two prototypes were ordered in September 1941. The XP-67 utilised the latest ideas in airframe design and a new engine – the inverted-Vee, turbo-charged Continental I-1430.

After the delayed engines were finally delivered and overheating problems appeared to have been solved, the aircraft took to the air. McDonnell test pilot Edward E. Elliott was not enthusiastic about the aircraft. Although it was easy to handle, the XP-67 had a slower rate of climb than anticipated and required a long runway from which to get airborne. In the 43 hours of testing, the 'Bat' never flew with its I-1430 engines at their design rating and thus never reached its intended top speed.

Meanwhile, the USAAF (the former USAAC) had decided to order the North American P-51 Mustang for the long-range escort role. The XP-67 programme ended in 1944.

Initially it was envisaged that the 'Bat' would be very heavily armed with fewer than 10 guns: six 12.7-mm (.50 cal.) machine-guns and four 20-mm cannon. During the detail design stage, however, this was changed to an equally formidable six 37-mm cannon mounted in the inboard wing sections.

Despite their intended 1007-kW (1,350 hp.) rating, the XP-67's engines never produced more than 790 kW (1,059 hp.) in flight.

The only completed XP-67 runs up its engines. The first of several fires, on 8 December 1943, was fortunately put out before causing serious damage.

Once flight trials got under way, handling was improved by moving the tailplane 30.5 cm (12 in.) upwards, increasing its dihedral by 2° and adding a small dorsal fin.

The turbo-superchargers fitted to the new 1007-kW (1,350-hp.) Continental XI-1430 12-cylinder, inverted-vee engines were a constant source of trouble. Even during tethered tests cooling was a problem, and they were prone to catching fire. The second XP-67 was to have been powered by two Rolls-Royce Merlin engines.

The XP-67's designers attempted to maintain true aerofoil sections over most of the airframe by 'blending' the centre fuselage and engine nacelles together to give a bat-like appearance.

211677

As it was intended as a high-altitude interceptor, the XP-67 had a pressurised cockpit for the pilot. Although described as easy to handle, the 'Bat' did not perform to specification.

A great deal of the semi-monocoque, Alclad-covered aluminium fuselage was used to store fuel. The aircraft was designed to have a range in excess of 3800 km (2,350 mi.) and a service ceiling of 11400 metres (37,400 ft.). However, flight tests revealed a slow rate of climb and a lower than expected top speed.

XP-67

Of the two XP-67s ordered, 42-11677 was the only one to be completed and flown. It was destroyed by fire on 6 September 1944.

XP-67

Type: single-seat long-range fighter

Powerplant: two 1007-kW (1,350-hp.) Continental XI-1430-17/19 liquid-cooled 12-cylinder inverted-Vee piston engines

Maximum speed: 652 km/h at 7620 m (404 m.p.h. at 25,000 ft.)

Cruising speed: 435 km/h (270 m.p.h.)

Landing speed: 150 km/h (93 m.p.h.)

Initial climb rate: 792 m/min (461 f.p.m.)

Maximum range: 3837 km (2,400 mi.)

Service ceiling: 11400 m (37,400 ft.)

Weights: empty 8049 kg (17,708 lb.); loaded 10031 kg (22,068 lb.); max take-off 11521 kg (25,346 lb.)

Armament: (planned) six 37-mm fixed forward-firing cannon

Dimensions:
span	16.76 m	(55 ft.)
length	13.65 m	(44 ft. 8 in.)
height	4.80 m	(15 ft. 4 in.)
wing area	38.46 m²	(414 sq. ft.)

COMBAT DATA

ARMAMENT

One of the notable features of the XP-67 was its six-cannon armament, which would have made it one of the most heavily-armed fighters of the period. The four 20-mm cannon fit of the Welkin was typical of other RAF fighters at the end of World War II. The Focke-Wulf Ta 152H-1 had three cannon, but was not used in the high-altitude role for which it was intended.

XP-67 — 6 x 37-mm cannon

WELKIN F.Mk 1 — 4 x 20-mm cannon

Ta 152H-1 — 1 x 30-mm cannon / 2 x 20-mm cannon

RANGE

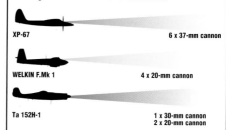

The XP-67 boasted an impressive range of over 3800 km (2,400 mi.), almost twice that of the Westland Welkin and Ta 152. However, the need for a new aircraft of this type disappeared with the adoption of the P-51, an aircraft that had already entered service with the RAF. The XP-67 had the least impressive ceiling performance.

XP-67 3837 km (2,400 mi.)

WELKIN F.Mk 1 1931 km (1,200 mi.)

Ta 152H-1 2012 km (1,250 mi.)

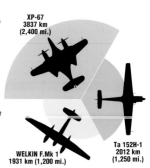

Long-range fighter prototypes of 1945

■ **LOCKHEED XP-58 CHAIN LIGHTNING:** This two-seat escort fighter was a development of the highly successful P-38. The lack of a suitably powerful engine hampered development.

■ **NORTHROP XP-61E BLACK WIDOW:** Based on the P-61 night-fighter, the E-model had a bubble canopy and no dorsal turret or radar. Two prototypes were built.

■ **FISHER XP-75 EAGLE:** An order for 2,500 of these single-engined fighters, fitted with a mid-mounted Allison V-3420 24-cylinder engine, was placed in June 1944. It was later cancelled.

■ **CONVAIR XP-81:** Powered by a turboprop and a turbojet, the P-81 would have escorted bombers in the Pacific. The first XP-81, with a Packard V-1650 piston engine, flew in 1945.

MCDONNELL

XF-85 GOBLIN

● Parasite fighter ● Early swept-wing jet ● Experimental aircraft

T he McDonnell XF-85 Goblin was designed for an incredible job – to be a 'parasite' fighter, carried by a giant B-36 bomber and released and retrieved in mid-air. This bizarre mission was never carried out operationally, but it dictated the unorthodox shape of the XF-85, a mid-wing monoplane with stubby, swept wings, a 'skyhook' in the nose and an X-shaped tail designed to fit into the bomb-bay of the B-36.

▲ *The diminutive Ed Schoch was the only man to fly the XF-85. Due to the compactness of the design, the aircraft could not be flown by anyone over 1.75 metres (5 ft. 8 in.) in height.*

MCDONNELL XF-85 GOBLIN

▲ **Tail feathers**
The XF-85's fuselage was so short that it required no less than six tails to keep it stable.

▲ **Stub fighter**
It was amazing that the tiny barrel shape of the fuselage could hold a pilot, engine, armament and fuel.

▼ **Snug fit**
There were not many inches to spare when fitting the XF-85 into the B-29 mothership.

▲ **Prepared for flight**
The Goblin required just as much maintenance as any other fighter of the period, despite its compact size.

▲ **Loading pit**
In order to load the XF-85, it was lowered into a pit. The B-29 was positioned overhead, allowing the Goblin to be raised.

Ready to go ▶
Nestling in the Superfortress weapon bay, the XF-85 is ready for flight. There was not a great deal of ground clearance for taxiing.

FACTS AND FIGURES

➤ The Goblin's escape system consisted of a T-4E powder charge fitted to the pilot's seat, which reclined at 33°.

➤ Two XF-85s were built, but the first aircraft completed only one test flight.

➤ A Boeing C-97 transported the XF-85 from Missouri to California in 1947.

➤ The XF-85 required a pilot 'not more than 1.75 m (5 ft 8 in tall) and weighing not more than 90.71 kg (200 lb).'

➤ Pilot Ed Schoch survived a belly landing following the XF-85's first flight.

➤ The Goblin was shorter than the wing span of an F-104 Starfighter.

PROFILE

Pocket-sized dogfighter

The McDonnell XF-85 Goblin was the only US Air Force aircraft conceived from the outset as a 'parasite' fighter, to be carried as an onboard escort aboard bombers, just as the converted Republic RF-84K Thunderflash was years later. In 1947, tests were carried out to evaluate the mating of a Goblin and a B-36 mock-up. The first XF-85 flew the following year, but it was plagued by conceptional and mechanical problems. Ed Schoch, the only man to pilot this strange aircraft, flew it from the bomb-bay of a B-29 Superfortress.

The XF-85 flew well enough by itself, but the whole concept of parasite fighters was flawed. Of about a dozen test flights four resulted in serious mishaps, with the hooking and unhooking sequence proving extremely unsafe. Though the 'parasite' concept was revived with the RF-84K a decade later, it was an on-off project for Strategic Air Command and General Curtis LeMay, who despised fighters. By this time, fighters were no longer needed to escort bombers, and the XF-85 Goblin finally became a museum piece.

Left: The XF-85 was aerodynamically advanced for its day, featuring a swept-back wing for good transonic performance. The wingtip fins provided yet more area to try to keep the aircraft directionally stable, adding to the six surfaces mounted on the rear of the fuselage.

Right: For moving the Goblin on the ground a special four-wheel transport dolly was built. As the aircraft was to have been recovered by its mothership in the air, it had no need for wheels.

XF-85 Goblin

Type: single-seat parasite fighter

Powerplant: one 13.35-kN (2,995-lb.-thrust) Westinghouse J34-WE-7 turbojet engine

Maximum speed: 1042 km/h (646 m.p.h.) at sea level

Initial climb rate: 3135 m/min (10,283 f.p.m.)

Endurance: 32 minutes at cruising speed

Service ceiling: 14691 m (48,186 ft.)

Weights: empty 1807 kg (3,975 lb.); max take-off 2540 kg (5,588 lb.)

Armament: none installed; four 12.7-mm (50 cal.) Browning machine-guns with 300 rounds of ammunition per gun would have been installed on a production version

Dimensions:
span	6.44 m	(21 ft.)
length	6.40 m	(21 ft.)
height	3.35 m	(11 ft.)
wing area	9.30 m²	(100 sq. ft.)

XF-85 GOBLIN

In the late 1940s the fighter was the main threat to bombers. As a means of countering this, the USAF studied the concept of bombers carrying their own defenders on ultra-long-range missions.

Just forward of the cockpit was a large, retractable hook which attached the Goblin to the mothership. This was retracted for operations, and then extended again for recovery.

Flight control was undertaken using standard ailerons on the wings, and rudder/elevator surfaces on four of the tails. The ventral fin and wingtip fins were added after the disastrous first flight in an unsatisfactory attempt to improve stability during the hook-up procedure.

The two prototype XF-85s did not have any armament fitted, but installations were provided for the carriage of four 12.7-mm (.50 cal.) Browning machine-guns in the upper sides of the fuselage.

Power was supplied by a single Westinghouse J34-WE-7 turbojet, mounted in the lower part of the fuselage. This engine was low on power but reliable by early jet standards. It was one of the few areas of the Goblin which did not give the engineering team problems.

Fuel was crammed into any available space within the tiny fuselage. Total capacity was 760 litres (200 gal.), used up by the thirsty J34 engine in about 30 minutes.

The swept-back wings gave the XF-85 a respectable speed, but the general performance and agility were way down on the conventional fighters of the period.

The lower tail and low-set dihedral wings allowed the XF-85 to make a reasonably safe belly landing in the event that it could not hook back up. This was just as well: in the course of the XF-85's flights, pilot Ed Schoch had to make four belly landings.

PARASITE FIGHTERS

AIRSHIP FIGHTERS: The first attempts to provide parasite fighters were made in the 1920s by hanging aircraft from special mounts on airships. The aircraft shown here is a Gloster Grebe being carried by the British airship R.33. These fighters had to land on the ground.

VAKHMISTROV'S NEST: The Russians produced the most impressive parasite combinations with the Zveno (nest) concept of the 1930s, pioneered by Vakhmistrov. This was the ultimate Zveno, a Tupolev bomber carrying five fighters.

FICON: Following the Goblin trials, the USAF continued with parasite fighter concepts, notably the FICON (Fighter Conveyor) programme. This involved an F-84 slung under a Convair B-36. This combination was used for a series of reconnaissance missions in the 1950s.

Recovering the Goblin

■ **APPROACH:** The XF-85 approaches the B-29 Superfortress mothership from below. The trapeze is already extended.

■ **STABILISATION:** The pilot Ed Schoch attempts to stabilise the XF-85 before slowly approaching the bar on the trapeze. On all of the Goblin's flights this proved near-impossible due to the air turbulence produced by the bomber and the instability of the small fighter.

■ **THE MOMENT OF TRUTH:** With great skill and a good deal of luck, Schoch managed to get near the bar on the first hook-up attempt. Unfortunately, in the process it hit the canopy, necessitating a belly landing – not a safe procedure in a tiny fighter like the Goblin.

■ **SUCCESS:** Despite the severe buffeting that occurred, Schoch accomplished a handful of successful hook-ups during the short flight trial programme.

McDonnell Douglas

F-4 Phantom II Sageburner

● Multiple speed/altitude records ● US Navy fighter prototypes

PHOTO FILE

McDonnell Douglas Phantom II Sageburner

▲ **Demonstrated for the President, April 1961**
The air-to-ground capabilities of the F4H-1 were demonstrated to President Kennedy when this aircraft dropped live bombs at Fort Bragg, NC.

▲ **Carrier trials for the sixth Phantom**
While a few airframes were singled out for record attempts, others were involved in service trials. Here the sixth Phantom is catapulted from the USS Independence.

World speed record in Skyburner ▶
Equating to Mach 2.43, the world absolute speed record set by the second YF4H-1 stood for just over six months, until broken by a Soviet pilot in his Mikoyan Ye-166.

▼ **'Grim Reapers' Sageburner**
Phantom 145307 carried the markings of US Navy Fighter Squadron VF-101, Detachment A. Named the 'Grim Reapers' this unit had been assigned to the training role in 1958 and from 1960 was part of the Atlantic Fleet F-4 Readiness Air Group (RAG).

▲ **Preserved by the NASM**
Seen during 1991 at Andrews Air Force Base, near Washington DC, Sageburner is largely intact after more than 20 years in storage.

The F-4 Phantom has set more records than any other fighter in history. While still being readied for squadron duty, before it even entered service, McDonnell's incredible F-4 (at the time called the F4H-1F) entered the record books with altitude, endurance, closed-circuit and absolute speed marks. One of the best remembered was a 3-km (1.86-mi.) closed-circuit record set in 1961 in the eighth Phantom built, named Sageburner.

▲ *Several individual US Navy and USMC pilots and pilot/navigator teams were hand-picked to fly early production F4H-1s to new record marks.*

FACTS AND FIGURES

➤ Pilot Lt. Hardisty later commanded US naval forces in the Pacific and in 1997 was president of Kaman Aerospace.

➤ The *Sageburner* speed record was achieved at a height of just 38 m (125 ft.).

➤ Felsman's *Sageburner* flight had been attempted below 38 m (125 ft.).

➤ F4H-1s were notable in being close to production standard, rather than being high-speed prototypes, like the Ye-166.

➤ F4H-1s flew in Project Lana, a multi-plane cross-country air race, in May 1962.

➤ Few of the first 47 Phantoms survive; the third and 47th airframes are preserved.

PROFILE

Phantom – multiple record breaker

A speed of 1452.826 km/h (900.75 m.p.h.) was reached on 28 August 1961 when Lieutenant Huntington Hardisty and Lieutenant Earl H. 'Duke' De Esch flew their F4H-1F Phantom II, nicknamed Sageburner, on its history-making speed dash.

Earlier, on 18 May, another Phantom, also called Sageburner, had disintegrated during a record attempt. It was torn to pieces after it entered a pilot-induced oscillation (PIO), and the pilot, Commander J. L. Felsman, was unfortunately killed.

Starting in December 1959, the US Navy had set a number of records in their early-production F4H-1/1Fs. That month the second YF4H-1 had been flown to a height of 30041 metres (98,534 feet) (Project Top Flight). And in September 1960 closed-circuit speed records over 500 km (310 miles) and 100 km (62 miles) were set, culminating in Hardisty and De Esch's August 1961 record.

However, the Navy did not stop there and was keen to show off the capabilities of its new fighter. A sustained altitude record (20252.1 m/66,427 ft.) was set on 5 December, and on 22 December the second prototype (named Skyburner) was in action again, setting a world absolute speed record of 2585.086 km/h (1,603 m.p.h.) on a flight from Edwards Air Force Base with Lieutenant Colonel Robert B. Robinson in the pilot's seat.

Finally, in 1962, a number of 'time-to-climb' records were set during Project High Jump.

Below: Lieutenant Huntington Hardisty and Lieutenant Earl De Esch set the 3-km closed-circuit speed record on 28 August 1961 at an average speed of 1452.826 km/h (900.75 m.p.h.).

Above: Sageburner made its record-breaking flight over the desert near Edwards AFB, California.

F4H-1F Phantom II

Type: two-seat all-weather carrier-based fighter

Powerplant: two 71.6-kN (16,109-lb.-thrust) General Electric J79-GE-2/2A afterburning turbojet engines

Maximum speed: 2585 km/h (1,042 m.p.h.) at altitude

Range: 1100 km (680 mi.)

Service ceiling: 16770 m (55,000 ft.)

Weights: empty 11235 kg (24,717 lb.); maximum take-off 23885 kg (52,547 lb.)

Armament: production aircraft equipped to carry four AAM-N-6 Sparrow III or AAM-N-7 Sidewinder air-to-air missiles

Dimensions:
span	11.71 m	(38 ft. 5 in.)
length	18.95 m	(62 ft. 2 in.)
height	5.03 m	(16 ft. 6 in.)
wing area	49.24 m²	(530 sq. ft.)

McDONNELL RECORD BREAKERS

JF-101A Voodoo: The sole JF-101A – the 'J' prefix signifying a temporary change for test purposes – was built to evaluate the more powerful Pratt & Whitney J57-P-53 engines chosen for the F-101B. This needed little internal modification, but did require a large extension of the jetpipe to accommodate the longer afterburner section. In Operation Fire Wall on 12 December 1957, Major Adrian Drew of the US Air Force flew this aircraft to a new world speed record from Edwards AFB in California. The Voodoo reached 1943.43 km/h (1,205 m.p.h.), taking the record from the British Fairey Delta 2. After the flight Drew immediately flew to Los Angeles International Airport to receive the Distinguished Flying Cross from General McCarty, commander of the 18th Air Force.

F4H-1 PHANTOM II

F4H-1 Phantom 145307 was, in fact, the second Sageburner aircraft, the first (145316) having crashed in a speed record attempt in May 1961. Number 145307 was later preserved by the National Air and Space Museum.

Both the world absolute height and speed records of 1959 and 1961, respectively, were set in the second Phantom prototype, 142260. The height record lasted just eight days, being broken by a USAF pilot in an F-104C, which reached 31513 metres (103,363 ft.).

F4H-1 Phantom 145307 was the eighth aircraft off the line at McDonnell's St Louis factory and the sixth pre-production example. In 1961 the first 47 aircraft became F4H-1Fs, with the survivors becoming F-4As in 1962.

The first 18 F4H-1s were readily distinguished from later machines by a smaller nose radome (housing a 61-cm [24-in.] reflector compared to the 81-cm [32-in.] reflector fitted to later aircraft) and a lower profile cockpit canopy, which restricted the crew's field of view.

Although aircraft which made record attempts flew in 'clean' condition to reduce drag, the F4H-1 was intended to have between five and nine pylons fitted under the wings and fuselage for a variety of air-to-air and air-to-ground stores, including Sparrow missiles.

Like all but the F-4Ks and F-4Ms built for the Royal Navy and RAF, the F4H-1 was powered by two General Electric J79 afterburning turbojets which, in their -2/-2A form, produced 71.6 kN (16,109 lb.-thrust) each.

F-15A 'Streak Eagle': Designed and built after the amalgamation of McDonnell and Douglas, the 'Streak Eagle' was an F-15A that was specially modified for an attempt on the world time-to-climb class records for jet-powered aircraft. Non-mission critical systems and the paintwork were removed to reduce the aircraft's weight by 816.46 kg (1,796 lb.). During the winter of 1974/75 the aircraft broke a total of eight records, the most spectacular of these being a climb to 30000 m (98,400 ft.) in 207.8 seconds on 1 February 1975. Flown by Major Roger Smith, this attempt overcame the previous record of 243.86 seconds held by a Soviet MiG-25 'Foxbat'.

Record-breaking fighters of the 1950s

■ DOUGLAS F4D-1 SKYRAY: At 1211.48 km/h (751 m.p.h.), the US Navy captured the world speed record on 3 October 1953. The previous record was held by a British Swift Mk 4.

■ NORTH AMERICAN YF-100A: This aircraft bettered the Skyray by less than 4 km/h (3 m.p.h.) just 26 days later. However, it took almost 22 months for an F-100C to gain this record.

■ LOCKHEED F-104A STARFIGHTER: In May 1958 the USAF broke the 2000 km/h (1,400 m.p.h.) barrier. An F-104A hit 2259.18 km/h (1,400.69 m.p.h.), taking the record.

■ CONVAIR F-106 DELTA DART: On 15 December 1959 an F-106A pushed the world absolute speed record to 2455.74 km/h (1,522.55 m.p.h.). This was beaten by Phantom 142260.

McDonnell Douglas

F-15 STREAK EAGLE

● Record breaker ● World-class performance ● Jet fighter

PHOTO FILE

McDonnell Douglas F-15 STREAK EAGLE

▼ Blast off
With engines blazing, the Streak Eagle leapt in to the sky after having all additional weight removed. The aircraft was secured by a cable while the engines reached full power.

▲ Proud history
Having broken the record, the Streak Eagle received grey camouflage and was retired to a museum.

▼ Future funding
Despite having no real tactical use, the Streak Eagle programme brought huge publicity to the F-15 Eagle and helped McDonnell Douglas receive many orders.

▲ Test pilots
Three test pilots were used during the Streak Eagle program, with each attempting specific records.

◄ All metal bird
Removing the standard 'eagle grey' paint saved 22.67 kg (50 lb.) of the overall weight. The resulting aircraft was a mass of bronze and silver panels covered with yellow primer, the only markings were the company logo and the Streak Eagle name.

The Streak Eagle was a one-of-a-kind record smasher – flown in 1975 by three US Air Force test pilots who used this exciting airplane to attack world climb records for jet aircraft. The Streak Eagle – a stripped, unpainted F-15A Eagle fighter – was unarmed and weighed far less than operational fighters. This made the Streak Eagle a hot rod, enabling its pilots to experience incredible speed and acceleration.

▲ Proudly displaying
the Streak Eagle logo on the nose, a test pilot prepares to set another record-breaking flight – proving to the world that the McDonnell Douglas Eagle was the best.

FACTS AND FIGURES

➤ The record attempts were a partnership between the USAF and the manufacturer, McDonnell Douglas.

➤ The Streak Eagle was the 19th production F-15.

➤ Radar, missiles and the cannon were all removed from the aircraft.

➤ A flight by Major Roger Smith on 1 February 1975 overcame a previous record by a Soviet MiG-25 'Foxbat'.

➤ Flights were mounted from Grand Forks AFB in North Dakota.

➤ Following the successful attempts, the Eagle was retired to the USAF museum.

PROFILE

St Louis' streaking bird

In 1975, this modified F-15A attempted a world climb record and demonstrated the F-15 fighter's acceleration – a big asset in combat.

The Streak Eagle's climb record attempts were mounted from Grand Forks AFB, North Dakota, to take advantage of the cold temperatures. Three pilots made eight record attempts – the most dramatic was a climb to 30,000 metres (98,400 ft.) in 207.8 seconds from brake release. This flight on 1 February 1975 by Major Roger Smith

broke a previous record of 243.86 seconds set by a Soviet MiG-25 'Foxbat'.

These flights were like firing a bullet upwards into the sky – the Streak Eagle simply kept climbing until it ran out of inertia and went 'over the top', actually reaching about 31,394 meters (102,970 ft.) Its high rate of climb was one reason the F-15A Eagle was later chosen for the Air Force's ASAT (anti-satellite) platform, which flourished briefly in the 1980s.

Above: With all unnecessary equipment removed, including the underwing pylons, the F-15 Eagle is a noticeably large aircraft.

Right: Seen here just after take-off, the Streak Eagle was unrivalled in its climbing ability.

F-15 Streak Eagle

Tarnished and covered in yellow primer, the F-15 Streak Eagle was an outstanding performer despite its battered appearance. Everything possible was done to reduce the weight of the aircraft.

Pilots ran the engines up to full military power before the aircraft was released from its cable attachment. Only the barest essental cockpit instruments were provided for the pilot; all equipment associated with the radar was removed.

The Streak Eagle made eight successful record attempts. These records were broken by a specially adapted Sukhoi Su-27 'Flanker' flown by Russian test pilots.

The aircraft was stripped down to its bare essentials, resulting in the removal of the grey camouflage paint. This gave the aircraft a particularly weather-beaten appearance. The different materials required to make the aircraft could be clearly seen.

To reduce weight, the large radar was removed, leaving just an empty nose cone. An instrument boom was installed to track the record attempt.

The aircraft carried few markings; the largest were the patriotic Streak Eagle logos either side of the nose.

Pilots had to retract the undercarriage quickly after the release of the brakes as soon as the aircraft was airborne.

All pylons under the wings were removed from the aircraft to offer the best possible climb rate. To save weight, the fuel load was restricted to allow just enough for each record attempt.

A secure cable was attached to the rear of the fuselage to hold back the aircraft. It was released only when the pilot had signalled that he had reached full power on both engines. Following this, the aircraft lifted off and the pilot quickly retracted the undercarriage

F-15 Streak Eagle

- **Type:** Single-seat superiority fighter
- **Powerplant:** Two 106.01 kN (14,680-lb.-thrust) Pratt & Whitney F100-P-100 turbofans with afterburner
- **Maximum speed:** 2655 km/h (1,646 m.p.h.); cruising speed 917 km/h (569 m.p.h.)
- **Record climb rate :** 30,000 m (98,400 ft.) in 207.8 seconds from brake release
- **Record ceiling:** 31,394 m (102,972 ft.)
- **Weight:** 12,157 kg (26,745 lb.) for record-breaking flights
- **Dimensions:** Span: 13,05 m (42 ft. 9 in.)
  Length: 19,43 m (63 ft. 9 in.)
  Height: 5,63 m (18 ft. 6 in.)
  Wing area: 56,48 m² (608 sq. ft.)

Rapid-climb record breakers

World time-to-altitude records: Showing significant advantage over McDonnell Douglas' other product, the F-4 Phantom, Streak Eagle was only beaten at the time by the Apollo space rocket. Profile for the record flight was for the F-15 to fly straight up until it ran out of inertia. Following this, the aircraft would roll over the top and return to Earth. The flights were made from Grand Forks AFB because its cold air temperature allowed the Eagle's engines to perform at their optimal level.

Metres (Feet)

Streak Eagle

Apollo moonshot

30 000 m (100,000 ft.)

25 000 m (85,000 ft.)

20 000 m (65,000 ft.)

F-4B Phantom

15 000 m (50,000 ft.)

12 000 m (40,000 ft.)

9000 m (30,000 ft.)

6000 m (20,000 ft.)

3000 m (10,000 ft.)

20   60   100   140   180   220

Seconds

Climbing for records

F-4 PHANTOM: Quick to publicise the capability of its new fighter, the Navy achieved a succession of records with their new Phantom fighter, including the altitude record.

E-266M 'FOXBAT': Cold War tensions saw the Russians make numerous record attempts for propaganda reasons. The 'Foxbat' broke the F-4's mark in 1977.

Su-27 'FLANKER': Continuing the seesaw battle between the Russians and Americans, a specially prepared 'Flanker' achieved a series of records, stealing the record from the F-15.

MCDONNELL DOUGLAS

F-15S/MTD

● **Short take-off** ● **Technology demonstrator** ● **Super agile**

Developing techniques for flying from damaged runways, the McDonnell Douglas F-15S/MTD (STOL and Maneuver Technology Demonstrator) is a derivative of the hot combat fighter that blasted the enemy in Operation Desert Storm. It uses advanced technology to explore many kinds of low-speed flying. A newer, updated MTD is back in use, researching the effects of vectored thrust for enhanced manoeuvrability.

▲ *Originally developed purely to operate from short runways, the F-15S/MTD has been resurrected thanks to the new emphasis on vectored thrust to enhance agility in combat aircraft.*

MCDONNELL DOUGLAS **F-15S/MTD**

◀ **Paddle turning**
With its canard foreplanes in full deflection and nozzles deflected, the S/MTD pulls into a tight turn. It can easily outmanoeuvre a standard F-15C.

▼ **Braking stop**
With its canards acting as a brake and the engine gases vented forwards, the S/MTD could decelerate very quickly, a useful ability in combat.

◀ **Damaged runway**
Operation from a short strip of damaged runway was the original reason for the development of S/MTD. New designs have been influenced by it.

▼ **Resurrected**
With emphasis on enhanced manoeuvrability, the S/MTD has resumed flight testing. The short take-off capability will be fulfilled by the new JAST/Joint Strike Fighter.

◀ **Trick engines**
In addition to the moving nozzles, the S/MTD had special vanes to allow engine gas to be vented forwards to reverse thrust.

FACTS AND FIGURES

➤ The S/MTD Eagle made its final flight for several years on 12 August 1991.

➤ The S/MTD first flew on 7 September 1988 with Larry Walker at the controls.

➤ The two-dimensional nozzles were fitted to the S/MTD in 1989.

➤ Test pilot Lt Col Felix Sanchez said, 'The S/MTD proves that it is more important to fly slow than to fly fast.'

➤ This aircraft was originally built as one of the prototype two-seat Eagles.

➤ The canard foreplanes for the S/MTD were derived from the F-18's tailplane.

PROFILE

Vectored thrust Eagle

McDonnell Douglas' F-15S/MTD is flying again after a successful programme several years ago that used vectored thrust and canard foreplanes to improve low-speed performance. This aircraft tested high-tech methods for operating from a short runway – important in wartime, when airfields are likely to be cratered and under constant attack.

Originally, this modified F-15B Eagle was part of an ambitious effort to improve ABO (air base operability), the survival of warplanes and fighting capability at airfields under attack. A variety of measures – point defences, construction teams, decoys and other deceptions – give airfields a high likelihood of remaining in use in the midst of a war. The F-15S/MTD tested ways to improve this situation by demonstrating the ability to land and take off from wet, bomb-damaged runways. The aircraft used a complex flight control system with a combination of reversible engine thrust, jet nozzles that could be deflected by 20° and canard foreplanes.

Initially costing $400 million to convert from an existing F-15, the S/MTD was used to validate some of the principles behind the X-31 fighter demonstrator. A new MTD is again in use, as a response to Sukhoi's Su-35 with thrust-vectoring nozzles.

Below: With a formidable reputation as a potential dogfighter even in its standard form, the S/MTD held much promise.

Above: With the technology in the S/MTD, large fighters like the F-15 can fight with agile light fighters like the F-16. The new F-22 also has thrust vectoring.

F-15S/MTD

Type: research aircraft

Powerplant: two Pratt & Whitney F100-PW-220 turbofan engines each rated at 64 kN (14,387-lb.-thrust) dry and 106 kN (23,828-lb.-thrust) with afterburning, equipped with Pratt & Whitney two-dimensional nozzles which can vector through 20° up to 20° down and provide reverse thrust

Maximum speed: Mach 2.1 or 2655 km/h (1,650 m.p.h.) at 10975 m (36,000 ft.)

Ferry range: 4415 km (2,743 m.p.h.)

Service ceiling: 17750 m (58,234 ft.)

Weights: empty 11966 kg (26,325 lb.); loaded 20201 kg (44,442 lb.); maximum take-off 32000 kg (70,400 lb.)

Armament: none carried

Dimensions:
span	13.05 m	(98 ft. 7 in.)
length	19.43 m	(63 ft. 9 in.)
height	5.63 m	(18 ft. 5 in.)
wing area	56.49 m²	(608 sq. ft.)

F-15S/MTD

In 1984, the USAF contracted McDonnell Douglas to convert an F-15B to explore the use of combined thrust vectoring, advanced flight control software and advanced pilot/aircraft interfaces.

Most of the avionics in the S/MTD were those developed for the advanced F-15E Strike Eagle, including multi-function displays and revised instrument layout.

Extensive modifications were made to the flight control system to co-ordinate the action of the foreplanes, engine nozzles and tailplane.

The most obvious feature of the F-15S/MTD was the large canard foreplanes, which could operate differentially for roll control or together for pitch. To save money, they were based on a design which McDonnell Douglas was used to – the tailplane of the F/A-18 Hornet fighter.

The emblem on the tail is a special 'maneuver Eagle' design that was only used by the F-15S/MTD. The tailplane worked in concert with the foreplanes and nozzles.

U.S. AIR FORCE

AF71290

To assist with measuring data precisely, the S/MTD had a prominent pitot probe in the nose. This allowed accurate readings to be taken by the aircraft's complex telemetry gear.

Research into improved undercarriages was also carried out with the S/MTD in order to allow operations more safely from damaged airstrips.

Unlike any other F100 engine, the S/MTD version had a two-dimensional paddle-type nozzle at its trailing edge, and vanes in the tailpipe that can be turned to vector thrust forwards to reverse thrust.

AGILE PROTOTYPES

This canard Phantom was fitted with experimental foreplanes and a fly-by-wire flight-control system. Neither of these was ever fitted to an operational Phantom, and after the test programme finished this aircraft, number 62-12200, was sent to the USAF museum.

Known as AFTI (Advanced Fighter Technology Integrator), this F-16 demonstrated such features as helmet-mounted sights, voice-command operated systems, terrain avoidance and the ability to perform 'flat turns' thanks to its downward pointing canards.

Perhaps the most radical wing design since the war, the Grumman X-29 tested forward-swept wing technology using new materials and flight-control software. Displaying stunning agility and low-speed handling, the X-29 has been retired from flight testing.

How the S/MTD works

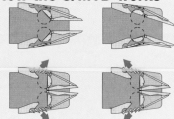

NOZZLES: Using a combination of the movable nozzles and vanes in the jet pipe, the S/MTD pilot can direct engine gas forwards, outwards or at an angle of up to 20° to the axis of the aircraft.

COMBINED EFFECT: With its highly advanced flight control software, the S/MTD co-ordinates the movement of the forward canards to give up-force, and the tailplane and nozzles to produce a down-force when manoeuvring.

FAST STOP: By vectoring engine gas from above and below the nozzles and turning the canard foreplanes to act as giant airbrakes, the S/MTD could decelerate very rapidly. This kind of manoeuvre is often useful in a dogfight.

McDONNELL DOUGLAS

F/A-18 EXPERIMENTAL

● Thrust vectoring ● Weapons testing ● High angle of attack

◄ Mud mover and fleet defender
The versatility of the F/A-18 was one of its major original trump cards. It was one of the few aircraft which was both a dedicated attacker and fighter.

▼ Weapons testing
Based at China Lake, in the Mojave Desert, the Naval Air Weapons Center operates a number of Hornets for weapons' trials and research and development.

▼ Sparrow capability
A major advantage of the F/A-18 over the A-7 was its medium-range missile capability.

▼ Hotrod Hornet
Based on the failed YF-17, the Hornet retained its predecessor's excellent performance and was the hottest thing around in the late 1970s.

◄ Carrier trials
Hornet No. 3 was the first to be used for trials aboard a carrier, USS America. The aircraft made 32 landings, catching the number 3 wire 75 per cent of the time.

A single McDonnell Douglas F/A-18 Hornet was modified by NASA (the National Aeronautics and Space Administration), to help develop the incredibly manoeuvrable fighters of the future. The special research version of the Hornet is called the F/A-18 HARV (High-Alpha Research Vehicle), with 'Alpha' being jargon for 'angle of attack'. Since the mid-1970s, several Hornets have been retained for development work by various agencies.

▲ *Five F/A-18A prototypes were initially procured and used for extensive testing throughout their lives. Indeed, the trials were reported as being among the most successful ever.*

FACTS AND FIGURES

➤ Th HARV Hornet actually began high 'Alpha' flights in 1987, before being modified with thrust-vectoring paddles.

➤ Besides the HARV, NASA operates a number of the prototype Hornets.

➤ Because it carries no armament, the HARV is lighter than fleet Hornets.

➤ The Hornet proved the prime candidate for HARV because of its already high angle of attack capability.

➤ Thrust vectoring has had little effect on the F/A-18's range or weaponload.

➤ The HARV completed a second phase of research flights during 1991.

PROFILE

A new era in manoeuvrability

Below: NASA's test fleet of F/A-18s include the very first prototype and Hornet Nos 3, 4, 6, 7, 8 and 11. These have supplanted the old F-104 Starfighters.

I n November 1990, at the very time standard F/A-18 Hornets were preparing to fight in Operation Desert Storm, a very different Hornet began flying at NASA's Ames-Dryden facility at Edwards Air Force Base, California.

The F/A-18 HARV was fitted with three spoon-shaped paddle vanes around each engine exhaust. The paddles were designed to re-channel, or vector, the engine thrust, enabling the aircraft to fly at angles of up to 70 degrees.

Flying at a high angle of attack is the key to manoeuvring in a small area, thus winning in a close-quarters dogfight.

In the early 1990s, the F/A-18 HARV made dozens of flights at high 'Alpha,' using smoke generators and yarn tufts to enable this remarkable manoeuvring to be studied and photographed. Today, even more advanced high-'Alpha' aircraft have emerged, including the Rockwell X-31 and the Lockheed Martin F-22 Raptor, both of which benefit

Above: After the successful trials conducted aboard USS America, *No. 3 was acquired by NASA at Edwards.*

tremendously from the scientific knowledge gleaned from the HARV Hornet. Any future fighter will have some form of thrust-vectoring fitted to improve performance in a dogfight, thanks to this extraordinary NASA research.

F/A-18 HARV

Type: NASA research aircraft

Powerplant: two 71.2-kN (16,000-lb.-thrust) afterburning General Electric F404-GE-400 turbofan engines

Maximum speed: 1915 km/h (1,190 m.p.h.) at 12190 m (40,000 ft.)

Combat radius: 1060 km (659 mi.)

Service ceiling: 15240 m (50,000 ft.)

Weights: empty 10455 kg (23,049 lb.); loaded 17690 kg (39,000 lb.)

Armament: unarmed for research flights

Dimensions:

span	12.34 m	(40 ft. 3 in.)
length	17.06 m	(56 ft.)
height	4.66 m	(15 ft. 3 in.)
wing area	37.16 m²	(400 sq. ft.)

F/A-18A HORNET

This aircraft was one of the first Hornets built and, after its development work with McDonnell Douglas was complete, it was assigned to NASA Dryden at Edwards Air Force Base, where it continues to fly.

Housed within the large dorsal fairing are the main fuel cells. Because of the design of the airframe, space for fuel was limited and thus a short range has remained the Hornet's Achilles' heel since the beginning. The centre and rear fuselage sections were built by Grumman.

The tail units are mainly constructed from graphite/epoxy skins over an aluminium core. Above each rudder are single emergency fuel dump pipes. The F/A-18 can dump large quantities of fuel in a short space of time.

Between the vertical tails is the airbrake. Mounting it well aft, unlike on the F-15, reduces the degree of pitch when the airbrake is extended in flight.

In the interests of greater performance and weight elimination, the NASA F/A-18s had their cannons removed.

Early Hornets featured the Hughes APG-65 multi-mode pulse-Doppler radar. This has nine air-to-air modes and, with Doppler beam sharpening, can illuminate individual enemy aircraft within a tight formation.

Ease of maintenance was considered important at an early stage and approximately 238 of the F/A-18's 268 access panels can be reached by a single man at ground level.

Because Mach 2 performance was not required for the F/A-18, the aircraft features a very simple intake design without variable intake ramps.

Powering the F/A-18A are twin General Electric F404-GE400 afterburning turbofans. The engines are identical and are also fully interchangeable, unlike some others.

ACTION DATA

MAXIMUM SPEED

Although having the fastest overall speed of the then new jet fighters, the YF-17 Cobra failed to secure a military contract. With the additional weight of operational equipment, the F/A-18 entered front-line operations with restricted speed capability.

F/A-18 HORNET	1915 km/h (1,190 m.p.h.)
YF-17 COBRA	2124 km/h (1,320 m.p.h.)
F-5E TIGER II	1700 km/h (1,056 m.p.h.)

SERVICE CEILING

Though a twin-engined design, the lightness of the YF-17 Cobra allowed the aircraft to operate at a exceptionally high altitude. Northrop's lightweight F-5E Tiger II, though a less capable aircraft, operated at a higher altitude than the F/A-18 Hornet.

F/A-18 HORNET 15240 m (50,000 ft.) — YF-17 COBRA 18288 m (60,000 ft.) — F-5E TIGER II 15590 m (51,150 ft.)

THRUST

With all the designs employing a twin-engined layout, the thrust of the F/A-18 Hornet was the greatest of the three. Technological improvements allowed the thrust to be increased still further, but early models suffered problems.

F/A-18 HORNET	142.4 kN (32,028-lb.-thrust)
YF-17 COBRA	128.16 kN (28,824-lb.-thrust)
F-5E TIGER II	44.4 kN (9,986-lb.-thrust)

Former combat jets in NASA service

■ **GENERAL DYNAMICS F-111A:** A single F-111A was modified by NASA with a special supercritical wing for the Transonic Aircraft Technology (TACT) programme.

■ **MARTIN B-57E CANBERRA:** A number of ex-USAF B-57s were employed at NASA Dryden, including this example which was used for Clear Air Turbulence (CAT) testing.

■ **McDONNELL DOUGLAS F-15A EAGLE:** This early F-15A was modified for testing the Space Shuttle's thermal protection tiles. These can be seen on the starboard wing.

■ **VOUGHT F-8C CRUSADER:** One of two Crusaders based at NASA Dryden, this F-8 was modified with a digital fly-by-wire system to mimic handling qualities of other aircraft.

McDonnell Douglas
YC-15

● Advanced STOL design ● Some technology used in the C-17

O n 11 April 1997, the first prototype YC-15A flew again, for the first time in 19 years. The aircraft had been retired to the US Air Force Aerospace Maintenance and Regeneration Center (AMARC) at Davis-Monthan Air Force Base (AFB) in 1978 and was now beginning a new career as a research platform for advanced transport aircraft technologies. The aircraft might even act as the basis for a new USAF special forces multi-role transport.

▲ During the mid-1970s the YC-15 represented the cutting edge of tactical airlifter technology. While it did not succeed as a C-130 replacement, it did contribute much invaluable information to the C-17 project and now looks set for a new career as a research platform.

McDonnell Douglas YC-15

STOL performance ▶
One of the keys to the remarkable short take-off and landing performance of the YC-15 was its use of wide-span, double-slotted flaps, blown by the efflux from the underwing turbofan engines, to give the wing 'powered' lift.

◀ Flight refuelling
During in-flight refuelling trials, the second YC-15, with its larger wing and tactical paint scheme, connects with a USAF Boeing KC-135A Stratotanker.

Engine trials ▶
During the second phase of flight testing, a new powerplant, the CFM International CFM56 turbofan, was fitted to the outboard port pylon of the first prototype in February 1977.

◀ Civil project
McDonnell Douglas made extensive modifications to the structure of the YC-15 for a planned civil production version, which was later cancelled.

Proof of concept ▶
Although not put into production, the YC-15 proved in flight trials that the jet STOL transport was a realistic project, and has since provided the basis for the C-17.

FACTS AND FIGURES

➤ In four years of flight tests, the YC-15 proved the short-field technology now employed by the C-17 Globemaster III.

➤ On 26 August 1975 the first of two YC-15s made its initial flight.

➤ The YC-15's cargo capacity was 32 per cent greater than the Lockheed C-130's.

➤ A developed YC-15A may meet a USAF requirement for a stealthy gunship/special operations/tanker aircraft.

➤ A DC-10 cockpit, optimised for operation by two pilots, was used by the YC-15.

➤ A US Army evaluation of the YC-15 was performed at Fort Bragg in 1975.

PROFILE

Advanced STOL transport

Below: The YC-15's rugged main undercarriage came from the C-141 StarLifter, but had longer-stroke legs. A modified DC-8 undercarriage member was used at the nose.

Above: Visibility from the YC-15's cockpit was excellent. The addition of a pair of lower windows on each side of the nose improved the crew's forward and downward view during short-field landings.

To give the US Air Force an advanced medium short take-off and landing transport (AMST), principally to replace the C-130 Hercules, the McDonnell Douglas YC-15 and Boeing YC-14 were developed during the mid-1970s.

To a typical transport aircraft fuselage configuration of rear loading ramp, heavy-duty retractable landing gear, and a T-tail, the YC-15 added a wing of advanced design. The aircraft's Short Take-Off and Landing (STOL) capability focused on a partnership between wing and

powerplant. The 'supercritical' wing incorporated huge flaps over 75 per cent of its span which, when fully deployed, were blown by the efflux from the engines.

Both the YC-15 and YC-14 provided a wealth of research data, but plans to order one of the aircraft as a replacement for the long-serving Lockheed C-130 Hercules proved premature. With the competition abandoned, the aircraft were retired into AMARC storage at Davis-Monthan AFB, Arizona, from where the first YC-15 was

moved to the Pima County Air Museum in 1981.

Both YC-15s, now referred to as YC-15As, are to be leased back to McDonnell Douglas and will be instrumental in proving systems for the transport aircraft of the next century.

YC-15

Type: four-engined, turbofan-powered assault STOL transport prototype

Powerplant: four 71.17-kN (16,000-lb.-thrust) Pratt & Whitney JT8D-17 turbofan engines. The engine pylons could accept other powerplants such as the 80.07-kN (18,000-lb.-thrust) JT8D-209 or the 97.86-kN (22,000-lb.-thrust) CFM56

Maximum speed: 805 km/h (500 m.p.h.)

Range: 740 km (460 mi.) on a STOL mission with a 12258-kg (26,968-lb.) payload

Ceiling: 7925 m (26,000 ft.)

Weights: empty 47627 kg (104,779 lb.); maximum take-off 99,418 kg (218,720 lb.)

Accommodation: flight crew of two pilots and one loadmaster; capacity to carry 90 per cent of US Army divisional combat vehicles, maximum payload 28122 kg (61,998 lb.)

Dimensions: span 41.05 m (134 ft. 8 in.)
length 38.45 m (126 ft. 2 in.)
height 13.40 m (44 ft.)
wing area 161.65 m² (1,739 sq. ft.)

YC-15

The YC-15 was one of five proposals put forward by US companies to meet a USAF requirement for an Advanced Medium STOL Transport aircraft.

A new flying control system for STOL operations saw lateral control provided by a combination of ailerons and triple inboard wing spoilers. The system is connected to the modified flight deck of a McDonnell Douglas DC-10 airliner.

A large, uninterrupted cabin allows for a 28122-kg (61,868-lb.) maximum weight cargo payload to be carried. Alternatively, it can accommodate 150 fully equipped troops. Passenger doors are provided on either side of the fuselage with a large ramp on the underside of the rear fuselage for cargo loading.

A conventional semi-monocoque structure was chosen for the fuselage, with a cantilever T-tail and swept parallel fin and rudder. The high-set, all-metal wing is swept by nearly 6°. The engines are mounted on forward-projecting pylons.

A wide rear loading ramp that lowered from the rear fuselage permitted a wide range of military vehicles and bulky cargo to be loaded into the transport and quickly off-loaded at the destination.

For STOL landings the YC-15 had long stroke main undercarriage units to allow for high sink rates, while twin nosewheels and four-wheel bogie main units were fitted for operations from rough, unprepared surfaces.

COMBAT DATA

MAXIMUM SPEED

In STOL configuration the YC-14 was barely faster than the turboprop-powered Hercules, but the YC-15 offered a high maximum speed useful for long flights with small payloads.

YC-15 — 805 km/h (500 m.p.h.)
YC-14 — 649 km/h (402 m.p.h.)
C-130H HERCULES — 621 km/h (385 m.p.h.)

FIELD LENGTH

A field length for safe operations of no more than 610 m (2,380 ft.) was required by the AMST specification. For a take-off to 15 m (50-ft.) height, the fully laden C-130H needs a clear run of 1573 m (5,160 ft.). The C-130H is possibly the more versatile machine.

YC-15 610 m (2,380 ft.)
YC-14 610 m (2,380 ft.)
C-130H HERCULES 1573 m (5,160 ft.)

RANGE

In its specification the USAF required a 740-km (460-mile) range with a 12258-kg (26,968-lb.) payload. With a similar payload, the C-130H has a far superior range but cannot match the STOL performance of the jets, leading to a compromise between long range and payload weight.

YC-15 740 km (460 mi.)
YC-14 740 km (460 mi.)
C-130H HERCULES 3791 km (2,350 mi.)

STOL technology

POWERED LIFT: McDonnell Douglas's design team chose a four-engined configuration with externally blown flaps. The jet efflux was spread over the wing to the rear, giving the YC-15 exceptional STOL capability.

BLOWN FLAPS: With the wide-span two-section trailing-edge flaps fully lowered and the engine exhaust blown onto them, the high-velocity airflow provides powered lift. Thus the YC-15 can take off with a 12258-kg (26,943-lb.) payload in 610 m (2,380 ft.).

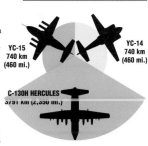

GOOD RANGE: The USAF required the YC-15 to be able to carry 12258 kg (26,968 lb.) out of a short field, climb steeply and carry the cargo over a 740-km (460-mi.) radius. It must then land in 610 m (2,380 ft.).

MESSERSCHMITT

ME 209

● World speed record holder for 30 years ● Fighter developments

I n November 1937 a Bf 109 fighter prototype set a new world air speed record for landplanes of 610.5 km/h(379 m.p.h.). By now Willy Messerschmitt was already working on a pure high-speed machine. Designated Me 209, it was intended to break the absolute speed record of 709 km/h (440 m.p.h.), held by a Macchi seaplane. What Messerschmitt did not know when he started was that his great rival, Ernst Heinkel, was aiming at the same target.

▲ Willy Messerschmitt (left) and his record-breaking test pilot Fritz Wendel: the Me 209's handling prompted Flugkapitän Wendel to describe it as a 'vicious little brute' and a 'monstrosity'.

MESSERSCHMITT ME 209

▼ Snake markings on V4
With markings for propaganda photographs, Me 209 V4 was an attempt to utilise V1 experience to design a Bf 109 replacement.

▲ Messerschmitt's 'other' Me 209
Referred to as the Me 209 II or Me 209A, this was an attempt to build a replacement for the Bf 109.

Record breaker ▶
Designed from the outset as a high-speed aircraft, the Me 209 was not intended to serve operationally. Constraints centred around the DB 601 engine and the need to accommodate a pilot.

◀ Evaporative cooling
Like the racing seaplanes of the period, the Me 209 employed wing-mounted radiators to provide cooling for the powerful DB 601ARJ.

Me 209 V5 ▶
The first of the Me 209 IIs to fly, SP+LJ was known as Me 209 V5. Intended to use Bf 109G components, the aircraft would have been known as the Me 209A in production.

FACTS AND FIGURES

➤ It was proposed eventually to install 30-mm cannon in the Me 209 fighter: one in the propeller hub and one in each wing.

➤ Me 209 V2 was written off in a landing accident after its engine failed.

➤ Originally, Me 209 V3 was to be used for the world record attempt.

➤ To give the impression that it was a variant of the Luftwaffe's fighter, the Me 209 was referred to as an 'Me 109R'.

➤ The V4 Me 209 fighter prototype in fact preceded the third machine into the air.

➤ Fritz Wendel noted that on landing the Me 209 swerved if brakes were applied.

Messerschmitt's 'vicious little brute'

With its small wings, a fuselage barely big enough to house the DB 601 engine and rear landing wheel mounted on the bottom of the tailfin, the Me 209 was much more compact than the Bf 109. Surface evaporation cooling, with condensers in the wings instead of conventional radiators, helped keep the airframe aerodynamically clean.

First flown in June 1938, the Me 209 proved extremely difficult to control and prone to overheating. The second prototype was lost after the oil cooling system failed and the engine cut out suddenly.

Messerschmitt had intended to use the third prototype (V3) for the record attempt. The plan was changed at the end of March 1939, when a modified prototype of Heinkel's He 100 fighter reached a new absolute record of 746 km/h (463 m.p.h.).

Instead, Messerschmitt used the first prototype fitted with a boosted engine ordered for the attempt, which was capable of delivering 1156 kW (1,550 hp.) with methanol injection and 1715 kW (2,300 hp.) in a one-minute burst. After a long wait for calm weather Flugkapitän Fritz Wendel finally succeeded in setting a new record of 755.138 km/h (469.22 m.p.h.) on 26 April 1939. This record stood for 30 years.

Above: By the time the Me 209 had been modified for service use it was little faster than a Bf 109F.

Me 209 V1

Type: single-seat high-speed aircraft

Powerplant: one 1156-kW (1,550-hp.) (1715-kW [2,300-hp.] with methanol injection) Daimler-Benz DB 601ARJ liquid-cooled piston engine

Maximum speed: 755 km/h (469 m.p.h.)

Weights: gross 2515 kg (5,533 lb.)

Dimensions:
span 7.80 m (25 ft. 7 in.)
length 7.25 m (23 ft. 9 in.)
wing area 10.60 m² (114 sq. ft.)

Me 209 V4

Type: single-seat high-speed fighter prototype

Powerplant: one 895-kW (1,200-hp.) Daimler-Benz DB 601N liquid-cooled piston engine

Maximum speed: about 600 km/h at 6000 m (372 m.p.h. at 19,700 ft.)

Cruising speed: 500 km/h (310 m.p.h.)

Initial climb rate: 1125 m/min (3,690 f.p.m.)

Service ceiling: 11000 m (36,080 ft.)

Weights: gross 2800 kg (6,160 lb.)

Armament: one 20-mm MG FF/M cannon and two 7.9-mm MG 17 machine-guns

Dimensions:
span 10.04 m (32 ft. 11 in.)
length 7.24 m (23 ft. 9 in.)
wing area 11.07 m² (119 sq. ft.)

Left: Me 209 V4 had little, other than its basic airframe, in common with the three earlier aircraft. As well as an entirely new wing, it had a larger tailfin.

Me 209 V4 was fitted with a hub-mounted cannon and had twin machine-guns above the engine. Plans to fit guns in the wings were abandoned for lack of space.

Among Fritz Wendel's complaints about the Me 209's handling were an excessive take-off run, 'vicious' take-off handling, instability during the climb and a tendency to roll on its back during banking.

ME 209 V4

First flown on 12 May 1939 carrying the civil registration D-IRND, Me 209 V4 was later adorned with these colourful snake markings, for propaganda photography purposes.

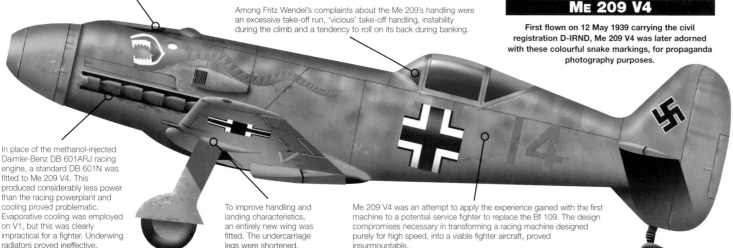

In place of the methanol-injected Daimler-Benz DB 601ARJ racing engine, a standard DB 601N was fitted to Me 209 V4. This produced considerably less power than the racing powerplant and cooling proved problematic. Evaporative cooling was employed on V1, but this was clearly impractical for a fighter. Underwing radiators proved ineffective.

To improve handling and landing characteristics, an entirely new wing was fitted. The undercarriage legs were shortened.

Me 209 V4 was an attempt to apply the experience gained with the first machine to a potential service fighter to replace the Bf 109. The design compromises necessary in transforming a racing machine designed purely for high speed, into a viable fighter aircraft, proved insurmountable.

POWER

The DB 603-powered V5 version had a power rating closer to that of the Me 209 racer than the Me 209 V4 fighter. Both types were considerably more powerful than the Heinkel He 100.

Me 209 V1 1715 kW (2,300 HP.)	Me 209 V5 1417 kW (1,900 HP.)	He 100 V1 670 kW (900 HP.)

MAXIMUM SPEED

Me 209 V1 set a new world speed record of just over 755 km/h (469 m.p.h.) in April 1939, beating the previous mark of 746 km/h (463 m.p.h.) set by the He 100. The Me 209 II (V5) was not as fast.

Me 209 V1	755 km/h (469 m.p.h.)
Me 209 V5	745 km/h (462 m.p.h.)
He 100 V1	746 km/h (463 m.p.h.)

GROSS WEIGHT

By maintaining a similar gross weight to that of the He 100, but increasing engine power, Messerschmitt was able to produce a faster aircraft. The Me 209 II (V5) was considerably heavier since it was equipped as a service fighter.

Me 209 V1 2515 kg (5,533 lb.)	Me 209 V5 4085 kg (8,987 lb.)	He 100 V1 2500 kg (5,500 lb.)

Other Messerschmitt prototypes

Me 261: Designed to make non-stop flights from Germany to Japan, the Me 261 was considered for the maritime reconnaissance role.

Me 263: To address the shortcomings of the Me 163 Komet, Messerschmitt gave the Me 263 more fuel capacity and retractable landing gear.

Me 264: One of a number of aircraft put forward for the transatlantic bombing role, the 'Amerika-Bomber' first flew in 1942.

P.1101: Largely complete by VE Day, this swept-wing jet served as the basis for the Bell X-5 variable-geometry prototype.

MIL

V-12

● Twin rotor ● Heavylift helicopter ● Unbroken records

Everything about the V-12 was enormous. The twin-rotor giant shattered every record for helicopter payload, and made every previous rotary-wing machine seem like a toy. But the problems of operating such a machine were also enormous and, despite the ingenuity of the design, it was not really a viable machine for commercial use. After a memorable appearance at the Paris Air Show, the V-12 rarely flew again.

▲ Mikhail Mil, son of a mining engineer, was perhaps the best helicopter designer ever. The V-12 was his greatest creation, but only two machines were produced.

MIL V-12

'Hook' power ▶
The engines, gearbox and rotors were all taken from the Mi-6 'Hook', albeit with some changes; rotor rpm was reduced to 112.

▼ Big wing
A large wing helped to offload the main rotors in forward flight. Its trailing-edge flaps were fixed after early trials.

▲ Loading ramp
Practical touches like the rear clamshell doors and loading ramp showed that the V-12 was not just a record breaker. The fuselage interior also had four cargo winches and a reinforced floor structure.

▲ Room at the top
The immense cockpit held a pilot, co-pilot, electronics operator and engineer, with the navigator and radio operator seated above.

▼ Paris performance
The Paris Air Show was the V-12's greatest moment, attracting enormous attention. But there was little interest in the machine from foreign customers.

FACTS AND FIGURES

➤ The enormous D-25 turboshaft engines were also used in other very large Mil helicopters like the Mi-6 and Mi-10.

➤ The one remaining V-12 can be seen at the Monino air force museum in Moscow.

➤ The V-12 had hydraulic flight controls, but it could also be flown manually.

➤ Fully loaded, the V-12 was as heavy as nine Mi-24 'Hind' gunships, or more than twice as heavy as an Mi-6.

➤ The main cabin of the V-12 was 28.15 m (93 ft.) long and 4.4 m² (47 sq. ft.).

➤ Optional ferry tanks could be carried inside the V-12 for maximum range.

Hundred-tonne helicopter

Produced by the man who had built the world's previous largest helicopter, Mikhail Leontyevich Mil, the V-12 was a giant. With a maximum take-off weight of over 100 tonnes, it was bigger than many transport aircraft.

Developed with the engines, transmission and rotors of the Mi-6, but in double pods outboard of a long reverse-taper wing, the V-12 had a huge fuselage space that contained one-tonne cargo hoists and seats could be fitted for more than 100 passengers. The V-12 even had a split-level flight deck, with pilots and flight engineer below and navigator and radio operator above.

The first V-12 was damaged in a crash in 1967, caused by resonance and control system problems. The second appeared at the Paris Air Show, and went on to break many helicopter payload records, most of which remain to this day. But despite its stunning performance and size, the V-12 was not really economical to use, and Mil

Above: Twin-rotor power was a new concept for the Mil company. Despite overcoming many of the technical difficulties, the V-12 was plagued by problems with resonance.

Below: The Soviet obsession with having the biggest and fastest of everything was manifest in the V-12. Mil turned his attentions to the more successful Mi-26 after the problems with the V-12 became apparent.

decided to develop the Mi-26 for heavy cargo work instead, leaving the V-12 in a museum.

V-12

Type: twin-rotor heavy transport helicopter

Powerplant: four 4847-kW (6,495-hp.) D-25V turboshafts driving in pairs with transverse shafting

Maximum speed: 260 km/h (161 m.p.h.)

Cruising speed: 240 km/h (149 m.p.h.)

Range: with max payload 500 km (310 mi.)

Service ceiling: 3500 m (11,480 ft.)

Weights: maximum payload 25 tonnes (24 tons); vertical take-off 30 tonnes (29.5 tons); maximum take-off 105 tonnes (103 tons)

Armament: none

Dimensions:

span	19.55 m	(64 ft.)
length	19.10 m	(63 ft.)
height	4.88 m	(16 ft.)
wing area	52.49 m²	(565 sq. ft.)

V-12

Number '21142' was the second Mil V-12 twin-rotor helicopter. In 1969, carrying a payload of 40204 kg (88,448 lb.), it was flown to 2255 metres (11,224 ft.) by V. P. Koloshchyenko.

The pilot flew the V-12 with the aid of an autostabilisation system. A ground-mapping radar was fitted under the nose.

The podded engines had access panels on their undersides to allow easy maintenance. The whole engine assembly was mounted at a 4° nose down angle. Fuel was carried in the outer wing section.

The large central tailfin gave the V-12 some much needed stability in forward flight, supplemented by auxiliary tailfins outboard.

АЭРОФЛОТ   МИ   СССР-21142

Fuel was carried in two external tanks as well as the outer wing structure.

The engine and wing were suspended with complex bracing. Vibration of the rotors through this bracing to the undercarriage caused many of the V-12's problems.

Light vehicles could be loaded through its rear doors, and a side door allowed access for passengers.

ACTION DATA

PAYLOAD

The V-12 could carry a huge load, even more with a running take-off in which it benefited from transition effect (like all helicopters). The Mi-26 carries almost as much using a single rotor and has trouble-free handling.

V-12	CH-53E	Mi-26 'HALO'
25000 kg (55,000 lb)	16330 kg (35,926 lb.)	20000 kg (44,000 lb.)

POWER

Using four engines from the Mil-6, the V-12 had awesome power. The modern Mi-26 has almost the same power from two more modern engines, which drive through a less wasteful transmission. The CH-53E is driven by three relatively small engines.

V-12	CH-53E	Mi-26 'HALO'
4 x 4847 kW = 19388 kW (4 X 6,495 hp. = 25,980 hp.)	3 x 3266 kW = 10798 kW (3 X 4,376 hp. = 13,129 hp.)	2 x 8380 kW = 16760 kW (2 X 11,229 hp. = 22,458 hp.)

MAXIMUM TAKE-OFF WEIGHT

The V-12 had a maximum take-off weight of 105 tonnes, or more than a loaded Vulcan bomber. The CH-53 is dwarfed by the much larger Mil helicopters, but is an impressive machine. The Mi-26 is almost as heavy as a fully loaded C-130 Hercules at maximum all-up weight.

V-12	CH-53E	Mi-26 'HALO'
105000 kg (231,000 lb.)	33400 kg (73,634 lb.)	56000 kg (123,458 lb.)

Mil's family of helicopters

■ **Mi-4 'HOUND':** Still in service in some Third World countries, the Mi-4 can carry a load underslung of 1300 kg (2,860 lb.) or an internal load of 1740 kg (3,820 lb.). Thousands of Mi-4s were built, including licence production in China.

■ **Mi-6 'HOOK':** The Mi-6 was the largest helicopter in the world for many years. It could carry 8 tonnes (8 (7.8 tons) internally or 12 tonnes (11.8 tons) underslung. It used fixed wings to offload the rotors in forward flight.

■ **Mi-8 'HIP':** Using the same gearbox and rotors as the Mi-4, the Mi-8 has been produced in thousands and is the most widely used helicopter in the world. The Mi-8 could lift 4 tonnes (3.9 tons) internally or externally.

■ **Mi-10 'HARKE':** Using the same engines as the Mi-6, the Mi-10 was developed as a flying crane with an long undercarriage for lifting bulky cargo. The Mi-10 could lift 15 tonnes (14.7 tons) internally or 8 tonnes (7.8 tons) underslung.

MILES

M.35/M.39 LIBELLULA

● Tandem wing ● Naval fighter design ● High-speed bomber

▲ Despite the unique wing layout, the M.35 handled well in tests after early longitudinal stability problems had been solved. Unlike the later M-39, the M-35's canard wing was mounted behind the cockpit.

I n 1941 Miles Aircraft decided to investigate the use of tandem wings to overcome the problem of visibility from the cockpits of land-based fighters adapted for operation from aircraft-carriers. The tandem-wing layout, with tailfins on the ends of the rear wings and an engine in the rear fuselage, would allow the cockpit to be in the extreme nose. Subsequently, the idea was developed further to include high-speed bomber projects.

MILES M.35/M.39 LIBELLULA

▼ From fighter to bomber
After the M.35 fighter had been snubbed, Miles decided to compete for a specification requesting a high-speed, unarmed bomber. The M.39B was a scale model of the bomber which Miles proposed in 1943.

▲ Tandem wings
After testing a number of scale models, Miles settled on a tandem wing layout. The rear wing was 1.7 times larger than the front wing.

Naval fighter design ▶
The M.35 was designed to overcome the problem of visibility when approaching a carrier. The tandem wing design allowed the pilot to be placed in the nose, giving a superb field-of-view.

◀ A rocky ride
The fuselage of the M.39 was not sufficiently stiffened and caused the nose, containing the pilot, to oscillate from side to side.

Wooden mock-up ▶
The only M.35 produced was a tiny mock-up of what would have been the final design. With a maximum take-off weight of less than 850 kg (1,870 lb.), it was conceived and constructed in less than a year.

FACTS AND FIGURES

➤ Both designs were ultimately rejected, partly because of Miles' unpopularity within the Air Ministry.

➤ On its first flight the M.35 suffered from severe longitudinal stability problems.

➤ The M.39 was a scaled prototype for a tri-jet high-altitude bomber for the RAF.

➤ The Royal Aircraft Establishment proposed a similar 'tail first' bomber design with jet engines; it was not built.

➤ The Libellula name came from the zoological name for the dragonfly genus.

➤ The M.35 was designed, built and flown within six weeks of work commencing.

Dragonfly for the Royal Navy

The first step in the development was the construction of a wooden flying model to check whether the design would be controllable in flight. Designated M.35 and named Libellula, this was built in secret using various parts from the company's Magister trainer. When it flew for the first time in May 1942, it proved to be very unstable but demonstrated that the configuration was flyable.

When Miles submitted its tandem-wing naval fighter proposal, the company was reprimanded for building an aircraft without official permission and the idea was rejected. A scheme for a heavy bomber using six piston engines, which were intended to be replaced by jets, was also rejected.

The next tandem-wing project was the M.39 high-altitude bomber. This model had a low front wing and a high rear wing, which was intended to carry the two Hercules or Merlin engines. Three jet engines were envisaged as the ultimate powerplants.

Although the M.39 never got beyond wind-tunnel tests, Miles decided to build another flying model, the M.39B. This flew in July 1943 and underwent official trials, but there were no production aircraft.

Above: With engines fitted just behind the cockpit, an emergency escape would have involved crawling along the fuselage to avoid the propellers.

Above: Although impressed by the design, the Air Ministry rejected the M.39B and severely rebuked the Miles company for designing and flying an aircraft without permission.

M.39B

Type: experimental bomber mock-up

Powerplant: two 104-kW (130-hp.) de Havilland Gipsy Major four-cylinder air-cooled in-line engines

Maximum speed: 264 km/h (164 m.p.h.)

Climb rate: 427 m/min (1,400 f.p.m.) at sea level

Take-off run: 133 m (436 ft.)

Landing roll: 151 m (495 ft.)

Weights: empty 1105 kg (2,431 lb.); maximum take-off 1270 kg (2,794 lb.)

Accommodation: pilot only

Dimensions: span (forward) 6.10 m (25 ft.)
span (rear) 11.43 m (37 ft. 6 in.)
length 6.76 m (22 ft. 4 in.)
height 2.82 m (9 ft. 1 in.)
wing area (total) 23.15 m² (249 sq. ft.)

M.39B

The only M.39 was a five-eighths' scale model of the proposed bomber. After initial trials as the U-0244, in 1944 it was sent to the Royal Aircraft Establishment at Farnborough where it became SR392. It was later returned to Miles and became the U4.

The single-seat cockpit had a fairly basic layout. The flaps on both wings were operated by two hand-wheels mounted on the starboard side of the cockpit.

Compared to the earlier M.35, the M.39B possessed a front wing which was smaller than the rear wing. The wing position was also reversed, with the front wing in the lower position.

Two de Havilland Gipsy Major IC engines powered the M.39B. If it had entered production it was intended to be powered by either two Rolls-Royce Merlins or three turbojet engines.

Flaps were fitted to both wings. Because of the disparity in wing loading it was impossible for the rear wing to stall, which made the aircraft fairly safe to fly.

The twin rudders were positioned well outside the slipstream and were highly effective, especially at low speeds when the ailerons became ineffective.

INNOVATIVE MILES AIRCRAFT

M.57 Aerovan and H.D.M.105: Converted from a civil Aerovan passenger and freight aircraft (54 of which were built from 1945), the H.D.M.105 featured a high aspect ratio wing designed by French company Hurel-Dubois. The standard Aerovan transport carried between six and nine passengers at 200 km/h.

M.77 Sparrowjet: Rebuilt from the prototype piston-engined, single-seat Sparrowhawk racing aircraft of the 1930s, the M.77 Sparrowjet utilised two 1.47-kN (330-lb.-thrust) Turboméca Palas turbojets, one in each wingroot. Capable of 367 km/h (228 m.p.h.), the M.77 won the King's Cup race in England in 1957.

M.100 Student: Built as a private venture and evaluated by the RAF as a trainer, the Student was a Turboméca Marboré-powered side-by-side two-seater. Only one was built and first flew in 1957. In 1985 the M.100 was restored to flying condition, but crashed later that year. It is to be restored to fly yet again.

Unconventional wing designs of World War II

JUNKERS Ju 287: This remarkable bomber design had only reached prototype stage at the end of the war. With forward-swept wings and four turbojets it completed successful flight trials.

KYUSHU J7W SHINDEN: The Shinden was the only aircraft of canard configuration to be ordered into production during World War II.

NORTHROP XB-35: Northrop's long-range flying wing bomber programme began in 1941 and four scale mock-ups were built. After extensive development the first XB-35 flew in 1946.

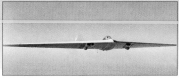

WESTLAND DELANNE: This development of the Lysander had an enlarged tailplane to provide extra lift for the installation of a turret.

MITSUBISHI/LOCKHEED MARTIN

FS-X (F-2)

● Japanese close-support fighter ● F-16C derivative ● In service in 1999

▲ Concerns have been raised about US involvement in the FS-X/F-2 programme and about the escalating costs; unit cost of early examples will be US $120 million.

Japan's successor to the Mitsubishi F-1 close-support fighter is a derivative of the F-16C. Known as the FS-X during its development, it has since gained the service designation F-2. Work on the project started in 1987, the first aircraft flying in October 1995. Slightly longer than the F-16C and with a bigger wing and tailfin for improved manoeuvrability, it will use a new radar of advanced design and will have an internal electronic warfare system.

PHOTO FILE

MITSUBISHI/LOCKHEED MARTIN FS-X (F-2)

Resemblance to the F-16 ▶
Though the FS-X was to feature vertical canards for agility, weight savings led to their deletion. As a result the F-2 looks more like a standard F-16.

▼ Blade aerials
Four blade aerials forward of the cockpit are believed to be associated with an IFF system.

▲ Well armed
Here the first FS-X/XF-2A prototype, serialled 63-0001, is seen on an early test flight. Rails on the wing tips are expected to carry AIM-9L Sidewinders or Japanese-designed AAM-3 short-range air-to-air missiles in service.

▼ Clay mock-up
Prior to construction of the four prototypes, this clay mock-up was constructed by Mitsubishi.

▲ Brake parachute-equipped
Unlike USAF-operated F-16s, the F-2 features a landing parachute deployed from a fairing at the rudder's base. Brake 'chutes reduce landing runs and brake wear.

FACTS AND FIGURES

➤ Initial F-2A unit cost is expected to be US $120 million; if all 130 examples are built this price will drop to US $80 million.

➤ Total expenditure on the F-2 between 1988 and 1995 was US $3.27 billion.

➤ The F-2's digital fly-by-wire system was developed jointly with Bendix-King.

➤ Fuji builds the upper wing skins, wing fairings, radome, flaperons, engine air intakes and tail unit of the F-2.

➤ F-2Bs may be used by the JASDF to replace the Mitsubishi T-2.

➤ General Dynamics proposed a twin-engined F-16 for the FS-X requirement.

PROFILE

Japan's home-grown 21st century F-16

Like the F-1, the F-2 will have protection of Japan's sea lanes as its main task. The new fighter's principal weapon will be the Mitsubishi ASM-2 anti-ship missile. For self-defence it will carry AIM-7 Sparrow medium-range and either AIM-9L or AAM-3 short-range missiles.

A new construction technique being used on the F-2 allows the composite wing skin and internal wing structure to be made as a single component, removing the need to rivet individual wing sections together. The F-2's wing is longer and 25 per cent larger

in area than that of the F-16C, but the new manufacturing technique reduces weight by about one third. This change and the use of larger tailplanes, enabled Mitsubishi to dispense with the vertical canards that were planned originally.

The aircraft will be built in single-seat F-2A and two-seat F-2B versions. Flight testing of four prototypes, two of each version, by the Japanese Self-Defence Agency began in 1995.

Delivery of production aircraft began in 2001 after some structural problems. The Japan Air Self Defence Force plans to

buy up to 130 examples. Initially 72 single-seaters will replace F-1s in three support Hikotai (3rd and 8th at Misawa and 6th at Tsuiki). F-2Bs will equip an operational conversion unit.

Left: The F-2 is now entering service in Japan after a rocky start. It will be used mainly in the anti-ship role. This aircraft is the first of two XF-2B conversion trainer prototypes.

Right: The F-2 programme has been entirely managed and funded by the Japanese and represents their most ambitious defence project to date. The end of the Cold War brought calls for cuts.

F-2A

Type: single-seat, close support fighter

Powerplant: one 131.6-kN (29,598-lb.-thrust) General Electric F110-GE-129 IPE afterburning turbofan

Maximum speed: Mach 2

Weights: empty equipped 12000 kg (26,455 lb.); maximum take-off 22100 kg (48,722 lb.)

Armament: (projected) one M61A1 Vulcan 20-mm rotary cannon plus a variety of air-to-air missiles (AIM-7F/M Sparrow and AIM-9L Sidewinder or AAM-3), anti-ship missiles (ASM-1 or ASM-2), 227-kg (500-lb.) or 454-kg (1000-lb.) bombs, cluster bombs and rocket launchers on 13 external stations

Dimensions:
span	11.13 m (36 ft. 6in)
length	15.52 m (50 ft. 11 in.)
height	4.96 m (16 ft. 3 in.)
wing area	34.84 m² (375 sq. ft.)

COMBAT DATA

THRUST
With the same General Electric F110 turbofan as late-production F-16Cs, the F-2 has similar performance to the American aircraft. The F110 engines give twice the installed thrust as the powerplants of the earlier twin-engined Mitsubishi F-1.

F-2A 131.6 kN (29,598 lb.thrust)	F-1 64.98 kN (14,615 lb.-thrust)	F-16C FIGHTING FALCON 131.6 kN (29,598 lb.thrust)

INTERNAL FUEL CAPACITY
More use is made in the F-2 of internal fuel tankage, leaving more pylons available for external weapons carriage. The Lockheed Martin F-16, the basis for the F-2's design, carries little more internal fuel than the Mitsubishi F-1, which the F-2 is intended to replace from 1999/2000.

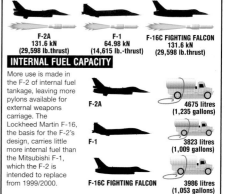

F-2A	4675 litres (1,235 gallons)
F-1	3823 litres (1,009 gallons)
F-16C FIGHTING FALCON	3986 litres (1,053 gallons)

MAXIMUM TAKE-OFF WEIGHT
The F-2 is a marginally larger and heavier aircraft than the Fighting Falcon. This reflects its fuel and weapon-carrying capacity in the close support role for which it was designed. Both have maximum take-off weights much greater than that of the F-1.

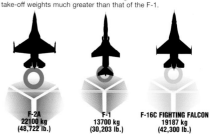

F-2A 22100 kg (48,722 lb.)	F-1 13700 kg (30,203 lb.)	F-16C FIGHTING FALCON 19187 kg (42,300 lb.)

XF-2A

Four flying prototypes were ordered, 63-0001 being the first of two XF-2As. Rolled out on 12 January 1995, it flew for the first time on 7 October. Two XF-2B prototypes followed in 1996.

Unlike the F-16, the F-2 has a two-piece cockpit canopy with a slightly different profile. This houses the pilot in a cockpit featuring largely Japanese avionics.

Construction of the F-2's airframe is subcontracted to several firms. While Mitsubishi builds the forward fuselage and wings, Fuji, Kawasaki and Lockheed Martin build other components.

An important aspect of the F-2 programme has been the technology transfer between the US and Japan. This has been a two-way process, the US gaining access to several advanced technologies developed in Japan, including the advanced composite wing.

As well as a Vulcan cannon, the F-2 sports up to 13 stores stations for a variety of air-to-air and anti-ship missiles, bombs, cluster munitions and rocket launchers.

F-2s have a slightly longer nose than the F-16C, to house a new radar (a Mitsubishi Electric active phased-array set) and other avionics. To the left of the cockpit is an M61A1 Vulcan 20-mm rotary cannon, as fitted to the Fighting Falcon.

To improve the aircraft's stealthiness, radar-absorbent material (RAM) was incorporated in the wing leading edges, nose cone and engine intake.

Power for the F-2 comes from the General Electric F110 afterburning turbofan as fitted to late-model F-16s. A shorter jet pipe is fitted to the F-2; the fuselage has a longer mid-section.

Aviation look-alikes

ISRAEL AIRCRAFT INDUSTRIES KFIR: After the French government banned the export of Mirage Vs to Israel, the Israelis 'acquired' plans for the design and built their own version known as Nesher. From this was developed the J79-engined Kfir.

LISUNOV Li-2: Originally designated PS-84, the Soviet Li-2 was a licence-built version of the Douglas DC-3. However, almost 1,300 engineering changes were introduced during the production life of the aircraft; variants included bombers and minesweepers.

MARTIN B-57: When the USAF needed an aircraft to replace the B-26 Intruder in the light bomber role, the British Canberra was chosen for licence production by Martin. Changes were made to the design for the intruder and reconnaissance roles.

MYASISHCHEV

M-17/M-55 'MYSTIC'

● Balloon interception ● Reconnaissance ● Geophysical survey

I n 1982 Western intelligence reported the
sighting of an unidentified Russian high-
altitude reconnaissance aircraft. Satellite
photographs of the Zhukhovskii flight test
centre showed an aircraft with twin tail fins and
long, unswept wings, suggesting that it was a
Soviet counterpart of the American U-2.
It was known as 'Ram-M', and several years
passed before the mysterious aircraft was
finally identified as the Myasishchev M-17.

▲ Russia's answer to
the U-2 has not achieved the success or
infamy of its American equivalent. The
M-17s and M-55s have performed useful
environmental research, however.

MYASISHCHEV M-17/M-55 'MYSTIC'

Record breaker ▶
*During 1990 the single-engined M-17 Stratosphera
set a total of 25 speed/climb/height records.*

▼ Environmental research
*The M-55 Geofizika was developed to help to study
the problems of ozone depletion.*

M-55 Geofizika ▶
*The M-55 can carry equipment for Earth-resource missions,
agricultural surveying, ground mapping and ice reconnaissance.*

▲ Air show star
*Geofizika has appeared in
the West at the Paris and
Farnborough air shows.*

Mystic power ▶
*Two 88.30-kN (19,865-lb.-thrust)
Soloviev D-30-10V turbofans
power the M-55.*

FACTS AND FIGURES

➤ Subject 34 was cancelled when the CIA
stopped using high-altitude balloons as
reconnaissance platforms.

➤ Eduard Chyeltsov flew the first M-17
Stratosphera on 26 May 1982.

➤ In 1992 an M-17 'Mystic-A' investigated
the Antarctic ozone hole.

➤ Chyeltsov also flew the M-55 Geofizika
on its maiden flight on 16 August 1988;
at least three more have flown since.

➤ A projected M-55UTS trainer was to have
a periscope to aid back-seat vision.

➤ The M-55 'Mystic-B' can climb to 21 km
(13 miles) in 35 minutes.

Master of the stratosphere

Originally planned in 1967 as an interceptor of high-altitude reconnaissance balloons under the designation Subject 34 and known as the Chaika (Gull), Myasishchev's new aircraft was first seen by NATO in the unarmed 'Mystic-A' form. Known as the Stratosphera in Russia, the M-17 retains some of its original mystery.

It resembles the U-2 in having a single engine with intakes on the sides of the forward fuselage, and was designed for a similar strategic reconnaissance role. But it has a greater wingspan and is slightly longer overall, with a shorter, deeper fuselage and a long tailplane carried on twin fins.

It was intended to replace the Yak-25RD, but one of the two M-17s that were built is now housed in a museum. The second aircraft has been used to investigate the ozone layer and pollution in the upper regions of the atmosphere.

Since 1994 a twin-engined version, the M-55 Geofizika ('Mystic-B'), has appeared at Western air shows. Designed specifically for environmental and geophysical research, it can carry a 1500-kg payload and has an endurance of seven hours.

From its operational altitude of 21500 metres, the M-55 can photograph an area 120 km (75 mi.) wide, and can also glide for a distance of 200 km (120 mi.).

Below: One of the two prototype M-17 Stratospheras (17103) survives in Aeroflot colours at the Monino aerospace museum near Moscow.

Above: According to Russian sources, development of the 'Mystic-B' as a strategic reconnaissance platform for military service is continuing.

M-17 Stratosphera 'Mystic-A'

Type: single-seat high-altitude reconnaissance and research aircraft

Powerplant: one 68.65-kN (15,450-lb.-thrust) RKBM Rybinsk RD-36-51V turbojet

Maximum speed: 743 km/h at 20,000 m (460 m.p.h. at 65,600 ft.)

Take-off run: 875 m to 10.5-m (2,870 ft. to 35-ft.) altitude

Endurance: 2 hours 25 min

Range: 1,315 km (815 mi.)

Service ceiling: 21,550 m (70,700 ft.)

Weights: max take-off 19,950 kg (43,890 lb.)

Dimensions:
span	40.32 m	(132 ft. 3 in.)
length	22.27 m	(73 ft. 1 in.)
height	5.25 m	(17 ft. 3 in.)
wing area	137.70 m²	(1,482 sq. ft.)

M-17 STRATOSPHERA 'MYSTIC-A'

Although it achieved a number of world records, the prospect of the M-17 becoming a Soviet counterpart of the U-2 faded. The aircraft moved on to investigation of the Antarctic ozone problem.

The M-17's single pilot is seated on a K-36L ejection seat, under an upward-hinging canopy. Carried just behind the pilot are two oxygen canisters.

Compared to the unusual inverted gull wing of the Subject 34 interceptor, the M-17's wing is much more conventional in layout. The engine is started by a turbo-starter and fed with fuel from five separate wing tanks, which hold a total of 10,000 litres (2,650 gallons).

The M-17s were built at Kumertau, Bashkiri, primarily from lightweight metals. The entire aircraft is comprehensively ice-protected for high-altitude operations. In normal conditions the reconnaissance-configured M-17 would have carried 1000 kg (2,200 lb.) of advanced cameras and sensors.

This M-17, serial CCCP-17401, was the aircraft used during trials and preparation work for the M-55. It flew missions to monitor Antarctica's atmosphere. A number of environmental slogans were subsequently added.

'Mystic-A' carries a PRNK-17 navigation system radio compass and an RSBN Kobalt radar. These were also used in the M-55 'Mystic-B'.

A novel feature of the M-17 'Mystic-A' is its retractable landing lights, stowed under the front of the tail booms.

Designed for high altitudes, the RD-36-51V is based on the engine core from which the MiG-31's powerplants were derived.

Both the M-17 Stratosphera 'Mystic-A' and M-55 Geofizika 'Mystic-B' feature an unusual twin-boom tail, with vertical surfaces bridged by a long horizontal stabiliser.

ACTION DATA

MAXIMUM TAKE-OFF WEIGHT

With its high maximum take-off weight, the M-17 is capable of lifting heavier loads to altitude than either of its most direct rivals. It does not have the high-tech avionics of the U-2R, however.

M-17 STRATOSPHERA 'MYSTIC-A'
19,950 kg (43,890 lb.)

U-2R
18,733 kg (41,213 lb.)

STRATO 2C
13,350 kg (29,370 lb.)

CEILING

Grob's all-composite Strato 2C uses specially tuned high-altitude piston engines to achieve its exceptional altitude capabilities. It is used solely as a research vehicle.

STRATO 2C
26000 m (85,300 ft.)

U-2R
24385 m (80,000 ft.)

M-17 STRATOSPHERA 'MYSTIC-A'
21550 m (70,700 ft.)

ENDURANCE

With its two-seat cabin the Strato 2C is equipped for missions of long duration. Its engines are extremely fuel-efficient but do not deliver the climb and speed performance of the jet aircraft.

M-17 STRATOSPHERA 'MYSTIC-A'
2 hours 25 min

U-2R
12 hours

STRATO 2C
48 hours

Changing roles of the 'Mystic'

Since its conception in 1967, the 'Mystic' has seen its role change from balloon interceptor to research platform.

INTERCEPTOR: Armed with a turret-mounted GSh-23 cannon and two air-to-air missiles, the single-seat Subject 34 was intended to destroy spy balloons.

M-17 'MYSTIC-A': In its design role the M-17 would have flown high-altitude strategic reconnaissance missions over sensitive foreign installations.

M-55 'MYSTIC-B': An unusual role adopted by the M-55 is the conversion of hail into rain by the use of chemicals. Such weather alteration avoids excessive crop damage, helping the struggling Russian economy.

MYASISHCHEV

VM-T ATLANT

● Spacecraft carriage ● Converted bomber ● Heavylift specialist

MYASISHCHEV VM-T ATLANT

▲ Fuel tank aboard
Heaving aloft the massive Energiya fuel tank was no mean feat despite more powerful engines.

▲ Shuttle transport
The VM-T could also carry the Buryan re-usable space vehicle. The American Space Shuttle is carried on a Boeing 747.

▲ Flying to Baikonur
The VM-T was very busy, making over 150 flights to the Baikonur launch station from the factories.

▼ New engines
The VM-T was fitted with non-afterburning VD-7M engines (from the Tu-22 bomber) for extra thrust.

▲ Standard 'Bison'
Instantly recognisable, even from below, because of its single tailfin, the 'Bison' served until the late-1980s as a tanker and reconnaissance aircraft.

While the USA and Europe have developed various 'Guppy'-type aircraft with outsize fuselages to carry large rocket assemblies, the Soviet Union uses several converted bombers as piggyback transports for complete aircraft wings and other large loads. The VM-T, or Atlant, is a version of the M-3M 'Bison-B' bomber which has been modified to carry bulky loads on top of its fuselage in support of the Soviet space programme.

▲ Dismissed as a failed bomber that was short of range, the Mya-4 'Bison' became a capable all-round aircraft used for inflight-refuelling, ocean reconnaissance and transporting outsize cargoes for the space industry.

FACTS AND FIGURES

➤ The first flight of the VM-T Atlant carrying a payload was by A. Kuryurchenko and his crew in January 1982.

➤ Myasishchev died in 1978, shortly after beginning work on the VM-T conversion.

➤ Two VM-Ts (also known as 3M-T) were completed and first flew in 1980.

➤ Myasishchev also proposed a twin-deck military cargo variant of the 3M bomber, but this was never built.

➤ A proposed civil 380-seat airliner variant of the 'Bison' was also not produced.

➤ The 3M version of the 'Bison' bomber was a redesign with a new wing shape.

PROFILE

The Soviet big lifter

Never a great success as a bomber, only about 200 'Bisons' were built, and many of them were converted into tankers or maritime reconnaissance platforms.

More unusually, two examples of the M-3M 'Bison-B' version were adapted for transporting some of the structures produced as part of the Soviet space shuttle programme. To accommodate extremely long assemblies and to provide enough directional stability to cope with the unusual sizes and shapes, the standard tail surfaces were removed. These were replaced by twin rectangular tailfins and rudders mounted on the ends of a new horizontal tailplane.

In this configuration the Atlant has been used to carry the Soviet Buryan space shuttle and sections of the Energiya launcher, including complete fuel tanks. They are secured on pylons mounted at various points on the front, centre and rear fuselage.

As the Atlant's payload is limited to 40 tonnes, the Buryan had to be stripped down before it could be carried, with the tail fin, orbital manoeuvring engines and other systems removed. The more recent An-225 Mryia can carry the complete shuttle orbiter on its back.

Above: The wide tailfins of the Atlant were necessary to cope with the turbulence from the Energiya fuel tank. The Atlant had quite good handling qualities.

Right: The Atlant used the airframe of the later 3MS 'Bison', recognisable by its longer nose profile. Only one of the aircraft had a flight-refuelling probe. The aircraft has the Cyrillic logo 'Aviaspetstrans' just above the Aeroflot badge.

VM-T ATLANT

RF-01502 was one of the two Atlant conversions of the Myasishchev 3M 'Bison' bomber used for carrying Energiya fuel tanks and Buryan shuttle bodies.

VM-T Atlant

Type: four-engine special transport aircraft converted from strategic bomber

Powerplant: four 93.2-kN (20,966-lb.-thrust) RBKM VD-7M single-shaft turbojets with afterburner removed for increased dry power rating

Maximum speed: 930 km/h (577 m.p.h.)

Take-off run: (3MS) 2950 m (9,676 ft.)

Range: 12,000 km (7,450 mi.) unloaded

Service ceiling: 14,900 m (48,875 ft.)

Payload: 40,000 kg (88,000 lb.)

Weights: (3MS-2) empty 75,740 kg (166,628 lb.); loaded maximum 192,000 kg (422,400lb.)

Dimensions:
span	53.14 m (174 ft.)
length	58.70 m (193 ft.)
height (approx.)	4.10 m (46 ft.)
wing area (est)	320 m² (1,050 sq. ft.)

The main modification to the Atlant was the fitting of a seven-metre fuselage extension, which was angled slightly upwards, and large fins on a dihedral tailplane. The majority of the design work was carried out after studies on three 3MN airframes.

The fuel tank was mounted on huge trusses at the front and rear of the fuselage.

The 3M bomber had RBP-4 radar located in the nose fairing. A flight-refuelling probe was fitted in the tip of the nose.

The Atlant nose was the same as the 3M bomber with the navigator located in a glazed nose compartment.

The Atlant and M3 used VD-7M engines unlike the Mikulin AM-3s and RD-3s in the early 'Bisons'.

РФ-01502

АТЛАНТ

ACTION DATA

PAYLOAD

With its uprated engines and redesigned fuselage, the Atlant could carry a much heavier payload than a standard 'Bison'. The Boeing 747 could carry even more, but is a much bigger and more powerful aircraft which was designed 10 years after the 'Bison'.

VM-T ATLANT	40,000 kg (80,000 lb.)
3MS 'BISON-B'	24,000 kg (52,800 lb.)
MODEL 747	70,000 kg (154,000 lb.)

Myasishchev designs

■ **DVB-102:** The first of the Myasishchev designs not to use the name of another design bureau, the DVB-102 was a fast light-bomber prototype. It flew in prototype form only, was delayed by the outbreak of war and was finally abandoned in 1944.

■ **M-17 'STRATOSPHERA':** Designed initially as a fighter to shoot down CIA high-altitude reconnaissance balloons, the M-17 was then converted to the high-altitude reconnaissance role itself. It was later used for ozone-layer research and geosurvey flights.

■ **M-50 'BOUNDER':** The M-50 had the biggest wing of any supersonic aircraft except for the American XB-70. The aircraft was designed as a strategic missile launcher, but engine development problems and limited range meant that it did not enter service.

NACA/NASA

X-2 – X-15

● Rocket and jet power ● Experimental aircraft ● Flying at the limit

▲ Flying experimental aircraft has always been considered glamorous. Publicity shots showing dashing pilots give no indication of the extreme risks that are being taken, however.

owadays aircraft manufacturers test experimental designs thoroughly using computer models long before the planes are flown by a test pilot. Up until the 1970s this was not the case, however, with simulators and wind tunnels providing only an idea of what might happen when an experimental design was taken aloft. NASA has conducted some of the most spectacular and dangerous of these experimental aircraft projects.

NACA/NASA X-2 – X-15

McKay's misfortune ▶
Test pilot John McKay had a serious landing accident in the X-15, but it was rebuilt to X-15A-2 standard with huge external propellant tanks.

▲ Ill-fated X-15
In 1967 Aircraft 56-6671 broke up at Mach 5 and at an altitude of 38100 metres (125,000 ft.); pilot Major Adams was killed.

▼ VTOL success story
Although primarily a USAF programme, NACA also became involved with the Ryan X-13.

▲ Long-serving Bell
After initial problems with the USAF, the X-14 was passed to NASA. The aircraft was re-engined and served for almost 25 years.

▲ First of the swingers
The X-5 was designed to investigate variable-geometry wings. Although one machine was lost in a fatal crash, others provided useful data.

FACTS AND FIGURES

➤ In 1958 NACA was redesignated as NASA (National Aeronautics and Space Administration).

➤ Bell used data from the Messerschmitt P.1101 when building the X-5.

➤ The X-6 never flew, but an NB-36H with a reactor onboard was flown by NACA.

➤ With the use of speedbrakes the X-4 could simulate the flying characteristics of other aircraft.

➤ Test pilots from all over the world experienced VTOL flight in the X-14.

➤ Astronaut Neil Armstrong flew several missions in the X-15.

Rocket ships and VTOL

The test pilots of the National Advisory Committee for Aeronautics (NACA), and later NASA, often flew at the edge of the known envelope and beyond. They investigated new airframe configurations, including swing-wings and tailless deltas, exotic materials and kinetic heating effects in high-speed and high-altitude flight.

Projects like the X-15 are the most well known because of the aircraft's amazing performance. The X-15A-2 flew higher and faster than any other

conventionally winged machine, and several pilots qualified for their astronaut wings because of the altitude achieved.

Less glamorous aircraft such as the Bell X-14 and the Ryan X-13, which were both used to test vertical take-off and landing technology, also provided a great deal of useful information, as did the nuclear-powered X-6.

Danger was inherent during every test flight. Aircraft were often rocket-powered and usually tricky to handle, which led to the death of some pilots and a number of serious accidents.

Built to test the tailless delta layout, the X-4 was one of the safest and most predictable X-planes to fly. The large wing flaps also acted as split airbrakes and gave the aircraft variable stability characteristics.

But the advances made in aviation due to NACA's and NASA's test pilots cannot be overestimated.

Both the windscreen arrangement and cockpit space suggested that the X-14 should be a two-seater. The aircraft had a limited thrust-to-weight ratio, however, and could not have taken off with a second crewmember.

In order to speed up production of the X-14 and to keep costs to a minimum, several parts from other aircraft were used. The wings, undercarriage and ailerons were those of a Bonanza and the tail section was from a T-34A Mentor.

The entire airframe was constructed from aluminium. It was conventional and was built with weight-saving and cost-cutting measures to the fore.

X-14B

Type: VTOL research aircraft capable of simulating the hovering characteristics of other VTOL types

Powerplant: two 13.4-kN (3,015-lb.-thrust) General Electric J85-GE-19 non-afterburning turbojets taken from the abandoned Lockheed XV-4 and fitted late in the X-14 programme

Maximum speed: 277 km/h (172 m.p.h.)

Range: 480 km (300 mi.)

Service ceiling: 5500 m (18,000 ft.)

Weights: empty 1437 kg (3,160 lb.); maximum take-off 1934 kg (4,255 lb.)

Dimensions:
span	10.30 m	(33 ft. 9 in.)
length	7.92 m	(26 ft.)
height	2.68 m	(8 ft. 9 in.)
wing area	16.68 m²	(179 sq. ft.)

Mounted side-by-side in the nose, the engines exhausted through vectoring nozzles mounted in the lower, rear fuselage.

The cockpit was basic, with just a windscreen for pilot protection. Weight-saving considerations forced the exclusion of an ejection seat and roll-over bar.

As an experimental aircraft the X-14 constantly evolved. It was originally powered by Armstrong Siddeley Viper turbojets. It then became the X-14A with General Electric J85-GE-5s and later the X-14B with J85-GE-19 engines.

In its original configuration the X-14 could not take off vertically. The engine arrangement resulted in air being pulled down onto the aircraft, which created low pressure beneath and the X-14 was literally sucked onto the runway. The solution was to fit longer undercarriage legs.

All fuel was stored in two 464-litre (123-gallon) external underwing tanks, which meant that the fuel was positioned close to the centre of gravity. This is an important consideration in VTOL flight.

X-14B

Many experimental aircraft were funded and flown by more than one agency. The X-14 was one such machine and variously wore NASA, USAF and US Army titles. The aircraft was retired in 1981.

ACTION DATA

MAXIMUM SPEED

Not all of the NACA/NASA X-plane projects worked as planned. The Douglas X-3 Stilletto was designed to study sustained high-speed flight at Mach 2 and above. It was underpowered, however, and was overtaken by contemporary fighter developments. Both the X-2 and X-15 were stunningly fast, and the X-15A-2 remains unsurpassed.

X-2	3370 km/h (2,090 m.p.h.)
X-3	1136 km/h (704 m.p.h.)
X-15A-2	7297 km/h (4,524 m.p.h.)

MAXIMUM ALTITUDE

Several X-planes demonstrated greater performance than had been expected. This was true of both the X-15 and X-2. The X-15 reached considerably higher altitudes than predicted.

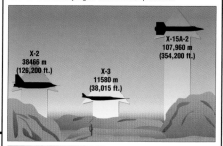

X-15A-2 107,960 m (354,200 ft.)
X-2 38466 m (126,200 ft.)
X-3 11580 m (38,015 ft.)

POWERED ENDURANCE

With its turbojet engines the X-3 performed conventional take-offs and was always powered in flight. The rockets engines of the X-2 and X-15 rapidly exhausted their limited fuel supply.

X-2 10 min 55 sec
X-3 1 hour
X-15A-2 2 min 36 sec

The fatal crash of X-2 46-674

1 **27 SEPTEMBER 1956:** Captain Mel Apt launched successfully from the EB-50D 'mothership' for his first X-2 flight. The aircraft achieved 145 seconds of rocket burn.

2 **ACCELERATION TO MACH 3.2:** After reaching 17,000 m (55,800 ft.), Apt accelerated in a 6° dive.

3 **INVERTED FLAT SPIN:** After turning the unpowered X-2 back towards Edwards Air Force Base, Apt used right aileron to correct an increasingly steep left bank. This created excessive drag on the right wing and the aircraft entered an inverted spin at Mach 3.

4 **FATAL ACCIDENT:** NACA instrumentation recorded instantaneous changes in stress between +6/-6g during the spin. The X-2 broke into three pieces when it hit the ground.

NASA/AMES

AD-1

● One-off prototype ● Pivoting wing ● Advanced home-build

I n 1978, NASA turned to the Ames Industrial Corporation to manufacture one of the most exotic flying machines ever built. The Ames-Dryden AD-1 was a small, lightweight research aircraft intended to test the pivoting wing, also known as the oblique wing – a unique way of improving aircraft performance at varying speeds. The AD-1 was tested, but ambitious plans for an improved version did not proceed.

▲ NASA has inspired a number of highly unusual, one-off aircraft designs, but few have been as odd as the AD-1. The machine provided a great deal of valuable research information.

PHOTO FILE

NASA/AMES AD-1

▼ **Navy interest**
An artist's impression illustrates the slender fuselage and twin podded engines of the AD-1. In addition to tests at NASA Dryden, flights were conducted by the Navy at Patuxent River.

▲ **Truly unique**
One of the strangest-looking machines ever to take to the air, the AD-1 nevertheless proved useful for research into oblique wing technology.

Supersonic benefits ▶
Due in part to its unique design, the AD-1 offered many potential advantages for future supersonic aircraft, including reduced engine power on take-off and reduced noise levels, an important environmental issue.

◀ **Conventional position**
While on the tarmac and during take-off and landing, the wing is kept in a conventional position for greater stability at low speed.

Maximum sweep ▶
Seen early in 1979, the then-incomplete AD-1 demonstrated the wing at its full oblique angle, which could be achieved only while flying at cruising speed.

FACTS AND FIGURES

➤ The AD-1 stemmed from research into a supersonic airliner/transport featuring a similar type of pivoting wing.

➤ Flight testing was conducted at NASA's Dryden facility between 1979 and 1982.

➤ A maximum oblique angle of 60° could be achieved while the aircraft was in flight.

➤ NASA provided the entire blueprints for the design; Ames was tasked purely with construction of the single AD-1.

➤ Gross weight of this bizarre machine is an incredibly low 816 kg (1,795 lb.).

➤ After years of inactivity, the AD-1 flew once again at Oshkosh in 1997.

PROFILE

Stranger than fiction

The principle behind the AD-1, designed by Burt Rutan, was similar to that of 'swing-wing' aircraft like the F-111, F-14 and Tornado. For operation at low speeds and during take-off and landing, the AD-1's wing was positioned in a 'normal' configuration. For flight at higher speeds, the wing pivoted to form an oblique angle of up to 60° – roughly the equivalent of shifting to greater sweep-back on a jet fighter – reducing drag and making possible greater speed and range with no noticeable increase in fuel consumption.

In tests, the AD-1 took to the air and flew with its wing at increasingly large angles, successfully demonstrating that the pivoting-wing principle worked as expected.

In 1986, NASA launched an effort to develop a short-span, 'joined wing' version of the AD-1. The new aircraft would have had removable wingtip panels, enabling it to be progressively modified for different wing sweep and angle configurations. This experiment did not proceed, but the AD-1 was a useful vehicle for research into such advanced concepts.

Left: High above the Californian desert, the AD-1 cruises with the wing pivoted. The large cockpit canopy gave outstanding visibility.

After increasing the angle of the wing during successive tests, NASA finally reached the full oblique of 60° during a flight on 24 April 1981.

Construction of the AD-1 comprised a semi-monocoque structure with a special foam core and glass-fibre epoxy for light weight.

For landing and take-off, the wing was kept at a conventional 90° to the fuselage. For the first few flights the wing remained in this position and it was only on the ninth flight that the angle was gradually increased.

AD-1

Only a single example of the NASA/Ames AD-1 was ever built. Construction at the Ames plant in Bohemia, New York, began in 1978, and this unusual creation took to the air for the first time in March 1979.

The cockpit was extremely long but very cramped, though excellent visibility was offered by the large canopy. The pilot sat very far back with his legs stretched out. Although nothing like it had ever flown before, the aircraft had surprisingly good handling qualities.

For such a small and light machine, a suitable powerplant had to be devised. A pair of extremely compact Ames TRS 18-046 turbojet engines proved the ultimate solution.

A conventional tricycle undercarriage was fitted, featuring single tyres on all three units. Ground clearance was minimal and landings were often quite bumpy.

In comparison to the unique main wing the tail unit was surprisingly conventional, with a standard vertical rudder and delta-style horizontal stabilisers featuring long elevators mounted on the trailing edges.

AD-1

Type: single-seat oblique-winged research aircraft

Powerplant: two rear-mounted 0.98-kN (153-lb.-thrust) Ames Industrial (Microturbo) TRS 18-046 turbojet engines

Maximum speed: 322 km/h (200 m.p.h.)

Service ceiling: 3600 m (11,800 ft.)

Weight: maximum take-off 907 kg (2,000 lb.)

Fuel capacity: 303 litres (80 gal.)

Accommodation: one pilot

Dimensions:
span	9.75 m	(32 ft.)
span (oblique)	4.93 m	(16 ft. 2 in.)
length	11.68 m	(38 ft. 4 in.)
height	1.98 m	(6 ft. 6 in.)
wing area	8.64 m²	(93 sq. ft.)

NASA OBLIQUE WING PROPOSALS

LOCKHEED SUPERSONIC JET TRANSPORT: Dating from about 1975, this proposal from Lockheed Georgia and NASA was for an aircraft with a pivoting oblique wing. Studies undertaken by that time had shown that such a wing would provide benefits at supersonic speeds, notably reduced drag and fuel consumption. This ambitious project was later shelved, though the information gathered proved useful for the much smaller AD-1. NASA is currently still studying the concept of oblique-wing aircraft.

OBLIQUE-WING F-8 CRUSADER: With the AD-1 programme drawing to a close in 1982, NASA began to look for alternative testbeds on which to continue development. It was particularly interested in the slew-winged concept applied to a larger machine. One proposal involved modifying the Administration's fly-by-wire Vought F-8 Crusader with an oblique wing. Rockwell International's North American Aircraft division was awarded a contract for development of the project, but it was not built.

Studies into variable-geometry wings

■ **MESSERSCHMITT P.1101:** Captured by the Americans at the end of World War II, this unusual aircraft featured 'movable wings' which had to be altered manually on the ground.

■ **BELL X-5:** Taking the idea of the P.1101 a stage further, the X-5 featured true variable-geometry wings. In practice the design proved dangerous, one example being lost after entering a spin.

■ **GRUMMAN XF-10 JAGUAR:** Developed with operational service in mind, the Jaguar demonstrated the potential offered by swing wings, but it was years before the idea took off.

NORD

GRIFFON

● Interceptor prototype ● Rocket and turbojet power ● Only one built

After the Korean War, several air forces decided to review their aircraft requirements in the light of the first real jet-combat experience. France perceived a need for a high-performance lightweight interceptor and, with seemingly endless government funding available, three prototypes were built. Nord produced the fabulous N 1500 Griffon, Sud-Est the unusual SE.212 Durandal, and Dassault the all-conquering Mirage III.

▲ *During the 1950s, the French aerospace industry produced a considerable number of prototypes, designed to satisfy particular operational requirements or to investigate some specific area of aviation research. Of these, the Nord Griffon was one of the most spectacular.*

NORD GRIFFON

Radical design for radical performance ▶
In order to meet the performance requirements of the French air force, Nord employed radical technology which resulted in a highly unusual airframe/powerplant configuration. Of note are the fixed foreplanes, retrospectively fitted to Mirage IIIs decades later to improve their manoeuvrability.

◀ In flight
In its N 1500-02 form the Griffon acquired a combined turbojet/ramjet powerplant. Here it is powered by the Atar turbojet; the ramjet was used only during high speed flight.

▲ Fiery interceptor
With the ramjet in operation, a distinctive ring of flame was emitted from the annular exhaust.

▼ N 1500-01
In its original form, the Griffon had a slimmer fuselage and a distinctive tailpipe.

▲ Pure delta
Nord selected a pure delta wing planform with forward fuselage canards for the Griffon.

FACTS AND FIGURES

➤ On 27 October 1958, the Griffon II became the second European aircraft to exceed Mach 2 on turbojet power.

➤ As the N 1500 the Griffon was registered F-ZWTX; as the N 1500-02 it was F-ZWUI.

➤ The Griffon II is preserved at the Musée de l'Air at Le Bourget.

➤ Dassault's Mirage III exceeded Mach 2 on turbojet power alone, three days before the Griffon II.

➤ A European absolute speed record was set by the N 1500-02 at Mach 2.18.

➤ Nord retired the Griffon soon after the October 1959 absolute speed record.

Nord's fiery Griffon

Flying first as the Guépard on 20 September 1955, the N 1500 was renamed Griffon. It was powered initially by a 40.2-kN (9,044-lb.-thrust) SNECMA Atar 101G21 turbojet, but was later re-engined with a 37.2-kN (8,369-lb.-thrust) Atar 101F. Trials were successful, but the aircraft was soon grounded for extensive airframe and powerplant modifications.

On 23 January 1957 the N 1500-02 Griffon II emerged powered by an Atar turbojet mounted within a Nord-built ramjet. The new configuration kept the swept delta wing of the N 1500 and its fixed foreplanes, but the fuselage was now wider to accomodate the ramjet.

On 27 October 1958 the aircraft exceeded Mach 2 for the first time, and on 25 February 1959 it set a new 100-km (62-mi.) closed-circuit record at 1643 km/h (1,018 m.p.h.). Over the course of 200 test flights, the Griffon II's speed was restricted only by kinetic-heating effects. It did not have the military potential of the Mirage III, however, and was therefore never destined to enter production as an interceptor.

The Griffon I had a traditional clear-view cockpit canopy. Attainable speeds were far lower than those of the Griffon II, so that kinetic heating was not a problem.

Fixed canard foreplanes kept the aircraft trimmed at all speeds. These advanced features were later to become popular on aircraft such as the Kfir and Mirage III.

While the Griffon's unusual powerplant gave it superb performance, it also gave it a very hot jet pipe. This would have been a perfect target for the new generation of heat-seeking missiles.

Leading edge sweep angle was 60º and the wing was unusually clean, without fences, notches or any other aerodynamic devices.

In order to shorten the landing roll, a braking parachute was fitted in a cylindrical fairing near the fin root.

Elevons at the trailing edge of each wing moved differentially for rolling movements and simultaneously for pitch control.

N 1500-02 Griffon II

Type: ramjet- and turbojet-powered interceptor prototype and research aircraft

Powerplant: one 34.32-kN (7,720-lb.-thrust) SNECMA Atar 101E3 turbojet mounted centrally within a Nord-built ramjet

Maximum speed: 1500 km/h at 3300 m (930 m.p.h. at 10,800 ft.)

Initial climb rate: 5200 m/min (17,056 f.p.m.)

Weights: maximum take-off about 6000 kg (13,200 lb.)

Accommodation: pilot only

Dimensions:
span	7.93 m (26 ft.)	
length	14.00 m (45 ft. 11 in.)	
height	5.00 m (16 ft. 5 in.)	

N 1500-02 GRIFFON II

Only one example of the remarkable Griffon was built, but it flew in two radically different configurations. As a ramjet/turbojet-powered research machine it had the potential for remarkable performance.

Since the Griffon II was expected to reach extreme speeds, it was fitted with a revised canopy which was mostly of metal. This allowed it to withstand kinetic heating.

In keeping with its high-speed performance, the Griffon had a long, sharply pointed nose. Little thought was given to the carriage of radar or fire-control systems, however, since the airframe design was not suitable for an operational type.

In N 1500-02 form, the intake of the Griffon was grossly distorted in order to feed air to the ramjet and turbojet. The Mirage III was superior to the Griffon, but the Dassault machine also featured compound power units for high-speed, high-altitude performance.

Low-pressure tyres and a robust undercarriage gave the potential for rough-field operations. The aircraft required an unusually long take-off run, however.

DELTA DEVELOPMENTS

NORD N 1042B GERFAUT II: Both the Gerfaut and Gerfaut II were used to collect data for a high-powered, delta-winged fighter which France intended to build. Two examples were built and modified many times, one becoming the first European aircraft to exceed Mach 1 in level flight without an afterburner.

DASSAULT MIRAGE III: Having investigated the delta-wing concept with the Gerfaut, the French industry moved on to producing submissions for the new interceptor. Dassault entered the fray rather late, having studied the experiences of other manufacturers to produce a thoroughly practical Mach 2 design.

SUD-EST SE.212 DURANDAL: Competing with the Griffon and Mirage III, the Durandal was severely handicapped by its inability to exceed Mach 1.5. The Griffon offered by far the best performance of the three designs, but while the Durandal fell short on speed, the Griffon lost out on practicality.

Nord design diversity

■ **N 3202:** Fifty examples of the N 3202 (a production derivation of the N 3200 primary trainer) were built for French service, followed by a second batch of 50 more powerful N 3202Bs.

■ **N 2501 NORATLAS:** Perhaps the most successful and well known of Nord designs, the Noratlas acquitted itself well in operations around the world.

■ **N 2200:** Designed to meet a French naval requirement for a cannon- and rocket-armed interceptor, the Nene-engined N 2200 was cancelled in favour of the Sea Venom.

■ **N 2100 NORAZUR:** An unusually configured 10/12-seat airliner prototype, the Norazur was designed in the same class as the de Havilland Dove. It was not a success.

NORD

GERFAUT

- Time-to-height record breaker ● Delta-wing research aircraft

T hree Nord Gerfaut test airplanes were among the many strange and ambitious prototypes created by France's aviation industry in the 1950s. Accused of building the ugliest airplanes ever to take to the skies, France could draw some comfort from the achievement of the Gerfaut when, on August 3, 1954, it became the first European aircraft to fly faster than sound in level flight without the help of an afterburner.

▲ Nord's N.1042 Gerfaut was a stubby-looking jet-powered delta research aircraft. The original version was the first European aircraft to exceed Mach 1 in level flight without an afterburner.

NORD GERFAUT

Flight trials ▶

The Gerfaut underwent extensive flight trials during 1954 and 1955. The two bulges at the base of the fin house an anti-spin parachute (above) and a braking parachute (below), which were vital for safety during trials.

◀ Afterburning Gerfaut

The Gerfaut II, which first flew in 1956, was fitted with the afterburning SNECMA Atar G engine, as revealed by the jet-pipe nozzle.

Northern Falcon▶

The Gerfaut (Northern Falcon) prototype was purely experimental, but it was intended for the aircraft to go into full-scale production as a rocket fighter.

▼ Delta design

Designed by Jean Galtier, the Gerfaut started the trend in French aviation for producing delta-wing fighters, culminating in the Mirage 2000 and Rafale of today.

FACTS AND FIGURES

➤ Nord used experience gained from this aircraft to develop a more advanced test plane, the N.1500 Griffon.

➤ At one point in the 1950s, 13 types of jet test aircraft were flying in France.

➤ A manned glider, the Nord 1301, was used to test the Gerfaut concept.

➤ The N.1402B, with improved engine and afterburner, made its first flight on April 17, 1956.

➤ The Gerfaut first flew in its original form on January 15, 1954.

➤ The Gerfaut was the first French delta-wing jet airplane.

PROFILE

Delta force, French style

In the late 1940s and early 50s, the French aviation scene was wild, wacky and wonderful. By building dozens of experimental aircraft, France was able to compensate for being held back during the World War II and pushed air exploration to the limits. The first unassisted level supersonic flight was only one of the achievements of the Nord Gerfaut research airplanes. It looked unorthodox, but pushed scientific knowledge forwards.

Gerfaut test pilot Andre Turcat called this ship a 'bullet with a motor in it,' although the airplane actually resembled a wedge or an arrowhead. The initial version was redesigned and was 80 percent new when it flew with an afterburner for the first time. During February 1957, Turcat established five time-to-altitude records in the rebuilt Gerfaut, the greatest of which was 15,000 metres (49,200 feet) in just three minutes 36 seconds.

Today, the Gerfaut is but a footnote in aviation history, but during the 1950s, when the speed envelope was being pushed, this aircraft did its part of the shoving.

Left: In the hands of André Turcat, who was later the French project pilot of the Concorde program, the Gerfaut II established five time-to-altitude records, helping to establish French fighter designs in the world market.

Right: When the Gerfaut was developed, delta-wing jet fighters were in their infancy. It was hoped that the aircraft would be produced as a fast-climbing bomber interceptor, however the fuel capacity in such a small airframe was never enough to achieve the necessary range.

Gerfaut N.1412 B

Type: delta-wing research aircraft

Powerplant: one 25 kN (6,177-lb.-thrust) SNECMA Atar 101C turbojet engine (N 1402A prototype); one 25 kN (6,177-lb.-thrust) Atar 101D turbojet (N 1402B); one 36 kN (8,825-lb.-thrust) Atar 101G21 turbojet with afterburning (N 1405)

Maximum speed: 1590 km/h (988 m.p.h.)

Range: 201 km (125 mi.)

Service ceiling: 17,250 m (56,600 ft.)

Weights: empty 2863 kg (6,311 lb.); normal load 3592 kg (7,920 lb.); max load 4526 kg (9,979 lb.)

Dimensions:
Span	6.6 m (21 ft. 7 in.)
Length	11 m (36 ft.)
Height	5.5 m (18 ft.)
Wing area	26 m² (282 sq. ft.)

GERFAUT IA

The Nord Gerfaut was France's first delta-wing jet and was fitted with a non-afterburning turbojet. This example was the first prototype and conducted extensive flight trials in the mid 1950s.

The pilot sat in a pressurized cabin built above the fuselage as a separate superstructure. The canopy hinges to the rear and an ejection seat is fitted for emergencies.

The cantilever tail unit has a high-mounted variable-incidence tailplane of delta planform. The two blisters at the base of the fin contain a braking parachute and an anti-spin parachute.

The landing gear is retractable with the main wheels folding inward into the wings. The nose wheel rotates through 90 degrees to lie flush in the fuselage beneath the air inlet duct.

The stubby barrel-shaped fuselage is of all-metal monocoque construction. Air brakes, which are used to slow the Gerfaut, are fitted on each side of the rear fuselage.

The Gerfaut's delta wing is made of all-metal construction and is very thin. Unlike conventional wing shapes, both the ailerons and elevators are inset in the trailing edges.

Power is provided by a SNECMA Atar 101D turbojet. The air intake is in the nose of the aircraft, and fuel is drawn from two tanks in the fuselage.

ACTION DATA

SPEED

The Gerfaut IA was not fitted with an afterburner, but could still easily exceed Mach 1. Its lightweight aerodynamic design made it one of the fastest aircraft in the world at that time. When fitted with an afterburner it could go even faster.

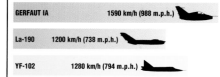

GERFAUT IA	1590 km/h (988 m.p.h.)
La-190	1200 km/h (738 m.p.h.)
YF-102	1280 km/h (794 m.p.h.)

CLIMB RATE

Because it was designed as a fast-climbing bomber interceptor, the Gerfaut had an amazing initial rate-of-climb. Although fitted with an afterburner, the YF-102 could not match the Gerfaut in a climb.

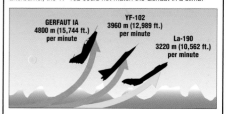

GERFAUT IA 4800 m (15,744 ft.) per minute
YF-102 3960 m (12,989 ft.) per minute
La-190 3220 m (10,562 ft.) per minute

RANGE

The main drawback with the Gerfaut was its noticeable lack of range. Despite increasing the fuel capacity, it was never viable as an operational aircraft. Although not as quick or fast-climbing, the YF-102 had excellent range and was the only one put into production.

GERFAUT	201 km (125 mi.)
La-190	1147 km (713 mi.)
YF-102	1796 km (1,116 mi.)

Experimental French jets

SUD-EST GROGNARD: The bloated looking Grognard was intended as a ground-attack aircraft; only two were built.

SUD-EST BAROUDEUR: Intended for tactical support, the Baroudeur took off from a wheeled trolley and landed on skids.

NORD N.1601: The N.1601 was a Rolls-Royce powered aerodynamic research vehicle testing 33 degree swept wings.

SUD-OUEST TRIDENT: This record-breaking rocket-powered research aircraft had an additional turbojet fitted to each wingtip.

NORTH AMERICAN

F-107A

● Experimental supersonic fighter-bomber ● Unique dorsal intake

O riginally designated the YF-100B, this new fighter-bomber was developed from the successful F-100A Super Sabre, only to lose out to Republic's F-105 Thunderchief in the race to secure a major USAF production order in the early 1950s. This failure marked the end of North American Aviation's early lead in the jet fighter field, the three YF-107A prototypes being the last new fighters to be built by the company for the USAF.

▲ The YF-107 had a unique engine intake, situated above and behind the cockpit, to feed its big J75 turbojet. The pilot had an excellent view over the short, steeply-raked nose.

NORTH AMERICAN F-107A

▼ **High landing speed**
A penalty of having been designed for maximum speed in combat operations, the YF-107 had a high stalling speed and therefore a very high landing speed compared to the YF-105.

▲ **Supersonic speeds**
The first prototype YF-107A achieved a speed in excess of Mach 2 very early in its flight trials.

▼ **Armament**
The F-107 was to have had four 20-mm fixed forward-firing cannon and underwing ordnance of up to 4536 kg (9,980 lb.).

▲ **No ailerons**
Highly manoeuvrable, the F-107 solved the problem of aileron reversal at high speeds by dispensing with ailerons.

◀ **Bifurcated intake**
As well as being situated above the fuselage, the YF-107's engine intake was divided in two and was the first to have a controlled variable flow inlet.

FACTS AND FIGURES

➤ The YF-107 was the last fighter plane built by North American Aviation after the successful P-51, F-86 and F-100.

➤ First flown on 10 September 1956, the YF-107 soon exceeded Mach 2.

➤ The F-107 has been dubbed 'the best American fighter to be cancelled'.

➤ In all, nine YF-107s were ordered; however, only three were built, test flying being terminated in 1957.

➤ The three prototypes were tested for only six months before cancellation.

➤ With no ailerons, lateral control was achieved by differential wing spoilers.

PROFILE

NAA's 'super' Super Sabre

As North American's rival to Republic's F-105 Thunderchief the F-107 was designed to overcome all the problems of the F-100 Super Sabre, from which it was developed.

The new fighter-bomber was fitted with a Pratt & Whitney J75 afterburning turbojet, developing 108.99-kN (24,520-lb.) of thrust. It was notable for its large variable flow dorsal intake, one-piece 'slab' tailplane and lateral control by spoilers in place of conventional ailerons. Originally designated the

YF-100B, the Type NA.212 (as it was known to NAA) was so extensively redesigned to meet the USAF's Operational Requirement GOR.68 that it was redesignated YF-107A when ordered on 8 April 1954. Built as an all-weather fighter-bomber for Tactical Air Command, the F-107 would have had radar, good weapons carriage and delivery, and advanced avionics.

The first prototype was flown on 10 September 1956, with the other two flying before the end of the year. Cancelled in March 1957, when the F-105 was

ordered instead, two of the YF-107As were used by NACA (National Advisory Committee for Aeronautics, the forerunner of NASA) for high-speed research. One of the prototypes has survived and was placed on display at the USAF Museum.

Below: With no large engine intake in front, the pilot had a good view over the YF-107's nose during its high-speed landing.

Above: No ailerons were fitted to the YF-107, with lateral control being achieved by the use of flaps and differential spoilers above and below its swept wings.

YF-107A

Type: single-seat supersonic fighter-bomber prototype

Powerplant: one 108.99-kN (24,520-lb.-thrust) Pratt & Whitney J75-P-9 afterburning turbojet

Maximum speed: 2084 km/h (1,292 m.p.h.)

Initial climb rate: 12162 m/min (39,900 f.p.m.)

Range: 1268 km (790 mi.)

Service ceiling: 16215 m (53,200 ft.)

Weights: empty 10295 kg (22,650 lb.); maximum take-off 18841 kg (41,450 lb.)

Armament: four fixed internal 20-mm cannon, plus up to 4536 kg (9,980 lb.) of external stores

Dimensions: span 11.15 m (36 ft. 7 in.)
length 18.84 m (61 ft. 9 in.)
height 5.99 m (19 ft. 8 in.)
wing area 34.93 m² (376 sq. ft.)

YF-107A

Aircraft 55-5119 was the second of the three YF-107As built by NAA and is today exhibited in the USAF Museum. All flew for the first time between September and December 1956. Six other pre-production aircraft were cancelled.

A single-seat cockpit had a specially strengthened windscreen and a one-piece canopy, which gave the pilot good views on three sides. A long pitot tube, with gust detectors, extended from the pointed nose.

A bifurcated air intake for the Pratt & Whitney YJ75 engine was located on top of the fuselage and immediately behind the cockpit. Its central knife-edge splitter created angled shock-waves to slow down the airflow entering the engine at supersonic speeds.

The YF-107's conventionally manufactured fuselage followed 'area rule' design principles. Hydraulically actuated airbrakes were fitted on either side at the rear. A centre-line fuel tank was recessed into the bottom of the fuselage.

Although the same shape as the F-100's fin and rudder, that of the YF-107 had a taller single-piece, fully powered fin that combined both functions. The aircraft also had a single-piece 'slab' tailplane set on the bottom of the rear fuselage.

U.S. AIR FORCE

55119

F-107A

The YF-107A's tricycle undercarriage had its nosewheel retracting forwards into the fuselage below the cockpit and specially strengthened mainwheels that retracted into the fuselage.

Developed from the F-100's very thin, swept wing, the YF-107A's was similar in construction but it had no ailerons on the trailing edges. These were replaced by spoilers.

A fuel tank of 946 or 1893 litres (250- or 500-gallon) capacity could be stowed in a recessed bay on the fuselage centreline. Weapon loads could include bombs and 'special stores' (nuclear devices).

ACTION DATA

MAXIMUM SPEED

Though the YF-107 was developed from the F-100, it was a radically redesigned aircraft. It had a much higher top speed than the F-100, though at altitude this was exceeded by the F-105.

YF-107A	2084 km/h (1,292 m.p.h.)
F-100D SUPER SABRE	1390 km/h (862 m.p.h.)
F-105D THUNDERCHIEF	2237 km/h (1,387 m.p.h.)

THRUST

Republic's F-105D shared its massive Pratt & Whitney J75 engine with the F-107. It produced considerably more thrust than the F-100's smaller J57 engine.

YF-107A	108.99 kN (24,520-lb.-thrust)
F-100D SUPER SABRE	75.40 kN (16,960-lb.-thrust)
F-105D THUNDERCHIEF	108.99 kN (42,520-lb.-thrust)

CLIMB RATE

An area in which the YF-107 performed well was climb rate, being appreciably better in this respect than the F-105. Both had a much better climb rate than the North American Super Sabre, the F-107's being almost three times better.

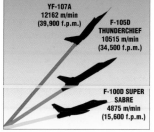

YF-107A 12162 m/min (39,900 f.p.m.)

F-105D THUNDERCHIEF 10515 m/min (34,500 f.p.m.)

F-100D SUPER SABRE 4875 m/min (15,600 f.p.m.)

Experimental designs from North American

YAT-28E: A turboprop version of the T-28 Trojan combat trainer, the YAT-3E was designed for armed counter-insurgency operations.

XB-70A VALKYRIE: The XB-70A was to be a Mach 3 strategic bomber to replace the B-52. Only two prototypes were flown.

YF-93A: A fighter development of the F-86 Sabre, it was powered by a Pratt & Whitney J48 turbojet with flush NACA intakes.

NAC.60: This was North American's submission for the USA's Supersonic Transport Program in the mid-1960s.

NORTH AMERICAN
X-15

● **Fastest aircraft in history** ● **World's highest flier**

T he North American X-15 is still the fastest, highest-flying winged machine man has yet produced, even though it has not flown for more than a quarter of a century. First dropped from its B-52 mothership in the late 1950s, the sinister-looking blue-black bullet pushed the boundaries of aviation to the edge of space and beyond. Without the data the X-15 collected, America's manned space programme might never have succeeded.

▲ The X-15A-2 is about to be dropped from beneath the wing of a B-52 launch plane. The white colour was a special thick coating developed late in the programme. It was designed to protect the plane from the extreme temperatures of hypersonic flight.

PHOTO FILE

NORTH AMERICAN X-15

◄ The bullet
The X-15 was a blunt-nosed projectile, shaped like an extended bullet. Tiny wings provided all necessary lift and control at the immensely high speeds the aircraft could attain.

▲ Record Breaker
The fuel in the X-15A-2's external tanks added 70 per cent to the rocket's time under power and an extra 1600 km/h (1,000 m.p.h.) to its top speed.

Power of the rocket ▶
The rocket motor which powered the X-15 on its record flights burned more than 15 tonnes of rocket fuel in under three minutes.

▼ Shuttle forerunner
Many of the lessons learned in the 199 X-15 flights were to be applied 20 years later to America's Space Shuttle.

▲ Astronaut wings
Pilots who, like these, regularly flew the X-15 above 85 km (53 mi.) were awarded astronaut wings for their feat.

◄ Risky business
Flying the X-15 was not without risk, as John McKay's emergency landing shows. McKay survived to make many more flights.

FACTS AND FIGURES

➤ The X-15's speed record of 7297 km/h (4,534 m.p.h.) is more than double the speed of the Lockheed SR-71 Blackbird.

➤ Its altitude record of 108000 m (354,000 ft.) is triple that of the Soviet Ye 266M.

➤ The X-15's engine provided four times more thrust than contemporary fighter engines.

➤ The three X-15s flew 199 missions, more than any other rocket research aircraft.

➤ There was only one fatality, when Major Michael Adams crashed in November 1967.

➤ In all, twelve pilots flew the X-15 on its 199 flights, including moon lander Neil Armstrong.

Faster than a speeding bullet

Man's greatest aviation obsession is the quest for speed. In October 1947, Major Chuck Yeager piloted the Bell X-1 beyond Mach 1 for the first time. Over the next 12 years a line of rocket-powered record breakers followed, climaxing in the North American X-15. A sleek black rocket with tiny wings, the X-15 flew higher and faster than anything before or since.

Most of the 199 powered missions between 1960 and 1968 probed the limits of possibility, smashing all previous records in the process. In October 1967, Captain William J. Knight piloted the X-15 to an absolute winged speed record more than six times faster than Yeager's mark, reaching a speed of

nearly 7300 km/h (4,536 m.p.h.). The X-15 also flew higher than any other airplane, climbing 108 km (67 mi.) out of the atmosphere to the edge of space.

Although overshadowed by the Mercury, Gemini and Apollo programmes, the X-15 contributed its share to the exploration of space, and even more to the understanding of practical hypersonic flight. The knowledge gleaned by the North American's manned bullet was to be a vital factor in the success of the Space Shuttle.

The X-15 could not take off under its own power. It was taken aloft beneath the wing of a specially modified Boeing B-52 heavy bomber (left). At 15000 m (49,212 ft.), the motor was ignited and the superfast rocket was released.

In the first years of its test programme the X-15's cockpit had oval windows. These were replaced by more conventional rectangular panes in later rebuilds.

The wedge-shaped tailplane provided directional stability at altitudes around 30000 m (98,000 ft.), but at 100 km (60 mi.) the X-15 was in space and control could only come from small reaction motors.

X-15A-2

Type: single-seat hyper-velocity rocket-powered research aircraft

Powerplant: one Thiokol (Reaction Motors) XLR99-RM-2 single-chamber throttleable liquid-propellant rocket engine, with a thrust rating of 26000 kg (57,200 lb.) at 14000 m (46,000 ft.) altitude and 32000 kg (70,400 lb.) at 30000 m (98,400 ft.)

Max speed: 7297 km/h (4,534 m.p.h.)

Maximum altitude: 107960 m (354,000 ft.)

Time to height: 140 sec. from launch at 15000 m (49,212 ft.) to 100000 metres (320,000 ft.)

Range: 450 km (280 mi.) on a typical test flight

Weights: loaded 25460 kg (56,000 lb.)

Dimensions:
span	6.81 m (22 ft. 4 in.)
length	15.47 m (50 ft. 9 in.)
height	3.96 m (12 ft. 11 in.)
wing area	18.58 m² (200 sq. ft.)

X-15A-2

Seriously damaged in a 1962 crash landing, the second X-15 was re-built with more fuel capacity. This increased burn-time and top speed.

NASA

66671

U.S. AIR FORCE

LOX JETT
H₂O JETT

H₂O VENT

The X-15 was mainly titanium and stainless steel, while its skin was a special nickel alloy to withstand friction temperatures of 650°C (1,200°F). The tiny cockpit windows were of dual-pane, heat-resistant glass.

The disposable external fuel tanks increased the burn time of the X-15's rocket motor from just over a minute to nearly two and a half minutes.

To save weight, the X-15 was equipped with a retractable skid instead of conventional landing gear.

ACTION DATA

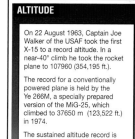

ALTITUDE

On 22 August 1963, Captain Joe Walker of the USAF took the first X-15 to a record altitude. In a near-40° climb he took the rocket plane to 107960 m (354,195 ft.).

The record for a conventionally powered plane is held by the Ye 266M, a specially prepared version of the MiG-25, which climbed to 37650 m (123,522 ft.) in 1974.

The sustained altitude record is held by the Lockheed SR-71, at 25908 m (85,000 ft.).

747	F-16	U-2	SR-71	X-15
11000 m (36,000 ft.)	16000 m (52,492 ft.)	21500 m (70,537 ft.)	25908 m (85,000 ft.)	107960 m (354,195 ft.)

MAXIMUM SPEED

X-15	MACH 6.72
SR-71	MACH 3
MiG-25	MACH 2.8
F-15	MACH 2.5
747	MACH 0.8

If the X-15 could carry enough fuel to sustain its maximum speed, it would be able to cross the Atlantic – a seven-hour journey in an airliner like the 747 – in less than 50 minutes.

Beyond the stratosphere

1 LAUNCH: As the carrier B-52 reaches launch altitude and position, the X-15 pilot completes his pre-flight checks and ignites his motor. On release, he opens the throttle wide.

2 ACCELERATION: In seconds, the X-15 pulls ahead of the B-52. Climbing at between 20° and 40°, it zooms skywards in what one of its pilots called a sustained 'kick in the butt'.

3 GOING BALLISTIC: After the rocket fuel is exhausted the X-15 follows a ballistic arc beyond the atmosphere. As it re-enters the thicker air it experiences maximum heating from atmospheric friction.

4 LANDING: The X-15 makes an unpowered descent to land. It comes in very fast – more than 320 km/h (198 m.p.h.) – and steeply, since with its tiny wings it has all the gliding capacity of a brick.

NORTH AMERICAN
XB-70 VALKYRIE

● Mach 3 strategic weapon system ● Fastest bomber ever flown

F lying at three times the speed of sound at 30 km (19 mi.) altitude to deliver a nuclear attack was the role of the unique XB-70 Valkyrie. This massive delta with six enormous engines would have been uncatchable, and it worried Soviet generals. But the cost of the project spiralled, and problems culminated in a disastrous crash during flight trials. And then surface-to-air missile developments made the XB-70 obsolete at a stroke.

▲ The XB-70 was the ultimate high-altitude bomber, with a performance that has never been matched. But it was a dead end; the future of the bomber lay in stealthiness and low-level penetration.

NORTH AMERICAN XB-70 VALKYRIE

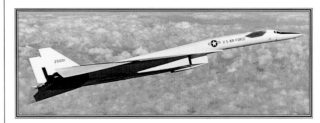

▲ Vortex death trap
No-one knows why F-104 pilot Joe Walker collided with the XB-70, but it is thought that the tiny F-104 got caught in the huge tip vortices generated by the XB-70's large delta wings.

◄ Canard design ▲
A combination of the large canard foreplanes and trailing-edge elevons controlled pitch. The four-man crew sat in a special ejection capsule, which was the only way to survive an ejection at the heights the Valkyrie flew at.

▲ Giant delta
Like the YF-12A and the MiG-25, the XB-70 needed a very thin delta wing with large twin tailfins for stability in Mach 3 flight.

▲ Jet blast
Stealth was the last thing the XB-70 had in its design brief. Both its radar and infra-red signatures were immense.

◄ On display
The surviving Valkyrie made its last flight in February 1969 to the USAF museum, where it remains on display to this day.

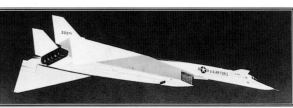

FACTS AND FIGURES

➤ The Valkyrie was used for 'sonic boom' trials flights in support of the American Supersonic Transport project.

➤ During one test flight the XB-70 covered almost 1600 km (1000 mi.) in 33 minutes.

➤ Ethyl borane was planned to fuel the XB-70, but was found to be too expensive.

➤ Colonel Joe Cotton described flying the XB-70 as 'like driving a Greyhound bus around the racetrack at Indianapolis'.

➤ The project had cost $500 million by the time the XB-70 crashed.

➤ The folding wingtips were designed to use aerodynamic 'shock wave' effects.

PROFILE

The fastest bomber ever built

Even today, no aircraft can match the staggering performance of the XB-70 Valkyrie. The aim of the aircraft was to fly so fast and high that interception was impossible and nuclear strikes on the Soviet Union could be threatened.

In order to evade the latest Mach 2 Soviet fighters, North American designed the huge bomber to cruise at Mach 3 for long distances at extreme altitude. The result was a six-engined delta that burned special fuel, and had wingtips that folded in flight. The machine had to be built from special materials to cope with the heat stress of high-speed flight. The prototype first flew in 1964, and a second aircraft began trials the following year. At first all went well, and the XB-70 demonstrated that it could do everything promised, including flying at around 3200 km/h (1,988 m.p.h.).

Tragedy struck during a test flight in June 1966. A Lockheed F-104 Starfighter in formation with the XB-70 for a photo

The Valkyrie was a stunning piece of engineering, but the cost of the Vietnam War made it hard to justify spending more money on it.

shoot accidentally crashed into the Valkyrie, and both aircraft were destroyed. Only one of the Valkyrie crew ejected. There was a political storm about the incident and the Valkyrie was cancelled, partly because new Soviet air defence missiles had, by the mid-1960s, made high-level bombers a thing of the past.

XB-70A Valkyrie

Type: prototype supersonic strategic bomber

Powerplant: six 133.38-kN (32,651-lb.-thrust) General Electric YJ93-GE-3 afterburning turbojets

Maximum speed: 3220 km/h (2,000 m.p.h.); test aircraft reached 3250 km/h (2,019 m.p.h.)

Range: 13300 km (8,283 mi.) unrefuelled

Service ceiling: test aircraft reached 22550m (73,982 ft.)

Weights: maximum take-off 250000 kg (550,000 lb.)

Armament: no defensive armament; planned bombload 23000 kg (50,600 lb.) of free-fall nuclear bombs or of conventional weapons

Dimensions:
span	32.04 m (105 ft. 2 in.)
length	57.61 m (189 ft.)
height	9.14 m (29 ft. 11 in.)
wing area	585 m² (6,295 sq. ft.)

The delta wing, which contained large fuel tanks, was designed to create a shock wave that the aircraft could 'ride' on, giving vastly increased lift.

To resist kinetic heating, the fuselage and wing structure were built almost entirely from stainless steel and titanium.

XB-70 VALKYRIE

Two prototype XB-70 Valkyrie bombers were produced, flying between September 1964 and February 1969. Number 62-207 was destroyed, and 62-001 is now an exhibit at the USAF museum.

The canards were essential for control of the XB-70 at low speed, as the elevons would have been masked by the wing at high angles of attack.

The six massive J93-3 turbojets would have made the Valkyrie the most powerful aircraft ever built, and probably also the noisiest.

The Valkyrie's fatal crash was caused by an F-104 striking the right fin and ripping most of it off. It then hit the left fin before finally smashing down on top of the left wing and exploding. The Valkyrie flew straight and level for several seconds before spinning to destruction.

Like the wings, the fins had fixed and moving sections. The leading edge was fixed and the rear section could move slightly.

The cockpit gave very little visibility to the crew, but there was little to see at the altitudes the XB-70 travelled at.

A large black anti-glare panel was painted in front of the cockpit. The overall paint scheme was a nuclear blast reflective white, which did not stand up well to Mach 3 kinetic heating.

Operational B-70s would have had a four-man crew, consisting of two pilots and two systems operators, all housed in the cockpit escape capsule.

The intake design was all-important, as control of the shock waves it produced greatly affected thrust. The massive intake box had a huge radar signature.

A long central weapons bay between the intake ducts could carry up to 14 free-fall thermonuclear weapons. No defensive weaponry was carried, as the survival of the Valkyrie depended on high speed and advanced electronics.

The variable-position wingtips could be set at 25°, or 65° for high-speed flight.

Last ride of the Valkyrie: 8 June 1966

■ **PUBLICITY SHOT:** Five aircraft powered by General Electric engines were flying in formation for a publicity shot when a NASA F-104, piloted by Joe Walker, strayed too close to the massive vortex generated by the Valkyrie's downturned wingtip, sucking it in.

■ **TRAGEDY:** The tiny F-104 was hurled across the XB-70's wing, smashing one tailfin and then exploding. The Valkyrie flew on for several seconds before tumbling out of control and crashing into the Mojave desert miles below.

ACTION DATA

MAXIMUM SPEED

The XB-70 was one of only three aircraft designed to reach Mach 3 operationally. The Soviet MiG-25 was designed primarily to intercept the massive American bomber, although it could not sustain its high speeds for nearly as long as the Valkyrie. Only the amazing SR-71, which was a smaller aircraft, could fly faster.

MiG-25	Mach 3
SR-71	Mach 3.5+
XB-70	Mach 3.08

NORTHROP

XP-79

● Flown once ● Flying wing fighter ● Prone pilot position

▲ With its twin
Westinghouse J-30 turbojets, the XP-79B experimental flying wing had the pilot lying in a prone position in a central glazed cockpit. The engines were situated on either side of the fuselage, just behind the cockpit.

Northrop introduced several new concepts with its all-wing jet-fighter. Extensive use was made of magnesium in its structure and the aircraft was expected to fly close to the speed of sound on the power of a single rocket engine. Eventually, it was completed with two turbojets as the XP-79B and the idea emerged of using the machine to destroy enemy bombers by ramming them, although this had not originally been planned.

NORTHROP XP-79

▲ **Before the XP-79**
As the first rocket-powered US aircraft, the MX-324 was a powered glider and pioneered many of the features which were incorporated into the XP-79.

▲ **Short first flight**
The full capabilities of the XP-79B were never tested, as it went out of control after 15 minutes during its first flight from Muroc Test Center. This shot is a cleverly constructed montage showing how the aircraft might have looked in regular service.

▲ **Fighting flying wing**
Northrop XP-56s were similar in basic concept to the XP-79, but used pusher propellers.

▼ **Low drag**
The prone pilot position gave the XP-79 a very low frontal area and an unusual appearance.

▲ **Rocket project**
Northrop did not know when planning the XP-79 that the German Me 163 tailless rocket fighter had first flown in 1941.

FACTS AND FIGURES

➤ Originally, the XP-79 was intended to fly as a conventional fighter – the ramming concept came later.

➤ The XP-79B was the fourth turbojet-powered aircraft to fly in the US.

➤ During taxiing tests, the XP-79B blew several tyres.

➤ During the XP-79B's one and only take-off run, a fire engine crossed the runway ahead of the aircraft just before lift-off.

➤ A single 8.89-kN (2,176-lb.-thrust) Aerojet rocket would have powered the XP-79.

➤ The pilot's compartment of the XP-79B was armoured but not pressurised.

Northrop's flying wing fighter

Continuing Northrop's long association with the flying wing, the XP-79 used a configuration which recurs today in the B-2 Spirit stealth bomber.

The XP-79 was to have been a rocket-powered, prone-pilot interceptor, capable of speeds of over 800 km/h (497 m.p.h.). Its rocket engine would have been hazardous in operation, since it used corrosive nitric acid and monoethylaniline (aniline) as propellants. After continuous delays with rocket development, the fighter emerged as the XP-79B with two jet engines.

Northrop test pilot Harry Crosby, who had flown earlier

flying-wing prototypes and was planning to retire to his farm in California, took off on 12 September 1945 and flew 'a beautiful demonstration' (as recalled by Jack Northrop).

Unfortunately, a relatively simple problem caused the XP-79B to enter a nose-down spin, from which it did not recover. Crosby, in the prone position, attempted an escape, but was trapped in the aircraft's slipstream and his parachute did not open. This fatal crash was later attributed to trim control problems that could have been easily resolved, but the project was cancelled.

Designed for 'high-g' flight, the flying surfaces of the XP-79B were very strong and smooth with a thick, welded magnesium alloy skin.

Bellows-operated, split horizontal control surfaces were located in the outer wings. Air for the activation of the controls came via control valves in the oval-shaped wingtip ducts.

The intakes for the XP-79's two turbojets were situated to the sides of the glazed nose. They considerably impaired the pilot's view to left and right.

Twin vertical fins and rudders were necessary to give the flying wing sufficient lateral stability and control when turning, and at low speed for landing.

In order to keep frontal area to a minimum and to give the pilot greater g-tolerance, a prone piloting position was adopted. This meant that the pilot had to lie on his stomach on a specially designed 'couch'.

352437

It was originally planned to power the XP-79 with an 8.89-kN (1,998-lb.-thrust) Aerojet XCAL-200 rocket motor, but instead two Westinghouse J30 turbojets were fitted with exhaust pipes on either side of the cockpit nacelle.

A four-wheeled landing gear was fitted. The front, steerable wheels retracted into the engine nacelles while the large mainwheels retracted into the lower surface of the wing.

XP-79B

Only one example of the XP-79B was completed and it was destroyed on its first flight. With World War II over, the USAAF lost interest in the project.

XP-79B

Type: single-seat, flying-wing interceptor and ramming aircraft

Powerplant: two 6.07-kN (1,364-lb.-thrust) Westinghouse Model 19-B J30 axial-flow turbojet engines

Maximum speed: 880 km/h (547 m.p.h.)

Cruising speed: 772 km/h (479 m.p.h.)

Climb rate: 4 min 42 sec to 7620 m (25,000 ft.)

Range: 1598 km (993 mi.)

Service ceiling: 12192 m (40,000 ft.)

Weights: normal take-off 3932 kg (8650 lb.)

Armament: provision for four fixed 12.7-mm Browning M3 machine-guns with 250 rounds each in the wing centre-section, two on each outboard side of the jet engines

Dimensions:
span	11.58 m (37 ft. 11 in.)
length	4.26 m (13 ft. 11 in.)
height	2.13 m (7 ft.)
wing area	25.82 m² (278 sq. ft.)

COMBAT DATA

MAXIMUM SPEED

Although it had been designed for high speed, the XP-79B was soon overtaken by more conventional designs which proved much more suitable for service.

XP-79B	880 km/h (547 m.p.h.)
F-86A SABRE	1093 km/h (680 m.p.h.)
P-80A SHOOTING STAR	898 km/h (558 m.p.h.)

THRUST

Powered by two small jet engines, not its intended rocket engine, the XP-79B had far less thrust than the single-engined Sabre and was marginally less powerful than the P-80A.

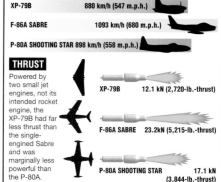

XP-79B	12.1 kN (2,720-lb.-thrust)
F-86A SABRE	23.2kN (5,215-lb.-thrust)
P-80A SHOOTING STAR	17.1 kN (3,844-lb.-thrust)

ARMAMENT

As the XP-79B project matured, it became clear that its machine-gun armament would be a secondary offensive tool, when compared to the airframe itself.

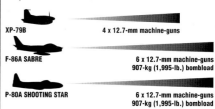

XP-79B	4 x 12.7-mm machine-guns
F-86A SABRE	6 x 12.7-mm machine-guns 907-kg (1,995-lb.) bombload
P-80A SHOOTING STAR	6 x 12.7-mm machine-guns 907-kg (1,995-lb.) bombload

Northrop's flying wing fighters

FAMILY EVOLUTION: All Northrop's flying wing designs, including the XP-79B and B-2A, have their origins in The Wing of 1929. The Wing of 1930 was a modification of the earlier design.

FIGHTER LINE: After the N-1M Jeep was flown in its original configuration, development split along three lines. The XP-56/XP-79 fighter line proved to be a dead end in 1945, and the MX-324/JB-1 powered glider line reached the same conclusion in 1944. Only the bomber line has proved successful.

| THE WING, 1929 | THE WING, 1930 | N-1M JEEP, 1940 | N-2B (XP-56), 1943 | XP-56, 1944 | XP-79, 1945 |

NORTHROP

X-4

● **Flying wing** ● **Transonic research** ● **Tailless design**

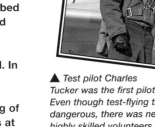

▲ *Test pilot Charles Tucker was the first pilot to fly the X-4. Even though test-flying the X-planes could be dangerous, there was never any shortage of highly skilled volunteers to do the job.*

Northrop's X-4 was one of a series of post-war 'X-planes' which probed the boundaries of flight beyond anything which had been seen before, exploring the performance of tailless aircraft at close to the speed of sound. In more than 100 flights this pure-white bantamweight produced a wealth of information, broadening understanding of airflow movement over flying surfaces at high speeds.

PHOTO FILE

NORTHROP **X-4**

▲ Swept-wing wonder
The X-4 was an extremely clean design when its gear and flaps were retracted, resulting in a high Mach number from quite low thrust.

▲ Flying wing
The X-4 owed much of its design to wartime German research as well as to earlier Northrop flying-wing projects.

◀ Design study
The Northrop design team started by building a wooden mock-up in 1946.

Hinged fuselage ▶
Mechanics could open the fuselage just behind the wingroot for ease of engine maintenance.

▼ Futuristic design ▶
The bubble canopy gave a superb view, and was similar to that of 1970s designs. The split flaps were another new feature.

▼ White lightning
The X-4 was usually finished in a brilliant white paint scheme with USAF insignia, a standard finish for early X-planes.

FACTS AND FIGURES

➤ The X-4 first flew on 16 December 1948 at Muroc in the California desert.

➤ The X-4 was so small that an average person could peer into its cockpit while standing on the ground.

➤ The landing gear was based on that of the F-89 Scorpion.

➤ On 24 January 1951, Scott Crossfield made the fastest X-4 flight, to more than Mach 0.92.

➤ Both X-4 aircraft survived and are on museum display in the United States.

➤ Northrop developed many tailless aircraft designs, including the modern B-2.

PROFILE

Northrop's tiny flying wing

The diminutive X-4 tested the tailless configuration at speeds of Mach 0.85 and higher. Drawing on experience gleaned from Northrop flying wings of the 1940s – and sharing some characteristics with today's B-2 stealth bomber – the two X-4s accumulated a wealth of data for the US Air Force and the National Advisory Committee for Aeronautics (NACA, the forerunner to NASA).

The X-4 had a unique bubble canopy which, along with its supporting frame, opened upward on rear hinges. This gave excellent visibility to test pilots like Chuck Yeager and Pete Everest who pushed the X-4 to its limits above Muroc in the California desert.

They found that the X-4 had some handling problems, and tended to go out of control at Mach 0.88 or faster. As a result it was considered that the X-4 had proved that tailless swept-wing aircraft were unsuitable for high-

speed flight. But technology has changed. Today the tailless B-2 flies very well – bearing the Northrop name.

The X-4 is test-flown over Edwards flight research centre, the X-planes' home in the deserts of California; the area was ideal, as it was largely unpopulated. The X-planes often produced sonic booms – or crashed.

The fuel tanks were built into the fuselage and wings of the X-4. Leaking tanks were a persistent problem in its development programme.

Split flaps could be opened out together as air brakes, or as a conventional landing flap.

There were no horizontal tail surfaces on the X-4, pitch authority being controlled by the wingtip 'elevons'.

X-4 BANTAM

The Northrop X-4 Bantam number 6677 was the second of two aircraft built. It was first flown in August 1950 by the man who broke the sound barrier in the Bell X-1, Chuck Yeager, who went on to fly it a further six times. In total, it made 82 flights.

In order to collect as much flight data as possible, the inside of the cockpit contained advanced instrumentation and telemetry equipment.

The X-4 wing was of conventional construction, but was magnesium-skinned for lightness. It could withstand a stress of 8g, and allowed fast loops by test pilots.

A large pitot probe was essential to accurately measure speed and Mach number for research. Differences of as little as Mach .02 caused radical handling departures in the flight regimes explored by X-planes.

Undercarriage locking problems plagued the first X-4s. Due to this the aircraft was grounded after only four flights.

Tailless configurations were designed to eliminate shock wave interaction at transonic speeds, between wing and tailplane surfaces. However, tailless designs produced as many problems as they solved when the aircraft approached the sound barrier.

X-4 Bantam

Type: single-seat experimental research aircraft

Powerplant: two 7.12-kN (1,600-lb.-thrust) Westinghouse XJ30-WE-7 turbojets; later two Westinghouse J30-W-9 turbojets, using standard JP-4 jet engine fuel

Maximum speed: Mach 0.92 or 1123 km/h (630 m.p.h.) at 10000 m (33,000 ft.) under extreme test conditions

Range: 676 km (420 mi.)

Service ceiling: 13906 m (42,300 ft.)

Weights: empty 2294 kg (5,507 lb.); normal loaded 3175 kg (6,985 lb.); max loaded 3547 kg (7,803 lb.)

Dimensions:
span	8.18 m (27 ft.)
length	7.19 m (23 ft.)
height	4.58 m (15 ft.)
wing area	18.58 m² (300 sq. ft.)

COMBAT DATA

MAXIMUM SPEED

The X-4 was one of the first jets to operate regularly at high subsonic speeds. It was faster than the similarly configured Me 163 of five years before, but had no real advantage over the F-86 Sabre fighter then in development. Unlike the X-4, the Sabre had a conventional tailplane and handled much more reliably.

X-4 BANTAM	1123 km/h (630 m.p.h.)
Me 163 KOMET	960 km/h (595 m.p.h.)
F-86 SABRE	1100 km/h (682 m.p.h.)

SERVIVE CEILING

The X-4's swept wing gave it a good high-altitude performance, and it could operate effectively at considerably greater altitude than preceding piston-engined aircraft. It could climb higher than the rocket-powered Messerschmitt, although not as rapidly.

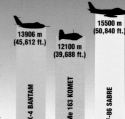

- X-4 BANTAM 13906 m (45,612 ft.)
- Me 163 KOMET 12100 m (39,688 ft.)
- F-86 SABRE 15500 m (50,840 ft.)

RANGE

As a test aircraft operating almost exclusively over California's Muroc Dry Lake, the X-4 did not need vast range. But its clean, efficient design meant that what little fuel it did carry took it almost as far as a Sabre on internal fuel – although the Sabre could travel much further when carrying external tanks.

- F-86 SABRE 835 km (518 mi.)
- X-4 BANTAM 676 km (420 mi.)
- Me 163 KOMET approx. 100 km (60 mi.)

Northrop's no-tail experiments

N-1M: Flown from Muroc Dry Lake (now Edwards Air Force Base) in 1940, the N-1M was the world's first powered flying wing.

XP-56: The XP-56 of 1943 was an attempt to use the low-drag tailless configuration to get an 800-km/h (500-m.p.h.) piston-engined fighter.

MX-324: Flown in great secrecy in 1944, the prone-piloted MX-324 was America's first manned rocket-powered aircraft.

XP-79: The heavily armoured jet-powered Flying Ram of 1945 was designed to slice the wings and tails off enemy bombers.

NORTHROP
XB-35/YB-49

● Flying-wing bombers ● Piston and jet-power ● B-2 predecessor

Those beautiful flying-wing bombers of the late 1940s, the propeller-driven XB-35 and the jet-powered YB-49—realized a dream for Jack Northrop, who had designed, tested and promoted 'all-wing' designs for a decade. The USAF's Strategic Air Command was gearing up for the B-49 when a crash intervened—and Northrop's dream had to be set aside until the B-2 Spirit stealth bomber of the 1990s entered the USAF inventory.

▲ *Jack Northrop was secretly briefed in 1980, shortly before his death, on the B-2 Advanced Technology Bomber concept. He said afterward, 'Now I know why God has kept me alive these last 25 years.'*

NORTHROP **XB-35/YB-49**

▲ The first YB-49 conversion
The first of two XB-35s converted to jet-powered YB-49s; 42-102367 first flew as such in October 1947.

▲ XB-35s become YB-49s
At Northrop's factory in 1948, a number of B-35 airframes are seen being converted to all-jet B-49 configuration. Only one was completed before cancellation.

▲ Secret N-9M prototype
Four N-9s, including a two-seat N-9MB, were built as scale models of a projected bomber and flew in 1942. The N-9MB was restored by a California museum over 11 years and flew in 1994. They had Menasco piston engines.

▲ N-1M Jeep
The first true all-wing aircraft to fly was the N-1M of 1940. Despite appearances, it flew well, and in 1945 was modified with straightened wingtips.

Northrop pair ▶
Seen in formation with a company chase aircraft, a Northrop P-61C Black Widow, the XB-35 prototype is seen here on an early test flight.

FACTS AND FIGURES

➤ During trials, XB-35s/YB-49s proved difficult to track by radar. This natural 'stealthiness' led to the B-2.

➤ The first XB-35 propeller-driven bomber made its initial flight on June 25, 1946.

➤ The first YB-49 was an XB-35 converted to jet power. It flew in October 1947.

➤ Jack Northrop hated the YRB-49's 'podded' engines, but range was better with more room in the wings for fuel.

➤ Northrop also developed two flying-wing fighters, the XP-56 and the XP-79.

➤ Production B-35s were to be fitted with seven gun turrets comprising 20 guns.

PROFILE

The wing's the thing

After an 'all-wing' YB-49 crashed in June 1948, a halt was called to Northrop's efforts to produce large flying-wing bombers for the U.S. Air Force in the early years of the atomic age. Had events unfolded differently, squadrons of B-49s might have been in service by the early-1950s.

Exploring the advantages of a swept wing shape with no fuselage or tail became the lifetime pursuit of Jack Northrop,

who worked on the Douglas Dauntless before he began with his 'all-wing' series with single-seat test ships in the late 1930s. The unique design offered low drag and a good load-carrying capability, but was slower than more convential, supersonic jet bombers.

Northrop's XB-35 bomber was ready shortly after World War II. It was one of the largest military aircraft in the world, and despite its unique shape, encountered

few problems in tests. The early decision was made to proceed with a jet version, the YB-49, but a crash and the importance attached to the Consolidated B-36 Peacemaker bomber ended the program. Northrop himself, who had dreamed of one day building a flying-wing airliner, lived just long enough to see the concept revived in today's B-2.

With a massive wing area of just under 371 m² (4,000 sq. ft.), the XB-35 had a gross weight of 94.8 tons. Empty weight was just over 40 tons.

XB-35

Type: seven-seat heavy bomber prototype

Powerplant: four 2238 kW (3,000-hp.) Pratt & Whitney R-4360-17/-21 radial piston engines

Maximum speed: 628 km/h (390 m.p.h.)

Ceiling: 12,192 m (40,000 ft.)

Range: 16,057 km (9,978 mi.) with full bomb load (projected)

Weights: max takeoff 94,800 kg (208,562 lb.)

Weapons: 20 .50 cal. (12.7-mm) machine guns; plus up to 4545 kg (10,000 lb.) of bombs

Dimensions:
Span	52 m (172 ft.)
Length	16.15m (53 ft.)
Height	6.09 m (20 ft.)
Wing area	371 m² (3,998 sq. ft.)

Vertical fins above and below the wing trailing edge on the YB-49 compensated for the loss of side force from the propellers and engine housings.

XB-35

The first of the 'flying-wing' bombers, 42-13603, was the prototype XB-35 and first flew on June 25, 1946. A second XB-35 and 13 YB-35s were built.

The flying wing concept was compromised to accommodate a canopy for the pilot's position.

The YB-49 replaced four piston engines with eight Allison J35 turbojet engines. One YRB-49 reconnaissance prototype was built with four internal J35s and two in external pods. J35s were also fitted to early-build F-84 Thunderjets.

The XB-35 prototype was built with four pusher contra-rotating propellers. The second prototype and the 13 YB-35s had single-rotation propellers.

With no fuselage markings, the 'star and bar' and serial number were painted on one of the engine nacelles.

Without conventional control surfaces, the B-35 used two sets of decelerons, elevons (for pitch and roll) and split flaps for landing.

A crew of up to nine would have manned a service B-35, consisting of a pilot, co-pilot, bombardier, navigator, flight engineer, radio operator and three gunners. On long missions a relief crew of six could also be carried.

The single nose wheel retracted to the left into the wing, while the two large tires and the main gears retracted rearward into the wing.

The massive propellers of the XB-35 were powered by four Pratt & Whitney R-4360 Wasp Major radial engines that also equipped the Boeing B-50 and Convair B-36.

ACTION DATA

RANGE

The XB-35 had a massive range capability that pushed its crew to the edge of their endurance, which necessitated carrying a relief crew for longer missions. Its competition was the B-36. Aircraft like the Soviet Tu-85 did not perform as well.

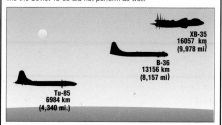

XB-35
16057 km
(9,978 mi)

B-36
13156 km
(8,157 mi)

Tu-85
6984 km
(4,340 mi.)

Northrop's 'flying-wing' family

■ **N-2B (XP-56):** In 1940, the USAAC launched a design competition for a new fighter using an unusual layout. Northrop's entry was the N-2B.

■ **MX-324/-334:** The first American rocket aircraft, the MX-334 had a 90 kg (200 lb.)-st. thrust engine, but started life as a glider.

■ **JB-1A:** This was a powered bomb similar in concept to the German V-1 of World War II. It had a two-ton warhead.

■ **XP-79B:** The jet-powered and heavily built P-79 was intended to ram and slice the tails off enemy bombers. A crash ended the scheme.

NORTHROP

YF-17

● Lightweight fighter ● Only two built ● Led to the F/A-18 Hornet

▲ *In 1974 Northrop entered one of the most competitive procurement battles in aviation history. Although the aircraft did not win the contract it was one of the most capable aircraft ever built.*

Northrop's YF-17 sacrificed many accoutrements deemed essential to a jet fighter. It had no radar and no significant capacity to carry bombs, but it was a highly capable combat aircraft with great potential. Built to win production contracts in the early-1970s, the YF-17 lost in a hard-fought competition to the now-famous F-16. But this light, nimble Northrop fighter laid the foundation for the McDonnell Douglas F/A-18 Hornet.

NORTHROP YF-17

Fighter-bomber ▶
Although not fitted with a sophisticated weapons system, the YF-17 was tested in the ground-attack role and showed great potential.

▲ Gunfighter
The first YF-17 test fires its M61 Vulcan cannon on a low-level strafing run near Edwards AFB.

▲ Cobra design
Northrop began designing its advanced lightweight fighter in 1966. By 1971 this P.530 design had been named Cobra.

◀ Futuristic layout
The YF-17 was the state-of-the-art in fighter design, being able to fly at unprecedented angles of attack.

▲ Round-the-clock flying
Making its first flight more than five months after the YF-16, the YF-17 had to fly every hour possible with ground crews working triple shifts.

FACTS AND FIGURES

➤ In September 1974 McDonnell Douglas agreed to build a navalised YF-17, which became the F/A-18 Hornet.

➤ The first YF-17 made a delayed, but successful, maiden flight on 9 June 1974.

➤ Northrop pursued sales of the land-based YF-17, but never won an order.

➤ The YF-17 is reported to have flown simulated combat against MiG-17s and MiG-21s from a secret US squadron.

➤ The two YF-17s completed more than 600 flights and were flown by 60 pilots.

➤ A twin-fin tail design was deemed essential for directional stability.

PROFILE

Northrop's lightweight contender

In a bid to cut the costs of fighters that were growing relentlessly more expensive, the Northrop YF-17 took to the air in the 1970s. Its competitor, the YF-16, won the 'deal of the century' and became NATO's standard fighter, while Northrop's craft was rejected. However, many believed the YF-17 should have been the winner.

Although it never achieved sales success, the YF-17 was highly regarded by the test pilots who flew it, indeed one pilot was quoted as saying: 'It is the best dogfighter I ever flew'.

Based on years of research by Northrop designer Lee Begin

and on an unbuilt design called the Cobra, the YF-17 ushered in a new era of fighter design with its accent on close-quarters combat manoeuvring at high angles of attack ('high-Alpha'). Unhindered by weighty radar and electronics, the YF-17 was a superb air combat machine.

Also evaluated for the US Navy and in a land-based version for pre-revolutionary Iran, the YF-17 never got the orders it deserved. It is remembered as the aircraft which introduced leading-edge root extensions (LERX) to modern fighter design, and as the forerunner to the excellent F/A-18 Hornet.

After the YF-17 lost out to the YF-16, the second airframe became the prototype F-18 which was eventually purchased by the US Navy.

The full-span leading-edge and half-span trailing-edge flaps produced good low-speed performance. Ailerons and differential tailerons provided roll control.

The two General Electric YJ101 turbojets were mounted close together to minimise the asymmetric effects on handling in the event of an engine failure.

The leading-edge root extensions gave the aircraft excellent stability at a high angle of attack.

YF-17 No. 2

The second YF-17, 72-01570, is seen in the two-tone colour scheme it wore during flight tests at the Lightweight Fighter (LWF)/Air Combat Fighter (ACF) Joint Test Force based at Edwards AFB.

The conventional, well laid-out cockpit incorporated a simple head-up display (HUD). The flight instruments were well positioned in the centre of the instrument panel.

The semi-monocoque fuselage was composed largely of a light alloy structure with some graphite composites.

The twin tailfins were canted outwards to keep them out of the wake from the wing. The rudders were fairly small reaching only halfway up the fins.

The M61 Vulcan cannon was located on the centreline under the nose. The only other armament carried for the ACF competition was two wingtip-mounted AIM-9J Sidewinder missiles.

The centrally mounted control column operated conventionally for pitch control, hinging from the base on the cockpit floor. For roll control it was unusually articulated just below the grip.

The very simple landing gear had single shock struts and high-pressure tyres. An airfield arrester hook and a dorsal airbrake were added later.

From Cobra to Hornet

■ **F-18 COBRA II:** After losing to the YF-16, Northrop changed the name to F-18 Cobra II and continued to market the aircraft.

■ **F-18 HORNET:** In October 1974 McDonnell Douglas assumed development of a naval version of the YF-17, which was called the Hornet.

■ **F/A-18D HORNET:** McDonnell Douglas gained significant sales. The latest version to enter service is the 'Night Attack' Hornet.

■ **F/A-18E HORNET:** The 21st century Super Hornet is currently under flight testing and is likely to become the US Navy's most important type.

YF-17

Type: single-seat fighter prototype

Powerplant: two 64.08-kN (14,415-lb.-thrust) General Electric YJ101-GE-100 turbojet engines with afterburning

Maximum speed: 2124 km/h at 12192 m (1,316 m.p.h. at 40,000 ft.)

Range: 4500 km (2,790 mi.)

Service ceiling: 18288 m (59,800 ft.)

Weights: empty 9527 kg (20,960 lb.); maximum take-off 13894 kg (30,567 lb.)

Armament: one 20-mm General Electric M61A1 'Vulcan' cannon in nose and two AIM-9 Sidewinder air-to-air missiles on wingtip launch rails; provision for two Mk 84 bombs

Dimensions:
span	10.67 m (35 ft.)
length	16.92 m (55 ft. 6 in.)
height	4.42 m (14 ft. 6 in.)
wing area	32.51 m² (350 sq. ft.)

COMBAT DATA

MAXIMUM SPEED

The YF-17 had a slightly higher top speed than the YF-16. The F-5E, on which some of the YF-17's features had been based, was significantly slower.

YF-17	2124 km/h (1,316 m.p.h.)
YF-16	2070 km/h (1,283 m.p.h.)
F-5E TIGER II	1700 km/h (1,050 m.p.h.)

SERVICE CEILING

The YF-17 had excellent performance at altitude because of its powerful engines and efficient wing. The YF-16 could not climb as high and had a similar ceiling to the less advanced F-5E.

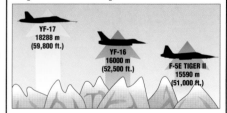

YF-17 18288 m (59,800 ft.)

YF-16 16000 m (52,500 ft.)

F-5E TIGER II 15590 m (51,000 ft.)

THRUST-TO-WEIGHT RATIO

Thanks to its impressive thrust-to-weight ratio, the YF-17 could climb at a faster rate than the rival YF-16. A ratio of better than 1:1 is regarded as essential for modern fighter aircraft.

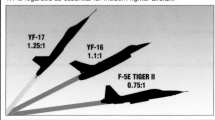

YF-17 1.25:1

YF-16 1.1:1

F-5E TIGER II 0.75:1

NORTHROP/MARTIN
HL-10/X-24

● Wingless flight ● Space shuttle research vehicles ● Rocket-powered

▲ As with all US research projects in the 1960s and 1970s, USAF and NASA pilots faced huge risks, flying untried aircraft in harsh flight regimes. Neither the HL-10 nor the X-24 was involved in any serious accidents.

While the problems of putting a re-usable spacecraft into orbit occupied the minds of many National Aeronautical and Space Administration (NASA) engineers, several others were working on a means of returning the craft safely to Earth. Research suggested that a lifting body design offered the best compromise between re-entry capability and in-atmosphere flight performance. The HL-10 and X-24 tested this radical theory.

PHOTO FILE
NORTHROP/MARTIN HL-10/X-24

Three-fin stability ▶
While the X-24A's middle fin was merely for stability, the outer fins carried large, thick, rudder-like surfaces. Each surface was split and could be used as separate upper and lower parts depending on the pilot's control inputs.

▲ NASA sponsorship
NASA funded Northrop's HL-10 and the similar but less successful M2-F2 illustrated here.

▲ Flat bottom and nose extension
The X-24A was rebuilt as the X-24B to test an alternative aerodynamic layout.

▼ Blue body
Unlike the natural metal X-24A, the X-24B was finished in a blue and white paint scheme.

▲ Launching the X-24A
Moments after launch, the X-24A has already attained the nose-high attitude that was typical of the aircraft in flight.

FACTS AND FIGURES

➤ When the USAF first flew the X-24A, NASA had already been working on lifting body designs for 10 years.

➤ NASA first flew the Northrop HL-10 on 22 December 1966.

➤ Eight control surfaces kept the X-24A in the air and on course.

➤ When the X-24B was retired in the mid-1970s, it marked the end of 30 years of US rocket-powered research types.

➤ Since 19 November 1976 the X-24B has been on display at the USAF museum.

➤ The X-24B had an unusual nose-down attitude on landing.

PROFILE

Testing for the shuttle

Several unmanned launches were performed with sub-scale lifting bodies at extreme speeds and altitudes, before a series of PILOT (PIloted LOw-speed Tests) was initiated in 1969.

Martin used the unmanned SV-5D as the basis of its much larger SV-5P, which was later designated X-24A. Powered by a 37.72-kN (8,485-lb.-thrust) rocket motor, the aircraft was taken to altitude under the wing of an NB-52B. The first gliding flight was made on 17 April 1969 and 28 powered flights were completed before the aircraft was modified to become the X-24B.

Before the X-24B flew, however, Northrop's HL-10 (Horizontal Lander design number 10), and similar M2-F2, had been launched. They proved difficult to fly, but were successfully modified. The HL-10 flew a number of useful simulated space shuttle approach patterns.

Further research into the flight characteristics of these unusual aircraft was required in order to determine their suitability for shuttle application. The X-24B went on to perform a number of flights at increased speeds and altitudes, but its proposed successor, the Mach 7 X-24C, was not built. It had become clear that the lifting body design was not suitable for the shuttle.

Left: Although it appeared to be a short, fat and slow aircraft, the X-24A used a similar engine to that of the X-1 but was 320 km/h (198 m.p.h.) faster.

Below: After a serious landing accident in which pilot Bruce Peterson was severely injured, the M2-F2 was rebuilt as the M2-F3.

X-24B

Type: lifting body aircraft for research into reusable spacecraft approach patterns

Powerplant: one 43.64-kN (9,820-lb.-thrust) Thiokol XLR-RM-13 four-chamber regeneratively-cooled rocket engine, plus two 2.22-kN (500-lb.-thrust) hydrogen peroxide rocket engines for increased lift during landing and for high-speed taxi trials

Maximum speed: 1873 km/h (1,161 m.p.h.)

Maximum ceiling: 22595 m (74,100 ft.)

Weights: maximum 6260 kg (13,772 lb.)

Accommodation: pilot on a zero-zero ejection seat allowing escape throughout the flight envelope

Dimensions: span 5.80 m (19 ft.)
length 11.43 m (37 ft. 6 in.)
height 3.15 m (10 ft. 4 in.)
lifting surface area 30.66 m² (330 sq. ft.)

Flight control of the X-24A was by conventional control column and pedals. A three-axis stability augmentation system was also fitted to make the aircraft easier to fly. Should the pilot need to leave his pressurised cockpit, he could do so on a zero-airspeed/zero-altitude ejection seat.

A number of cameras were carried to record various aspects of the X-24A in flight. Tufting on the right fin-tip and lower flaps, the engine area and the instrument panel, as well as the view forwards from the nose, were all filmed.

A long instrumented pitot boom was carried ahead of the X-24A. Together with several other sensors, it collected a huge amount of data on each flight and sent telemetry back to the ground. Even more information was recorded by an on-board tape recorder.

X-24A

Three pilots made a total of 28 flights in the X-24A, before it was converted to X-24B standard by the addition of an extended nose. The programme was USAF sponsored.

In its X-24A form, the aircraft had a rounded top and bottom fuselage, giving it a bulbous appearance. The bottom flattened out at the mid-fuselage point. The whole fuselage provided lift.

In some flight regimes it was desirable to explore increased rates of roll. This was accomplished by using an aileron to rudder interconnect, which operated the two surfaces simultaneously.

Four flap-like control surfaces were attached to the rear fuselage of the X-24A. Each flap had its own hydraulic actuator, allowing the flaps to be operated separately or in unison. Differential deflection allowed control in roll, while simultaneous deflection controlled changes in pitch.

ACTION DATA

MAXIMUM ALTITUDE

With greater thrust from its modified main engine, the X-24B was able to reach higher altitudes than the X-24A. Although the HL-10 was powered, it flew mostly as a glider. In this configuration its maximum altitude at launch was 13716 metres (45,000 ft.).

X-24A 21763 m (71,383 ft.)	X-24B 22595 m (74,100 ft.)	HL-10 13716 m (45,000 ft.)

MAXIMUM SPEED

A combination of increased power and greater altitude performance allowed the X-24B to reach higher speeds than the X-24A. Both vehicles outperformed the X-1 in its original form, in spite of their unusual configuration, but neither had performance approaching that of the returning Orbiter. In the event, the shuttle did not take lifting body form, but the research vehicles provided useful data for the project.

X-24A	1667 km/h (1,033 m.p.h.)
X-24B	1873 km/h (1,161 m.p.h.)
HL-10	724 km/h (449 m.p.h.)

Lifting body re-entry theory

THROUGH THE ATMOSPHERE: Engineers believed that a blunt body would be more capable than a conventional aircraft shape of withstanding the frictional heating which occurs during re-entry.

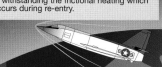

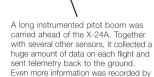

CONVENTIONAL AIRCRAFT: The nose of a conventional aircraft generates a shock-wave which causes heat. This moves back along the airframe and affects the leading edges of the wings.

BLUNT BODY: The requirement to develop a blunt-nosed vehicle without wings but with the capability of atmospheric flight led to creation of the lifting body. Initial contact with the atmosphere causes a shock-wave and heating at the nose, as with the conventional layout.

BOUNDARY LAYER: In this case, however, the shock-wave moves from the nose to surround the craft as a boundary layer, without making contact with it, and so protects the body from severe heating.

MAXIMUM LAUNCH WEIGHT

None of these aircraft was capable of a conventional take-off. All were launched from a modified X-15 pylon beneath the starboard wing of an NB-52B. Launch weight typically included a large amount of fuel, although flights were of limited duration.

X-24A 5194 kg (11,427 lb.)	X-24B 6260 kg (13,772 lb.)	HL-10 4080 kg (8,976 lb.)

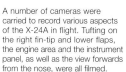

NORTHROP/McDONNELL DOUGLAS

YF-23

● Ultra-stealthy ● Air superiority ● Agile dogfighter

Had it entered service, the startling YF-23 would have been named Black Widow II. The high-tech fighter was one of two aircraft competing hard for the US Air Force's Advanced Tactical Fighter (ATF) production contract. But although the YF-23 promised to be faster and more stealthy than its competitor, it finished in second place, losing the ATF competition to the Lockheed F-22.

▲ *Built in competition with the YF-22, the YF-23 was in many respects a superior design, but it was more expensive to produce and eventually fell foul of government politics.*

PHOTO FILE

NORTHROP/McDONNELL DOUGLAS YF-23

▼ **Flying for NASA**
With no future as a combat aircraft ahead, the two YF-23 prototypes may become project demonstrators for NASA. The abilities of the YF-23 are unmatched by anything else in the NASA inventory.

▲ **Smooth lines**
The blended shape of the YF-23 was designed to give the lowest possible radar cross-section. The engines are actually above the wing, with the inlets below, feeding them through ducts.

▼ **Grey ghost**
The first prototype (with YF119 engines) wore a dark-grey low-visibility paint scheme with small national markings.

▼ **Northrop roll-out**
The loss of the ATF competition was keenly felt at Northrop, design leaders of the YF-23, which badly needed more fighter work.

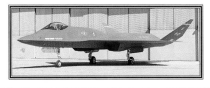

▲ **Stealthy engines**
The YF-23 had fixed nozzles where the rival YF-22 has vectoring nozzles. Both the YF119 and YF120 engines could drive the fighters past Mach 1 without afterburning.

FACTS AND FIGURES

➤ High-speed taxi tests of the YF-23 began on 7 July 1990, and the maiden flight took place on 27 August.

➤ The second YF-23 made a 44-minute first flight at Edwards AFB on 26 October 1990.

➤ The two service-test prototypes logged 219 flying hours in 23 months.

➤ The first YF-23A was powered by Pratt & Whitney YF119 engines, the second by General Electric YF120s.

➤ The two YF-23s have been turned over to NASA, but are not expected to fly again.

➤ The stealthy YF-23 made extensive use of composite materials.

PROFILE

Stealth fighter contender

In many ways the YF-23 was a better fighter than the successful YF-22. Both aircraft were a generation ahead of anything else flying, but the Northrop design would probably have been faster and stealthier, with low-speed handling the only area where the Lockheed aircraft was superior.

To save money, the YF-23 prototypes used more conventional components than its rival. The Lockheed YF-22 had a sidestick controller like that in the F-16, but the YF-23 had a more orthodox centre stick. The YF-23 used the forward cockpit of the F-15E Strike Eagle, but was longer and wider than an F-15C.

Both advanced tactical fighters met most of the US Air Force requirements, but ultimately it was industrial performance which mattered. The two main partners in the consortium managing the F-23 were under considerable strain. Northrop's B-2 bomber was delayed and suffering cost overruns, and McDonnell

The YF-23 would have been a lethal opponent for any of today's fighters, able to attack without warning and dogfight well too.

Douglas was having even greater problems with the A-12 naval bomber.

Lockheed, by contrast, had developed the F-117 Stealth Fighter on time and under budget, which probably proved decisive in the Pentagon's choice of aircraft.

Pitch and yaw stability at high angle of attack and low airspeed are mainly generated by the forward fuselage chine, which acts much like a leading-edge root extension.

YF-23

Type: advanced-technology fighter

Powerplant: two 155.69-kN (35,000-lb.-thrust) Pratt & Whitney YF119 or General Electric YF120 advanced technology engines

Maximum speed: Mach 1.6 with non-afterburning 'supercruise'; Mach 1.8 with afterburning

Range: not disclosed, but over 4500 km (2,790 mi.)

Service ceiling: over 19000 m (65,000 ft.)

Weights: empty 16783 kg (36,900 lb.); loaded 29030 kg (63,866 lb.)

Armament: four or six AIM-7 Sparrow or AIM-120 AMRAAM radar-guided and four AIM-9 Sidewinder infra-red missiles, plus an M61A1 Vulcan rotary 20-mm cannon

Dimensions:
span	13.29 m	(44 ft.)
length	20.54 m	(67 ft.)
height	4.24 m	(14 ft.)
wing area	87.80 m²	(945 sq. ft.)

YF-23

The two YF-23 prototypes began flying in August 1990 in a two-year demonstration/evaluation. The aircraft lost to the rival Lockheed/Boeing YF-22 in the ATF programme.

The YF-23 has a radar and an infra-red search and track system.

Although the prototypes contained no gun armament, production F-23s would have carried the familiar Vulcan M61 20-mm cannon in the starboard fuselage.

The wide, flat exhaust nozzles are designed to dissipate the hot engine gases as quickly as possible to reduce the aircraft's infra-red signature. The nozzle has a fixed lower ramp with a small moveable upper ramp.

The wing has large trailing- and leading-edge flaps which assist in roll control, and also deploy simultaneously to give 'straight ahead' aerodynamic braking and lift augmentation.

Normal protruding pitot tubes were fitted to the prototypes, but the production aircraft would have had ports only to reduce radar signature.

To reduce costs, the YF-23 used the standard F-15 nosewheel unit.

Primary armament of the YF-23 would have been six AIM-120 missiles, stowed in an internal weapons bay to hide them from radar.

The inlets on the underside of the aircraft are curved so that the compressor faces of the engines, a major source of radar returns, are shielded from enemy search radars.

The main undercarriage was taken from the McDonnell Douglas F/A-18 Hornet, also to reduce development costs.

COMBAT DATA

SPEED AND STEALTHINESS

Both the advanced fighter demonstrators made extensive use of composite and radar-absorbing materials. This made them far stealthier than fighters like the F-15, which was 100 per cent visible on radar. With high agility and advanced weapons, they also promised an almost unbeatable air combat performance. The YF-23 was never able to demonstrate its full speed potential, but computer simulations indicated that it would be faster than the rival YF-22. Neither could match the F-15 for sheer speed, but with supercruise both could maintain supersonic speed for hours rather than the minutes which an Eagle on full afterburner can sustain.

YF-22 RAPIER 50% Mach 1.7

F-15 EAGLE 100% Mach 2.5

YF-23 40% Mach 1.8

Superfighters that didn't make it

■ **F-107A:** A strike fighter developed from the F-100, the F-107 fell victim to industrial politics and to the appearance of the even better F-105.

■ **XF8U-3 'CRUSADER III':** A superb radar- and missile-armed development of the F-8, the 'Crusader III' was beaten by the F-4 Phantom.

■ **F-111B:** The F-111 was originally intended to be a Navy aircraft as well as a USAF bomber, but the F-111B was too heavy for carrier use.

■ **YF-17:** Beaten by the F-16 for the USAF Lightweight Fighter contract, the YF-17 formed the basis for the US Navy's larger and heavier Hornet.

■ **F-20 TIGERSHARK:** It performed superbly, but Northrop could not sell the F-20 because of US government support for the rival F-16.

RAVEN

DOUBLE EAGLE II

● Gas balloon ● Atlantic crossing ● Seaworthy capsule

I n the 18th century the Montgolfier brothers launched their first manned balloon, carrying Jean François Pilâtre de Rozier. He therefore became the world's first aeronaut. Almost 200 years later, the Double Eagle II gas balloon, piloted by L. Abruzzo, Maxie L. Anderson and Larry M. Newman, entered the record books by becoming the first balloon of any type to cross the Atlantic. This flight also set new world distance and endurance records.

▲ Unlike today's more common hot-air balloons, Double Eagle II was filled with helium gas. Helium-filled balloons do not have to carry heavy fuel, which can give them longer endurance.

DOUBLE EAGLE II

◀ **Final descent**
After passing over the south coast of England, Double Eagle II began its final descent into northern France.

▼ **Airborne advertising**
Based in northern Germany, this Colt 90A hot-air balloon is sponsored by a computer company.

▲ **US Navy research**
Filled with helium, this US Navy balloon carried two naval observers during high-altitude experiments in November 1956.

▼ **Height record**
In 1957 another US balloon took a world record. This view of Minnesota was taken by Major D. Simons from 31090 m (101,975 ft.).

◀ **British manufacturer**
Cameron is the largest hot-air balloon manufacturer in Europe. This example is a medium-sized model V-56.

FACTS AND FIGURES

➤ Crew member Maxie Anderson was unsuccessful in a round-the-world record attempt in 1981.

➤ The Double Eagle II capsule is displayed at the Smithsonian Museum, Washington.

➤ The subsequent Double Eagle V became the first balloon to cross the Pacific.

➤ In honour of the crew, an airport at their home town of Albuquerque, New Mexico has been named Double Eagle II.

➤ Double Eagle V's crew included Abruzzo and Newman from the D.E. II team.

➤ The Double Eagle II crew enjoyed almost perfect weather for their flight.

PROFILE

Crossing the ocean

On 12 August 1978 the three-man crew of the Double Eagle II gas balloon lifted off from Presque Isle, Maine, on a journey which would end five days 17 hours and six minutes later in northern France. This journey not only established new world distance (5001.22 km/3,100 mi.) and endurance records, but set up the crew as the first people to cross the Atlantic by balloon.

The intention had been to touch down at Paris's Le Bourget airport, the same arrival point as Charles Lindbergh after his record-breaking transatlantic flight of 1927. A lack of food and exhaustion forced the crew down short of their intended destination, but the record had been taken.

The route had taken the craft across the North Atlantic and over southern England before crossing the coast of Dorset. Once the balloon had crossed the English Channel it was greeted by hundreds of members of the public. They followed the balloon in cars through northern France for over 30 minutes, causing a massive traffic jam. The craft eventually touched down in perfect conditions near Evreux, with the Stars and Stripes and the French tricolour draped from its gondola.

Above: It was not until 1987 that the first successful transatlantic crossing in a hot-air balloon was accomplished, by the Virgin team.

Below: The varying sizes of today's hot-air balloons are evident here. The single-seat Cameron V-20 is dwarfed by the Cameron A-530.

DOUBLE EAGLE II

The one-off Double Eagle II was produced in conjunction with the well-established Raven balloon manufacturing company in the USA. It underwent rigorous testing before the record flight.

Transatlantic journey

2 FRENCH FINALE: As the craft approached the British Isles, the wind eased and progress was slow. The balloon passed over southern England and the English Channel before finally touching down at Miserey.

1 LIFT OFF: Departing from Presque Isle, Maine, the Double Eagle II used the prevailing west-to-east winds to carry it over Newfoundland. The winds enabled the craft to make good progress over the central area of the North Atlantic.

Double Eagle II

Type: record-breaking gas balloon

Crew: three

Endurance: 137 hr 6 min (on record flight)

Range: 5001.22 km (3,100 mi.) (on record flight)

The top half of the balloon was covered in a reflective material to help prevent the sun's rays from overheating the helium gas contained within the envelope.

CROSSING THE ATLANTIC

John Alcock and Arthur Whitten Brown – On 14 June 1919 Capt. Alcock and Lt Brown departed St John's, Newfoundland on the first successful non-stop flight across the Atlantic. In their modified Vickers Vimy, they touched down at Clifden, Northern Ireland.

Charles Lindbergh – On 20-21 May 1927 Capt. Lindbergh made the first non-stop solo air crossing of the North Atlantic Ocean in the Ryan NYP (New York Paris) high-wing monoplane, *Spirit of St. Louis*, covering 5810 km (3,600 mi.) in 33 hours 30 min.

Amelia Earhart – Exactly five years to the day after Lindbergh made his epic flight, Amelia Earhart became the first woman to make a solo crossing of the North Atlantic. She flew a Lockheed Vega monoplane from Newfoundland to Northern Ireland.

Control ropes operated from the capsule were used to release some of the gas when necessary. This helped the crew control the balloon's altitude during the long flight.

Contained within the large air-tight envelope was helium gas. Helium is lighter than air and therefore causes the balloon to rise. Before World War II hydrogen was used for airships and gas balloons, but the flammable nature of this gas caused a number of disasters and its use was abandoned.

The three-man crew spent over five days in the cramped confines of their capsule. The capsule was designed to be seaworthy in case the balloon had to ditch in the ocean. The lack of space restricted food stocks, and it was for this reason that the crew was eventually forced to land.

RFB

FANTRAINER

● Ducted fan trainer design ● Thai service ● Jet-powered derivative

Rhein-Flugzeugbau (RFB) was founded in 1956, and as an independent subsidiary of MBB pursued several original lines of development. One was a novel propulsion system which involved a fuselage-mounted ducted fan. The concept was applied to the Fantrainer, which was first flown in 1977 with a Wankel rotary engine and later with an Allison turbine. Sales of this pilot trainer were sluggish and although Thailand took delivery of a small fleet, it never realised its potential.

▲ Although a promising design, the unorthodox Fantrainer found only one military customer. It was exceptionally quiet and economical, but its lack of power was a drawback.

PHOTO FILE

RFB FANTRAINER

◄ **Airline pilot trainer**
In the mid-1980s, Lufthansa considered using the 600 to train instructors in aerobatics and special flight attitudes.

▼ **Unsuccessful Ranger 2000**
With Rockwell International, RFB (under the auspices of DASA) entered a jet-powered derivative of the Fantrainer, the Ranger 2000, in the USAF/USN JPATS trainer contest.

▲ **Luftwaffe evaluation**
Germany's defence ministry funded two Fantrainer prototypes and although the Luftwaffe evaluated the type, it did not place an order.

Sole Fantrainer customer ▼
No. 402 Sqn., Royal Thai Air Force operated 46 Fantrainer 400s and 600s in 1996.

▲ **Rotary-engined**
RFB's AWI-2 was the first member of the Fantrainer family. Powered by two Wankel rotary engines together rated at 224 kW, it flew in 1977 and was followed by the Allison turbine-powered ATI-2 in 1978.

FACTS AND FIGURES

➤ From 1984, the Royal Thai Air Force took delivery of 31 Fantrainer 400s and 16 Fantrainer 600s.

➤ Thailand uses its Fantrainers as lead-in trainers for operational F-5 pilots.

➤ In 1979 RFB proposed a Vought-built Fantrainer as a USAF T-37 replacement.

➤ Nowadays, RFB specialises in glass-fibre reinforced plastic (GFRP) and metal component manufacture for airliners.

➤ Composite wing parts have resisted deterioration in the damp Thai climate.

➤ RFB delivered most of the Royal Thai Air Force's Fantrainers in kit form.

PROFILE

Unorthodox ducted fan trainer

The ducted fan gave jet-like handling at an economical price. The airflow, lack of torque, thrust-change feel and single-lever control were all claimed to resemble those of jet aircraft, while the small turboshaft integrated into the fuselage reduced fuel consumption, noise and air pollution.

The Fantrainer was produced in two versions. The 400 was fitted with a 407-kW (545-hp.) Allison 250-C20B engine, while the 600 had the more powerful 250-C30. Both were bought by

the Royal Thai Air Force, which later replaced the original composite wings with metal airfoils.

In 1986 the Luftwaffe evaluated a modified Fantrainer, armed with gun and rocket pods, as a potential replacement for its Piaggio P.149Ds. Lufthansa also tried out the type as an aerobatic trainer for pilot instructors, but neither ordered the aircraft. In the early 1990s RFB teamed up with Rockwell to develop the Fanranger version, which was fitted with a conventional Pratt & Whitney

To prove the ducted fan concept, RFB flew the Fanliner in 1973. In 1976, this improved version was flown, but failed to enter production.

JT15D turbofan, for the JPATS competition for a new US military trainer. Unfortunately, one of the two prototypes crashed, and the renamed Ranger 2000 failed to win the competition.

The Fantrainer's four fuel tanks are installed in the wings, with the filler caps on the top surface.

The main wings have a 6° forward sweep to balance the long tandem cockpit section which is ahead of the front wing spar.

The Fantrainer 600 has the ability to carry four underwing 96-litre tanks.

Fantrainer 600

Type: two-seat primary/basic trainer

Powerplant: one 485-kW (650-hp.) Allison 250-C30 turboshaft driving a five-bladed Hoffman constant-speed ducted fan

Maximum speed: 417 km/h (259 m.p.h.)

Cruising speed: 370 km/h (230 m.p.h.)

Maximum climb rate: 914 m/min (3,000 f.p.m.)

Range: 1037 km (644 mi.)

Service ceiling: 7620 m (25,000 ft)

Weights: maximum take-off 2300 kg (5060 lb.)

Dimensions:
span	9.70 m	(31 ft. 9 in.)
length	9.48 m	(31 ft. 1 in.)
height	3.00 m	(9 ft. 10 in.)
wing area	14.00 m²	(150 sq. ft.)

FANTRAINER 600

D-EATR was one of several Fantrainer 600 development airframes flown by RFB. Ninety-two per cent of the 600's airframe is shared with the 400, the principal difference being a more powerful engine.

Two separate canopies over the tandem cockpits provide access for the instructor (in the rear seat) and pupil. Ejection seats are standard equipment.

The forward and centre fuselage are of light alloy with glass-fibre-reinforced plastic skins. These are joined to the metal cruciform tail section at three points.

An Allison 250-C30 turboshaft engine, rated at 485 kW (650 hp.), powered the ducted fan of the Fantrainer 600 from an engine bay behind the rear cockpit. This was fed from air intakes above the wing.

D-EATR

FANTRAINER

Fantrainers have conventional manually-operated controls and hydraulic retracting undercarriages. The nosewheel retracts forwards and upwards, while the main gear folds into the lower fuselage and wings.

The shroud for the ducted fan propulsion system dominates the rear fuselage. Hydraulically-actuated carbon-fibre airbrakes are fitted flush to the side of the shroud on both sides of the aircraft.

ACTION DATA

NEVER EXCEED SPEED

The Fantrainer 400's top speed is only slightly less than that of the Pilatus PC-7 turboprop trainer. It is considerably slower than jet designs like the Agusta (SIAI-Marchetti) S.211, however.

FANTRAINER 400	463 km/h (287 m.p.h.)
S.211	740 km/h (460 m.p.h.)
PC-7 TURBO TRAINER	500 km/h (310 m.p.h.)

SERVICE CEILING

Service ceiling is another area in which the Fantrainer does not compare favourably with other military trainers. The S.211 is able to climb to over twice the height for example. Although later Fantrainer variants improved on this, they were still inferior.

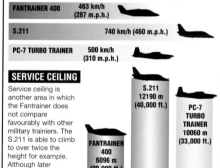

S.211 12190 m (40,000 ft)

PC-7 TURBO TRAINER 10060 m (33,000 ft.)

FANTRAINER 400 6096 m (20,000 ft.)

ENDURANCE

Powered by a small, comparatively economical turboshaft engine, the Fantrainer has good endurance, which allows longer training missions. Turboprop trainers, like the PC-7, have a similar endurance ability.

FANTRAINER 400 4 hours 36 min — 04:36:00

PC-7 TURBO TRAINER 4 hours 22 min — 04:22:00

S.211 3 hours 24 min — 03:24:00

Rhein-Flugzeugbau's original designs

■ **RW-3 MULTOPLAN:** RFB's earliest pusher-propeller product was the licence-built Multoplan, designed by Herr Fischer. Twenty-two were built between 1958 and 1961.

■ **RF-1:** An all-metal, six-seat STOL design, the RF-1 was powered by two piston engines driving a ducted fan. A prototype flew in 1960, but the design's complexity ruled out production.

■ **SIRIUS:** After purchase by VFW-Fokker in 1968, RFB developed this ducted fan-powered sailplane. The Sirius I had twin piston engines; the Sirius II (below) had two Wankel rotaries.

■ **X 114:** An experimental ground-effect craft, the six-seat X 114 was one of several similar designs developed by RFB. This model had a top speed of 150 km/h (93 mi.).

ROCKWELL

XFV-12

● Supersonic V/STOL design ● Advanced technology ● Unflown

PHOTO FILE

ROCKWELL XFV-12

▼ Ejector flaps
Flaps constructed from titanium honeycomb deflected engine air through the wing and canard augmentor systems.

▲ Tethered hover
A single XFV-12A prototype, with an F401 engine, was completed. It was used for hovering trials at Langley during 1977-78, but never flew free.

▼ Futuristic shape
Although it was a sleek and purposeful-looking aircraft, the XFV-12A was destined to fail.

▼ Funding fiasco
As the XFV-12A sank deeper into trouble, Congress became increasingly unwilling to provide funds.

▲ Naval optimism
Known by the US Navy designation, NR-356, this artist's impression shows the XFV-12A as it might have appeared in service, with modified wings and vertical tail surfaces. The aircraft would have been hugely expensive.

Technological and budgetary problems caused a series of delays to the XFV-12A programme, and it eventually faded away in the late 1970s. Designed to fly from small aircraft-carriers without catapults or arresting gear, the XFV-12A presented complex engineering problems that could not be solved within the restricted budget available, even though the concept of diverting engine thrust to provide jet-lift for take-off and landing seemed practical in theory.

▲ *The first flight of the XFV-12A had been planned for September 1974. The delays which led to its eventual roll-out in August 1977 were typical of this ill-fated programme.*

FACTS AND FIGURES

➤ A Rockwell advertisement of 1981 included a painting of XFV-12As battling against Russian MiG fighters.

➤ 'Borrowed' components for the XFV-12A included an F-4 Phantom wing box.

➤ A McDonnell Douglas Escapac zero-zero ejection seat was to be fitted.

➤ The XFV-12A's wing-mounted, blown-air scheme was totally different from the vectored thrust used by the Harrier.

➤ Small canards forward of the wing were fitted to improve manoeuvrability at speed.

➤ The tricycle undercarriage of the XFV-12A came from an A-4 Skyhawk.

PROFILE

Naval V/STOL disaster

Unfortunately, the XFV-12A only ever left the ground while suspended under the NASA Lunar Lander gantry in Virginia.

In order to save time and money, the XFV-12A was built using components from other aircraft, including the nose section of a Douglas A-4 Skyhawk and the intakes and wing box of the McDonnell Douglas F-4 Phantom II.

From the time of the first US Navy order in 1972, until the programme quietly disappeared at the end of the decade, the XFV-12A consumed several years of design and construction effort, all of it by experts who constantly struggled to make the concept work. Ironically,

the ships from which the XFV-12A would have flown remained hypothetical, since the US Navy did not have any real plans to build small aircraft-carriers or other warships that would have required an XFV-12A-type aircraft.

A special rig which rotated at high speed was built to test the Pratt & Whitney F401-PW-400 turbofan and its associated thrust diverter valve. The engine, mounted at the centre of the rig, produced thrust which was ducted to a complete wing assembly set on a long arm. Successful rig tests did not lead to a flight, however, and the US Navy eventually stated that it had 'learned all it could' from the Rockwell XFV-12A.

Above: This mock-up shows the XFV-12A as it might have appeared, armed with Sparrow missiles, and in the standard US Navy fighter colours of the period.

Louvred doors covered the intake, mounted in the upper fuselage. The fuselage was very deep and wide in order to house the large turbofan and its associated ducts and control systems. Canard surfaces were mounted low down on the fuselage sides. Each had full-span ejector-flaps like those of the wing, and full-span trailing-edge flaps for increased manoeuvrability in high-speed flight. All flight controls were hydraulically actuated.

XFV-12A

Only one functioning aircraft was completed. It conducted live engine runs while suspended from the Lunar Lander gantry, but reports suggest that even they may have been disappointing.

A long nose radome disguised the fact that the forward fuselage and cockpit area were from the Skyhawk. The pilot sat on a McDonnell Douglas Escapac zero-zero ejection seat in a pressurised and air-conditioned cockpit. No radar was fitted.

A conventional exhaust nozzle at the rear of the airframe was used in forward flight. The F401 engine employed advanced technology and was unusually powerful. When ducted to the ejector-flaps, the thrust was greatly increased by mixing it with ambient air, giving the potential of enormous lift and comparatively low exhaust temperatures.

Engine air was delivered via the lateral Phantom-derived intakes. During hovering or thrust-vectored flight at low speeds, the mass flow of air to the engine was insufficient, and auxiliary intakes above the fuselage were employed.

The Skyhawk undercarriage of the XFV-12A was fully retractable, with the main units retracting backwards into wingtip fairings and the nose gear retracting forwards.

Fixed to each wingtip was an endplate, which formed the vertical stabilising surfaces of the aircraft during forward flight. The upper section incorporated a fixed fin and rudder, that below only a fin. Each wing had full-span trailing-edge flaps.

XFV-12A

Type: experimental supersonic V/STOL research aircraft

Powerplant: one Pratt & Whitney F401-PW-400 advanced-technology turbofan engine in the 133.40 kN (30,000-lb.-thrust) range for lift and forward flight

Maximum speed: Mach 2.2 to 2.4 predicted

Take-off run: a 91-m (298-ft.) short take-off roll allowed an increase in maximum take-off weight to 11000 kg (24,200 lb)

Combat radius: in excess of 925 km (574 mi.) was predicted

Weights: basic operating weight 6259 kg (3,889 lb.); maximum vertical take-off weight (planned) 8845 kg (5,496 lb.); maximum short-field take-off weight 11000 kg (24,200 lb)

Armament: ability to carry air-to-air and air-to-ground weapons was planned; operational version would have had an internal gun in the lower fuselage

Dimensions:
span 8.69 m (28 ft. 6 in.)
length 13.39 m (43 ft. 11 in.)
height 3.15 m (10 ft. 4 in.)
wing area 27.20 m² (293 sq. ft.)

SUPERSONIC NAVAL V/STOL

HAWKER SIDDELEY P.1154: As early as spring 1963, Hawker Siddeley proposed an advanced project based on its experience with the P.1127 V/STOL tactical strike and reconnaissance aircraft, which would satisfy the needs of the Fleet Air Arm and Royal Air Force for a strike aircraft and interceptor. A short-sighted government cancelled the project before any of the highly supersonic aircraft were built.

YAKOVLEV YAK-141 'FREESTYLE': Designed as a replacement for the Yak-38 'Forger', the Yak-141 is capable of 1800 km/h and uses a single afterburning turbofan of 152.00 kN thrust for lift and forward flight. Since the first flight in 1989, the two prototypes have flown a successful test programme, including operations from carriers, although the second prototype was damaged in a landing accident. The 'Freestyle' may enter service as the Yak-41.

XFV-12A flight control

1 HOVERING: A diverter valve in the engine exhaust system forces the jet efflux into the duct system, which transfers air to the ejector-flap systems. Hot air passing downwards through these flaps pulls ambient air through from above in a 7:1 ratio, creating far more lift than from engine thrust alone.

2 TRANSITION: As the ejector-flaps begin to close, the aircraft moves gradually into forward flight. As speed increases and wing lift becomes sufficient for flight, the diverter valve is adjusted and the engine begins to exhaust through the rear nozzle. The louvred intakes above the fuselage, supplying engine air in the hover, also begin to close.

3 FORWARD FLIGHT: Ejector-flap systems are fully closed and the diverter valve is fully deflected so that all thrust is via the main exhaust nozzle. All engine air is supplied by the main fuselage-side intakes as long as forward air speed is sufficient. In flight, the upper ejector-flaps could be used as powerful airbrakes.

ROCKWELL
B-1A

● Mach 2 bomber prototype ● Four built ● Predecessor of B-1B Lancer

Rockwell's B-1A was the great white hope of the late-1970s while the Cold War was raging. This was a 'swing-wing' bomber, capable of supersonic speed and hauling heavy bombs, that would finally, belatedly, replace the B-52 Stratofortress. However, those who complained that the B-52 should have been retired long before were premature if they expected the B-1A to replace it. President Jimmy Carter had other ideas.

▲ *Rolled out on 26 October 1974 and first flown on 23 December, the first of four B-1A prototypes was 74-0158. The expense of the programme was the major factor in its cancellation.*

ROCKWELL **B-1A**

▼ Mach 2 top speed
The B-1A was designed from the outset to be capable of twice the speed of sound at altitude.

▲ Crew escape capsule
Like the F-111 before it, the B-1 employed a crew escape capsule rather than ejection seats to allow the crew to leave the aircraft in an emergency at high speed. Normal ejection at high speeds would be fatal.

Swing wings ▶
A key feature of the B-1 was its swing wings, fully forward (15° sweep) for low-speed flight and landing, and swept to 67° for high-speed dashes.

▼ Cockpit layout
The B-1 featured fighter-type control sticks, vertical scale flight instruments and TV screens for a forward-looking infra-red image.

Prototype tests ▶
The prototype first flew from Palmdale, California. Subsequent testing was carried out at Edwards AFB.

FACTS AND FIGURES

➤ The prototype B-1A first flew on 23 December 1974 and made 79 test flights totalling 405 flight hours.

➤ The second B-1A crashed on its 127th flight on 29 August 1984, killing the pilot.

➤ B-1As had a crew of four: two pilots and offensive and defensive systems officers.

➤ On 19 April 1976 the US Secretary of Defense, Donald Rumsfeld, flew a B-1A with a Rockwell test pilot.

➤ The second and fourth B-1As were used as test aircraft for B-1B development.

➤ On 5 October 1978, the second B-1A briefly hit a speed of Mach 2.22.

PROFILE

SAC's ill-fated Mach 2 bomber

Below: The B-1A's undercarriage retracted into the fuselage between the engine nacelles. Each main leg was supported by a four-wheel bogie.

The Rockwell B-1A was the bomber of the 1970s that paved the way for the Rockwell B-1B Lancer, 100 of which were built in the 1980s.

However, the B-1A differed from the Lancer in several important ways. It was designed to fly at Mach 2, bomb from high altitude and have only a limited low-level capability. It had greater wing sweep and bomb-carrying capacity and had a very different avionics fit.

From 1974 until 1977, three glossy-white B-1As flying at Edwards Air Force Base, California, were believed to

be prototypes of a new Strategic Air Command bomber, one that would supplant the ageing Boeing B-52 Stratofortress which was scheduled to retire in 1975.

A contract for the Advanced Manned Strategic Aircraft (AMSA) was awarded in 1970, with the first B-1A flying in 1974.

In 1977, President Carter struck what appeared to be a fatal blow by cancelling the B-1A programme. Concerns were raised regarding the huge cost of the 240 aircraft that SAC had requested. It was concluded that the job of striking at the Soviet Union could be carried out by

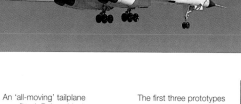

Above: Unusually, the first flight of the prototype B-1A was also the first flight of the YF101 turbofan. New engines are more often tested in an existing airframe before being flown in a new aircraft type.

B-52s armed with 'stand-off' weapons. Besides, any new manned bomber would have to be optimised for low-level flight. When Ronald Reagan became president in 1981, he revived the B-1 to create just such an aircraft, the B-1B.

B-1A

Type: strategic bomber

Powerplant: four 136.93-kN (30,716-lb.-thrust) General Electric F101-GE-100 turbofan engines with afterburning

Maximum speed: Mach 2.22 or 2351 km/h at 15240 m (1,458 m.p.h. at 49,987 ft.)

Range: 9815 km (6,085 mi.)

Service ceiling: 12000 m (39,360 ft.)

Weights: max take-off 176810 kg (388,982 lb.)

Armament: max of 52160 kg (114,752 lb.) of stores, including up to 24 1016-kg (2,235-lb.) AGM-69A Short-Range Attack Missiles (SRAMs), Air-Launched Cruise Missiles (ALCMs) and decoy missiles

Dimensions: span swept   23.84 m (78 ft. 2 in.)
span unswept 41.67 m (136 ft. 8 in.)
length   45.78 m (150 ft. 2 in.)
height   10.24 m (33 ft. 7 in.)
wing area   181.2 m² (1,950 sq. ft.)

B-1A

Glossy-white 74-0158 was the first of three B-1A prototypes built and test flown before cancellation in 1977. A fourth example flew in 1979 after the Carter Administration agreed to allow testing to continue.

In common with prototype aircraft under test, the first B-1 was fitted with a 'candy-striped' instrumentation boom on the tip of the nose radome.

Two of the three 4.57-metre long weapons bays were located ahead of the wings, the third being above the end of the engine nacelle. Fuel tankage was located in the wings and the rear fuselage. The B-1A was also able to refuel in the air.

The high-altitude bombing role of the B-1A was reflected in the 'anti-flash' white colour scheme applied to the prototypes. Anti-flash schemes are intended to reflect heat from a nuclear blast, protecting the airframe and crew.

An 'all-moving' tailplane was fitted. Below this, in the rear fuselage, was a large avionics bay. The B-1A was equipped with a comprehensive electronic countermeasures suite to provide some protection against Russian surface-to-air missiles and fighters. The B-1B relies on flying at low level for defence.

The first three prototypes carried the serials 74-0158, -0159 and -0160. The fourth aircraft, 76-0174, did not fly until 1979, after the B-1A programme was cancelled.

A blue ribbon decorated with stars and highlighting the Strategic Air Command emblem was wrapped around the nose.

Movable foreplanes either side of the nose below the cockpit were part of the Low-Altitude Ride Control (LARC) system. This was designed to make the often bumpy conditions during high-speed flight at low altitude more bearable.

Power for the B-1A was provided by four General Electric F101-GE-100 afterburning turbofans. This engine was test flown in such aircraft as the F-16 fighter and was the basis for the later F110 turbofan.

COMBAT DATA

MAXIMUM SPEED

The B-1A's Mach 2 capability was sacrificed in the B-1B in order to improve other performance features. Wing sweep was reduced and engine air intakes were simplified. Both types outperformed the ageing B-52, however.

B-1A   2351 km/h (1,458 m.p.h.)
B-1B LANCER 1324 km/h (820 m.p.h.)
B-52H STRATOFORTRESS   957 km/h (593 m.p.h.)

ARMAMENT

The B-1B was required to carry an even larger load than that of the B-1A and a wider variety of weapons. The B-52 can only carry about half this load, but over a greater range.

B-1A	B-1B LANCER	B-52H STRATOFORTRESS
52160 kg (114,752 lb.)	56699 kg (124,738 lb.)	22680 kg (49,896 lb.)

RANGE

The B-52's exceptional range is hard to better in an aircraft like the B-1. The B-52 was intended to carry a relatively light nuclear bombload over very long ranges. While the B-1A was short on range, the B-1B was an improvement.

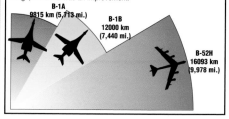

B-1A 9815 km (5,713 mi.)
B-1B 12000 km (7,440 mi.)
B-52H 16093 km (9,978 mi.)

USAF jet bomber prototypes

CONVAIR XB-46: Straight-winged, four-engined and the USAF's fastest bomber when it first flew, the B-46 did not reach production.

CONVAIR YB-60: Based on the B-36, the B-60 was Convair's 1950s bomber contender in the competition won by the Boeing B-52.

NORTH AMERICAN XB-70 VALKYRIE: Intended to replace the B-52, the Mach 3 XB-70 was cancelled in the late-1960s. Two were built.

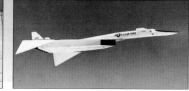

NORTHROP YRB-49A: One of the Northrop 'flying wing' family, the six-engined RB-49 would have been used as a reconnaissance bomber.

ROCKWELL/DASA

X-31

● Post-stall manoeuvrability research aircraft ● Amazingly agile

It may be futuristic and fast, but the streamlined X-31 is having an impact on aviation today because of its performance at low speeds. No matter how fast the aircraft, air combat almost invariably breaks down into low-speed turning matches. The X-31 Enhanced Fighter Manoeuvrability (EFM) aircraft uses new technology to exploit this low-velocity, high-angle manoeuvring.

▲ The X-31 does not look so very different from any of the current generation of delta-wing, canard-equipped superfighters, but it is exploring flight regimes that no other aircraft is equipped to enter.

PHOTO FILE

ROCKWELL/DASA X-31

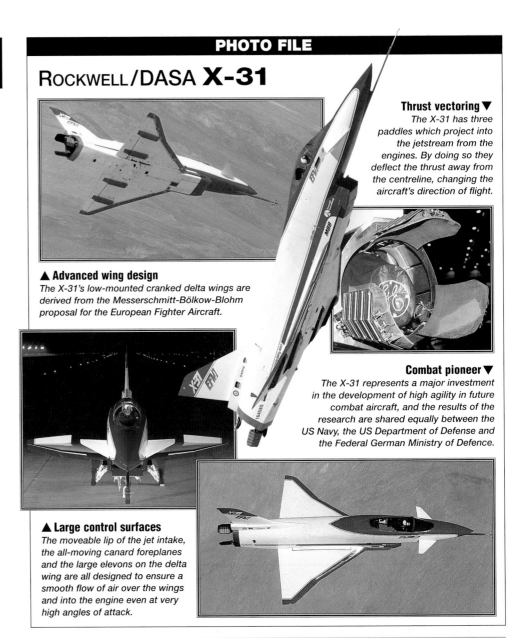

Thrust vectoring ▼
The X-31 has three paddles which project into the jetstream from the engines. By doing so they deflect the thrust away from the centreline, changing the aircraft's direction of flight.

▲ Advanced wing design
The X-31's low-mounted cranked delta wings are derived from the Messerschmitt-Bölkow-Blohm proposal for the European Fighter Aircraft.

Combat pioneer ▼
The X-31 represents a major investment in the development of high agility in future combat aircraft, and the results of the research are shared equally between the US Navy, the US Department of Defense and the Federal German Ministry of Defence.

▲ Large control surfaces
The moveable lip of the jet intake, the all-moving canard foreplanes and the large elevons on the delta wing are all designed to ensure a smooth flow of air over the wings and into the engine even at very high angles of attack.

FACTS AND FIGURES

➤ First flight of the X-31 occurred on 11 October 1990.

➤ The X-31 has repeatedly defeated the McDonnell Douglas F/A-18 Hornet in mock dogfights at close range.

➤ The X-31's German-designed clipped, double-delta wing makes extensive use of graphite epoxy materials.

➤ The thrust-vectoring system used on the X-31 is developed from a paddle system evaluated on an F-14 Tomcat spin test aircraft.

➤ The X-31 first reached its design limit of 70° of angle of attack on 18 September 1992 at NASA's Dryden Center in California.

PROFILE

Exploring the boundaries of flight

The X-31 is an aircraft intended to make future fighters more agile by exploring flight at high angles of attack. 'Angle of attack' is the engineer's term for the angle of an aircraft's body and wings relative to its flight path. At high angles of attack conventional aircraft stall, as their wings lose lift, airspeed drops and they become uncontrollable.

The X-31 uses three unique thrust vectoring paddles, which deflect its engine exhaust and can push the aircraft in any direction. Its canard foreplanes, coupled with a sophisticated digital flight computer, keep the aircraft under control. Thus the experimental X-31 can turn tighter and point at targets more quickly than any of today's front-line fighters.

It can achieve this super manoeuvrability at incredibly low speeds, speeds at which normal aircraft would fall from the sky. This is called 'post-stall manoeuvrability' and, while this is a capability planned for future fighters like America's F-22, only the X-31 has this ability today. At times the aircraft appears to defy the laws of nature and aerodynamics as it side-slips and pirouettes through the sky, but always under complete control.

The X-31 rolled out on 1 March 1990. An extensive test programme showed that it could more than hold its own in mock dogfights with the latest high-agility superfighters.

X-31A EFM

Type: single-seat research aircraft

Powerplant: one 53.38-kN (16,000-lb.) General Electric F404-GE-400 turbojet with a three-paddled vectored exhaust

Max speed: Mach 1.08 at sea level

Range: 380 km (240 mi.)

Service ceiling: 12384 m (40,000 ft.)

Weights: empty 5248 kg (11,400 lb.); loaded 7100 kg (15,900 lb.)

Capabilities: with its ability to manoeuvre at high angles, the X-31 can fly as slow as 45 km/h (28 m.p.h.) indicated air speed and turn in less than 100 m (330 ft.)

Dimensions:
span 7.37 m (23 ft. 10 in.)
length 13.25 m (43 ft. 4 in.)
height 4.51 m (14 ft. 7 in.)
wing area 21.02 m² (226 sq. ft.)

The X-31 can hold a 70° nose-up attitude while maintaining controlled forward flight.

X-31A EFM

Designed to meet the requirements of the joint US/German Enhanced Fighter Manoeuvrability programme, the X-31 is perhaps the most agile aircraft ever built.

The nose of the X-31, which on a combat jet would contain the radar, houses flight test equipment and air data sensors.

The ejection seat, instrument panel, stick and throttle are all standard equipment, taken from the McDonnell Douglas F/A-18 Hornet.

The basic structure of the X-31 is aluminium with some areas of composite honeycomb. The outer skin is almost entirely graphite epoxy, with titanium over the rear section of the fuselage.

X-31 is powered by a General Electric F404-GE-400 engine identical with those fitted to the F/A-18 Hornet. It delivers 53.38 kN (12,000 lb.) of thrust with afterburning.

The X-31's canard foreplanes are designed to control the flow of air over the wings and fuselage with the nose more than 50° from the horizontal while maintaining low-speed forward flight.

The landing gear is adapted from that of the Lockheed Martin F-16, although the wheels themselves came from a Cessna Citation and the tyres were originally Vought A-7 equipment.

COMBAT DATA

ANGLE OF ATTACK

The X-31's exceptional ability to point away from the line of flight is of great use in a short-range dogfight, enabling combat aircraft to take snap shots at targets directly above or to one side of the aircraft. The F-16 is more limited, not through aerodynamics but because its computer-aided controls restrict the pilot from making radical manoeuvres.

X-31 70°
MiG-29 'FULCRUM' 35°
F-16 FIGHTING FALCON 24°-26°

G-LIMITS

The X-31 is stressed to withstand nine times the force of gravity, which is standard for modern fighters since this is the maximum most human beings can take without blacking out. The MiG-29 is even tougher, although its pilots could not take such stress for more than a few seconds.

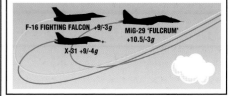

F-16 FIGHTING FALCON +9/-3g
MiG-29 'FULCRUM' +10.5/-3g
X-31 +9/-4g

Going beyond the 'stall barrier'

TURBOFAN POWER: In normal flight the X-31 uses the thrust from the General Electric F404-GE-400 engine like any other jet: the action of the hot gases, accelerated at great speed out of the jetpipe, cause a reaction in the aircraft, pushing it forward.

THRUST VECTORING: The three paddles act in concert to deflect the stream of hot gases by as much as 15° in any direction from the thrust line, forcing the aircraft to turn in the opposite direction.

BEATING THE STALL: The use of foreplanes, wing surfaces and vectored thrust mean that the X-31 is still creating lift and flying long after more conventional aircraft have stalled and fallen out of the sky.

ROCKWELL/NORTHROP
FLYING WINGS

● Radical design ● Jet bomber ● Cutting edge

▲ Although offering the potential of high speed coupled with long range, Jack Northrop's flying wings were continually hindered by lack of interest from the United States Air Force.

Recognising that an all-wing aircraft might represent the most efficient form of flying machine, Jack Northrop resigned from his job at Lockheed to form an independent company for the pursuit of his futuristic design dream. 'The Wing', the first of Northrop's designs, proved the concept's practicality when it took off in 1929. By the early 1950s, however, the idea appeared to have no future – until the B-2 appeared in 1988.

PHOTO FILE

ROCKWELL/NORTHROP FLYING WINGS

Tail-less fighter ▶
The XP-56 had an extremely troublesome flight testing phase, with this example overturning while taxiing, seriously injuring its pilot, John Myers.

▼ Ram fighter
Designed to attack enemy aircraft by knocking off their tails, the XP-79B did not see combat.

▼ Elegance in the air
The YB-49 was one of the most attractive aircraft ever to fly.

▲ Re-entry vehicles
The HL-10 Lifting Body was the highest-flying and fastest of the lifting body series and was used to test landing techniques that would be employed on NASA's Space Shuttle.

◀ Failed dream
Though more capable than the conventional bombers of the day the XB-35 Flying Wing was scrapped because of its unconventional design and the adoption of Convair's B-36 Peacemaker by SAC.

FACTS AND FIGURES

➤ Jack Northrop, creator of the 'flying wing' concept, originally worked for the Lockheed aircraft company.

➤ First flight of the N-1M 'Jeep' occurred on 3 July 1940; it was kept totally secret.

➤ A rocket powered flying wing, the MX-324, was constructed and test flown.

➤ The first variant of the XB-35 was fitted with contra-rotating propellers, but after problems these were replaced.

➤ An all-jet reconnaissance flying wing, the YRB-49, was developed from the bomber.

➤ No flying wings survived after the termination of the project.

PROFILE

Fifty years of flying wings

Back in the 1920s Jack Northrop considered that the Lockheed company's insistence on building aircraft with conventional wings and tail surfaces was too restrictive. He also thought that wooden construction was not the way for the future and used a metal stressed-skin design in his 'Wing'.

While even 'The Wing' was relatively conservative and retained small boom-mounted tail surfaces, the N-1M which followed it was a far more radical design and was far closer to being a pure flying wing. It was this aircraft which led, via the XB-35 and the YB-49, to today's Northrop/Grumman B-2A Spirit 'Stealth Bomber'.

A separate line of evolution led to the pusher-engined XP-56 fighters, the first flying in 1943 with a tiny dorsal fin. The second aircraft gained large dorsal and ventral surfaces, however, proving that Northrop's faith in the all-wing design had been misplaced in this case. The

jet-powered XP-79B which followed was also a bitter disappointment.

In addition, Northrop experimented with the MXP-1002 and MX-324 gliders, as well as the X-4 and HL-10 experimental aircraft. None of these became production types.

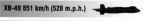

Left: On its dramatic entry into the public gaze the B-2A Spirit featured a span identical to that of its predecessor, the YB-49.

Above: With its bright yellow colour scheme the N-1M was unlike anything else in the skies. Protruding from the underside of the aircraft is the faired tailwheel.

XB-35

Type: strategic heavy bomber

Powerplant: four 2237-kW (3,000-hp.) Pratt & Whitney R-4360-17/-21 radial piston engines

Maximum speed: 629 km/h (390 m.p.h.)

Range: 16094 km (10,000 mi.)

Service ceiling: 12190 m (4,000 ft.)

Weights: empty 40624 kg (89,372 lb.) ; maximum take-off 94801 kg (208,562 lb.)

Armament: 20 12.7-mm machine-guns in seven turrets, up to 4536 kg (9,979 lb.) of bombs carried internally

Accommodation: seven crew

Dimensions:
span	52.43 m	(172 ft.)
length	16.18 m	(55 ft. 1 in.)
height	6.12 m	(20 ft.)
wing area	371m²	(3,991 sq. ft.)

XP-56 'BLACK BULLET'

The XP-56 would have provided the USAAF with a powerful attack aircraft, like no other fighter design of the period, but stability problems with this unique layout, saw the aircraft cancelled.

Visibility to the rear was extremely restricted for the pilot. The main worry for test-pilots was their chances of escape after an in-flight mishap. Many were concerned about being struck by the tail if they had to bail out.

Because of stability problems with the early versions of the XP-56 design, the fin height was increased in an effort to eliminate these problems, but handling was still hazardous.

Though not fitted, planned armament was for two 20-mm and four 12.7-mm guns in the nose, this would have allowed for an extremely concentrated and accurate field of fire to be achieved during combat.

238353

A conventional tricycle undercarriage was fitted to the aircraft, a feature of which was an exceptionally tall nose strut. The nose wheel was steerable.

The XP-56 also used a pioneering method in its construction. It was the first aircraft to be built entirely from thick magnesium alloy sections welded together in the Heliarc process.

The highly swept wings featured down-turned tips incorporating spoilers, which were normally recessed in the upper surfaces.

The XP-56 was powered by an impressive liquid-cooled sleeve-valve Pratt & Whitney H-2600. This engine drove a Curtiss Electric contra-rotating propeller. Later, a Double Wasp was installed.

Northrop's failed designs

■ **A-9A:** Developed to meet a requirement for a jet ground-attack aircraft for the USAF, the Northrop A-9A lost out to Fairchild's A-10 Thunderbolt II.

■ **YF-17 COBRA:** After losing out to the F-16 Fighting Falcon, the Cobra was developed into the F-18 Hornet with assistance from McDonnell Douglas, who by then owned Northrop.

■ **F-20 TIGERSHARK:** Trying to improve on the F-5 Freedom Fighter, Northrop developed the F-20 Tigershark. Though more capable than the F-16, no orders were received for the aircraft.

ACTION DATA

MAXIMUM SPEED

Despite its unique looks the XB-49 was not capable of high speed compared to more conventional bombers of the period. During this early period numerous design layouts were tested. The three-engined XB-51 was the fastest performer.

XB-49 851 km/h (528 m.p.h.)	
XB-46 877 km/h (545 m.p.h.)	
XB-51 1038 km/h (645 m.p.h.)	

OPERATIONAL RANGE

Range was the key factor that saw the development of the Flying Wing bombers. Capable of reaching targets at great distances with the minimum amount of fuel, the XB-49 offered a huge advantage over the XB-51, while the XB-46, with its huge wing span, was able to glide to a greater range still.

XB-49
4506 km
(2,800 mi.)

XB-51
2595 km
(1,612 mi.)

XB-46
4618 km
(2,870 mi.)

MAXIMUM TAKE-OFF WEIGHT

The huge span of the XB-49 also meant that the aircraft had one of the greatest take-off weights of any bomber of the period. Its ability to accommodate a vast bombload within its wings would have allowed the XB-49 to deliver a devastating attack.

XB-49
96617 kg
(212,557 lb.)

XB-46
3629 kg
(7,983 lb.)

XB-51
25367 kg
(55,807 lb.)

ROLLS-ROYCE

THRUST MEASURING RIG

● 'Flying Bedstead' ● Harrier forebear ● Vertical flight

By 1953, turbojet engine technology was sufficiently mature for engines to be able to produce more thrust than their installed weight. This effectively meant that they were able to lift themselves vertically, and Rolls-Royce designers were quick to recognise the significance of this characteristic for future military application. The company designed its Thrust Measuring Rig (TMR), universally known as the 'Flying Bedstead', to test the principle.

▲ The complex and unorthodox design of the 'Flying Bedstead' in no way reflected the benefits in the new dimension of vertical flight that the early test flights offered.

◀ **Proud heritage**
Harriers line up to demonstrate the developments made in the design of the vertical take-off fighter.

▼ **Up and away**
The test rig had to be capable of attaining a height of 15 m (49 ft.).

▼ **Tethered flight**
First flights of the rig were tethered while the handling characteristics were evaluated.

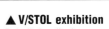

▲ **V/STOL exhibition**
Rebuilt for display purposes, the sole surviving test rig is exhibited in the FAA Museum at Yeovilton.

◀ **Vertical developments**
The Shorts SC.1 was a vast improvement over the test rig.

FACTS AND FIGURES

➤ The Thrust Measuring Rig made its first tethered flight on 9 July 1953 from Hucknall in England.

➤ Flight duration was restricted to only 15 minutes because of the limited fuel load.

➤ Two thrust rigs were constructed, both of which crashed during testing.

➤ Captain Ronnie Shepherd piloted the first free flight on 3 August 1954, achieving the first vertical take-off without rotors.

➤ Wg Cdr H.G.F. Larson was killed when he collided with a gantry during testing.

➤ The last flight of the Thrust Measuring Rig was on 27 November 1957.

PROFILE

Rolls-Royce's 'Flying Bedstead'

Aircraft designers and military planners had always been aware of the benefits of a combat aircraft capable of taking off vertically. Helicopters were suitable for a number of roles, but were limited in terms of performance and flexibility.

Having gained a great deal of jet engine experience during the closing stages of World War II and in the immediate post-war years, Rolls-Royce was at the forefront of engine technology and ideally placed to exploit the Vertical Take-Off and Landing (VTOL) potential of the turbojet.

The TMR featured two inward-facing Nene turbojets mounted within a simple unenclosed rig. Each jet exhaust was angled downward through 90° and divided into two equally sized pipes which directed the jet efflux vertically toward the ground from either side of the rig. This complicated arrangement of split jetpipes provided a considerable safety margin, since, in the event of a single engine failure, thrust was still provided on both sides. This safety feature was appreciated by the pilot, who sat in a crude seat on top of the rig.

Pitch control and a limited degree of directional control were provided by engine

bleed-air outlets mounted at the end of four long pipes arranged in a cruciform layout, protruding from the sides of the rig.

First flown from the Rolls-Royce Flight Test Centre in 1953, the TMR proved entirely successful. Although it did not have the thrust-vectoring capabilities of the later Pegasus-powered P.1127 and Harrier designs, it must be considered to have been a vital part of their successful development.

Right: Preparing for another test flight from Hucknall, the pilot waits while final checks are completed. Prominent in this view are the puffer pipes which controlled pitch, roll and yaw, allowing precise manoeuvres to be accomplished.

The pilot was seated above above the engines and was presented with rudimentary flight controls. Protection was limited and one pilot lost his life during flight testing.

THRUST MEASURING RIG

In the early 1950s Rolls-Royce, together with the Royal Aircraft Establishment, investigated the possibility of controlled vertical jet flight. The 'Flying Bedstead' paved the way for a whole new era of flight.

Thrust Measuring Rig

Type: experimental research aircraft

Powerplant: two 18.02-kN (4,054-lb.-thrust) Rolls-Royce Nene 101-IV turbojet engines coupled to one jet outlet

Maximum speed: 21 km/h (13 m.p.h.)

Endurance: 15 minutes

Fuel load: two 864-litre (228-gal.) fuel tanks

Service ceiling: 15 m (50 ft.)

Weights: 3404 kg (7,489 lb.) fully fuelled

A yaw vane was mounted on the front outrigger which fed the primitive flight instruments with data such as altitude, thrust and air speed. Controls for the pilot consisted of a control column and rudder pedals which enabled the rig to turn.

Two Rolls-Royce Nene 101-IVs powered the rig, and were mounted horizontally opposed to nullify gyroscopic torque. These engines remained the standard throughout the test phase.

The requirement for the test rig called for a thrust-to-weight ratio of 1.25 to 1. It had to be capable of carrying sufficient fuel for 15 minutes' testing, and be able to remain off the ground for at least five minutes without overheating.

Compared with its contemporaries in France and America, Britain's flying test rig was without question the most ungainly, but its achievements demonstrated that VTOL flight was possible.

The exhaust was directed downwards and the jet pipes were positioned near each other to minimise the effects of rolling and pitching. Although modifications were made throughout the developmental flights, this arrangement remained unchanged.

Control of pitch and yaw was achieved by air tapped from the compressors being fed to the puffer pipes at the corner of the rig. Nine per cent of the compressor delivery air was bled off one of the engines.

Problems were encountered initially with the undercarriage structure. The oleo legs did not extend evenly at first, resulting in landings that were particularly hazardous during early developmental flights.

EARLY VTOL FLIGHT

Designed in response to a US Navy request, the Ryan X-13 tested the feasibility of building a pure-jet VTOL fighter. It was first flown on 28 May 1956 by test pilot Pete Girard. Later flights proved the concept of the aircraft. The X-13 used a platform from which to launch from and recover to upon completion of its mission. Although proving the concept of VTOL flight, the aircraft required the abilities of a test pilot to recover to its platform. The only failing of the X-13 was that, for its time, it was too complex; simpler methods of VTOL were available.

Company representatives and members of the Royal Air Force watch another test flight of the Thrust Measuring Rig from Hucknall. Although never intended to enter service, the TMR paved the way for controlled vertical take-off and landing using jet engines. Later developmental aircraft such as the Short SC.1 were of a more conventional layout. Those later types relied on the proving trials made in earlier days which ensured that government backing would be forthcoming for future VTOL fighters.

Rolls-Royce testbeds

■ **HEINKEL He 70G:** A Rolls-Royce Kestrel V, offered improved performance over the German BMW-engined aircraft.

■ **GLOSTER METEOR:** The world's first propeller-turbine aircraft was powered by Rolls-Royce Trents. Fins were added to the tailplane.

■ **AVRO LANCASTRIAN:** Two Nene jet engines were tested, allowing the Merlins to be stopped. This was the world's first jet 'airliner'.

■ **AVRO VULCAN:** A Vulcan conducts icing trials on the Olympus engine that would be installed on the supersonic Concorde airliner.

RUTAN

VARIEZE/LONG-EZ

● Advanced construction ● Fully aerobatic ● Cheaper than a car

Aircraft for everyone: that is the goal of California inventor Burt Rutan, maker of unorthodox glassfibre lightplanes which can be constructed by amateurs and flown by ordinary people. Since 1968 Rutan has given the world the VariViggen, VariEze, Long-EZ and Quickie. All are affordable, unconventional, and easy to construct and operate.

▲ Burt Rutan's designs use advanced technology at astonishingly low cost and are highly original. The VariEze is fairly typical: a high-performance ship, appealing to the eye and offering simplicity with great strength.

RUTAN VARIEZE/LONG-EZ

◀ More space
The Long-EZ is an improved and enlarged VariEze, and has an astonishing maximum range of more than 3200 km (2,000 mi.).

▲ Foreplane control
Foreplanes in place of tailplanes offer a pilot considerable low-speed handling advantages. Aircraft like the Quickie do not stall at slow speeds; they simply 'parachute' downwards without changing attitude, and a touch on the throttle has them flying again.

▲ Viking Dragonfly
The pioneering VariEze influenced a whole generation of designers. In 1980 the Viking company introduced the Dragonfly, a highly successful two-seater which could be built for less than $12,000.

▼ Quickie
Burt Rutan has helped several companies with designs. The Quickie, which first flew in 1977, is an easy-to-build kit which bears the unmistakable Rutan stamp.

▲ VariViggen
Named after the Swedish fighter, which was one of the first to use a canard configuration, the VariViggen is one of the most manoeuvrable aircraft ever to have flown, able to slow-roll at speeds where other aircraft would stall.

FACTS AND FIGURES

➤ Some Rutan homebuilds use a sidestick controller, like the F-16 jet fighter.

➤ The first VariEze, the Model 31, was built in a 10-week period in 1975 and performed perfectly on its first flight.

➤ Rutan's Defiant is a bigger, four-seat, twin-engine craft.

➤ The Popular Flying Association gives advice on flying and building VariEzes.

➤ The Long-EZ holds world distance records for homebuilds; in 1981 it flew 7725 km (4,800 mi.) non-stop.

➤ The prototype Defiant reached an altitude of 8535 metres (28,000 ft.) during trials.

PROFILE

Planes for the people

The Rutan VariEze, the best known in a series of fine lightplanes designed by Burt Rutan, first flew in 1975. From the start it enabled ordinary enthusiasts to build and fly an exciting small aircraft which incorporates glassfibre composites and other cutting-edge technology.

The maker of the VariEze provides homebuilders with all raw materials and most component parts of this recreational aircraft, including the Plexiglas canopy, moulded glassfibre nosewheel, two- or four-cylinder lightweight piston engine and glassfibre cowling.

With little more than written directions and a spirit of adventure, almost anyone can transform drawings into an actual VariEze aircraft that is able to fling itself around the skies at almost 300 km/h (185 mi.).

Not everybody is ready for the homebuilt revolution, however, and the radical shape of the Rutan VariEze still seems startling to many. But to those ready for a voyage of discovery, constructing a VariEze is a realistic undertaking which can cost less than the price of a mid-sized saloon car.

Because Rutan designs are sold in kit form, they have been built all over the world. This VariEze is from Switzerland.

QUICKIE

The Quickie Aircraft Corporation of Mojave, California, asked Burt Rutan to use his VariEze experience in helping them to design an advanced composite aircraft for homebuilders.

The foreplane has marked anhedral – sloping downwards from the wingroots. The main wing, by contrast, has a small dihedral; it slopes upwards.

All flight surfaces are formed from glass-reinforced plastic (GRP) spars within a shaped core of low-density rigid foam. The outer skin is covered in a smooth layer of GRP.

A one-piece side-hinged canopy covers the single-seat cockpit. The Q2 has a wider cockpit, seating two side by side.

The Quickie's backward-sweeping tailplane is of similar construction to the wings, and is equipped with a single narrow-chord rudder.

The original Quickie was powered by a two-cylinder four-stroke engine delivering 13.5 kW (17 hp.) to a wooden two-blade fixed-pitch propeller.

Fixed undercarriage mainwheels are mounted in swept fairings at the tips of the downward-sloping foreplanes.

The Quickie's fuselage is of semi-monocoque construction. The banana-shaped body is formed from 25 mm (1 in.) of foam, surfaced by a thin layer of GRP for strength.

Built to a standard tailwheel layout, the Quickie has the rear wheel projecting to the rear and continuing the downward line of the fuselage.

VariEze Model 33

Type: two-seat sporting aircraft

Powerplant: one 74.5-kW (100-hp.) Continental O-200-B flat-four engine in the rear fuselage driving a two-blade pusher propeller

Max speed: cruising 313 km/h (195 m.p.h.); economy cruise 265 km/h (164 m.p.h.)

Stalling speed: 90 km/h (56 m.p.h.)

Take-off run: 275 m (900 ft.)

Range: 1126 km (700 mi.) at 75 per cent power; 1368 km (850 mi.) with max fuel at economy cruising speed

Service ceiling: 6705 m (22,000 ft.)

Weights: loaded 601 kg (1,320 lb.)

Dimensions:
span	7.96 m (26 ft. 11 in.)
length	5.12 m (16 ft. 9 in.)
height	2.40 m (7 ft. 7 in.)
wing area	7.62 m² (82 sq. ft.)

RUTAN SPECIALS

RUTAN MODEL 151 ARES

Burt Rutan was involved in design studies for the US Army to produce a low-cost battlefield aircraft, and used that experience in the design of the ARES. The name stands for Agile Response Effective Support and describes a lightweight jet armed with a 25-mm cannon, which has potential for anti-helicopter, close support, border patrol, drug enforcement and forward air control work.

BEECH STARSHIP

The Beech Starship takes all of Burt Rutan's characteristic design features and applies them to a business aircraft. The result is one of the most advanced and sophisticated private aircraft in the world: the Starship has jet-like performance and handling with the economy of a twin turboprop. The aft-mounted engines and pusher propellers give the eight passengers and two crew an extremely smooth ride.

A tradition of mould-breaking

■ **RUTAN DEFIANT:** In its first year, 150 sets of plans of the Defiant four-seater were sold to homebuilders.

■ **VIKING DRAGONFLY:** The Viking Aircraft Company's Dragonfly cruises at up to 275 km/h (170 m.p.h.).

■ **QUICKIE Q2:** The original Quickie was a single-seater. The Q2 is a side-by-side two-seater introduced in 1979.

■ **AT3:** Built by Scaled Composites, the AT3 is a 14-seat advanced-technology tactical transport.

■ **VARIVIGGEN:** Very easy to fly, the VariViggen can barrel-roll safely at speeds as low as 148 km/h (90 m.p.h.).

RUTAN

VOYAGER

● Ultra-long-range experimental craft ● Non-stop around the world

V oyager's glorious adventure enthralled millions in December 1986, when for the first time a crew of two pilots travelled around our entire planet without pausing or refuelling. With its bizarre shape, modern lightweight construction and enormous fuel capacity, this amazing aircraft was the right machine for a marathon endurance test. Its pilots were cramped but courageous throughout their incredible journey.

▲ Jeanna Yeager and Dick Rutan were the two pilots of the Voyager for its incredible globe-circling flight. Dick's brother Burt was the designer of the amazing contraption.

RUTAN VOYAGER

◄ Voyager pilot
Dick Rutan not only co-piloted the Voyager on its round-the-world flight, but also made the type's first flight on 22 June 1984. To prepare for the global flight, Rutan and Yeager flew a 111-hour warm-up.

Flying fuel tank ▶
The layout of the Voyager was set by the need to carry more than 4500 litres (1,200 gal.) of fuel. Every available space in the wings, booms and fuselage was used for tanks.

▲ Flexible wing
The wingtip was so flexible that it moved up and down through 3 metres (10 ft.).

▼ Voyager meets the press
This was the public roll-out at Mojave airport. The amazing shape of the aircraft included winglets, but these were damaged on take-off on the record-breaking flight and were deliberately shaken off by some vigorous manoeuvring.

▲ Safe return
After nine days, three minutes and 44 seconds, Rutan and Yeager landed Voyager at Edwards AFB to a tumultuous reception.

FACTS AND FIGURES

➤ Ninety per cent of Voyager's construction is of light but strong graphite fibre.

➤ B-52 Stratofortress bombers, the only other non-stop around-the-world fliers, needed inflight-refuelling.

➤ One of Voyager's fuel tanks is 9.04 m (30 ft.) long, longer than some small aircraft.

➤ Voyager carried more than four tonnes of fuel when it set off around the world.

➤ Voyager's wings scraped the ground on take-off, but the pilots jettisoned the damaged winglets and pressed on.

➤ Voyager is now on display in the Smithsonian museum in Washington.

PROFILE

Non-stop Voyager

Voyager pilots Dick Rutan and Jeanna Yeager lived inside a cocoon of futuristic graphite for nine days in December 1986 when they guided this fantastic aircraft 40252 km (25,011 mi.) around the world. Like seafaring explorers of the past, they had to rely on skill and daring.

Their strange aircraft was a marvel of shrewd design and 21st century technology. For its purpose of going higher and further than any flying machine before it, the Voyager needed

composite material for very light weight, a capacity for a giant-sized volume of fuel, and a graceful, sailplane-like shape which would allow it to be carried on its journey by the air and the wind.

The courageous pilots conquered dangerous weather, including Typhoon 'Marge' in the Pacific early in the flight. They used several methods of navigation to take their

When it lifted off for its around-the-world flight, Voyager used more than 4330 m (14,200 ft.) of the 4570-m (15,000-ft.) runway.

remarkable route around the Earth. After 216 hours in the air, they were greeted by an extraordinary welcome and by world acclaim.

One of the small wingtip winglets was lost on take-off, so the other was shaken loose in flight without incident.

Voyager's wings were like those of a high-performance sailplane. The main spar was solid Magnamite graphite composite, covered with a Hexcel paper honeycomb and skinned with Magnamite sheets and a composite of aramid/epoxy/graphite.

VOYAGER

Voyager was an aircraft built for a single task: to fly non-stop around the world. Designed by Burt Rutan and flown by his brother Dick and co-pilot Jeanna Yeager, it achieved its purpose in December 1986.

Voyager was powered by two Teledyne Continental piston engines, one of which was generally shut down for maximum economy during cruising flight.

The rear engine was slightly less powerful than the front, delivering 82 kW (110 hp.) against 97 kW (130 hp.). The propeller was fitted with a brake to stop it windmilling in the front engine's slipstream when in single-engine mode.

Voyager had two vertical fins, which were mounted on the end of the tailbooms.

The landing gear was fully retractable, but to save weight there was no power assistance: the wheels were pulled or wound up manually by the crew.

The cabin was just large enough for one pilot to sit to starboard while the off-duty crew member stretched out on a bunk alongside.

On the ground, the tips of Voyager's fuel-laden wings flexed nearly three metres downwards from their flight positions.

Voyager's fuselage and tailbooms were of Magnamite graphite/Hexcel honeycomb composite construction.

Only one of the two tailfins was fitted with a rudder.

N269VA

Voyager

Type: special mission (around-the-world, non-stop) aircraft

Powerplant: one 82-kW (110-hp.) Teledyne Continental Motors Voyager 200 liquid-cooled engine at the rear of the fuselage and one standard 97-kW (130-hp.) Continental Model O-240 air-cooled engine at the front

Normal speed: 193 km/h (120 m.p.h.); with tailwind 238 km/h (148 m.p.h.)

Range: 41840 km (26,000 mi.)

Weights: empty 842 kg (1,850 lb.); world flight take-off weight 4472 kg (9,900 lb.)

Dimensions:
span	33.83 m (111 ft.)
length	7.86 m (25 ft. 6 in.)
height	3.18 m (10 ft. 4 in.)
wing area	30.10 m² (324 sq. ft.)

WINGS AROUND THE WORLD

DOUGLAS WORLD CRUISER

In the early days of flight, the US Army planned a spectacular trip around the world to publicise military aviation. Four Douglas DT-2s were modified as Douglas World Cruisers, with excess equipment removed and extra tanks fitted. On 6 April 1924, the flight took off from Seattle on a route which would take them via Alaska across the Pacific, through Japan, China, Southeast Asia, India, the Middle East, Europe, Iceland and Greenland. One aircraft crashed in Alaska and one was forced to ditch in the Atlantic, but the two survivors completed the route on 28 September. The flight had lasted 175 days, with a total of 371 hours 11 minutes actual flying time.

BOEING B-52 STRATOFORTRESS

The US Air Force made the first non-stop flight around the world. On 2 March 1949 a Boeing B-50 fitted with the newly developed aerial refuelling capability completed a 94-hour flight which had required the services of six tankers. Eight years later mid-air refuelling had become commonplace, and three eight-engined B-52B bombers completed the journey in 45 hours and 19 minutes. They had flown 39146 km (24,270 miles) at an average speed of 860 km/h (530 m.p.h.), refuelling several times en route.

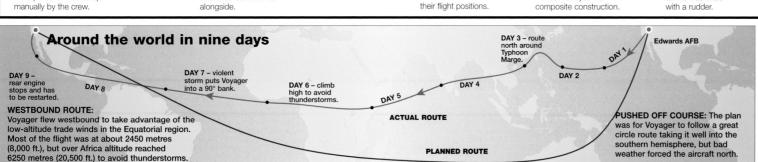

Around the world in nine days

DAY 9 – rear engine stops and has to be restarted.

DAY 8

DAY 7 – violent storm puts Voyager into a 90° bank.

DAY 6 – climb high to avoid thunderstorms.

DAY 5

DAY 4

DAY 3 – route north around Typhoon Marge.

DAY 2

DAY 1

Edwards AFB

ACTUAL ROUTE

PLANNED ROUTE

WESTBOUND ROUTE: Voyager flew westbound to take advantage of the low-altitude trade winds in the Equatorial region. Most of the flight was at about 2450 metres (8,000 ft.), but over Africa altitude reached 6250 metres (20,500 ft.) to avoid thunderstorms.

PUSHED OFF COURSE: The plan was for Voyager to follow a great circle route taking it well into the southern hemisphere, but bad weather forced the aircraft north.

RYAN

X-13

● Vertical take-off ● Jet-propelled ● Naval interest

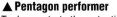
▲ Opening a new
era of flying manoeuvres, one of the
Ryan X-13s on a test flight is recorded by
cameramen. The US Navy was extremely
interested in the future of VTOL fighters.

The Ryan X-13 Vertijet was a 'tail sitter',
designed to take off vertically – and do
away with dependence on airfields and
runways. The X-13 was a research aircraft
(published reports of an XF-109 fighter version
are incorrect), but as a test vehicle it was able
to advance scientific knowledge. If the US Air
Force had proceeded with a vertically-
launched fighter, data provided by the X-13
would have been invaluable.

RYAN X-13

▼ Honourable retirement
Having survived the flight
test programme, one of the
X-13s was displayed at the
USAF Museum.

▲ Temporary undercarriage
To test the flight characteristics of the X-13, the aircraft was equipped
with a fixed tricycle undercarriage for early flights.

Conventional flight ▶
Ryan engineers watch a high-
speed pass by the small X-13.
Test pilots found the aircraft to be
extremely responsive in flight.

◀ Delicate touch
Test pilots required all their
skill to manoeuvre away
from the vertical support rig
used in the programme. To
assist in this delicate
operation, the pilot was
given a swivelling seat which
allowed him to view the rig.

▲ Pentagon performer
To demonstrate the potential of
vertical flight, Ryan flew its X-13 in
front of a specially assembled
group of defence officials.

FACTS AND FIGURES

➤ Two X-13s were completed by Ryan and
were allocated Air Force serial numbers
54-1619 and 54-1620.

➤ Although initially a naval contract, the
project was taken over by the USAF.

➤ Ryan installed a British Rolls-Royce Avon
turbojet in the X-13.

➤ During its demonstration to Pentagon
officials, the X-13 retraced the course
flown by Orville Wright.

➤ Total expenditure on the X-13 programme
amounted to $9.4 million.

➤ The first vertical flight took place on
11 April 1957 at Edwards AFB.

Vertical flying in the Vertijet

Ryan's X-13 was designed to explore the feasibility of pure-jet vertical take-off and landing operations. Ryan built two aircraft.

The X-13 was an 'X-plane', built to evaluate the concept of vertical flight at a bargain price. The pilot's seat, for example, was borrowed from a Navion civil aircraft. In the VTOL mode the X-13 employed no landing gear but instead had two small bumper skids on the fuselage and a retractable nose wheel.

After flying conventionally, test pilot Peter Girard flew the X-13 on the world's first jet-powered transition from vertical to horizontal flight on 28 November 1956. Many subsequent flights were made

while the aircraft was still tethered to the ground.

The two X-13s proved that VTOL flight on jet thrust alone was both feasible and practical. The ease with which the aircraft routinely transitioned from vertical to horizontal attitude, and back again, left little question of the value of the concept. Though they never led to an operational warplane, the X-13 test and evaluation aircraft stretched the borders of the flight envelope farther than ever.

Right: Pioneering for the period, the Ryan X-13 created immense interest wherever it performed. The aircraft provided a huge amount of data for future VTOL aircraft.

Below: To allow the pilot access to the cockpit of the X-13, a specially devised platform was utilised.

During every flight a cameraman was present to record the manoeuvres of the X-13. To aid filming, large reference markings were painted onto the aircraft.

X-13 VERTIJET

Despite its small size Ryan's X-13 proved to be one of the most successful experimental aircraft developed in America. It provided a host of data for future VTOL designers.

Ryan built only two X-13 Vertijets. Both survived the the extensive flight test programme. Eventually, one example was retired to the USAF Museum in Ohio.

A unique feature within the cockpit of the X-13 was a swivelling ejection seat. During early test flights the canopy was removed from the aircraft as a safety precaution for the pilot.

To allow the X-13 to attach itself to the vertical test rig, a large hook was positioned on the underside of the forward fuselage. This connected to a wire upon landing.

To allow pilots to explore the level flight characteristics of the X-13 a temporary tricycle undercarriage was fitted. After a short test period, this was removed.

To assist directional stability during vertical flight manoeuvres, small winglets were attached to the outer wings. These greatly improved handling at low speeds and during the transition stage.

U.S. AIR FORCE 41619

Ryan X-13 VERTIJET

X-13 Vertijet

Type: tail-sitting VTOL research aircraft

Powerplant: one 44.46-kN (10,000-lb.-thrust) Rolls Royce Avon RA.29 Mk 49 axial flow non-afterburning turbojet, allowing for 30 minutes of flight at full military power

Maximum speed: 777 km/h (482 m.p.h.) in level flight at optimum altitude

Range: 308 km (190 mi.)

Service ceiling: 9144 m (30,000 ft.)

Weights: empty 2419 kg (5,322 lb.); maximum vertical take-off 3317 kg (7,297 lb.)

Accommodation: one pilot seated on a swivelling ejection seat

Dimensions:

span	6.40 m (21 ft.)
length	7.14 m (23 ft. 5 in.)
height	4.63 m (15 ft. 2 in.)
wing area	17.74 m² (191 sq. ft.)

VERTICAL VISIONS

CONVAIR XFY-1: The product of a competition between Lockheed and Convair, the XFY-1 utilised a massive Allison engine driving a contra-rotating propeller. The Convair design was stubbier than the Lockheed offering, with large delta wings allied to massive upper and lower vertical surfaces in a cross-shaped layout. The project was eventually cancelled in 1955 because of handling problems.

SNECMA C.450-01 COLEOPTERE: This was an ambitious attempt to develop the technology for a compact combat aeroplane with very high performance. In 1952 this French company acquired the rights to the annular-wing concept pioneered by Zborowski. First flying in May 1959 using deflection of the jet exhaust for control, the aircraft proved too radical and the project was cancelled.

Rising stars in vertical flight

BELL X-14: Conceived as a research tool for the evaluation of jet-deflection for VTOL applications, the type was intended only for low-speed trials. It was therefore designed with an open cockpit and fixed undercarriage.

LOCKHEED XV-4A: Originating from a US Army Transportation Research Command contract for an experimental aircraft, the XV-4A achieved only limited success.

SHORT SC.1: This was the first fixed-wing VTOL aircraft built in the UK, and was produced as a flight platform for the newly developed RB.108 lift turbojet. The aircraft was an ungainly type with a low-set wing and fixed tricycle landing gear.

RYAN

XV-5A VERTIFAN

● Escort fighter ● Lift-fan engines ● V/STOL research aircraft

▲ In a new era of flight characteristics, the Ryan XV-5A was seen to present the United States Army with a highly capable aircraft. Roles envisaged were SAR and helicopter escort.

A high performance jet aircraft that was able to fly at more than 804 km/h (500 m.p.h.), yet hover, manoeuvre, land and take off like a helicopter was to many just a pipe-dream. But to the Ryan aircraft company all seemed possible with their XV-5A. Though retaining a conventional fighter configuration, the XV-5A, was anything but. The US Army showed great interest in the Vertifan as a potential SAR and attack aircraft.

PHOTO FILE

RYAN XV-5A VERTIFAN

▼ Test flight twins
The two developmental XV-5A Vertifans are seen undergoing routine maintenance between test flights at Edwards AFB.

▲ Rescue role
Replacing the helicopter in the search-and-rescue role, the XV-5A Vertifan removed the hazardous down-draft.

▼ Flying on fans
The two fans mounted in the wings were supplemented by a small extra fan positioned in the nose to help control the aircraft.

▲ Rising star
With airflow directed directly downward through the open vents in the wings, an early Ryan XV-5A lifts off to begin another series of handling tests. Pilots found the small jet to be highly responsive to control inputs.

Ryan in retirement ▶
Having proved unsuitable for US Army operations, one of the XV-5A Vertifans was passed to NASA pilots for further evaluation of the flight characteristics of the concept.

FACTS AND FIGURES

➤ The primary mission of the XV-5A Vertifan was to provide an armed escort for transport helicopters.

➤ A specialised casualty evacuation variant was proposed but not developed.

➤ For SAR test flights an instrumented mannequin was used as the 'survivor'.

➤ When in the hover, downward jet wash was very dissipated and so did not affect personnel underneath the Vertifan.

➤ Rescue operations were conducted over water and the desert.

➤ Ryan's other V/STOL aircraft was the jet powered X-13 Vertijet.

PROFILE

Flying on fan-power

Airfields have long been prime targets for enemy bombers. Their large concrete runways can easily be bombed, rendering conventional jet aircraft useless. It has long been a dream of aviation engineers to produce an aircraft that can land like a helicopter and fly like a jet.

One of the most innovative attempts to meet this requirement came from the Ryan aircraft company. Even though lift-fan propulsion was still in its infancy, Ryan mounted two fan engines in the wings of their small XV-5A Vertifan. Powered by two J85 turbojets and using the process of deflecting the jet exhaust, air was sucked through the jet inlet and diverted through the wing fans. These produced a column of air that would allow the XV-5A to hover like a helicopter. To return to normal flight the exhaust was switched through the twin tail-pipes, allowing the XV-5A to fly away.

Despite its obvious potential the Ryan XV-5A Vertifan failed to

Above: This publicity shot produced by Ryan demonstrates the capabilities of the Vertifan.

fulfll the dream for the US Army. The Vertifan ended its days as a research aircraft for NASA.

Below: With its lightweight tricycle undercarriage extended and all doors open, the XV-5A Vertifan hovers on fan-power alone. Ryan test-pilots were able to accomplish precision landings with the XV-5A.

XV-5A Vertifan

Type: VTOL fan-powered research aircraft

Powerplant: two 11.8-kN (2,655-lb.-thrust) J85 General Electric turbojet engines

Maximum speed: 804 km/hr (498 m.p.h.) (est)

Endurance: 2 hr 25 min for SAR mission

Initial climb rate: 670 m/min (2,200 f.p.m.)

Combat radius: 555 km (344 mi.)

Range: 2007 km (1,244 mi.)

Service ceiling: 12192 m (40,000 ft.)

Weights: empty 3199 kg (7,038 lb.); take-off 5669 kg (12,472 lb.)

Accommodation: two crew, one rescued airman

Dimensions: span 9.38 m (30 ft. 9 in.)
length 13.92 m (45 ft. 8 in.)
height 4.20 m (13 ft. 9 in.)

XV-5A VERTIFAN

Combining the performance of a jet fighter and abilities of a helicopter, the Ryan XV-5A Vertifan had enormous potential for the US Army but, despite this, remained an experimental test aircraft.

Positioned within the nose was a small auxiliary fan used for pitch and trim control. This was accomplished by a series of moveable louvres being positioned above the intake to direct the airflow.

The two crewmen of the Vertifan were seated side-by-side. A rescue variant of the Vertifan was to include an extra position behind the pilots to seat any downed pilot recovered during a mission.

Positioned on top of the fuselage were the two J85 turbojet engines. The jet exhaust from these engines could be diverted into the fans when the Vertifan was in the hover or re-directed out of the two tail-pipes for conventional flight manoeuvres.

A large high-set horizontal 't-tail' was programmed to adjust pitch trim during the critical transition from fan-supported flight to wing-supported flight. The elevators provided longitudinal control forces during conventional flight, although the pilot had the option to override the programme and adjust the elevator trim himself.

During early test flights a nose-mounted instrument boom was installed on the Vertifan. This provided data on the flight characteristics and handling of the Vertifan for the Ryan ground engineers who were monitoring all the flights.

One large fan was situated in each wing of the Vertifan. In forward flight these were covered by doors.

The two small jet-pipes were positioned on the lower side of the fuselage. Each jet-pipe was equipped with a thrust spoiler to enable the pilot to use full power at reduced flying speeds. This allowed transition from fan-supported flight to forward flight at full power.

STRAIGHT-UP SOLDIERS

LOCKHEED: Originating from a US Army request for a light transport aircraft, the Lockheed VZ-10 used a jet deflection principle. The exhaust was blown through 20 rows of nozzles within the fuselage, allowing the small aircraft to take off and land vertically. The first flight was made in July 1962 but after numerous test flights the programme was suspended.

RYAN: One of the most innovative aircraft programmes ever undertaken was also one of the most successful for Ryan. Investigating the principle of tail-sitting aircraft from 1947, Ryan undertook the construction of the small delta-winged X-13 Vertijet in the early 1950s. First flying in December 1955 the X-13 Vertijet operated from a special platform which allowed the aircraft to be raised to the vertical position for take-off. Although never entering service, the X-13 provided valuable data.

Revolutionary Ryans

■ **FR-1 FIREBALL:** Using both a piston engine and a booster turbojet, the Fireball was built in limited quantities.

■ **FLEX WING:** Hailed as a new mobility concept for the US Army, the Flex Wing was seen as a future transport aircraft.

■ **VERTIPLANE:** One of a number of experimental aircraft for the STOL transport role, it used an all-moving-wing layout.

SAUNDERS-ROE

SR.53

● Experimental rocket-powered interceptor ● Outstanding performance

▲ After serving as a testbed, the original SR.53 was passed to RAF Cosford. Restored to original condition, the aircraft was placed on display in 1981.

One of many fighter prototypes with combined powerplants built during the 1950s, the SR.53 displayed the dazzling performance for which designers were desperate. Combining a rocket and a turbojet with an advanced delta wing, it seemed to be the way to higher speeds. But development was protracted, and marred by a fatal crash, and as better jet engines were produced in the late 1950s, the mixed power concept fell out of favour.

SAUNDERS-ROE SR.53

▼ **Rocket engine**
An unusual aircraft, the SR.53 could have been a fantastic interceptor – but for government interference.

▲ **Unique propulsion**
A small, graceful aircraft, the SR.53 was powered by a de Havilland Viper turbojet and a Spectre rocket motor. Main propulsion came from the latter, with the low-powered turbojet being used for take-off and for returning to base.

▼ **First flight**
This aircraft, XD145, was the first of two prototypes to take to the air. It is seen here in the spring of 1957, prior to performing its first flight piloted by Sqn Ldr Booth.

▲ **Sad finale**
When the second SR.53 was destroyed in 1958, the first aircraft was grounded and never flew again. By that stage, interest in the programme had waned.

◄ **Missiles**
Two de Havilland Firestreak missiles could be carried by the SR.53, though they were seldom seen during early flight testing.

FACTS AND FIGURES

➤ The idea for the SR.53 stemmed from great Allied interest in the Messerschmitt Me 163 rocket fighter of World War II.

➤ First flight of the SR.53 took place on 16 May 1957.

➤ Two SR.53s (XD145 and XD151) were completed. A third aircraft was not built.

➤ The second prototype was destroyed in a fatal accident during take-off on 15 June 1958.

➤ XD145 is currently displayed in the Aerospace Museum at RAF Cosford.

➤ A larger derivative, the SR.177, was proposed, but the project was cancelled.

PROFILE

Saro's rocket fighter

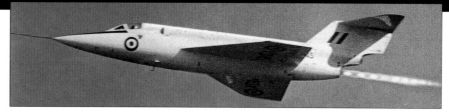

Above: Seen just after take-off, the first SR.53 displays the characteristic flame efflux from the Spectre rocket.

Like the MiG Ye-50 and the Sud-Ouest Trident, the SR.53 was a hybrid powerplant fighter concept using a rocket and a turbojet. Inspired by the advanced Me 163 rocket-engined fighter used by the Luftwaffe, the SR.53 was developed in response to a request for a rocket-powered short-range defence aircraft, with the emphasis on low cost and simplicity. Saunders-Roe decided to add a turbojet engine to the original concept, opting for the new Viper engine as a supplement to the Spectre rocket, giving the aircraft the capability of returning to base under power. Armament was also advanced, including de Havilland Blue Jay air-to-air missiles, although the aircraft was not originally designed to carry radar.

Gradually, the specification became more advanced as the designer, Maurice Brennan, could see an increasing need for radar and a more capable engine. The SR.53 flew in May 1956, quickly displaying Mach 1.33 capability and an extremely high rate of climb. Disaster struck in June 1958, when the aircraft crashed on take-off, but

a more capable SR.177 was already under development. This attracted considerable interest from the USA and West Germany. Just when the prospect of hundreds of export orders seemed likely, the British government's 1957 Defence Review cancelled all manned fighter aircraft development and condemned the project to death, despite its potential.

Above: With both rocket and turbojet power, the SR.53 was a superb performer. This performance was extremely hard to match, even by most aircraft of the 1970s.

SR.53

Type: single-seat short-range interceptor

Powerplant: one 7.3-kN (1,640-lb.-thrust) Armstrong Siddeley Viper turbojet and one 35.6-kN (8,008-lb.) Spectre rocket

Maximum speed: Mach 2.2

Endurance: 7 minutes at full power

Initial climb rate: 132 seconds to 16000 m (52,500 ft.)

Turn radius: 2757 m (9,043 ft.) at Mach 1.6

Service ceiling: 20000 m (65,600 ft.)

Weights: loaded 8363 kg (18,400 lb.)

Armament: two Firestreak or Blue Jay infra-red homing missiles

Dimensions:		
span	7.65 m	(25 ft. 1in.)
length	13.71 m	(10 ft. 5in.)
height	3.30 m	(10 ft. 10 in.)
wing area	25.45 m²	(274 sq. ft.)

SR.53

The first SR.53, XD145, is still in existence. After the programme was terminated, the aircraft was used as a testbed by the Rocket Propulsion Establishment. It was acquired by the RAF Museum in 1978.

A small, narrow cockpit was a feature of the SR.53, with the pilot sitting on a conventional ejection seat.

A mid-mounted delta wing with cropped ends was a feature of both the SR.53 and the proposed SR.177. It incorporated large slotted flaps and leading-edge slats as well as ailerons for exceptional manoeuvrability and control at low speed.

Mounted below the turbojet was the main power unit, the de Havilland Spectre rocket engine. At the time, the idea of a rocket-propelled fighter was revolutionary and research into rocket propulsion was at best limited. Despite this, and the highly volatile mixture it required, the SR.53 enjoyed successful and trouble-free flight testing.

A distinctive feature of the aircraft was its very squat vertical tail and high-mounted horizontal stabilisers.

XD145

The SR.53 carried no radar, yet the Central Flight Establishment concluded that one must be fitted. This resulted in the larger, more powerful SR.177 which was to incorporate an AI 23 air intercept radar.

Originally, the SR.53 was to have no internal landing gear, just a skid and a detachable trolley. This idea proved too expensive and a conventional tricycle undercarriage was adopted instead.

Two de Havilland Blue Jay infra-red missiles were the planned armament for the SR.53, though in the end this was changed to twin Firestreaks which could be mounted on the wingtips.

An unusual exhaust configuration characterised the SR.53 At the top was mounted the Viper turbojet. It was designed to supplement the Spectre rocket during take-offs and to enable the aircraft to get home after a mission.

SAUNDERS-ROE PROJECTS

SR.45 PRINCESS: The only Princess to take to the air, is seen here flying over Farnborough during an SBAC display. Making its maiden flight on 20 August 1952, the Saunders-Roe design was destined to fail because of the improving capability of landplanes for long-range intercontinental services. After numerous demonstrations and much interest, no orders were forthcoming. Despite their elegant design and capable performance, the three aircraft were eventually broken up and sold as scrap.

SR.A/1: Designed for the island-hopping battles in the Pacific during World War II, the SR.A/1 was too late to see service in the war, however the project was proceeded with. First flight of the SR.A/1 occurred on 16 July 1947 and an additional three aircraft were constructed, two of which were lost in landing accidents. Although unique in design, the SR.A/1 attracted no interest and the project was eventually dropped in 1951. One example was preserved and is displayed at the Southampton Hall of Aviation.

Hybrid fighters of the 1950s

■ **DASSAULT MIRAGE IIIA:** A contemporary of the SR. 53, this aircraft went on to become the successful and widely exported Mirage IIIC.

■ **McDONNELL XF-88B:** Designed to test high-speed propellers, the XF-88B incorporated three engines and used a huge amount of fuel.

■ **REPUBLIC XF-91:** Loosely based on the F-84F Thunderstreak, this was powered by a conventional turbojet and rocket motors.

■ **RYAN FR-1 FIREBALL:** One of a number of turbojet/piston-engined aircraft, the Fireball was operated by the US Navy for a brief period.

SAUNDERS-ROE

SR.A/1

● Jet flying-boat fighter ● Three built ● Planned Pacific war use

SAUNDERS-ROE SR.A/1

Smooth finish ▶
To preserve laminar flow over the wing, Saro applied a fine Titanine finish over the flush rivetted skin of the aircraft. To this was added the RAF and prototype markings.

◀ On the Thames in 1951
With little doubt the first SR.A/1 prototype is the only jet aircraft ever to have landed on the River Thames.

Minor early problems ▶
TG263's first flight was virtually trouble-free, though the test pilot noted a slight 'snaking' tendency in flight. This was cured by fitting a small acorn fairing at the junction of the tailplane and fin. A tendency to roll, another early problem, was also rectified.

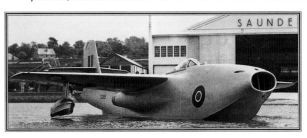

▲ Isle of Wight factory
Seen in 1947, TG263 is tied up near the Saunders-Roe factory at East Cowes on the Isle of Wight. In order to reduce drag while in flight, the retractable underwing floats folded inward to a semi-recessed position.

Three E.6/44s ▶
Impressed by Saro's proposals, the Ministry of Aircraft Production ordered three SR.A/1s to jet flying-boat fighter specification E.6/44, which was written around the SR.A/1 fighter design.

I nspired by the 'island hopping' nature of the Allies' Pacific campaign during World War II, Saunders-Roe (Saro) produced a radical solution to the problem of providing fighter cover during a mobile campaign where land air bases were invariably bombed. The jet-powered SR.A/1 was a sensational flying-boat fighter which showed considerable promise in testing. However, the end of the war in August 1945 removed any need for the aircraft.

▲ Like so many military designs of the late war years, the SR.A/1 was destined to remain at the prototype stage and was the only British jet-powered flying-boat to take to the air.

FACTS AND FIGURES

➤ TG263, the first SR.A/1, was preserved by the Imperial War Museum and is displayed at Southampton's Hall of Aviation.

➤ During the Korean War an SR.A/1 variant was proposed with new engines.

➤ Only 11 Beryl engines were built, enough for three aircraft with five spares.

➤ After TG263 was passed to the College of Aeronautics, one Beryl engine was used in Donald Campbell's Bluebird speedboat.

➤ SR.A/1s were displayed at the 1947 and 1948 SBAC air shows.

➤ The third aircraft, TG371, was lost when it hit a semi-submerged object off Cowes.

PROFILE

Flying-boat fighter for the Pacific war

Left: After prototype TG263 lost its bubble canopy during a test flight, it was fitted with a metal replacement.

Traditionally, waterborne fighters had proved inferior to land-based aircraft which were unencumbered by drag-reducing floats or the extra weight of a planing hull. The SR.A/1 addressed this problem by utilising two of the then-new turbojet powerplants, about to make their combat debut over Europe. Though a comparatively heavy aircraft, the power of the two Metropolitan-Vickers F.2/4 Beryl axial-flow engines gave the 'Squirt' (as it was known) a healthy turn of speed.

In 16 July 1947 the TG263, the first of three SR.A/1s built, flew. Test flying showed that the 'Squirt' was not only fast, but performed well both on the water and in the air. On only its fifth flight, TG263 reached speeds of over 644 km/h (400 m.p.h.) watched by military and industry officials. Improvements to the engines, which in their final form produced 17.13 kN (3,855-lb.-thrust) each, allowed the aircraft to top the 800-km/h (500-m.p.h.) mark. Other innovations included a pressurised cockpit and a Martin-Baker ejection seat.

However, with World War II over and the RAF reduced in size, official interest in the type (never very great) waned. Two crashes sealed its fate, even though neither of these was attributable to a flaw in the aircraft. Engine supply was also a problem post-war.

One SR.A/1 survives, owned by the Imperial War Museum.

Above: Saunders-Roe test pilot Geoffrey Tyson perfected a short take-off technique which allowed the SR.A/1 to lift off in the relatively short space of 460 m (1,500 ft.).

SR.A/1

Type: single-seat flying-boat fighter

Powerplant: two 14.4-kN (3,237-lb.-thrust) to 17.1-kN (3,844-lb.-thrust) Metropolitan-Vickers F.2/4 Beryl turbojets

Maximum speed: 824 km/h (510 m.p.h.)

Endurance: 1 hr 48 min without slipper tanks; 2 hr 24 min with slipper tanks

Initial climb rate: 1768 m/min (5,800 f.p.m.)

Service ceiling: 13110 m (43,000 ft.)

Weights: maximum weight 8633 kg (19,000 lb.)

Armament: (planned) four Hispano 20-mm cannon, plus up to 907 kg (2,000 lb.) of bombs, rockets, smoke floats and slipper fuel tanks

Dimensions:
span	14.02 m (46 ft.)
length	15.24 m (50 ft.)
height	5.11 m (16 ft. 9 in.)
wing area	38.55 m² (415 sq. ft.)

TG263's engine air intake was fitted with a 25.4-cm (10-in.) extendible snout intended to prevent water ingestion on take-off and landing. Trials proved the snout unnecessary.

Among modern features in the SR.A/1's cockpit were pressurisation, which activated automatically at 2745 m (9,000 ft.) altitude, provision for a *g*-suit and an ejection seat. The latter was the first delivered to an aircraft manufacturer from the Martin-Baker works.

Metropolitan-Vickers's F.2/4 Beryl turbojet was Britain's first axial-flow jet powerplant. A promising design when it first ran in January 1945, it was far more compact than the centrifugal-type engines then being built in much greater numbers.

For control of the aircraft on the surface, a water rudder was fitted to the rear of the hull which was connected to the air rudder while taxiing.

TG263

Four 20-mm cannon ports were a feature of the first prototype, though the guns were never installed. However, rocket projectile installations and bomb racks were fitted.

To ease mooring, the SR.A/1 was fitted with a hook in the nose, below the keel just under the waterline. This was controlled by the pilot and engaged a cable which dragged the aircraft to a suitable dock.

SR.A/1

Three SR.A/1s were built, TG263 being the first. Apart from having more powerful engines, the later aircraft were essentially similar. The second and third aircraft were written off in accidents; TG263 survives.

COMBAT DATA

MAXIMUM SPEED

The Saunders-Roe SR.A/1 was a markedly slower type than early land-based jet fighters. However, the aircraft was expected to perform well in combat against the Japanese piston-engined fighters of the Pacific war.

SR.A/1	824 km/h (510 m.p.h.)
SEA VENOM FAW.Mk 22	925 km/h (574 m.p.h.)
METEOR F.Mk 4	975 km/h (605 m.p.h.)

INITIAL CLIMB RATE

Compared to the jet fighters entering service in the years shortly after World War II, the SR.A/1 had a marginally slower climb rate, though it was only slightly less than that of the carrier-based de Havilland Sea Venom Mk 22.

SR.A/1 1768 m/min (5,800 f.p.m.)	SEA VENOM FAW.Mk 22 1798 m/min (5,900 f.p.m.)	METEOR F.Mk 4 2240 m/min (7,350 f.p.m.)

SERVICE CEILING

SR.A/1s were expected to operate at high altitudes and were thus fitted with pressurised cockpits. The Sea Venom operated at a slightly lower altitude, while the Meteor Mk 4 had a 450-m (6,000-ft.) advantage over the SR.A/1.

SR.A/1 13110 m (43,000 ft.)	SEA VENOM FAW.Mk 22 12192 m (40,000 ft.)	METEOR F.Mk 4 13563 m (49,200 ft.)

RAF fighters too late for World War II

■ **DE HAVILLAND VAMPIRE:** First ordered in May 1944, the Vampire entered service in 1946 as the RAF's second jet type, initially joining Fighter Command and Second Tactical Air Force.

■ **HAWKER F.2/43 FURY:** A lightweight development of the Tempest, this was Hawker's fastest piston-engined design. In April 1944, 200 Centaurus-engined examples were ordered.

■ **MARTIN-BAKER M.B.5:** Powered by a 1745-kW (2,340-hp.) Rolls-Royce Griffon engine, the M.B.5 flew in May 1944. Despite an amazing performance, the type failed to gain an order.

■ **SUPERMARINE SPITEFUL:** First flown in June 1944, featuring a laminar-flow wing and 795-km/h (493 m.p.h.) top speed, Spiteful was intended to replace the Spitfire; 17 were built.

SAUNDERS-ROE

PRINCESS

● Last of the great passenger flying-boats ● Magnificent failure

▲ The Princess, like the Brabazon, was another example of a technological wonder that had almost no relevance at all to the requirements of airlines in the 1950s and should never have been built.

A vision of a futuristic age of air travel that might have been, the Saunders-Roe SR.45 Princess was a magnificent flying-boat of the post-war era, and was to be the world's largest pressurised aircraft and turboprop. It was an enormous technical achievement, but the Princess suffered from nagging problems with its powerplant and it arrived on the scene after flying-boats no longer offered advantages over landplanes.

SAUNDERS-ROE PRINCESS

◀ Clean design
The Princess was powered by engines located in pairs in the wing, driving the propellers via long shafts. This was an elegant aerodynamic solution, but it made the wing very complex and heavy.

▲ Air show star
The Princess flew at Farnborough to delight the crowds. At higher speeds the floats would have been retracted into the wingtips.

◀ Saunders-Roe slipway
The Princess shared its slipway at Cowes with the SRA-1 fighter. The Princess handled well on water, but the need for large flying-boats, like floatplane fighters, did not really exist.

▼ Under construction
The huge size of the Princess meant that it was built more like a ship than an aircraft. The twin pressurised hulls were constructed first, mounted one on top of the other, and the rest of the airframe was then assembled around them.

▲ Waiting for engines
The technical snag with the Princess was the disastrous Bristol Proteus turboprop. Even when the airframe was complete, the engines were delayed and were much weaker than expected.

FACTS AND FIGURES

➤ The first Princess made a delayed maiden flight on 22 August 1952.

➤ The 65920-litre (17,140-gal.) fuel capacity was housed entirely in wing tanks.

➤ By 1952 British Overseas Airways Corporation, the only potential customer, decided to operate landplanes only.

➤ A proposition to use six Tyne turboprops would have solved any power problems.

➤ The US Navy seriously considered using the three Princess prototypes to test an atomic powerplant.

➤ The only Princess to fly was towed to a salvage yard in 1967 and scrapped.

PROFILE

Britain's magnificent maritime failure

As the Princess thundered over Southampton Water on an early test flight, it looked down on the ocean liners it was designed to replace. This huge, majestic aircraft with its double-deck fuselage and 10 engines in six nacelles was intended as an ocean liner of the sky, to offer luxurious travel to the privileged and the discerning.

The dream died because no turboprop engine available in 1950 could offer the power the Princess needed – and because land-based aircraft then coming along, including the Boeing Stratocruiser, offered a similar standard of service at far lower cost to the operator.

The ambitious thinking behind the Princess led, in fact, to plans for a landplane version, as well as a 'Twin Princess' with two full-sized fuselages and 14 engines which would have been used as a cargo-hauler.

In the end, these grandiose plans came to nothing. At one stage the three Princess prototypes were to be converted into RAF troop transports. But this dream also died, and only the first prototype was ever flown.

The Princess belonged to the maritime world of Southampton. In many ways it had more in common with the ocean liners which it flew over than with the airliners with whom it would have shared the airways.

Princess prototype

Type: long-range passenger flying-boat

Powerplant: 10 2386-kW (3,200-hp.) Bristol Proteus 600 turboprops (eight in coupled units, plus two single units)

Maximum speed: 579 km/h (360 m.p.h.)

Range: estimated 9000 km (1,860 mi.)

Service ceiling: estimated 10000 m (33,000 ft.)

Weights: take-off 156492 kg (344,282 lb.)

Accommodation: flight crew of two pilots, two flight engineers, one navigator and one radio operator. As conceived for trans-ocean airline travel, the Princess would have handled 105 passengers in first class; as an RAF troop transport it would have carried 200 fully-equipped combat soldiers and all their equipment

Dimensions:
span	66.90 m	(219 ft.)
length	45.11 m	(148 ft.)
height	17.00 m	(56 ft.)
wing area	487 m²	(5,240 sq. ft.)

The Princess was an incredible sight. But no matter how majestic its appearance, it was doomed to fail, beaten by the harsh demands of economics and market forces.

SR.45 PRINCESS

The Princess prototype, G-ALUN, was the only one that flew out of the three built. The other two were put into storage on completion.

The flight deck housed two pilots, a navigator, two flight engineers and a radio operator.

Passenger accommodation was divided between two decks, with spiral staircases between them fore and aft. The rear cabin even had pull-down beds in the area where modern airliners have overhead baggage lockers.

The wing leading edges were de-iced thermally, using air piped from the exhaust manifolds.

The tailplane was de-iced by kerosene-burning heaters with their own fuel supply, fed by an air intake in the base of the fin.

Powered control units in the rear of the hull operated the three-section electro-hydraulically operated rudder and twin-section elevators.

The Princess used a capacious hold in the lower hull to carry cargo and baggage.

The hull bottom was an efficient hydrodynamic design. Take-offs and landings were notably smooth.

Giant cargo carrier

■ One of the more outlandish schemes to salvage the Princess programme was to develop a giant cargo carrier. Joining a pair of hulls with a common central wing would have created a transport able to carry 400 troops or 50 tonnes of cargo.

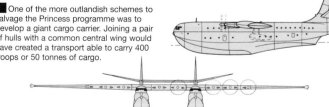

Princess landplane

■ A more practical proposition involved redesigning the hull with wheels and a rear loading ramp. Power would have been provided by six Tyne turboprops. Although the resulting airlifter would have been highly capable, the plans perished with the rest of the Princess programme.

ACTION DATA

TRANSATLANTIC TIME

To be fair to the aviation committees of the 1940s which first planned the Princess and the equally large but futile Brabazon, few people could have foreseen the revolution that the jet would bring to airliner performance. But by the early 1950s the Comet had sounded the death knell for such monsters, and the superb Boeing Model 707 was in the air less than two years after the first flight of the Princess.

PRINCESS	BRABAZON Mk I	BOEING 707
11 hours	14 hours	7 hours

SCALED COMPOSITES

RUTAN 151 ARES

● Lightweight ● Unique design ● Only one built

SCALED COMPOSITES RUTAN 151 ARES

◀ Flying cannon
In some respects, the ARES represented a scaled-down A-10 Thunderbolt II, with a huge and tremendously powerful gun in the nose. Firing tests on this weapon began in 1991.

▼ Military transport, Rutan style
Another of Rutan's ambitious projects was the AT3 Advanced Tactical Transport. Like the ARES, it failed to win any orders.

▲ New standard in economy
Intended as a replacement for the Beechcraft Bonanza, the Catbird was an ultra-efficient five-seater light aircraft.

Demonstrator experience ▶
In the past, Scale Composites had built many advanced prototypes.

◀ Too advanced?
An excellent aircraft in its own right, demonstrating superb performance and agility, the Rutan 151 ARES was perhaps too radical to succeed. It was nevertheless a very valuable research tool and demonstrator.

When Fairchild designed an aircraft around a single, big, multi-barrelled cannon, it materialised as the massive, tank-like A-10. Facing the same challenge, maverick designer Burt Rutan came up with something completely different. The Agile Response Effective Support (ARES) which his Scaled Composites company produced in the late 1980s matched a US Army requirement for a low-cost close air support aircraft. The emergent aircraft was unique.

▲ *Rutan began studies on a light, low-cost battlefield support aircraft in 1981 and the result was the ARES. Customers were sought, but to no avail, and the project was shelved in 1995.*

FACTS AND FIGURES

➤ Scaled Composites was bought from Burt Rutan by Beech Aircraft but later sold back to him in June 1985.

➤ Design on the ARES began in 1981, yet it did not fly until 1990.

➤ Initially, the project was private, with no additional funding from outside firms.

➤ The gun installation was designed so that the blast impinged on the forward fuselage and counteracted recoil.

➤ The single ARES prototype was finally grounded during 1996.

➤ A two-seat trainer variant was proposed but unfortunately never built.

PROFILE

Beyond frontiers and the battlefield

The reason for the location of the ARES turbofan engine on the left side of the aft fuselage was to keep the intake clear of the gases generated when the gun was fired. The gun itself was mounted at the aircraft's centre of gravity in a depression on the fuselage side, ensuring that the powerful recoil forces were balanced by the muzzle blast.

Aerodynamically, the aircraft used forward-swept canard foreplanes, a compound wing swept back 50° on the inboard sections and 15° outboard, and twin fins mounted on booms.

Low observability was another consideration. Although advanced stealth techniques were avoided to escape export restrictions, the position of the engine meant that its compressor blades were shielded from ground-based radars, while the twin fins masked the IR emissions of the exhaust.

The ARES flew for the first time in February 1990 and went on to complete live firing tests. However, the end of the Cold War meant the US Army no longer needed large numbers of low-cost ground attack aircraft, and the developing countries which were another target market generally opted for more versatile designs.

Distinctive canards are a feature of many Rutan designs, although, during flight testing, those on the Model 151 ARES were found to limit the angle of attack.

Extensive use was made of lightweight materials, notably carbon-fibre and poly vinyl chloride, resulting in a very light airframe.

RUTAN 151 ARES

Only one Model 151 was ever built. Allocated the serial N151SC (the last two letters indicating Scale Composites), it first flew in 1990 and began armament firing tests a year later. It is currently in storage.

From the outset, the entire aircraft was designed around the General Electric GAU-12 rotary-barrelled cannon. Despite its proximity to the cockpit, the pilot encountered few problems during gun firing, and a special shield protected him from the blast.

A clear one-piece bubble canopy offered superb all-round visibility, better than perhaps any combat aircraft, production or otherwise. For escape, the pilot sat on a UPC SIIS-3ER ejection seat.

Offsetting the single Pratt & Whitney JT15D-5 to port prevented gun gases being ingested by the air intake. Despite its location, the thrust line was central, being corrected by a curved jet pipe.

During flight testing, the Model 151 was cleared to carry a variety of ordnance. Two AIM-9 Sidewinder air-to-air missiles could be carried on the wing stations for air defence, or four of the smaller AIM-92 Stinger missiles.

One of the few conventional features of the ARES was the landing gear. Single wheels were fitted to each oleo and retracted backwards. The nose unit retracted into the fuselage and the main units retracted into the forward sections of the twin tail booms.

Mounting the fins and rudders on short tail booms resulted in the engine being shielded, making it less likely to be hit by ground fire.

SPECIFICATION
Rutan Model 151 ARES

Type: experimental anti-helicopter and close air support aircraft

Powerplant: one 13.12-kN (2,949-lb.-thrust) Pratt & Whitney JT15D-5 turbofan

Maximum speed: 695 km/h (431 m.p.h.)

Range: better than 1850 km (1,149 mi.)

Internal fuel capacity: 771 kg (1,696 lb.)

Weights: empty (unarmed) 1308 kg (2,877 lb.); maximum take-off 2767 kg (6,087 lb.)

Armament: one General Electric GAU-12 25-mm cannon with 220 rounds of ammunition plus two Stinger or Sidewinder missiles

Dimensions:

span	10.67 m (35 ft.)
length	8.97 m (29 ft. 5 in.)
height	3.00 m (9 ft. 10 in.)
main wing area	17m² (188 sq. ft.)
canard area	3.19 m² (34 sq. ft.)

ACTION DATA

MAXIMUM SPEED

Powered by a turbofan, the Model 151 had decent performance. It was faster than the twin-engined turboprop-powered Rockwell OV-10 Bronco, but slower than the single-engined Cavalier Turbo-Mustang that was derived from the famous World War II P-51.

MODEL 151 ARES	695 km/h (431 m.p.h.)
OV-10D BRONCO	463 km/h (287 m.p.h.)
TURBO MUSTANG III	869 km/h (540 m.p.h.)

RANGE

Both the ARES and the Turbo Mustang had a range greater than 1850 km, which in a war scenario would give them considerable time over the battlefield if required. The Bronco, which was the only one of these three to enter service, ironically had the shortest range of all.

MODEL 151 ARES 1850 km (1,150 mi.)
OV-10D BRONCO 1297 km (805 mi.)
TURBO MUSTANG III 1850 km (1,150 mi.)

MAXIMUM TAKE-OFF WEIGHT

Extensive use of lightweight materials resulted in one of the lightest aircraft ever devised for the battlefield support role. Both the Bronco and the Turbo Mustang were real heavyweights by comparison and probably less suitable for the role.

MODEL 151 ARES 2767 kg (6,087 lb.)
OV-10D BRONCO 6552 kg (14,414 lb.)
TURBO MUSTANG III 6350 kg (13,970 lb.)

Failed battlefield support aircraft

■ **CAVALIER MUSTANG II:** Derived from the civilian Cavalier, the Mustang II proved unsuitable for the close-support role.

■ **CONVAIR 44 CHARGER:** One of two designs evaluated by the USAF in the 1970s, the Charger lost out to the OV-10 Bronco.

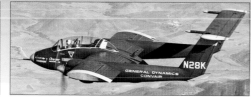

■ **ILYUSHIN Il-102:** An unusual design, the Il-102 was an attempt at a simple, very low-cost close-support aircraft.

SHORT

MAYO COMPOSITE

● Long-range record holder ● Floatplane and mothership ● Mailplane

▲ An ingenious attempt
at solving the problem of establishing
a high-speed transatlantic mail route,
the remarkable Short Mayo Composite
performed brilliantly.

Short's Mayo Composite was an attempt to provide long-range air mail services by using two aircraft teamed together to carry out a single mission. This was a daring concept which looked bizarre. It was also a challenge to pilots, but it worked. During its brief moment of glory in the late-1930s, the Short Mayo combination established a long-distance duration record for seaplanes that will probably never be broken.

PHOTO FILE

SHORT MAYO COMPOSITE

▼ Pylon support
A complicated pylon structure held the 'Mercury' securely on the S.21's back until separation.

▲ Short S.20 'Mercury'
'Mercury' was a completely new design and emerged as a sleek, four-engined floatplane with a long range.

Combining the aircraft ▶
Ground crew secure 'Mercury' on top of its 'Maia' mothership. Fully laden with fuel and 454 kg (1,000 lb.) of mail, the S.20 could not take off under its own power.

▼ Separation
'Mercury' was released at cruising altitude by the S.21. Although potentially dangerous, this operation never caused problems.

▲ Eight-engined take-off
A vital component of the Mayo Composite, the S.21 was based on the design of the successful 'Empire' flying-boat.

FACTS AND FIGURES

➤ With all eight engines running for take-off, the Short Mayo Composite had a total power output of 3760 kW (5,040 hp.).

➤ The normal cruising range of the loaded 'Mercury' was 6116 km (3,800 mi.).

➤ 'Mercury' was launched over Dundee, Scotland, for the record-breaking flight.

➤ On 6 February 1938 'Mercury' completed its first commercial, non-stop journey to Montreal in 20 hours 20 minutes.

➤ Changes in aerospace technology mean that the S.20's record may stand for ever.

➤ The second separation of the Mayo Composite was performed for the press.

PROFILE

Unique transatlantic mailplane

For its time it was one of the most incredible records in aviation history: 9652 km (5,984 mi.), from Dundee to the Orange River in South Africa.

In the 1930s, tests proved that an Imperial Airways 'Empire' flying-boat could achieve a transatlantic crossing if its entire payload only consisted of fuel, leaving no room for cargo or passengers. Since an aircraft can fly at a greater weight than at which it can take off, Robert Mayo proposed that a small, heavily loaded mailplane could be carried to operational altitude above a larger 'mother-plane'

and then released to complete its long-range task.

Short designed and built a composite unit by modifying an 'Empire' flying-boat to carry the S.20 long-range twin floatplane. The system was a success, but World War II ended any further development.

'Maia' receives attention at its moorings. The S.21 flying-boat was destroyed by enemy action in May 1941, while the S.20 'Mercury' survived the war but was later broken up.

MAYO COMPOSITE

Short Brothers built only one each of the S.20 'Mercury' (G-ADHJ) and the S.21 'Maia' (G-ADHK). Both aircraft were finished in their natural metal colour with Imperial Airways titles.

Napier Rapier H engines, each of 254-kW (340 hp.), drove two-bladed propellers to power the S.20. On the flight to South Africa a cowling broke away adding extra drag to the problems posed by headwinds.

An ingenious design, the pylon had to hold 'Mercury' securely but hinder the launch sequence as little as possible. This composite may have inspired the German Mistel projects.

'Mercury' was flown by a pilot and co-pilot, the latter also acting as the radio operator. For the record-breaking flight to South Africa the small S.20 weighed 12474 kg (27,443 lb.) on separation.

Three-bladed propellers fitted to Bristol Pegasus radial engines drove the S.21. The lower aircraft was only required to fly the short distance for launch before it returned to base.

For the long-distance record attempt the floats were modified to hold extra fuel. Headwinds caused greater than expected fuel consumption, however.

To give the optimum water performance and to make lift-off as easy as possible, 'Maia' had a smooth two-step flying-boat hull.

S.20 'Mercury'

Type: long-range floatplane mail carrier

Powerplant: four 254-kW (340-hp.) Napier Rapier H piston engines

Maximum speed: 339 km/h (210 m.p.h.); 314 km/h (194 m.p.h.) at maximum weight

Normal range: 6116 km (3,800 mi.)

Extended range: record flight 9652 km (5,984 mi.)

Weights: empty 4614 kg (10,150 lb.); maximum 7030 kg (15,466 lb.); normal Mayo Composite launch 9443 kg (20,775 lb.); record launch 12474 kg (26,752 lb.)

Payload: 454 kg (1,000 lb.)

Dimensions:
span 22.20 m (73 ft.)
length 15.50 m (51 ft.)
wing area 56.80m² (611 sq. ft.)

SPECIFICATION S.21 'Maia'

Type: flying-boat mother-plane for long-range upper component

Powerplant: four 686-kW (919-hp.) Bristol Pegasus XC radial piston engines

Maximum speed: 322 km/h (200 m.p.h.)

Range: 1360 km (843 mi.)

Service ceiling: 6100 m (20,000 ft.)

Weights: empty 11234 kg (24,715 lb.); max take-off 17252 kg (37,954 lb.); maximum for Mayo Composite launching 12580 kg (27,676 lb.)

Dimensions:
span 34.70 m (114 ft.)
length 25.90 m (85 ft.)
wing area 162.50 m² (1,748 sq. ft.)

The Mayo Composite concept

1 TAKE-OFF: Too heavily loaded to lift-off under its own power, the S.20 'Mercury' was hauled aloft by the S.21 'Maia'. Immediately after launch the 'mother-plane' returned to base.

2 SEPARATION: 'Mercury', still with a large fuel reserve, was released by 'Maia' at cruising altitude.

3 'MERCURY' LANDS ALONE: At the end of its long flight the S.20 landed on any suitable stretch of water. Return flights had to be made in stages since the 'mother-plane' was not available to carry 'Mercury' to altitude. This would have been a problem if the composite had entered regular service.

Record-breaking flight

DUNDEE

FLIGHT TO SOUTH AFRICA: Flying from Dundee, Scotland, to South Africa was a hazardous journey. Problems en route prevented 'Mercury' reaching its intended destination of Cape Town, and the crew were perhaps lucky to reach the Orange River unscathed.

ORANGE RIVER

SHORT

SC.1

● Vertical take-off pioneer ● Lift engines ● Single-seater

▲ A major weakness of the SC.1 concept was the lift jets themselves. These took up valuable fuselage space and used large amounts of fuel, but were needed only for take off and landing. It was easy, therefore, to see the attraction of the single-engined P.1127 which would ultimately enter service as the Harrier.

Hawker's P.1127, powered by the Rolls-Royce Pegasus turbofan delivering thrust through swivelling jet nozzles, was to make the concept of separate vertical lift jet engines impractical. That said, the SC.1 was a pioneer in VTOL flight. In transitioning from vertical to horizontal flight it was only narrowly beaten by the American Bell X-14. Its 10 years of flying also provided experience in the design of 'puffer' control jets as used on the Harrier.

SHORT SC.1

▲ **Football pitch landing**
During an early flight test a landing was made on a football pitch, slightly scorching the grass. Operating from 'unprepared' surfaces was dependant upon the engine not ingesting debris.

▲ **Farnborough debut**
XG905 made its first public appearance at the Farnborough Air Show in September 1959. At this stage transitional flight had yet to be accomplished.

Maiden flight ▶
The first SC.1, XG900, completed its initial flight on 2 April 1957. The undercarriage legs were angled forwards during conventional flight.

▼ **Hovering SC.1**
After initial engine runs at Short's Belfast factory the SC.1 was taken by sea to England. The first flights were made from the Royal Aircraft Establishment's airfield at Boscombe Down.

▲ **Long legs**
The undercarriage legs were equipped with long-travel hydraulic oleos, which provided cushioning for potentially heavy vertical landings. These gave the SC.1 an ungainly appearance on the ground.

FACTS AND FIGURES

➤ XG905, the second SC.1, tragically crashed in October 1963, killing its pilot, J.R. Green; the aircraft was repaired.

➤ The SC.1 developed from plans for a delta-wing supersonic airliner using lift jets.

➤ The RB.108 engine had a thrust-to-weight ratio of 8:1; advanced for the 1950s.

➤ XG900 was flown to the 1961 Paris Air Show in seven stages over four days, the first jet-lift aircraft to fly the Channel.

➤ XG900, displayed at the Fleet Air Arm Museum, is a Science Museum exhibit.

➤ The SC.1's landing gear oleos withstood a descent rate of 5.5 m (18 ft.) per second.

PROFILE

Britain's jet-lift VTOL pioneer

By the early-1950s turbojet engines were producing enough thrust to make vertical jet-lift feasible. Rolls-Royce's 'Flying Bedstead' Thrust Measuring Rig demonstrated the concept in 1953.

Rolls-Royce then designed a small turbojet lifting engine, and at the same time the Ministry of Supply issued specification ER.143. This was for a research aircraft that could take off vertically by jet lift alone, accelerate into forward flight and become fully wing-

supported in cruise with lift engines inoperative. It was also required to decelerate and land vertically.

Short Brothers was awarded a contract to build two SC.1s, the first making a conventional flight in April 1957. It was not until three years later, in April 1960, that the first transition from vertical to horizontal flight occurred.

Flown until 1971, these odd-looking aircraft provided a great deal of valuable data, especially relating to vertical take-off and

landing (VTOL) handling techniques. However, by November 1960 the P.1127, predecessor of the famous Harrier, had shown the way of future VTOL development using a more practical single engine with swivelling exhaust nozzles.

The SC.1's fairly conventional delta wing had elevators inboard and ailerons outboard. No flaps were fitted.

The tailfin and rudder were very small compared to conventional jet aircraft of the period. Control was maintained by large flaps and the vertical lift jets.

The four vertical lift engines were centrally-mounted in pairs and could be tilted fore and aft through 35 degrees to assist the transition from vertical to conventional flight. The main air intake in the tip surface of the fuselage was protected by a wire-mesh guard to prevent the ingestion of debris.

SC.1

Type: single-seat delta-wing VTOL research monoplane

Powerplant: five 8.89-kN (2,000-lb.-thrust) Rolls-Royce RB.108 turbojet engines, four mounted vertically in the fuselage and one horizontally in the tail

Maximum speed: 296 km/h (184 m.p.h.)

Range: 240 km (150 mi.)

Weights: empty 2720 kg (5,984 lb.); all-up (vertical take-off) 3495 kg (7,689 lb.) ; all-up (short take-off) 3650 kg (8,030 lb.)

Dimensions:
span	7.16 m (23 ft.)
length	9.10 m (30 ft.)
height	3.25 m (11 ft.)
wing area	13.18 m² (142 sq. ft.)

JET VTOL PIONEERS

ROLLS-ROYCE THRUST MEASURING RIG: Known as the 'Flying Bedstead', this amazing craft took to the air in 1953, the first machine to demonstrate the potential of jet VTOL. Two Nene turbojet engines were centrally mounted, with their exhausts directed vertically downwards. Compressed air piped to 'puffer' jets provided directional control.

SC.1

XG905 was the second SC.1. It is displayed in the Ulster Folk and Transport Museum, Holywood, Northern Ireland. The first aircraft, XG900, is at the Fleet Air Arm Museum, Yeovilton.

The cockpit was initially fitted with a Folland lightweight ejector seat, but later it was replaced by a Martin-Baker 'zero-zero' seat.

XG905

Short SC1

Important work carried out by the 'Flying Bedstead' and SC.1 pioneered the use of 'puffer' jets to control the aircraft's attitude. These used air 'tapped' from the engines and ejected downwards through valves at the nose, tail and on the wingtips.

Fuel tanks were installed along the wing leading edge and in 'bag' tanks fitted between the main wing spars.

Each fixed undercarriage leg carried a pair of castoring wheels, the rear ones being fitted with disc brakes. Long-stroke oleos were used on the legs to cushion vertical landings.

The angle of the rear undercarriage legs could be moved through 15° according to the type of flight to be made: forward for conventional take-off and landing and to the rear for vertical flight.

One 8.89-kN (2,000-lb.) Rolls-Royce RB.108 turbojet was installed in the rear of the airframe for horizontal flight. As this engine was designed for vertical mounting, it had to be slanted at 30° so that its lubrication system would function properly.

BELL X-14: This VTOL pioneer was the first aircraft to transition between vertical and conventional flight on 24 May 1958. Unlike the SC.1, it used vectored thrust through swivelling nozzles to achieve the transition, like the later P.1127.

Two approaches to VTOL flight

1 LIFT-JET POWER: The SC.1's four separate lift jets drew air in the top of the fuselage and expelled it downwards to provide lift.

FORWARD THRUST: Once airborne the tail-mounted engine provided the thrust to accelerate the SC.1 forwards; the lift jets were now redundant.

2 VECTORED THRUST: The P.1127 used one engine for lift and flight, thrust being expelled through four swivelling nozzles on the fuselage.

HAWKER P.1127: As a forerunner to the highly successful Harrier family, the P.1127 first flew untethered in November 1960. A number of test aircraft followed, successfully demonstrating the operational potential of VTOL. The Harrier finally entered RAF service in 1969 and still operates.

SNECMA

COLÉOPTÈRE

● VTOL research ● Annular wing ● Only one aircraft built

▲ *One of the most distinctive aircraft designs ever, the Coléoptère proved that this line of VTOL research was a dead end and that the future lay with vectored thrust.*

Sitting on an ejection seat attached to the front of a vertically mounted turbojet engine would not be most people's choice of a way to go flying. But that was the formula for the Atar Volant (flying Atar), a vertical take-off and landing (VTOL) research aircraft produced by SNECMA in the mid-1950s. By 1959 the basic idea had been developed into the tail-sitting Coléoptère, with an annular wing surrounding the engine.

SNECMA COLÉOPTÈRE

◀ **Retractable foreplanes**
Lying horizontally on its launch rig, the C.450-01 reveals a number of its details. The retracted foreplanes are clearly seen in the nose section, as is the side window.

Sleek design ▶
Despite its strange looks, the C.450 was a streamlined aircraft, an impression accentuated by its natural metal colour scheme. No markings were applied during its brief flying career.

▲ **Preparing for launch**
A special trailer was constructed to transport the Coléoptère and to erect it for launch. Runway damage caused by the hot engine efflux was a distinct possibility.

◀ **Nose glazing**
Clear panels in the sides and on the undersides of the nose allowed the pilot a reasonable view in all directions during vertical flight.

Military service ▶
Had the Coléoptère entered service, all operations would have involved recovery to this vertical position.

FACTS AND FIGURES

➤ Both Convair and Lockheed also produced tail-sitting VTOL prototypes and abandoned them as impractical.

➤ Powered by an Atar 101DV engine, the C.400 P-1 had annular lifting surfaces.

➤ The C.400 P-2 completed 123 flights before being lost in an accident.

➤ All of the Coléoptère's successful flights were accomplished vertically, its one attempted transition resulting in a crash.

➤ SNECMA achieved a thrust:weight ratio of 1.4 for the C.450-01.

➤ SNECMA had hoped to use the C.450 as the basis for a ramjet-powered fighter.

PROFILE

Rising vertically on an annular wing

As a major French aero-engine manufacturer, SNECMA (Société National d'Étude et de Construction des Moteurs d'Aviation) was keen to investigate direct-lift applications of turbojet engines. The company acquired European rights for an annular wing design by Professor von Zborowski, seeing this innovation as an ideal basis for VTOL research.

Work on a remote-controlled test aircraft led to the first flight of the Atar Volant C.400 P-1 in 1956. A programme of 206 flights paved the way for the piloted Atar Volant C.400 P-2. A fatal accident was suffered by the ejection seat-equipped P-2, ending its career. SNECMA continued its research with an improved P-3 version which featured a more powerful 34.3-kN thrust Atar engine.

By 1959 SNECMA and Nord Aviation had produced the C.450-01 Coléoptère. Based on Professor von Zborowski's design, it used the annular wing for lift and four fins for directional control once it had lifted off vertically and made the transition to horizontal flight. The direction of the engine thrust was controlled pneumatically and, powered by a 36.3-kN (8,160-lb.-thrust) Atar 101 turbojet, the aircraft flew untethered for the first time on 6 May.

Predictably, despite all the test flying, the transition from vertical to horizontal flight continued to pose problems. On 25 July the pilot lost control at a height of about 75 m (246 ft.). He ejected to safety but the machine was destroyed and the project was effectively dead.

Like the Americans, the French were quick to realise the problems of flying tail-sitting aircraft in regular service. Large items of specialised support equipment would be needed for ground handling and maintenance, while pilots would be forced to land looking over their shoulders!

C.450-01 COLÉOPTÈRE

Only one aircraft was built and this flew successfully on a number of occasions. Disaster occurred on 25 July 1959 during the only transition from vertical flight. The pilot ejected successfully.

With its ability to provide lift in all directions, the annular wing might have been ideal for VTOL aircraft. Several designs were mooted using such surfaces, few of which went beyond artists' impressions. The Coléoptère's wing seems to have performed well, and the accident was the result of leaving vertical flight.

A head-on view illustrates the perfectly circular wing. In cross-section the wing thickness varied because of its aerofoil shape. This caused a distinctive bulge at mid-chord, giving the Coléoptère its barrel-shaped profile.

With its raised and extensively glazed cockpit, the C.450 gave its pilot a good view forwards and to the side. The huge wing would have severely restricted his view rearwards however.

Cruciform fins mounted on the sides of the mid-fuselage supported the annular wing. They appeared to be part of the outer fins but were in fact separate items, arranged in a similar cruciform pattern.

Large intakes were needed to supply the Atar with sufficient air at low speeds and potentially unusual attitudes. In general, the engine installation was quite conventional.

Movable fins gave the aircraft directional control in horizontal flight. Both the XFV-1 and XFY-1 also featured four fins for stability and directional control.

Had the C.450-01 been developed into an operational combat aircraft, its weight would have increased considerably, requiring a far more substantial undercarriage. A more powerful engine, probably with afterburning, would also have been necessary.

C.450-01 Coléoptère

Type: single-seat, annular-winged, turbojet-powered VTOL research aircraft

Powerplant: one 36.3-kN (8,160-lb.-thrust) SNECMA Atar 101E.5 V turbojet

Maximum speed: 800 km/h (497 m.p.h.)

Endurance: 25 min

Initial climb rate: 7800 m/min (25,590 f.p.m.)at sea level

Service ceiling: 3000 m (9,842 ft.)

Weights: max take-off about 3000 kg (6,600 lb.)

Dimensions: wing diam. outside 3.2m (10ft.6in.)
wing diam. inside 2.84m (9ft.3in.)
length 8.02m (26ft.3in.)
span over fins 4.51 m² (49 sq. ft.)

ACTION DATA

THRUST

By the late 1950s and early 1960s, it had become clear that vectored thrust was the key to successful VTOL aircraft. The P.1127 was to lead directly to the world-beating Harrier.

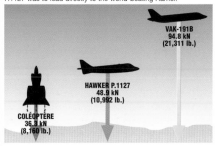

VAK-191B
94.8 kN
(21,311 lb.)

HAWKER P.1127
48.9 kN
(10,992 lb.)

COLÉOPTÈRE
36.3 kN
(8,160 lb.)

Flying the Coléoptère

1 VERTICAL LAUNCH: With engine thrust greater than its weight, the Coléoptère was able to rise vertically supported only by its jet efflux. The exhaust was deflected pneumatically to achieve the transition to horizontal flight once sufficient speed had been built up.

2 CONVENTIONAL FLIGHT: In horizontal flight air was to be fed into the intakes and ejected via the engine exhaust along the C.450's line of thrust as with any conventional aircraft (red arrows). The annular wing was to provide lift all around the aircraft, with air passing within and outside the ring.

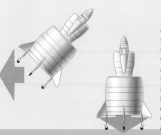

3 VERTICAL LANDING: As speed decreased, the engine exhaust was to be deflected, so that thrust-borne flight took over from wing-borne flight. Once established in a stable hover at low level, the pilot gently decreased thrust, effectively reversing the aircraft onto the ground.

SUKHOI

SU-35 'FLANKER'

● Multi-role advanced-technology fighter ● World-beating dogfighter

Sukhoi's Su-35 is dramatic evidence that Russia can still create advanced warplanes. It is a development of the Su-27 'Flanker' which gives Moscow a new Top Gun with no equal in the West. The Su-35 introduces new flight systems and the super-long-range KS-172 missile, able to span vast distances to destroy AWACS aircraft. This is one of the world's hottest fighters.

▲ The Su-35 is essentially a developed version of the superb Su-27 'Flanker', and retains the astounding speed and agility of its predecessor. It is regarded by most pilots as the standard to beat.

PHOTO FILE

SUKHOI SU-35 'FLANKER'

Armed to ▶ the teeth
The Su-35 is a lethal opponent, as it can carry up to 10 advanced air-to-air missiles as well as mounting the Gsh-30-1 30-mm cannon found in the MiG-29 fighter.

▲ Prototype
This Sukhoi T-10 can be seen at Monino museum near Moscow. At least one test pilot died in the trials flights for the T-10, which suffered from wing flutter and lacked engine power.

◀ New tail
The Su-35 can be easily distinguished from other Su-27 variants by its square-cropped tail fins, lengthened tail cone, and canard foreplanes. Other new features include a revised cockpit with multifunction displays and new ground-mapping and terrain-following radar system.

▼ Tight turn
The streaming vortices from the wingtips of the Su-35 show that this heavy fighter can dogfight as ably as any F-16. Unlike Western fighters, it also has helmet-mounted sights and missiles with thrust vectoring.

▲ Low and slow
Extending its massive dorsal airbrake, the Su-35 can dump speed dramatically. The superb fly-by-wire control system and dogfighter aerodynamics allow the Su-35 to be flown with carefree ease in the landing approach as well as in air combat, unlike the MiG-25 which needed great care.

FACTS AND FIGURES

➤ The Su-35 appears to have been chosen over the MiG-29M, even though the MiG offers similar capabilities at lower cost.

➤ Pavel Sukhoi died in September 1975 at the age of 80 and never saw his Su-35 fly.

➤ The Su-35 is capable of the tail-sitting 'Pugachev Cobra' manoeuvre.

➤ This fighter is a close relative of the Su-27K, a navalised 'Flanker' for operations from 'Kuznetsov'-class aircraft-carriers.

➤ The Su-35 has a retractable inflight-refuelling probe in the port forward fuselage.

➤ Electronic countermeasures pods have been noted on the wingtips of this fighter.

PROFILE

The best just gets better

If Russia can overcome economic hurdles and put this fighter into production, the Su-35 – recognised by its knife-like canard wings – will be a world-beater. Earlier 'Flankers' had outstanding agility and combat prowess, but needed improved radar and missiles. The Su-35 has the best of everything. A large jet fighter not nearly as heavy as it looks, the Su-35 is probably the world's best-manoeuvring aircraft in a dogfight.

The pilot of this incredible flying machine has a modern glass cockpit with video displays,

another improvement over the Su-27. Other improvements include a new fly-by-wire fighter control system and improved avionics allowing tracking of six targets simultaneously. Deadly at close quarters, the Su-35 also has greater 'reach' than any other fighter in Russia or the West, able to launch missiles that can strike a target far beyond visual range, more than 360 km (224 mi.) away.

So far, only a few Su-35s are flying. The Sukhoi design bureau's challenge will be to secure production money for this potentially great warrior.

SU-35 'FLANKER'

The Sukhoi Su-35 has some claim to being the world's most deadly fighter. It is the warplane that all of the new generation of Western superfighters must match.

The nose of the Su-35 contains the advanced N-011 radar, with the capacity to track enemy aircraft up to 400 km (250 mi.) away. It also has a very effective IRST – infra-red search-and-track – system.

The canard foreplanes on the Su-35 are the main identifying feature distinguishing it from the Su-27. They are also fitted to the Su-34 strike aircraft, which is now undergoing development trials and may enter service soon.

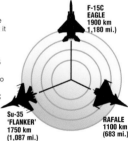

The Su-35 is known as 'Zhuravlik' ('crane') to Russian pilots, because of its drooping nose. The aircraft has not had the export success of its much cheaper competitor, the MiG-29.

Wingtip electronic countermeasures pods have replaced missile launch rails on at least two of the Su-35 development aircraft.

The fuselage of the Su-35 contains an enormous amount of fuel, which is why the aircraft is rarely seen with wing-mounted tanks. The airframe is mostly built of traditional welded alloys.

The R-77 is an excellent medium-range missile in the AMRAAM class, which is available with various types of infra-red and active radar seeker heads and a large warhead.

The tail of the Su-27 family has been redesigned several times. Early T-10s had canted fins, but later Su-27s had straight ones with a slanted profile tip. The Su-35 reverts to a flat-tipped tail, rather like the T-10.

The large tail 'sting' of the Su-35 houses ECM gear and a rear-looking radar.

The huge KS-172 missile has no Western equivalent. With a range estimated at 400 km (250 mi.), it is designed to destroy AWACS-type aircraft from beyond the range of escorting fighters.

The R-73 missile is a dogfight weapon, with greater manoeuvrability than the Sidewinder, thanks to its thrust-vectoring rocket nozzle.

Su-35 'Flanker'

Type: high-performance interceptor and fighter

Powerplant: two 130.4-kN (29,328-lb.-thrust) Lyul'ka AL-31FM afterburning turbofans

Maximum speed: 2280 km/h (1416 m.p.h.)

Range: at high altitude, 3680 km (2,400 mi.)

Service ceiling: 17700 m (58,070 ft.)

Weights: empty 18400 kg (40,565 lb.); loaded 26000 kg (57,320 lb.)

Armament: one GSh-30-1 30-mm cannon with 149 rounds; six R-27 (AA-10 'Alamo') and four AA-11 'Archer' or three Novator KS-172 AAM-L ultra-long-range missiles

Dimensions:
span	15.16 m (49 ft. 9 in.)
length	22.18 m (72 ft. 8 in.)
height	6.84 m (22 ft. 5 in.)
wing area	c.48.00 m² (516 sq. ft.)

COMBAT DATA

MAXIMUM SPEED

Su-35 'FLANKER'	2280 km/h (1,416 m.p.h.)
F-15C EAGLE	2655 km/h (1,649 m.p.h.)
RAFALE	2125 km/h (1,320 m.p.h.)

The 'Flanker' is not quite as fast as the American F-15, which was originally designed to intercept the Mach 3 MiG-25 'Foxbat'. But its supersonic manoeuvrability is at least as good, and its low-speed agility is even better than that of the American fighter.

COMBAT RADIUS

The Sukhoi Su 35's huge fuel capacity means that it can almost match the exceptional long-range performance of the McDonnell Douglas F-15 Eagle. However, the American fighter needs to carry extra tanks to achieve maximum range; the 'Flanker' does it on internal fuel alone. The Rafale is smaller and carries less fuel.

F-15C EAGLE 1900 km (1,180 mi.)

Su-35 'FLANKER' 1750 km (1,087 mi.)

RAFALE 1100 km (683 mi.)

ENGAGEMENT RANGE

Su-35 'FLANKER' 400 km (250 mi.)	F-15C EAGLE 50 km (31 mi.)	RAFALE 50 km (31 mi.)

With its normal air-to-air weaponry, the Su-35 has a similar engagement range to the AMRAAM-equipped F-15 and the MICA-armed Rafale. But the massive KS-172 anti-AWACS missile gives the enhanced 'Flanker' the ability to engage specialised targets at more than double the range of any other fighter in service today. It can also carry Russia's newest medium- and short-range missiles.

'AMRAAMSKI': The 50-km (30-mi.)-range R-27 missile (NATO designation AA-12) is inertially-guided with active radar homing. It can engage targets ranging from fast jets and manoeuvring helicopters to low-flying cruise missiles.

MULTI-MODE: The Su-35's radar can track up to 15 targets simultaneously, engaging six or more at the same time.

BEYOND VISUAL RANGE: Su-35s can detect targets beyond normal visual range with both radar and infra-red systems.

LOOKDOWN/SHOOTDOWN: The Su-35 can engage low-flying targets trying to hide in ground clutter.

Multiple target engagement

SUPERMARINE

S.6B

● High-speed floatplane ● Record breaker ● Schneider race winner

SUPERMARINE S.6B

▲ Taking to water
The S.5 makes a test flight at Calshot in preparation for the Schneider race of 1929. Its rival, the Macchi, is in the background.

Meeting the sponsor ▲
Lady Houston, who helped finance the prize-winning aircraft, meets members of the 1931 British team.

◄ Second winner
The original S.6 won the 1929 Schneider race. The engine was a 1417-kW (1,900-hp.) Rolls-Royce 'R', uprated in 1931 for the winning S.6B.

▼ Powerful engine
The S.6B needed the power of the 'R' series engine and special fuel, which was stored in the floats, to compete successfully.

▲ To be the best
The Supermarine company had a tradition of excellence, and built their aircraft to be the best. This attitude won them much acclaim, but meant that each aircraft required many man-hours on the production lines.

S upermarine's S.6B was the fastest aircraft of its time. The company entered racing with its 1919 Sea Lion flying-boat and reached a pinnacle of performance with the S.6B of 1931. The combined talents of design genius R. J. Mitchell and fuel technician F. Rodwell Banks achieved Schneider Trophy glory, in the process laying the foundations of Britain's aerial defences during World War II.

▲ The experience
of competing in the Schneider races not only gave British aviation much prestige, but the lessons learned about the technology anticipated the shape of World War II fighters to come.

FACTS AND FIGURES

➤ In the 1927 Schneider race two S.5 monoplanes took first and second places.

➤ H. R. Wagborn flew the Supermarine S.6 to a record 528.87 km/h (329 m.p.h.) in 1929.

➤ A generous endowment by Lady Houston provided the finances for Britain's racing entry in 1931.

➤ On 29 September 1931 the S.6B became the first aircraft to fly over 643.7 km/h (400 m.p.h.).

➤ The S.6B was a top tourist attraction in London's Science Museum.

➤ One of the first plastic models sold in the United States was a Supermarine S.6B.

Schneider Trophy winner

The principal achievements of the Supermarine S.6B are in the record book for all to see: 547.3 km/h (340 m.p.h.) to win the Schneider Trophy outright for the United Kingdom at Calshot on 13 September 1931, and 654.9 km/h (380 m.p.h.) to establish an absolute world speed record at Ryde on the Isle of Wight on 29 September. The flights were made by pilots J. N. Boothman and G. H. Stainforth. These incredible records were all the more impressive because Britain's entry into the race had no government support and the S.6B was a modification of the earlier S.6 rather than, like many of the contestants, a new aircraft.

Before the S.6B made its mark in 1931, the S.5 and S.6 were among early monoplanes on the air racing scene and logged impressive flying records in their own right.

The great designer R. J. Mitchell had by now settled upon the general configuration of a sleek, graceful, high-speed aircraft, and was to use lessons learned to design yet another – the immortal Spitfire.

Success of the S.6 series owed much to the superb Rolls-Royce 'R' series engine, a direct ancestor of the wartime Merlin that powered the Spitfire and Hurricane, and which eventually went on to become the Griffon.

S.6A

The original S.6 of 1929 was upgraded to S.6B standard for the 1931 race and was redesignated S.6A to distinguish it from the newer aircraft.

The thin wings were a good design for high-speed flight, but needed extra bracing to cope with the immense stress.

A small cockpit was another concession to high speed and low drag, but it was not a feature that pilots liked.

Taking off from water was safe enough, but pilots disliked using a periscope to see ahead. The aircraft were intentionally designed without a canopy to minimise drag and improve airflow.

Engine cooling was a serious headache for aircraft designers in the 1930s. Use of ethylene glycol in flush-fitting radiators built into the underside of the wings helped solve the problem.

The sleek profile and long engine of the S.6 showed how designers tried to reconcile the need for maximum power with minimum frontal area to reduce drag and gain top speed.

The stressed-skin construction used to build the S.6 series was to prove extremely valuable to Supermarine in building the Spitfire seven years later.

The very minimum amount of fuel needed to complete the race course was carried in the large floats. One pilot discovered this when he miscounted the number of laps he had flown, and ran out of fuel!

ACTION DATA

ENGINE POWER

The development of engine power during the decade after World War I was the key to the vastly improved performance of the aircraft competing for the Schneider Trophy. Output increased dramatically from the victorious Curtiss of 1923 through the Macchi of 1926 to the triumphant S.6B of 1931.

CR-3   346.8 kW (464 hp.)

M.39   657 kW (880 hp.)

S.6B   1752.4 kW (2,350 hp.)

MAXIMUM SPEED

Greater power and advances in aerodynamics saw the speeds achieved by Schneider Trophy competitors leap ahead. The lessons learned during the epic races were to stand the competitors in good stead as war clouds loomed in the 1930s.

1923 CR-3 285.6 km/h (177 m.p.h.)

1926 M.39 396.69 km/h (245 m.p.h.)

1931 S.6B 547.3 km/h (380 m.p.h.)

Previous winners

■ **DEPERDUSSIN (1913):** The first Schneider Trophy race was won at Monaco meet at an average speed of 73.63 km/h (45.65 m.p.h.).

■ **SUPERMARINE SEA LION (1922):** After two post-war wins by Italy the Sea Lion won at Naples, at a speed of 234.48 km/h (145.38 m.p.h.).

■ **CURTISS CR-3 (1923):** The US Navy's Curtiss seaplanes were a revelation at Cowes, winning at 285.6 km/h (177.07 m.p.h.).

■ **MACCHI M.39 (1926):** Ordered by Mussolini to win the trophy, the Italians built the Macchi M.39, which achieved 396.69 km/h (245.95 m.p.h.).

■ **SUPERMARINE S.5 (1927):** First of the great Supermarine 'S' series, the S.5 won in Venice at an average speed of 453.29 km/h (281.04 m.p.h.).

TUPOLEV

VAKHMISTROV ZVENO

● Composite aircraft ● Parasite fighters ● Combat operations

TUPOLEV VAKHMISTROV ZVENO

▲ **Combined attack**
The Zveno Z-6SPB consisted of a TB-3/AM-34RN with two I-16s beneath the wings.

Flying 'nest' ▶
The culmination of the Zveno concept was the extraordinary Aviamatka, comprising a TB-3 bomber and five fighters of three different types.

◀ **Parasite fighter**
The first Zveno design named Z-1 first flew in December 1931, carrying two Tupolev I-4 fighters above the wing.

▲ **Bigger and better**
Leading on from the Z-1 experiment, the Z-2 featured the larger TB-3 mother ship carrying up to three Polikarpov I-5s.

◀ **Extra power**
The two I-4 fighters fitted to the TB-1 in the Z-1 composite ran their engines at full power during the take-off run.

O ne of the strangest aircraft ever to have flown, the Zveno was from Vakhmistrov's series of composite bomber/fighter designs of the 1930s. Using the biggest bomber of the day, the Tupolev TB-3, different combinations of fighters or light dive-bombers were attached to the fuselage and/or wings, providing the aircraft with its own self-defence capability. One squadron of these strange Zveno (link) aircraft saw service in World War II.

▲ The Zveno series of experiments led to limited operational use during World War II. The I-16s mounted below the wing of this TB-3 flew dive-bombing missions with two 250-kg bombs.

FACTS AND FIGURES

➤ The first flight of the original Zveno Z-1 took place at Monino on 3 December 1931 with Vakhmistrov aboard the TB-1.

➤ On the first release the co-pilot detached one of the I-4s early, causing it to rear up.

➤ The first successful rejoin by an I-Z to the TB-3 occurred on 23 March 1935.

➤ One combat unit flew Zveno aircraft during World War II with six modified TB-3s and 12 I-16SPB dive-bombers.

➤ The Aviamatka successfully released all five aircraft in a flight in November 1935.

➤ Vakhmistrov proposed a tailless bomber design carrying eight ultra-fast fighters.

PROFILE

Vakhmistrov's bizarre composite designs

After experimenting with a glider attached to the wing of a Polikarpov R-1, Vladimir Vakhmistrov proposed an adaptation of this concept in one of the world's first 'parasite' schemes. He persuaded the Soviet air force that a bomber could carry fighters for its own protection and release them when necessary.

The first combination, called the Zveno 1 or Z-1, involved carrying a modified I-4 fighter above each wing. The aircraft were placed in position using wooden ramps and ropes to haul them onto the wing.

Initial trials proved successful and after the design had been adapted to carry two I-5 fighters as the Z-1a, the idea progressed to the much larger TB-3 'mother ship'. The Z-2 consisted of a TB-3 with three I-5s, one on each wing and a third above the fuselage. The TB-3 proved to be an excellent carrier platform.

The even more ambitious Z-5 featured a Grigorovich I-Z suspended beneath the TB-3 on a steel trapeze. The aircraft could

then be recovered after being released using a system similar to that used by the Curtiss F9C.

The culmination of the design was the incredible Aviamatka which carried two I-5s, two I-16s and an I-Z on the trapeze. Unexpectedly, the final combination, the Z-7, saw service during World War II, carrying two I-16SPB dive-bombers; it made one famous mission, destroying the Danube bridge at Chyernovod, Romania.

Two I-4s are released simultaneously from the TB-1 mother ship. The TB-1 remained remarkably steady throughout the release sequence.

TB-3/AM-34RN

Type: adapted version of TB-3 bomber used for carrying two I-16 dive-bombers beneath the wing

Powerplant: four 611-kW (819-hp.) Mikulin AM-34RN piston engines

Maximum speed: 245 km/h (152 m.p.h.)

Initial climb rate: 8 min to 1000 m (3280 ft.)

Range: 1000 km (620 mi.)

Service ceiling: 7740 m (25,393 ft.)

Weights: empty 11417 kg (25,117 lb.); loaded 18877 kg (41,529 lb.)

Armament: single 7.62-mm machine-guns in each of nose, ventral, dorsal and tail positions

Dimensions: span 41.80 m (137 ft. 1 in.)
length 25.10 m (82 ft. 4 in.)
wing area 234.50 m² (2,523 sq. ft.)

The co-pilot was tasked with releasing the main axle attachment on the I-5 once the pilot had released the rear fixture.

Above each wing was a Polikarpov I-5 fighter secured by a hold-down link on the undercarriage and a steel tripod fixture attached to the TB-3's wing.

Powered by four Mikulin AM-34 engines, the Tupolev TB-3 was the largest Soviet bomber of the period. The aircraft was developed from the earlier twin-engined TB-1.

The pilot of the TB-3 had the difficult task of keeping the 'mother ship' as steady as possible during the release sequence. The aircraft on the wings were released simultaneously to prevent the dangerous asymmetrical situation of having an aircraft on one wing but not on the other. The aircraft was extremely unmanoeuvrable when all aircraft were attached.

An I-16 fighter was attached beneath each wing of the 'mother ship'. Each was held in position by two large V-struts made from aluminium tubing.

Suspended beneath the fuselage of the TB-3 on a steel-tube trapeze, the I-Z fighter was the only aircraft which could be recovered in flight. The I-Z had a steel structure with a sprung hook in front of the cockpit, which the pilot guided into the trapeze.

The first in-flight coupling was achieved using a large steel trapeze beneath the fuselage.

ZVENO AVIAMATKA

As the most ambitious of the Vakhmistrov designs, the Aviamatka (mother aircraft) involved six aircraft of four different types (including the 'mother'). The arrangement was found to be impractical for military use.

COMBAT DATA

MAXIMUM SPEED

Of the three fighter designs carried by the Aviamatka the I-16 was undoubtedly the most capable, with a superior performance in both speed and rate of climb over the other two types. It was the Soviet Union's principal fighter of 1941.

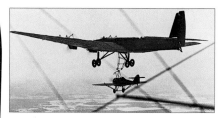

I-5	278 km/h (173 m.p.h.)
I-16 TYPE 24	490 km/h (304 m.p.h.)
I-Z	300 km/h (186 m.p.h.)

SERVICE CEILING

To be effective as a defence for a bomber, the 'parasite' fighters had to be able to match enemy fighters. The I-16 could climb the highest of these types and could therefore fly above the bomber to gain a tactical advantage over attacking enemy aircraft.

| I-5 | I-16 TYPE 24 | I-Z |
| 7500 m (24,606ft.) | 10210 m (33,496ft.) | 7000 m (22,965ft.) |

Composite aircraft designs

■ **CURTISS F9C SPARROWHAWK:** The F9Cs were attached to the airships USS *Macon* and *Akron* by a recoverable trapeze system.

■ **SHORT MAYO COMPOSITE:** Designed to provide long-range mail services, the Mayo broke a number of long-distance records.

■ **JUNKERS MISTEL:** Using a Ju 88 airframe as a flying bomb, a single fighter was attached to the fuselage and guided the Ju 88 to the target.

■ **CONVAIR B-36 FICON:** The B-36 bomber was used by the USAF to carry a GRF-84F reconnaissance fighter under the fuselage.

VFW-FOKKER

VAK 191B

● VTOL attack aircraft ● Fiat G91 replacement ● Prototypes only

▲ *The VAK 191B suffered because of NATO's changing requirements. High costs and a lack of US support saw a complete U-turn take place as VTOL was abandoned outside the UK.*

I n the 1950s and 1960s aeronautical engineers were fascinated by the possibilities of jet-powered vertical take-off and landing (VTOL) aircraft in combat roles. Germany, in particular, flew no fewer than three different types: a fighter, a transport and a ground-attack machine. Arguably, the most promising of them was the VAK 191B, an advanced VTOL attack aircraft employing vectored thrust and lift engines to achieve Mach 0.96 at 300 m (984 ft.).

VFW-FOKKER **VAK 191B**

▼ **FOD screens**
FOD (foreign object damage) was prevented during hovering trials by fitting screens to all four jet air intakes.

▲ **Reaction control jet rig**
To perfect the VAK 191's reaction control jet system, the SG 1262 hovering rig was built. It featured a row of five RB.108 lift jets.

▼ **Resemblance to P.1127**
From this angle, the VAK 191B's resemblance to the British P.1127 VTOL design was most apparent. VAK 191Bs shared the latter's four-nozzle vectored thrust arrangement but had a significantly smaller wing area than the P.1127.

▲ **Luftwaffe testing**
Starting with D-9564, the Luftwaffe undertook trials from its Manching test facility. D-9564 was airlifted from Bremen to Manching by a US Army CH-54 helicopter.

Shortcomings ▶
NATO commanders cited the VAK 191B's small size and lack of power as major shortcomings. Without STO (short take-off) ability the design had a limited weapons load.

FACTS AND FIGURES

➤ VFW-Fokker proposed VAK 191B Mk 2 and supersonic Mk 3 versions with more powerful engines and larger wings.

➤ Originally, there were to be six VAK 191B prototypes, including three two-seaters.

➤ D-9563, the first VAK 119B, is today displayed at the Deutsches Museum.

➤ A VAK 191B variant was proposed for the US Navy's Sea Control Ship V/STOL competition, won by Rockwell's XFV-12A.

➤ VAK 191B production was to be split 60:40 between German and Italian factories.

➤ The first SG 1262 test rig flight took place in 1966; it lasted 12 minutes.

PROFILE

VTOL G91's ill-fated replacement

Vertikalstartendes Aufklärungs- und Kampfflugzeug (vertical take-off reconnaissance and battle [i.e. attack] aircraft) 191B had its origins in requirement NBMR-3/169b of 1961. This aimed to find a replacement for the Fiat G91 reconnaissance and attack aircraft. The new machine had to be able to operate from a semi-prepared dispersed site, with no ground facilities other than fuel and ordnance, make a vertical take-off, fly at 150 m (500 ft.) and carry 907 kg (2,000 lb.) of ordnance at Mach 0.92 over a combat radius of 463 km (285 mi.).

Three design proposals were received, Britain's trend-setting P.1127 (the basis for the RAF's Harrier) being named as a reference point during design evaluation. Finally, the two countries using the G91, Germany and Italy, decided in July 1965 to proceed with Focke-Wulf's proposed Fw 1262 as the VAK 191B (the Hawker P.1127 and two other contenders were designated VAK 191A, 191C and 191D, respectively).

The successful design, with three engines – a vectored-thrust turbofan propulsion engine and two vertically-mounted lift turbojets for VTOL – was

developed by VFW, a merger of Focke-Wulf and Weser.

However, before an aircraft had flown, NATO abandoned VTOL on cost grounds in 1965, instead choosing to develop an aircraft to operate from conventional airfields. Thus, the MRCA (later Panavia Tornado) was chosen for the attack role in 1968. (Italy had withdrawn from the programme in 1967, having selected the Fiat G91Y.)

Three of six planned VAK 191Bs were built and flown, the first in 1971. One is preserved.

Left: Advanced for its day, the VAK 191B used triply-redundant fly-by-wire signalling for its flight controls, coupled to the auto-stabilisation system perfected on the SG 1262 rig.

Above: VAK 191B V2, D-9564, took to the air in 1971 bearing the logo of VFW-Fokker, the new company formed with the Dutch manufacturer in 1969.

VAK 191B

D-9563 was the first VAK 191B, emerging from the Bremen factory on 24 April 1970. After tethered flight testing that lasted over a year, the aircraft made its first free hover on 10 September 1971.

Much of the VAK 191B's fuselage was filled with fuel tanks for the aircraft's three thirsty engines. The forward group was situated directly behind the pilot and around the lift/cruise engines intake and had a capacity of 1150 litres (300 gal.).

Two lift turbojets were installed aft of the cockpit and in front of the tail fin. They could be started in a few seconds using bleed air from the lift/cruise engine just before a vertical take-off. Originally each engine was to have a fore/aft-deflecting nozzle ring. The air intakes were protected by folding 'clam shell' doors.

Small wings were a feature of the VAK 191B, providing the pilot with the smoothest possible ride at low altitude. However, a drawback was inferior combat manoeuvring, especially in the absence of in-flight thrust-vectoring.

VFW-FOKKER
VAK 191B
V1
D-9563

Avionics were housed in the VAK 191B's nose and in a compartment under the tailfin. Prototypes were fitted with a 1.68-m (5-ft. 6-in.) test instrumentation boom.

Main propulsion power was provided by Rolls-Royce's RB.193 turbofan, much to the disappointment of Bristol Siddeley who had proposed the Pegasus that powered the P.1127. Production was to be jointly undertaken by Rolls-Royce and, in Germany, by MTU.

Reaction control 'puffer' jets in the nose, tail and wingtips were fed by both the lift/cruise engine and lift engines. They were linked to an auto-stabilisation system which maintained the aircraft's stability during vertical take-off and landing modes, thus reducing the pilot's workload.

Thrust for VTOL

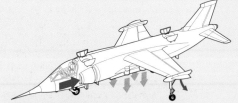

LIFT TURBOJETS: Focke-Wulf's approach to the VTOL problem was to employ a lift jet at either end of the VAK 191B's fuselage to provide vertical lift.

LIFT/THRUST TURBOFAN: The vectored thrust main propulsion engine provided lift during take-off and landing, as well as thrust for forward flight.

'PUFFER' JETS: Reaction control jets operated at speeds below 333 km/h (206 m.p.h.) and 'reacted' to control stick movements to keep the aircraft stable at low speeds and in the hover.

ACTION DATA

ENGINE POWER

Had the VAK 191B entered service it would have represented a major increase in aircraft power. However, a VTOL design requires significantly more installed thrust than a conventional aircraft just to take off – over four times that of the G91.

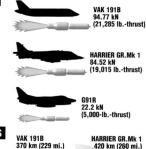

VAK 191B
94.77 kN
(21,285 lb.-thrust)

HARRIER GR.Mk 1
84.52 kN
(19,015 lb.-thrust)

G91R
22.2 kN
(5,000-lb.-thrust)

COMBAT RADIUS

Range was always a weakness of early variants of the RAF's Hawker Siddeley Harrier. The VAK 191B would undoubtedly have suffered from the same weakness, despite being a better performer in this respect than the Fiat G91. The VAK's engines had a large fuel requirement.

VAK 191B
370 km (229 mi.)

HARRIER GR.Mk 1
420 km (260 mi.)

G91R
320 km (198 mi.)

WEAPON LOAD

The VAK 191 weapon load requirement was modest; production aircraft would have carried larger loads. Using a short take-off run, something the VAK was unable to do, the Harrier GR.Mk 1 could carry over two tonnes of ordnance to a target.

VAK 191B   907 kg (2,000 lb.)

HARRIER GR.Mk 1   2268 kg (4,990 lb.)

G91R   1400 kg (3,100 lb.)

VICKERS

R.100

● Last British rigid airship ● Record-breaking flight ● Simple construction

▲ One of two
competing airship designs, the
privately funded R100 was a simple but sound
craft. It is best remembered for its record-
breaking endurance flight across the Atlantic.

Long range with a big payload and the
ability to operate safely in conditions
that would keep contemporary
aeroplanes on the ground were the main
attractions of the airship in the 1920s.
One of the most successful rigid airship
designs was the R.100, created by Barnes
Wallis and built by a Vickers subsidiary
called the Airship Guarantee Company.
During its brief career the R.100 made the
first transatlantic crossing by an airship.

VICKERS R.100

▲ First flight
Powered by conventional aero engines, the R.100 took to the air
for the first time on 16 December 1929, piloted by G.H. Scott.

▲ Last British Airship
When it was built the R.100 was one of
the largest rigid airships in the world.
Built at the Airship Guarantee
Company works in Howden, Yorkshire,
it was the last made in Britain.

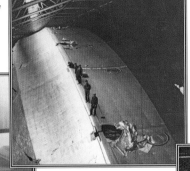

◄ Undignified end
No major problems
were ever found with
the design of the
R.100, though the
fate of its rival, the
R.101 resulted in the
airship concept
falling from favour
and to the R.100
being prematurely
scrapped.

◄ Fit for Royalty
The accommodation on the
R.100 was truly luxurious
and even boasted a formal
dining room capable of
seating 56 passengers.

Simple construction ►
The key factor in the
strength of the R.100 was
the geodetic design of
its structure.

FACTS AND FIGURES

➤ Barnes Neville Wallis designed the R.100
and later became famous for creating
the bouncing bomb during World War II.

➤ A disused RNAS air station was chosen
as the site for building the R.100.

➤ When the airship was scrapped, Vickers
had not covered all its costs.

➤ Geodetic construction used on the R.100
was later employed on the famous
Vickers Wellington medium bomber.

➤ Neville Shute later wrote of the Atlantic
crossing in his book *Slide Rule*.

➤ In 1924, the fixed price for the as yet
unbuilt R.100 was set at £350,000.

PROFILE

Britain's best and last

It was the need for better communications with far-flung colonies that persuaded the British government to finance the development of two airships, the Vickers R.100 and the R.101, which was built by the Royal Airship Works.

Barnes Wallis used some novel construction techniques, including a system of wire mesh netting to keep the gas bags from being damaged by rubbing against the structural girders. There were three decks, with cabins for 100 passengers, a promenade area and a dining salon for 56.

After making its maiden flight in December 1929, the R.100 set out for Canada on 29 July, arriving on 1 August after 78 hours in the air. On the way it survived a violent thunderstorm over the St Lawrence River. The fabric covering on the stabilising fins was ripped, but the crew carried out repairs in flight before eventually arriving at Montreal. The return journey, to Cardington, took 58 hours.

Unfortunately, the rival R.101 crashed in France with many fatalities two months later, after setting out on a proving flight to India. As a result, the R.100 was taken out of service and scrapped, although it had already proved to be a safe and reliable craft.

Above: Seen in company with a German Zeppelin, the R.100 sits quietly, tied to its mooring mast. The German craft were filled with hydrogen instead of helium.

Above: In order to make the airship as streamlined as possible, Barnes Wallis and his team arranged the accommodation on three decks in the lower portion of the hull. A viewing promenade was also featured.

R.100

Type: rigid airship

Powerplant: six 500-kW (670-hp.) Rolls-Royce Condor piston aero engines

Maximum speed: 130 km/h (81 m.p.h.)

Endurance: 80 hr

Date of completion: 1929

Price: £350,000

Gross lift: 158.50 tonnes (174.7 tons)

Accommodation: on three decks, with sleeping berths for up to 100 passengers located on the upper decks and a gallery lounge on the bottom deck.

Dimensions:
beam	41.15 m (135 ft.)
length	216.00 m (708 ft. 6 in.)
gas volume	147247.60 m³ (5,199,954 cu. ft.)

R.100

One of two designs submitted for a British long distance airship, the R.100 was completed in 1929. Built for use on the North American route, it completed only one, successful, flight before being withdrawn from service.

Although the R.100 was a relatively simple design, several construction techniques were pioneered on it. These included the use of wire mesh netting to contain the gas bags and prevent them from pressing on the main girders. The Vickers craft also had fewer main spars than other airship designs.

Barnes Wallis set out to build the R.100 in as straightforward and cost effective a manner as possible. The airframe was extremely strong and the Vickers craft proved to be much cheaper and easier to maintain than the entirely Government-funded R.101.

At the very tip of the nose were anchor points for attaching the craft to a gigantic mooring mast. This also made entry and exit for the passengers and crew much simpler.

Propulsion was by means of six Rolls-Royce Condor IIIB aero engines. It had originally been intended to use experimental kerosene fuel engines, but the eventual choice proved to be a shrewd move.

In order to achieve the best aerodynamic efficiency, the R-100's stabilisers were smoothly blended in to the main structure.

GOLIATHS IN THE SKY

SAGA OF THE R101: Rival to the R.100, though destined for the Far Eastern and African routes, was the ambitious R.101. Unlike the Vickers design, this giant airship was built by the Air Ministry at Cardington. It was a highly complex machine and no expense was spared during its construction. It suffered problems right from the beginning and proved to be underpowered and had poor handling. During its maiden voyage to India the R.101 crashed in France, bursting into flames and killing many of those aboard.

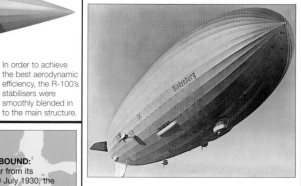

END OF AN ERA: After the R101 tragedy, Britain halted its development of long-range airships, though Germany persisted with the idea. The largest airship ever to emerge was the Graf Zeppelin Hindenburg. It was originally designed to use helium, but an international embargo resulted in highly flammable hydrogen being used instead. The Hindenburg completed 17 transatlantic crossings with success, though on a voyage in 1937, the huge airship burst into flames at Lakehurst in New Jersey, resulting in horrendous casualties. The era of the airship had finally ended.

The record-breaking journey

2 PROBLEMS STRIKE: While the R-100 was passing over the St Lawrence Seaway, a violent thunderstorm resulted in two damaged stabilisers and a hole being torn in the fabric. The crew made repairs in flight and the R.100 arrived safely.

3 JOURNEY HOME: The trip back took only 58 hours, though by this time the R.100 had made history by performing the longest-endurance flight ever by an airship.

1 OUTWARD BOUND: Slipping clear from its moorings on 29 July 1930, the R.100 set off from Cardington on its record-breaking flight to Canada. No problems were encountered for most of the journey, although strong head winds resulted in the trip taking slightly longer than anticipated.

MONTREAL

CARDINGTON

VOUGHT

XF5U 'FLYING PANCAKE'

● Naval fighter ● Flying wing design ● Compound propulsion

When Vought devised its revolutionary 'Flying Pancake' during World War II, the goal was to create an advanced naval fighter. At the time no one imagined that the saucer-shaped aircraft would fuel rumours that the US government was secretly testing a UFO (Unidentified Flying Object). The 'Flying Pancake' design did not succeed however, and never entered production or saw active service.

▲ The XF5U was the culmination of the many 'flying saucer' programmes led by Charles H. Zimmerman for Vought. Despite the ingenuity of the design, problems associated with the complex power transmission were insurmountable.

VOUGHT XF5U 'FLYING PANCAKE'

▲ **Tunnel test**
A model XF5U spent many hours in a wind tunnel, testing its aerodynamic properties.

▲ **'Flying Flapjack'**
Also known as the 'Flying Flapjack', the V-173 prototype was powered by two Continental flat-four piston engines.

Test flight ▶
During the test programme the V-173 showed that it was capable of landing at very low speeds and could manoeuvre almost like a helicopter.

▼ **Advanced construction**
The XF5U had very advanced propeller technology and was made from a Matelite balsa and aluminium sandwich, which proved extremely strong.

▲ **Ready for launch**
The XF5U was completed in March 1947, but became obsolete overnight by the sudden appearance of jet fighters.

FACTS AND FIGURES

➤ The XF5U-1, developed from the V-173, was shipped from the Connecticut factory to California via the Panama Canal.

➤ The estimated take-off distance for the XF5U-1 fighter was just 220 metres.

➤ The lightly powered V-173 made its maiden flight on 23 November 1942.

➤ The V-173 used two Continental A-80 engines and had the same 'wing' area as the XF5U-1.

➤ The V-173 had originally been designed for the pilot to lie prone.

➤ The XF5U-1 had many features in common with the recent B-2 bomber.

PROFILE

'Flying Pancake' takes to the sky

I t is a great disappointment that the Vought XF5U-1 never flew. When a test prototype, the V-173, took to the air it was unique. The V-173 and the XF5U-1 fighter were based upon a wing of circular shape, which was also the 'fuselage'.

Designed to be capable of vertical take-off and landing, as well as very high-speed flight, the 'Flying Pancake' used a very low aspect ratio wing offering high efficiency. This design was the brainchild of Charles Zimmerman, who had been researching such shapes since 1933. The wood-and-fabric V-173 performed well in tests during 1942, proving stall-proof.

The V-173 prototype was damaged in a crash caused by a fuel vapour lock. The aircraft was forced to land on sand and flipped over.

The all-metal XF5U-1 fighter, which used the same wing planform, would have gone further despite problems with its complex transmission. But, although the XF5U-1 was shipped to Muroc, California, for tests, it never flew. The jet age made propeller-driven fighters a thing of the past and the XF5U was scrapped.

An ejection seat was provided for the pilot. The cockpit contained a special propeller control lever and the canopy opening was electrically operated.

Either engine could drive both shafts in an emergency. The complexity of such a system, with right-angled drives, clutches and five-to-one reduction gearboxes, caused huge problems.

The contra-rotating propwash over the wingtip prevented the formation of wingtip vortices, thereby reducing induced drag to very low levels.

The massive propwash close to the large tail gave the XF5U very good control authority.

The engines were fitted inside the blended wing and fuselage and drove the propellers via shafts.

Propeller technology was of vital importance to the XF5U because of its large range of speed and its hovering requirement. Hydromatic propellers, similar to those used on the F4U fighter, were fitted originally.

Projected gun armament either side of the cockpit was not fitted. A combination of machine-guns and 20-mm cannon would have been used.

Provision was made for the XF5U to carry two drop-tanks under the inner fuselage.

NAVY 33958   XF5U-1

XF5U 'FLYING PANCAKE'

Just one XF5U was built and it only completed taxiing trials following the fitting of its articulated propellers. The V-173 prototype survived and is in the Smithsonian Museum in Washington.

XF5U-1 'Flying Pancake'

Type: single-seat vertical take-off naval fighter prototype and research aircraft

Powerplant: two 1007-kW (1,350-hp.)Pratt & Whitney Twin Wasp 14-cylinder air-cooled radial engines

Maximum speed: 811 km/h (504 m.p.h.)

Initial climb rate: 670 m/min (3,000 f.p.m.)

Range: 1465 km (910 m.p.h.)

Service ceiling: 9754 m (32,000 ft.)

Weights: normal loaded 7620 kg (16,764 lb.)

Armament: none fitted, but projected armament of six 12.7-mm machine-guns or four 20-mm cannon

Dimensions:
span 7.20 m (23 ft. 7 in.)
length 8.72 m (28 ft. 7 in.)
height 4.50 m (14 ft. 9 in.)
tail area 9.90 m² (106 sq. ft.)

ACTION DATA

MAXIMUM SPEED

For a propeller-driven fighter the XF5U had a very high speed, faster than any naval fighter of the war and not much slower than a post-war jet fighter. This was an enormous achievement in an aircraft that could also fly very slowly and was extremely agile.

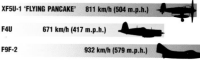

XF5U-1 'FLYING PANCAKE'   811 km/h (504 m.p.h.)

F4U   671 km/h (417 m.p.h.)

F9F-2   932 km/h (579 m.p.h.)

RANGE

With no seperate wings, the XF5U had less internal space for fuel. Heavy reduction gearing took up a great deal of room. Although the XF5U could carry external fuel tanks, these would have taken up the space reserved for the two bombs that would have been carried by operational aircraft flown by the navy.

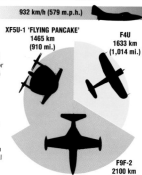

XF5U-1 'FLYING PANCAKE'
1465 km (910 mi.)

F4U
1633 km (1,014 mi.)

F9F-2
2100 km (1,305 mi.)

APPROXIMATE STALLING SPEED

Thanks to its unique aerodynamics the XF5U could almost float, and could be handled in a carefree manner without fear of going into a spin. It would have been much safer to fly than an F9F.

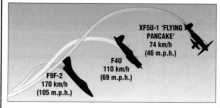

XF5U-1 'FLYING PANCAKE'
74 km/h (46 m.p.h.)

F4U
110 km/h (69 m.p.h.)

F9F-2
170 km/h (105 m.p.h.)

Blended wing and fuselage

■ **McDONNELL XP-67:** An attempt to produce a heavily armed high-altitude fighter, the XP-67 used a highly blended wingroot and fuselage for extra lift. One prototype was built.

■ **NORTHROP M2-F2:** Developed by NASA and Northrop, the M2-F2 was used to test the concept of re-usable space re-entry vehicles. The aircraft was drop-launched by a B-52.

■ **MARTIN MARIETTA X-24B:** This lifting body design proved the potential for aircraft to fly as fast as 1600 km/h (994 m.p.h.). It was very manoeuvrable and could fly at extreme altitudes.

■ **NORTHROP N-1M:** The first true flying wing design to fly, the N-1M had down-turned wingtips, the angle of which could be altered in flight to improve the aircraft's stability.

VOUGHT
XF8U-3

● Mach 2 all-weather interceptor ● Based on F8U Crusader

▲ The Crusader III, as it was unofficially dubbed by Vought, was a far more capable aircraft than the F8U. The Navy wanted both the F8U-3 and F4H-1, but funding was not forthcoming.

Although four decades have passed since it first flew, the Vought F8U-3 Crusader III remains one of the fastest and most formidable fighters ever to take to the air. The F8U-3 was also one of the biggest and heaviest single-seat fighters ever built. This powerful and robust warplane was not really a version of the F8U Crusader, as its name indicates, but was a brand-new aircraft seen by Texas-based Vought as the Navy's hope for the 1960s.

VOUGHT XF8U-3

▼ Familiar layout
The Crusader III retained the F8Us layout, but was a totally new aircraft.

▲ Different requirements
The F8U-3 lost out to the F4H-1 because it was designed to be only a fighter/interceptor, rather than a multi-role aircraft. Funding went to the more versatile Phantom.

◀ Missile armament
The F8U-3 was to be exclusively air-to-air missile armed. Guns were omitted altogether—the fashion at the time. The F4H Phantom II was also gunless, but experience over Vietnam resulted in cannon pods being added to this aircraft.

▼ Big intake for big engine
To feed the J75 engine a much larger air intake was necessary.

▲ Variable-incidence wing
The F8U-3 inherited the Crusader's variable-incidence mainplane, which tilted the leading edge upwards to increase lift during takeoff.

FACTS AND FIGURES

➤ Only the design of the F8U-3's windscreen prevented it from reaching its designed top speed of Mach 2.6 to 2.9.

➤ Of nine F8U-3 Crusader IIIs built, only three were flown before cancellation.

➤ The XF8U-3 prototypes completed 190 flights, logging an estimated 300 hours.

➤ Donald Engen, an F8U-3 test pilot, serves today as director of the National Air and Space Museum in Washington, D.C.

➤ The first flight of an XF8U-3 was accomplished on June 2, 1958.

➤ Some observers thought the XF8U-3 should have been redesignated F9U.

PROFILE

Uncrowned king of the Crusaders

In 1955, Vought (known for a brief period as LTV, the acronym for Ling-Temco-Vought) began design work on the spectacular F8U-3 Crusader III, seeking to create a state-of-the-art interceptor with unprecedented speed and climbing ability. The F8U-3 was more than one metre (3 ft.) longer and wider, and 50 percent heavier, than the Navy's F8U Crusader fighter of the period, and had much increased power. A planned rocket booster was never tested, but on jet power alone the Crusader

III had far more prowess than any fighter then in service.

The F8U-3 was one of the first Navy fighters designed without guns. It was expected to take off from an aircraft carrier, climb at incredible speed (thanks to its massive afterburning J75 turbojet) and engage its adversary from a distance, in all weathers, using air-to-air missiles.

The test program revealed few flaws. But the Navy chose to produce the fighter that was designed to compete with the F8U-3. That aircraft evolved into

the immortal McDonnell Douglas F-4 Phantom II.

Two XF8U-3s and a single F8U-3 test aircraft were built and flown; a further 13 test aircraft were cancelled in 1958.

Below: The first XF8U-3 stands next to the second XF8U-1 Crusader. The differences between the two were numerous.

Above: Notable among the features of the Crusader III were the prominent ventral stabilizing fins. These were folded horizontally for landing and take-off.

The three Crusader IIIs that were completed and flown carried a natural metal finish with Day-glo patches often added to the nose, wings and tail. The single F8U-3 had a black nose radome.

XF8U-3 Crusader III

Type: single-seat all-weather interceptor prototype

Powerplant: one 131-kN (29,515-lb.-thrust) Pratt & Whitney J75-P-6 turbojet engine

Maximum speed: 2340 km/h (1,454 m.p.h.)

Cruising speed: 924 km/h (574 m.p.h.)

Climb rate: 9903 m/min (32,492 f.p.m.) at sea level

Combat range: 1036 km (644 mi.)

Service ceiling: 18,288 m (60,000 ft.)

Weights: empty 9896 kg (21,817 lb.); max take-off 17,550 kg (38,691 lb.)

Weapons: (proposed) 4 AIM-7 Sparrow semi-active radar homing; 3 AIM-9 Sidewinder heat-seeking air-to-air missiles

Dimensions:
Span	12 m	(39 ft. 10 in.)
Length	17.8m	(58 ft. 7 in.)
Height	5 m	(16 ft. 4 in.)
Wing area	41.8 m²	(450 sq. ft.)

XF8U-3 CRUSADER III

The first of two XF8U-3 Crusader III prototypes constructed, 146340 flew for the first time on 2 June 1958. It exceeded the speed of sound on its sixth flight on June 11 and Mach 2 on 14 August.

A new and highly sophisticated radar and fire control system was fitted in a greatly enlarged radome above the engine air intake. Sparrow air-to-air missiles used radar guidance.

As used on later model French navy Crusaders and F-8Js rebuilt for the Navy, the F8U-3 was to use boundary layer control (BLC) to further increase lift by blowing hot air, bled from the aircraft's engine, over the wing.

Hydraulic actuators raised the variable-incidence wing for landing and takeoff. This arrangement allowed the fuselage to remain level on approach, improving pilot visibility and enabling a smaller, lighter undercarriage to be fitted.

After the Crusader III programme was cancelled, the three aircraft were transferred to NASA for high-speed, high-altitude trials.

The nose undercarriage of the XF8U-3 was offset to starboard to accommodate one of the AIM-7 Sparrow air-to-air missiles under the forward fuselage.

The F8U-3 had a much more powerful engine than the earliest versions of the Crusader, fitted with the Pratt & Whitney J57 turbojet. The J75 (also found in the USAF's F-105) was a considerably larger powerplant and necessitated a fuselage redesign in order to accommodate it.

Ventral stabilising fins were a major departure from the Crusader design. These were folded outward to a horizontal position during landing and take-off.

ACTION DATA

SPEED

The F8U-3 fighter-interceptor was an exceptionally fast aircraft with a formidable climb rate. It had a planned top speed above Mach 2.5, though this was not reached during test flights. The Crusader had a top speed less than Mach 2.

XF8U-3	2340 km/h (1,454 m.p.h.)
F4H-1 PHANTOM II	2385 km/h (1,482 m.p.h.)
F8U-2 CRUSADER	1773 km/h (1,102 m.p.h.)

WEAPONS

While later variants of the Crusader were able to deliver air-to-ground ordnance, the first versions and the F8U-3 were purely air-to-air aircraft. The Phantom II was a true multi-role aircraft, which made it a more attractive buy.

XF8U-3	7 x air-to-air missiles
F4H-1 PHANTOM II	7242 kg (15,965 lb.) of weapons, 8 x air-to-air missiles
F8U-2 CRUSADER	4 x 20-mm cannon, 4 x air-to-air missiles or 6 x 65-mm rockets

CLIMB RATE

A feature of the F8U-3 was its ability to zoom climb at high speed to intercept a hostile aircraft. Its climb rate was around 50 per cent better than that of the Crusader and faster than the F4H-1 Phantom II.

XF8U-3	9903 m (32,492 f.p.m.)
F4H-1 PHANTOM II	8534 m (28,000 f.p.m.)
F8U-2 CRUSADER	9144 m (30,000 f.p.m.)

Vought's jet-setting family

■ **F6U PIRATE:** Vought's first jet fighter was powered by a Westinghouse J34. Only 30 production examples were built for the Navy.

■ **F7U CUTLASS:** This unusual tail-less design was based on German wartime research. Four carrier fighter units operated the despised F7U-3.

■ **F8U-1/-2 CRUSADER:** The XF8U-3 based on the highly successful Crusader, served the US Navy aboard carriers for 30 years.

■ **A-7 CORSAIR II:** Operational from 1967, the A-7 replaced A-4 Skyhawks aboard Navy carriers. The type was finally retired in 1991.

WRIGHT
FLYER

● History's first powered heavier-than-air flight ● Home-built aircraft

H istory was made when the Wright brothers flew their 'Flyer' a few metres over the sands of Kitty Hawk, North Carolina, in 1903. This short hop, in an aircraft that was less powerful and slower than a modern motor scooter, began the age of powered flight in heavier-than-air aircraft. The flight was less than the wing span of a modern airliner, but it opened up a whole new era of aviation.

▲ Flying the first aircraft
was nothing like flying modern aeroplanes. The builders and pilots devised their own control systems, built their own engines and airframes, and all too frequently caused their own deaths.

WRIGHT FLYER

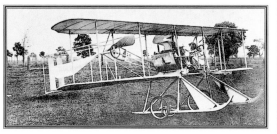

▲ **Rail-launched**
The Wright brothers' first experiments had been on dry sand which allowed take-offs on skids, but they had to find a way to reduce drag. One answer was a wooden railway, later replaced by wheels.

▲ **Gliding record**
In 1911, Orville returned to Kitty Hawk for the last time to set a world gliding record. He stayed aloft for 9 minutes and 45 seconds before landing safely.

▼ **On camera**
Keen to record their achievements, the brothers often filmed their flights. Here, Wilbur is seen photographing Orville during a test flight at Fort Myers in 1909.

▲ **Wheeled undercarriage**
The model 'R' was a sophisticated machine for its day, with twin propellers and wheels in place of the skids. The racing 'Baby Wright' was derived from this model.

◀ **Passenger carrier** ▶
The later Wright machines ('B' to 'R') could carry a passenger and had dual flying controls. The French aviation pioneer Paul Zens was Wilbur Wright's companion on this flight from Le Mans in 1908.

FACTS AND FIGURES

➤ The Smithsonian Institute refused to recognise the Wrights' achievement until the early 1950s.

➤ The Wright brothers opened their own flying school to train pilots.

➤ Wilbur Wright often kept his bowler hat on while flying his slow aircraft.

➤ Flyer III of 1905 had new propellers and a more powerful engine, and could be controlled easier than earlier 'Flyers'.

➤ Wilbur Wright had such a strong faith that he refused to fly on Sundays.

➤ The 'Flyer' Model D was a single-seater, two of which were sold to the US Army.

The first true powered aeroplane

Building experimental flying machines was a pursuit of cranks in the eyes of most people in 1903, but the Wright brothers were determined to achieve their goal of producing a practical, powered and controllable aircraft. Using the knowledge of previous aviation pioneers, they started building models and then small gliders, before rejecting many of the ideas as useless. With new plans of their own, such as controlling the aircraft with 'wing warping' and designing their own tiny engines, they produced the 'Flyer', a derivative of their 'Glider No. 1' of 1899.

Orville Wright took the controls of the 'Flyer' on 17 December 1903, a blustery day on the remote Kill Devil Hill. Mounted on a wooden railway track and watched only by a handful of local spectators, the 'Flyer' slowly climbed into the air and flew nearly 40 metres (120 ft.) before safely landing.

The brothers made four more flights that day, one lasting almost a minute.

Going on to demonstrate their flying machines to sceptical audiences all over Europe, they built bigger and better aircraft, cautiously correcting previous failures before going on to another flight. Thus, Wilbur Wright avoided being killed in an aeroplane crash like so many of his contemporary pioneers, instead succumbing to typhoid fever in his mid-40s.

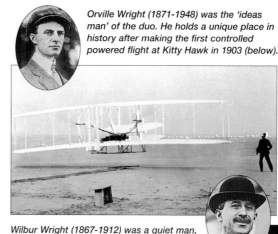

Orville Wright (1871-1948) was the 'ideas man' of the duo. He holds a unique place in history after making the first controlled powered flight at Kitty Hawk in 1903 (below).

Wilbur Wright (1867-1912) was a quiet man, who once said that a parrot, the bird that talked the most, did not fly very high.

Wright Flyer 1903

Type: experimental heavier-than-air powered biplane glider

Powerplant: home-built four-cylinder in-line piston engine delivering 9 kW (12 hp.)

Maximum speed: c. 50 km/h (31 m.p.h.)

Height on initial flight: c. 3 m (10 ft.)

Distance on initial flight: 36.5 m (120 ft.)

Duration of initial flight: 12 sec

Take-off weight: c. 340 kg (750 lb.)

Dimensions: span 12.29 m (40 ft.)
length 6.43 m (21 ft.)
height 2.81 m (9 ft.)
wing area c. 35.00 m² (510 sq. ft.)

WRIGHT FLYER

The Wright Flyer was based on earlier Wright glider designs. The 'Flyer' made history when Orville Wright flew it at Kill Devil Hill, Kitty Hawk, North Carolina, on 17 December 1903.

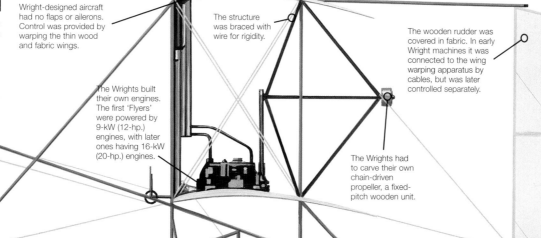

The 'elevators first' layout was soon dispensed with. This layout has recently found favour with aircraft designers, and can be seen on many fighters.

Early Wright gliders were fitted with skids rather than wheels, with the 'Flyer' being built to the same pattern.

Wright-designed aircraft had no flaps or ailerons. Control was provided by warping the thin wood and fabric wings.

The Wrights built their own engines. The first 'Flyers' were powered by 9-kW (12-hp.) engines, with later ones having 16-kW (20-hp.) engines.

The structure was braced with wire for rigidity.

The wooden rudder was covered in fabric. In early Wright machines it was connected to the wing warping apparatus by cables, but was later controlled separately.

The Wrights had to carve their own chain-driven propeller, a fixed-pitch wooden unit.

FIRST FLIGHTS

Man has probably dreamed of flight for as long as he has dreamed of anything. From the first caveman watching bats flitting out into the night, through the ancient Greeks and their myths of Daedalus and Icarus, to writers like Cyrano de Bergerac in the 17th century who fantasised about going to the moon in a carriage pulled by swans. But it was not until the 18th century, when the Montgolfier brothers harnessed the power of hot air in a balloon, that these dreams became an as-yet imperfectly achieved reality.

Dare-devils all over Europe followed the Montgolfier example, often with fatal results. Soon, people were experimenting with hydrogen to lift their balloons – much more controllable than hot air, but far more dangerous.

From there, the logical step was to fit some form of propulsion and steering mechanism. Experiments along these lines culminated in the last decade of the 19th century with steerable balloons, or dirigibles. Had anybody been taking bets in those days, most people would have put money on this being the future of flight. Few would have taken notice of the work being carried out by two mechanics in America, who were to achieve so much at Kitty Hawk in 1903.

The most important flight in history

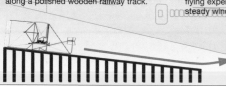

LAUNCH RAMP: The Wright Flyer had no wheels. It took off by skidding along a polished wooden railway track.

HEAD WIND: The Wrights had chosen Kitty Hawk, on the North Carolina coast, for their flying experiments because it had a consistent steady wind blowing in off the Atlantic.

INTO THE AIR: There was a headwind of 43 km/h (21 m.p.h.) when, with Wilbur Wright at the controls, the 'Flyer' lifted into the air from the end of the launch rail.

ONE SMALL STEP: Although Wright was in the air for only 12 seconds, during which time the aeroplane covered 36.5 metres (120 ft.), the short hop was one of the greatest events in history. For the first time, man had flown under power in a heavier-than-air machine, and the way was paved for the 20th century's aviation revolution.

YAKOVLEV

YAK-141 'FREESTYLE'

● First supersonic V/STOL fighter ● Stealth characteristics

▲ The Yak-141 is probably the most capable V/STOL aircraft ever built and has snatched many records previously held by the BAe/McDonnell Douglas Harrier II.

Designed to serve aboard the Soviet navy's 'Kiev'-class aircraft-carrying cruisers as a replacement for the Yak-38 'Forger', the Yak-141 first flew in March 1989. The novel layout included a large main engine supplemented by two smaller lift jets. Vectoring nozzles enable the 'Freestyle' to take off vertically, or after a very short roll, to hover and to land vertically. In conventional flight the aircraft has supersonic performance.

PHOTO FILE

YAKOVLEV YAK-141 'FREESTYLE'

▼ 'Foxbat' lookalike
A Yak-141 prototype in flight displays its unusual design, reminiscent of the Mikoyan MiG-25 family.

▲ 'Forger' links
Designed to replace the 'Forger' aboard the 'Kiev'-class ships, the Yak-141 has a great deal in common with its predecessor.

Setbacks ▶
As with several other Russian aircraft, Yak-141 development has been plagued by a lack of funds.

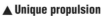

▼ Accident at Sea
The second prototype was severely damaged during carrier trials. The pilot ejected safely, however, and the aircraft was rebuilt.

▲ Unique propulsion
Unlike the Western Harrier II, the Yak-141 'Freestyle' incorporates, two vertically mounted Rybinski vertijets in addition to the main Soyuz turbofan engine. These are used only during vertical or short take-offs and landings.

FACTS AND FIGURES

➤ The Yak-141 is the world's first supersonic V/STOL fighter designed to operate from small aircraft-carriers.

➤ Radar and avionics equipment from the MiG-29 were incorporated into the design.

➤ The first flight of the aircraft took place in March 1989.

➤ After a landing accident on board a carrier in 1991, development was temporarily halted.

➤ The 'Freestyle' can be operated from small land sites and warship decks.

➤ Export partners have been sought because of a lack of funding.

PROFILE

Supersonic V/STOL fighter

For short take-offs, the nozzle of the Yak-141's extremely powerful main engine can be rotated to 65° and its thrust is augmented by the lift jets. Steel matting is needed to protect runway surfaces from the heat of the afterburner, and the procedure generates an immense amount of noise.

The lift jets can also be rotated backwards from their normal 15° angle to allow the aircraft to make the transition from vertical to forward flight more easily. Alternatively, they can be angled slightly forward to help slow the aircraft to a hover.

The Yak-141 cannot compete with the contemporary MiG-29 and Su-27 in terms of manoeuvrability, but it was designed to carry a similar avionics suite. This included a radar, laser and TV target designation system, and a helmet-mounted sight for the pilot. There were to be four weapons stations under the fixed part of the folding wings, and a pylon for a 2000-litre (440-gallon) fuel tank under the fuselage. Funding problems, however, meant the type never progressed beyond the technology demonstrator stage. The second aircraft built was

severely damaged in 1991 while conducting carrier trials aboard the *Admiral Gorshkov*. This aircraft was rebuilt, and the Yakovlev design bureau has continued flight development with its own funds.

Above: When the first prototype reappeared at Farnborough in 1992, it sported this new camouflage scheme and insignia.

Right: Two small nozzles are located behind the twin tails. These are yaw valves and are designed to aid control of the aircraft during hovering.

Yak-141 'Freestyle'

Type: single-seat V/STOL fighter

Powerplant: one 152-kN (34,170-lb.-thrust) Soyuz R-79 cruise/lift turbofan augmented by two 41.7-kN Rybinski RD-41 vertijets

Maximum speed: 1800 km/h (1,118 m.p.h.)

Range: 1400 km (875 mi.) on internal fuel; 2100 km (1312 mi.) with external fuel

Service ceiling: approx. 15000 m (49,212 ft.)

Weights: empty 11650 kg (25,630 lb.); loaded (STOL) 19500 kg (42,900 lb.)

Take-off run: 500 m (1,640 ft.)

Armament: one internal 30-mm gun and four AA-10/AA-11 'Alamo'/'Archer' AAMs

Dimensions:
span	10.10 m	(33 ft. 1 in.)
length	18.30 m	(60 ft.)
height	5.00 m	(16 ft. 4 in.)
wing area	31.70 m²	(341 sq. ft.)

YAK-141 'FREESTYLE'

No. 48 was the first prototype built and when the government froze development it was placed in storage. It re-emerged as No.141 and was painted in a new colour scheme.

As with many other Russian aircraft of the era, the cockpit of the Yak-141 features a conventional layout and dial instruments. Fully digital and automatic flight controls have been included, however, and give the aircraft exceptional agility. They also provide the capability to operate worldwide and in any weather conditions.

The twin Rybinski RD-41 vertijets are located under an airscoop behind the cockpit. During vertical flight the airscoop is opened from the rear to feed air into the vertijets, which are rotated at 12.5° to each other for maximum thrust.

Like its predecessor, the Yak-141 cannot carry a huge warload although it does have underwing provision for up to four AA-10/AA-11 air-to-air missiles.

The Yak-141 has a much more advanced avionics suite than the 'Forger', plus a laser target designator with a helmet-mounted sighting system. The radar is similar to that fitted to the MiG-29 'Fulcrum'.

The underside of the rear fuselage is coated in various heat-resistant materials to avoid damage to the airframe. The heat generated by the engines is so intense that it has damaged the surface of several runways during take-off and landing.

Large twin sponsons incorporating the tail units were required in order to provide sufficient clearance for the rotating nozzle of the main cruise/lift engine. This design feature gives the aircraft its boxy profile.

Yak-141 take-off

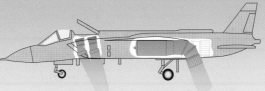

VERTICAL TAKE-OFF: Air is fed into the vertijets, angled at 12.5° to each other, via an intake behind the cockpit. The main engine thrust nozzle is rotated by 95° to provide maximum lift.

VULNERABILITY: Despite huge advances in technology, modern warplanes still remain vulnerable to attack during take-off and landing. The Yak-141 was designed to attain level flight as soon as possible. The combination of the main engine and twin vertijets enables rapid take-offs.

SHORT TAKE-OFF: For short take-offs both vertijets are rotated backwards for greater forward lift. In combination with the main R-79 engine they permit an easy and effective transition to forward flight.

COMBAT DATA

TOTAL THRUST

Although a more modern concept and arguably a more flexible and efficient aircraft, the BAe/McDonnell Douglas Harrier is considerably less powerful than either the Yakovlev Yak-38 or the newer Yak-141 'Freestyle'.

Yak-141 'FREESTYLE'	235.4 kN (52,917 lb.)
Yak-38 'FORGER-A'	130.42 kN (29,318 lb.)
HARRIER GR.Mk 7	96.75 kN (21,749 lb.)

BOMB LOAD

Both the Yak-38 'Forger' and its successor may be more powerful than their Western contemporaries (in this case the Harrier), but, like many Russian designs they are not as efficient, do not possess the same radius of action and are unable to carry as much ordnance.

Yak-141 'FREESTYLE' 2600 kg (5,720 lb.)	Yak-38 'FORGER-A' 2000 kg (4,400 lb.)	HARRIER GR.Mk 7 4173 kg (9,180 lb.)

MAXIMUM SPEED AT ALTITUDE

Speed is where the Yak-141 represents the biggest improvement over the other types. The 'Freestyle' is the only supersonic V/STOL aircraft in the world and in a combat scenario this factor alone would have provided a huge tactical advantage for the Russian navy (AV-MF).

Yak-141 'FREESTYLE'	1800 km/h (1,118 m.p.h.)
Yak-38 'FORGER-A'	1009 km/h (627 m.p.h.)
HARRIER GR.Mk 7	967 km/h (600 m.p.h.)

INDEX